Managing Finance

Managing Finance
A Socially Responsible Approach

David Crowther

ELSEVIER
BUTTERWORTH
HEINEMANN

AMSTERDAM · BOSTON · HEIDELBERG · LONDON · NEW YORK · OXFORD
PARIS · SAN DIEGO · SAN FRANCISCO · SINGAPORE · SYDNEY · TOKYO

Elsevier Butterworth-Heinemann
Linacre House, Jordan Hill, Oxford OX2 8DP
200 Wheelers Road, Burlington, MA 01803

First published 2004

British Library Cataloguing in Publication Data
Crowther, David
    Managing finance: a socially responsible approach
    1. Managerial accounting   2. Social responsibility of business
    I. Title
    658.1'511

Library of Congress Cataloguing in Publication Data
A catalogue record for this book is available from the Library of Congress

ISBN   0 7506 6101 1

For information on all Elsevier Butterworth-Heinemann publications visit our website
at http://books.elsevier.com

Typeset by Integra Software Services Pvt. Ltd, Pondicherry, India
www.integra-india.com
Printed and bound in Great Britain

Contents

Preface

All organisations make use of accounting. They are required to produce annual accounts, which are provided to shareholders to explain what actions have been taken on their behalf during the previous year and what the results of those actions have been in terms of profitability. These annual accounts are, however, widely used by other organisations and people to assess the financial health of a business. This might be important in order to decide whether or not to invest in the business or whether or not to lend money to it; it might be important in order to decide whether or not to do business with that company: will it pay its bills for example; for an individual it might even be important in order to decide whether or not to accept a job with the business. There are a multitude of uses to which the information contained in the annual accounts of a business can be put – if you understand what these accounts are telling you.

Accounting is used extensively not just in this way but also within a business, here it is used for planning and controlling operations, making decisions about how to manage the business and for measuring performance – of the business, of a department or unit within the business, or even of an individual. Budgets are used extensively for guidance in all of these aspects of the use of accounting. It is probably impossible for any manager within any business not to have familiarity with budgets, if with no other aspects of accounting use within a business. It is more likely though that every manager has greater experience of the uses to which accounting is put within his/her business than simply the budget.

In fact many people would say that accounting is the language of business which is used to communicate throughout the world of business. Through accounting it is possible to communicate about plans, actions and activity of an organisation to other people. These other people do not need to be present as accounting can communicate across national boundaries as it is an international language which is used in much the same way throughout the world. It is also a timeless language as it enables an understanding of what has happened in the past and also a forecast to be made of what will happen in the future.

So accounting is very important in the business world and is fairly central to managers of all types and in all organisations. No manager can really escape exposure to accounting. If you were to live in a foreign country, you would find it helpful to understand the language of that country and would consider it worthwhile to put some effort into learning that language. Well, accounting is the language of business and it is equally worthwhile to put some effort into learning this language. If you understand and can use the language of the country in which you live, you can manage your life better in that country. Equally, if you understand and can use the language of business, namely accounting, you can manage better and conduct yourself more effectively in the world of work. This book is designed to help you understand and make use of the language of accounting so that you can be more effective as a manager. And it is not, as you will see, a difficult language to learn and to use.

One of the things which accounting is used for, of course, is to identify the profit which an organisation makes from its activities. It is therefore generally considered that the role of accounting in any organisation is concerned with profit maximisation. But of course there are a lot of other objectives which an organisation might have and it is the role of accounting to be used to help an organisation to realise its objectives.

One aspect of the actions of an organisation which is very prominent at the present time is what is known as corporate social responsibility (CSR). It is often thought that profit and socially responsible behaviour – or at least the maximisation of profit and socially responsible behaviour – are incompatible with each other. This is not the case, however, and there is a lot of evidence to suggest that an organisation which behaves in a socially responsible manner actually improves its profitability (see Crowther 2002 for example). So an important question therefore is whether accounting can be used to support socially responsible behaviour as well as profit-maximising behaviour. The answer of course is that it can indeed, but that this aspect of accounting and business management is normally ignored by those writing textbooks about accounting.

A distinctive feature of this textbook therefore is not just that it is designed to enable managers to use accounting in the management of their business operations but that it is designed to show how to do this in a socially responsible way.

Reference

Crowther, D. (2002). *A Social Critique of Corporate Reporting*. Aldershot: Ashgate.

About the Author

David Crowther is a qualified accountant who worked as an accountant, systems specialist and general manager in local government, industry and commerce for 20 years. After a number of years in the financial services sector, including a spell in which he set up and ran a store credit card scheme, he decided to leave the business world and become an academic. In 1994, he joined Aston University as a lecturer in accounting. He obtained a PhD from Aston in 1999 for research into corporate performance and reporting before leaving to join the University of North London. He is now Professor of Corporate Social Responsibility at London Metropolitan University.

David is the author of several books and has also contributed over 100 articles to academic, business and professional journals and books. He has also spoken widely at conferences and seminars and acted as a consultant to a wide range of government, professional and commercial organisations. His research is into organisational performance with an emphasis upon social accounting and social responsibility.

1

Introduction to Accounting

Learning objectives

After studying this chapter you should be able to:

- describe the main features of a manager's job;
- outline the key elements of information provision;
- describe the nature and functions of financial and management accounting;
- discuss the relationship between performance measurement and accounting in a modern business environment;
- outline the relationship between ethical behaviour and business performance.

The role of a business manager

A manager of any modern business has a difficult job to perform. A crucial part of his/her job is to meet the objectives of the organisation of which he/she is a part and in order to do so he/she must pay attention to a number of important issues. We will look at these issues and ways in which accounting information can be used to help a manager during the course of this book. Although the exact nature of a manager's job may vary quite significantly from one organisation or department to another, so that the role of a marketing manager, a production manager or a manager of a supermarket may appear to be quite different. There is, however, considerable similarity in terms of the fundamental tasks to be performed.

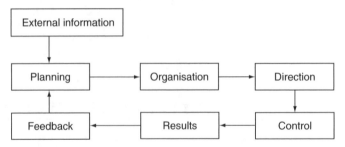

Figure 1.1 The tasks of management

These tasks can be categorised as shown in Figure 1.1.

Managers plan their work and the work of others as well as organising themselves and others, directing others as to what to do, motivating them and exercising control over situations and other people. The results are fed back into the planning process in order to modify future plans for the business.

All managers are concerned with working with people: those they work with, those they supervise, those they report to, and those who are the customers for the product or service which is provided by that area of an organisation which the manager is responsible for. All managers are therefore naturally concerned with the output for their particular area of responsibility and also with the inputs to their area of responsibility, whether these be raw materials, information or goods to be displayed and sold.

Using the information available, a manager must plan for the future of the business. In this context a manager must decide upon the courses of action which need to be taken in order to achieve the best results, and must consider what alternative courses of action are available, and what the consequences of any particular decision might be. Thus the manager of a restaurant, for example, will need to decide what its opening hours need to be and how these might affect possible customers who might want to dine when the restaurant is closed. The manager, however, needs also to decide upon the ingredients of the menu and how much of each to order; in doing so he/she needs to consider what the effect of not ordering enough of a particular item might be in terms of dissatisfied customers and the possible effect this might have upon the future of the business and also what the effects of overordering and having waste might be upon the profitability of the business. The manager therefore needs to consider alternatives and their consequences and decide what course of action to take after this consideration of the facts.

Decision-making is a crucial part of the job of any manager, and decisions need to be made between conflicting alternatives. These decisions are often to a large extent conflicting in their possible outcomes and there is a degree of uncertainty surrounding the consequences. Selecting the best possible decision to make is therefore often a difficult and skilful process but it is important that the decisions made are the right ones. Because of this managers need tools to help them to evaluate the consequences of the alternative decisions which they might make. These tools will assist them in making better decisions. Within most organisations a key dimension in decision-making is financial. In the case of a restaurant manager, for example, he/she will need to balance the cost of the ingredients bought against the income from providing meals. Accounting has been developed as one tool which can help managers in decision-making through helping them to assess the financial implications of any courses of action available.

The development of accounting

Virtually all commercial enterprises have some form of accounting function. Accounting has become the universally adopted system of communicating economic information relating to an organisation and its activities. The notion of accounting, however, is far from being a new phenomenon. Accounting records dating back to ancient civilisations have been located, including building accounts for the Parthenon in Athens which have been found on marble tablets. Similarly, ancient Greek records exist illustrating an early form of stewardship accounting known as 'charge and discharge accounting': charge representing the amounts received and discharge being the amount expended (de Ste Croix 1956). This system was further developed in Italy throughout the thirteenth and fourteenth centuries. The development included the practice of distinguishing between debit and credit entries and the use of two-sided accounting entries. The origins of double-entry bookkeeping system thus began to take form.

Widespread knowledge and use of a system of bookkeeping across Europe was facilitated by the publication in 1494 of a treatise by Luca Pacioli entitled *Summa de Arithmetica, Geometria, Proportioni et Proportionalita* ('All about arithmetic'). This work included a section headed 'Particularis de Computis et Scripturis' which described a method of double-entry bookkeeping. Pacioli's work received general recognition during the sixteenth century with many translations: the English translation appeared nearly 50 years after the first publication.

From the late 1700s onwards there were a number of influencing factors on the development of financial accounting theory in the UK.

Firstly, the Napoleonic Wars placed a huge financial burden on the UK. The government response to this was the introduction of taxes on income, including that of businesses. This new tax burden created an incentive for businesses to maintain detailed accounting records.

Secondly, the coming of the railways in the early 1800s created the demand for substantial funding, beyond the resources of any individual. To satisfy this demand, companies were formed whose shares were sold to the wider public. Widespread ownership of shares in the railway companies meant that it was no longer feasible for all shareholders to be involved in the active management of the enterprise: this task was delegated to professional company managers. The separation of the roles of ownership and management established a demand for accounting statements that would report on managers' stewardship of the enterprise.

Thirdly, a need arose to offer protection to shareholders and creditors in their dealings with limited liability companies: The Joint Stock Companies Act 1862 made this type of organisation common. Protection was offered in various forms:

1 The Railways Act 1868 provided for a standardised form of financial statements and accounting methodology to be adopted by railway companies.
2 In 1879 it became mandatory for banks to have their accounts audited by independent accountants and this requirement was extended to all companies some 20 years later.
3 In 1908 the publication of annual accounts was made a legal requirement for all companies.

The fourth factor affecting the development of accounting was the establishment of the professional accounting bodies: The Scottish Institute of Chartered Accountants was founded in the 1850s and its English counterpart some 30 years later. The accounting profession helped to develop accounting conventions including the distinction between capital and revenue expenditure and the preparation of financial statements capable of independent and objective verification.

The need for accounting information

It is impossible for managers to ignore the financial implications of any decision which they might make and so the evaluation of any decision in financial terms is a crucial part of the decision-making process. As accounting is the method by which a business records its operations, it is an important part of the business and cannot be ignored by any manager. Accounting information, however, takes time and effort to collect and process and so is costly to produce. Such information therefore is valuable to a business and so needs to be used to benefit that business.

In order for accounting information to benefit the business it needs to enable the users of that information (the managers) to alter their behaviour as a result of considering the information which has been provided. The information therefore needs to be meaningful to the recipient and also relevant to the purpose for which it is provided. It also needs to be provided at a time when it can be used to alter behaviour. The information also needs, naturally, to be accurate and provided in a format which is understandable by those receiving that information.

The key elements of information therefore are:

• meaningfulness
• relevance
• timeliness
• accuracy
• format.

Information can be distinguished from data, which is a set of facts which are not capable of influencing behaviour. In order to be useful, information must be communicated in a form which is understandable to the recipient and the quantitative nature of accounting information enables it to be more precisely understood.

Accounting information can be divided into two types according to its use:

1 External information is provided for people who need to know about the business but are not involved in the running of the business, such as shareholders, investors in the business and government departments (e.g. Customs & Excise or Inland Revenue).
2 Internal information is provided for use within the business and is the kind of information which managers need to help them make decisions in the running of the business.

Each of these types of information is provided by a different type of accounting.

 ## Different types of accounting

Accounting can be categorised into three distinct types, depending upon its function.

Financial accounting

This is concerned with the provision of external information about the business, with the determination of profit and with the production of the final accounts, which a business needs to produce on an annual basis. It is therefore concerned with meeting statutory requirements in this respect. Financial accounting is also concerned with the raising of finance for a business and with the acquisition of assets. It is largely historical in perspective and concerned with recording what has happened in the business and the effect which this has had upon the business.

The key functions of financial accounting therefore are:

- meeting statutory requirements;
- record keeping;
- production of final accounts;
- the raising of finance.

Management accounting

This is concerned with the internal informational needs of the business. Its focus is upon the future rather than the past and on the evaluation of alternative possible courses of action. It is therefore essentially a part of the management decision support system and also a part of the planning and control aspects of the business. Management accounting also enables performance to be measured and evaluated.

The key functions of management accounting therefore are:

- controlling business operations;
- decision support;
- business planning;
- performance measurement.

Cost accounting

This is often considered to be a part of management accounting and is the base from which management accounting was developed. In reality, however, cost accounting needs to be viewed as a separate branch of accounting which provides the basic information for both financial and management accounting. It is concerned with the identification and allocation of the various costs of production and with the determining of the valuation of the goods produced.

The key functions of cost accounting therefore are:

- identifying and attributing costs;
- cost accumulation for product costing;
- stock valuation;
- provision of source data for financial and management accounting.

This book is concerned with accounting as a tool for business management and decision-making and is therefore concerned with all three types of accounting. It is not intended to enable you to become an accountant as this requires extensive technical training. Instead it is intended to assist you as a business manager to understand and make use of accounting information. More importantly it is intended to help you become aware of the context in which accounting is used. Contrary to the general perception, accounting is not neutral but is built upon a set of assumptions which predetermine what is to be produced. Thus there are value judgements built in to the use of accounting and to the decisions made based upon the use of that information. One of these assumptions is that the only people who really matter are the shareholders of a business as the business is run for their benefit.

In the current environment the behaviour of organisations and their managers has been opened up for questioning and the accusation has been made that these organisations and their managers are exploiting others. Thus the term corporate social responsibility has come into popular use as a means of describing behaviour which differs from this perception. One of the major themes of this book therefore is to show how accounting can be used in a socially responsible manner to help managers plan and run their businesses in a different manner.

The objectives of a business

A business manager must be concerned not just with the internal running of the business but must also be concerned with the external environment in which the business operates – that is with the customers and suppliers, with competitors, and with the market for the products or services supplied by the business.

Such concerns of a business manager comprise the strategic element of the manager's job and a manager must therefore be familiar with this aspect of management, and with the way in which accounting can help in this area. This chapter therefore is concerned with a consideration of the external environment of a business and with the strategic part of a manager's job. First, however, we need to consider the various objectives which an organisation might have.

We have seen in our previous studies that management accounting exists as a tool to help the managers of a business in meeting their objectives, but the objectives of managers need to be considered in terms of their helping to meet the objectives of the organisations in which they work. While most business organisations aim to make a profit, this is not true of all; the not-for-profit sector of the economy is one which is increasing in importance, and making a profit is not the only objective of most organisations. Nevertheless, organisations do have objectives, and the following possible objectives of an organisation can be identified:

Profit maximisation

For organisations which exist to make a profit it seems reasonable that they should seek to make as large a profit as possible. It is not, however, always clear what course of action will lead to the greatest profit, and it is by no means clear whether profit maximisation in the short term will be in the best interests of the business and will lead to the greatest profit in the longer term. Thus profit maximisation may not be in the best interests of a business and it certainly may conflict with other objectives which a business may have.

Maximising cash flow

Cash flow is not the same as profit and an organisation needs cash to survive. In some circumstances this cash flow may be more important than profit because the lack of cash can threaten the survival of the organisation.

Maximising return on capital employed

This is a measure of performance of a business in terms of its operating efficiency and therefore provides a measure of how a business is performing over time. Comparative measures are useful in helping the owners and managers of a business to decide what course of action may be beneficial to the business.

Maximising service provision

This is the not-for-profit sector equivalent of maximising the return on capital employed and thus provides a similar means of evaluating decisions.

Maximising shareholder value

The value of a business depends partly upon the profits it generates and partly upon the value of the assets it possesses. These assets can comprise partly of tangible assets such as plant and machinery or land and buildings and partly of intangible assets such as brand names. Thus the value of Coca-Cola as a business far outweighs the value of its fixed assets because of the value of its brand name which is recognised worldwide. Maximising the value of the business to shareholders therefore involves much more than maximising the profit generated.

Growth

Growth through expansion of the business, in terms of both assets and earnings as well as the increase in market share which the business holds, is one object-ive which appeals to both owners and managers. If this is an objective of the business then it will lead to different decisions to those of profit maximisation.

Long-term stability

The survival of a business is of great concern to both owners and managers and this can lead to different behaviour and a reluctance to accept risk. All decisions involve an element of risk and seeking to reduce risk for the purpose of long-term stability can lead to performance which is less than desirable.

Satisficing

It must be recognised that all objectives of an organisation are dependent upon the people who set them and business behaviour cannot be considered with-out taking this into account. Satisficing is a way of reducing risk and taking multiple objectives into account by making decisions which are acceptable from several viewpoints without necessarily being the best to meet any particu-lar objective.

Any business is likely to seek to pursue a number of these objectives at any point in time. The precise combination of them is likely to vary from one organisation to another and from one time to another, depending upon the individual circumstances of the organisation at any point in time. The organi-sation will not, however, view all the objectives which it is pursuing at any particular time as equally important and will have more important ones to fol-low. These objectives will therefore tend to be viewed as a hierarchy, which may vary from time to time.

None of these conflict with socially responsible behaviour and there is growing evidence that social responsibility actually enhances the ability to achieve all of these objectives.

The principles of financial accounting

Accounting has often been described as the language of business and, as such, provides the means by which an organisation may represent its actions to its stakeholders and be universally understood. It is an international language which means that it can be understood by everyone concerned without worrying about translation difficulties. So profit is understood as profit, as reported by the organisation, whatever the native language of the user of that accounting information. This assertion is, however, a little simplistic. Whilst national comparison between companies is assisted by the requirement that all companies report according to a common standard, no such common framework has yet been established at the global level.

As world financial markets become more integrated, the number of investors who look abroad for stocks and shares to invest in has grown. A US investor considering investing in a German company will need to understand the way in which German companies report on their financial performance. However, the reporting standards[1] used in Germany differ from those used in America. Indeed, differences in reporting standards pertain in most countries. As an example of the problems that this can cause consider the following example. When in 1993 Daimler-Benz became the first German company to get a listing on the New York Stock Exchange, the accounts, which following German standards showed a healthy profit of just over DM150m, were converted to follow US accounting practice. Rather than showing a profit the reconstructed accounts showed a loss of close to DM950m. We mention this example to highlight the point that financial accounts are drawn up according to a set of rules and standards, and as these rules and standards differ so will the accounting information they provide.

All accounts are, however, prepared in accordance with a set of Accounting Concepts and Conventions. The purpose of these is to ensure, as far as possible, that transactions are recorded in a uniform manner. Thus to ensure consistency in the preparation of financial statements a set of rules have been agreed by the accounting profession, in the UK the Accounting Standards Board regulates these conventions. These conventions vary in different countries. We will not attempt here to review these differences, but when accounts are prepared under different standards in different countries then that the differences can be significant. Conventions which are important in the preparation of accounts are:

Business entity

The business and the owner are separate and the financial statements represent the activities of the business. This convention holds for all, and not just limited liability, companies.

Money measurement

The financial statements record only those transactions that have a monetary value. You should be aware of the limitations of this convention as outlined by Atrill, and the variations that have been suggested to overcome these limitations.

Cost

All transactions are recorded at their original cost to the business. The cost convention is based upon the accounting principle of prudence. This means that the lowest value is always that which is used.

There are two possible departures from the cost convention. The first is stock valuation, which should be valued at the lower of cost and net realisable value (sale value). There may be a situation where stock has been damaged and is no longer worth what was paid for it, then obviously it must be recorded at its new lower value. The second is in relation to property. Many large companies have properties, which increase in value, and the regulations allow these companies to revalue these properties to their new market value, subject to a number of restrictions.

Going concern

Accounting statements are prepared annually by businesses and unless there is evidence to the contrary, it is assumed they will continue for the foreseeable future.

Accruals

Accounting statements are normally prepared on an annual basis. It is important, therefore, to include all income and expenditure that is relevant to that time period, even if payment has not been made. This is the major difference between a cash flow forecast and a profit and loss account, the former is only interested in cash, and the latter does not concern itself with cash.

Prudence

It is a practice to recognise all possible losses in the financial statements, but not anticipating profit. An example of anticipating profit would be to include as a sale a transaction that had not been formalised, i.e. a customer rang and inquired about purchasing a consignment of goods but did not place an order. This cannot be recognised as a sale until the transaction has been formalised and both an order has been received and a sales invoice has been raised.

The accepted usage of this accounting language also means that the owners and managers of a business can communicate with each other, plan for the future, control the implementation of that planning and report upon the subsequent performance. Thus Robson (1992) provides a reminder of some of the qualities of accounting. He states that accounting should be explained as inscription to enable action at a distance. He explains that such inscription enables the translation of elements within their context and that viewed this way accounting has the following qualities: mobility by enabling the actor and his setting to be divorced; stability by the use of conventions which eliminate contextual dependencies thereby making information recognisable to all users; and combinability by enabling the accumulating and aggregating of data.

The development of management accounting

Thus far, however, we have only considered the historical development of book-keeping and financial accounting. The development of these preceded the development of management accounting. Cost accounting, the precursor of management accounting, appeared relatively late in the evolution of accounting systems but, just as financial accounting developed in response to the needs of its environment, so too did cost accounting emerge in order to satisfy different needs of business. Whereas financial accounting can be seen as concerned with controlling, recording and reporting upon transactions with, and to, stakeholders in the enterprise's external environment (primarily, shareholders and other investors), cost accounting has traditionally been seen as an internal control mechanism. Johnson and Kaplan (1987) suggest that the development of cost management was influenced by the decision of nineteenth-century entrepreneurs to arrange for processes, which had previously been organised and priced in the market, to be brought within the control of one organisation. For example, the process outputs for a textile business include spinning, weaving and finishing. In the past each of these activities had been carried out by separate craftsmen operating in their own right and with their process outputs being exchanged in the market via merchants. Entrepreneurs believed that bringing the various processes associated with a single activity, such as textiles, within the control of one centrally organised hierarchy would result in greater profits. In so doing, however, a need was created to control the efficiency of the processes when combined and to attach an internal price, or more precisely a cost, to the processes now performed within the hierarchy. These systems thus provided quasi-market metrics that enabled managers to gauge the efficiency of the economic activity taking place within the organisation.

These early cost management systems emphasised the need to control the level of input resources consumed per output unit. This was particularly true of labour, as a unit of resource consumed, because labour normally comprised the greatest factor – cost of production – in any nineteenth-century industrial organisation. Different industries developed control measures to serve their own particular requirements: thus for example railways used cost per ton-mile while distributors/retailers used gross margins and stock turnover. Johnson and Kaplan describe how other organisational and procedural changes that were occurring in the late nineteenth and early twentieth century spawned cost accounting developments to serve the needs created by these changes.

Procedural changes included the emergence of scientific management, which gave rise to F.W. Taylor's notion of 'one best way' of utilising labour and material resources, measured in terms of physical units. The natural evolution of this concept was to ascertain the standard cost of a process and the concomitant comparison of variances between actual and standard performance. The first description of a system of standard costing and variance analysis is generally ascribed to G. Charter Harrison. Organisational changes in the form of vertically integrated, and later divisionalised, businesses also led to the development of innovative forms of accounting. Thus for example return on investment (ROI) was developed in order to be used centrally in vertically integrated firms to guide decisions on capital allocation between various activities. At a later date, when divisionalised businesses delegated the responsibility for using capital efficiently to managers, ROI also came to be used to judge local performance. Similarly, flexible budgets were developed to assess and control business units subject to variations in output.

This brief historical review illustrates how management accounting methods evolved in response to the needs and challenges created by organisational and procedural changes which were taking place at the time. It has been argued, however, that whilst global competition and developments taking place in information technology, production procedures and technology are similarly calling for innovative and relevant responses from management accounting at the present time, these have not been forthcoming. Johnson and Kaplan note that all management accounting procedures known today were developed over 70 years ago and question their relevance in today's environment. Indeed Kaplan (1986) adds that accountants are now 'living off innovations in management accounting' that were developed in previous decades. They also state of management accounting systems that 'their original purpose of providing information to facilitate cost control and performance measurement in hierarchical organisations has been transformed to one of compiling costs for periodic financial statements'.

The lack of a response from management accounting to today's needs and the continued usage of obsolete methods are arguably causing a crisis in management accounting. In the next section we will consider the causes of this apparent crisis.

Despite these criticisms of management accounting as based in the past it can be seen that management accounting has to some extent adapted to meet the needs of the new business environment. The ways in which accounting has adapted, or failed to adapt, to the needs of both modern business and society as a whole, will be returned to at various points throughout this book. Similarly, the effectiveness of management accounting will be evaluated from a variety of perspectives at various points throughout this book.

The nature of management accounting

Management accounting is concerned with the analysis and reporting of financial information for managers within a business in order to assist them in the performance of their jobs. The collection of this financial information is crucial to management accounting, and cost accounting has a large part to play in this. Other sources of information are, however, needed and not all information will be expressed in financial terms. Information regarding quantities of resources (in terms of physical units) may be important, as may qualitative information and so this too falls within the scope of management accounting.

Management accounting is essentially a part of management decision-making and of use to all managers. It is used throughout the business rather than being focused within the finance department. Its use therefore is to help managers with decision-making in the following areas:

- *Planning*: what to produce and how best to meet the objectives of the organisation;
- *Control*: to ensure that the outcomes correspond to those planned;
- *Decision-making*: to decide between alternative courses of action by evaluating the consequences;
- *Measuring performance*: to decide if it matches the expectations set out in the plan and to take corrective action if not.

In this book we will investigate the types of problems which managers face in these three main areas and the way in which management accounting can be used to help solve these problems.

Accounting information systems

Management accounting information will be generated to a large extent by the accounting information system which the business possesses. As far as managers are concerned this system is a means of collecting information and communicating it to aid their decision-making. The system therefore needs to have been developed to meet the requirements of the managers of the business, along with its other function of satisfying the financial accounting and reporting requirements of the business. These requirements will vary greatly according to the nature of the business and according to the role which each individual manager plays in that business. The information needs of a warehouse manager will naturally be greatly different to those of a manager of a sales force, while a manager in a hospital will have quite different information reporting needs to those of a manager within a textile company. These informational needs will also be to some extent dependant upon the structure of the organisation, and the manager's place in that structure, and the culture of that organisation. Organisational structure and culture will tend to vary from one organisation to another, thus placing different demands upon the accounting information system.

The technology upon which an accounting information system is based will also vary greatly and will depend partly upon the size of the company. Nevertheless there are certain functions common to all such systems, namely:

Information collection and recording

This function ensures that the relevant information is identified and stored in a systematic way so that it can be used for the future.

Information analysis

This function involves the interpretation of information and the sorting of it into such a form that it can be used to help the manager in the business.

Information reporting

The relevant information needs to be communicated to managers in such a way that it enables them to use it to help make decisions. It is vital that information is reported in time to enable decisions to be made.

The tasks of a manager

We have seen how the role of a manager of a business will vary greatly according to his area of responsibility. We have also seen how the manager needs to help the organisation meet its objectives and that these can vary significantly from one organisation to another. The roles of different managers are therefore very different and the tasks which they undertake to perform their roles are also very different. Nevertheless we can classify these different tasks into one of several types according to their nature. These tasks can be classified as follows:

Planning

A manager needs to plan for the future in order to decide how best to meet the objectives of the organisation. He needs to decide what can be achieved and what inputs are needed to help him meet his plan. Planning therefore needs to be not just qualitative but also quantitative in order to evaluate the plan and determine inputs and outputs to the plan. All business processes can be considered as taking a set of inputs and performing operations in order to add value and transform them into outputs. The function of any business can therefore considered to be adding value through the transformations made during its processing. This can be illustrated as shown in Figure 1.2.

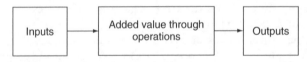

Figure 1.2 The transformational process

Planning needs to consider alternatives, not just in terms of alternative targets to set but also in terms of alternative methods of achieving these targets. Planning cannot be done in isolation but needs to take into account what effect the planning has upon the plans of other managers within the organisation. This is especially true when the inputs of this plan come from the outputs of the plan of another manager or when these outputs affect the planning of another manager. Thus a sales manager cannot plan how much to sell without taking into account the plan of the production manager concerning how much will be produced, and the production manager cannot make his plans for production without taking into account the planning of the sales manager regarding how much can be sold. The planning tasks of the manager therefore are important but cannot be made in isolation.

Control

Control is concerned with making sure that things happen in accordance with the plan. It therefore involves monitoring the plan, and progress being made in accordance with the plan. It also involves taking action when things are not going in accordance with the plan in order to attempt to change things so that the plan can be achieved. Control is, therefore, an ongoing activity for a manager and involves comparing actual performance with targets, providing feedback on actual performance and taking action to change performance when it diverges from the plan. Although the manager may be able to achieve this by physical observation and communication with people, it is likely that this will not be sufficient. He will probably need to rely to a large extent upon reports in order to exercise control. The reports which management accounting provides are, therefore, crucial in assisting a manager to exercise control.

Decision-making

One of the key aspects of a manager's job is concerned with making decisions. There is always more than one course of action which a manager can take in any particular situation (even if one of the courses is to do nothing!) and so he needs to decide between the alternatives in order to make the decision which is most beneficial. In order to make a decision the manager needs to identify the possible alternative courses of action open to him, to gather data about those courses of action and to evaluate the consequences of each particular alternative. The stages in the decision-making process are shown in Figure 1.3, which illustrates that the decision-making process is not complete when an alternative has been selected and implemented but that the outcomes of the decision need to be followed through into the control process.

In order to make a decision a manager needs information. Management accounting is one tool which exists to help the manager by providing information about the consequences of the alternatives open to him.

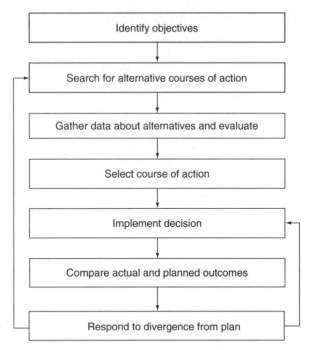

Figure 1.3 The decision-making process

Performance evaluation

While the performance of organisations is evaluated by such measures as return on capital employed, the organisation in turn needs to evaluate the performance of its units and the managers running these units. The managers in turn need to evaluate the actual performance of their tasks against that which has been planned. In order to evaluate performance there needs to be acceptable measures of performance. Measurement needs to be relative to be meaningful – to compare performance with plans and with past performance. Performance measures also need to be quantitative in order to enable comparisons to be made and financial information provides important data for the measurement of performance. Unless performance can be evaluated managers have no basis upon which to exercise control, to make decisions and to plan for the future. The role of management accounting in this context is therefore of crucial importance in enabling managers to carry out their tasks.

Communication

Information available to help managers in their tasks needs to be communicated to them, and managers in turn need to communicate their plans and decisions to others. Communication involves both the sender of information and its

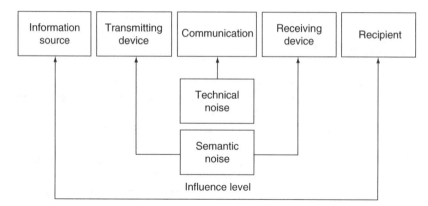

Figure 1.4 The communication of information

recipient, and for the information to be of value it needs to be understood by the recipient as intended by the sender. Any interference which prevents the message being received by the recipient is known as noise. Figure 1.4 shows that two types of noise prevent a message being received as transmitted.

Technical noise is that such as occurs on a telephone or radio which is concerned with the technical means of communication. A more crucial type of noise, however, is semantic noise which occurs because a message is not transmitted in a clear and unambiguous manner and so is not correctly understood by the recipient. Quantitative information is less likely to be misunderstood than qualitative information and this is one of the important features of accounting information. Management accounting therefore has an important part to play not just in enabling decisions to be made but also in the communication of this information.

The importance of performance measurement

In order for a business to be able to control its operations it is necessary that the managers of that business are able to measure the performance of the business and of individual parts of that business. We will look at examples of how management accounting can help a manager to do this. It is important, however, to remember that businesses, and the environment in which they operate, are continually changing. As the business environment changes so too must accounting in order to respond to this changed environment and to provide business managers with the tools needed to manage in such an environment. These changes can be expected to continue and there is a consequent need for managers to keep abreast of developments in order to be able to perform their jobs to optimal effect.

A significant feature of business management is the need to measure and evaluate performance, both of the business as a whole and of individual parts of that business. Of equal significance is the ability to evaluate the performance of individual managers. This is of importance to the business but particularly to the managers themselves, as their rewards are increasingly based, at least in part, upon an assessment of their performance. Thus management accounting needs to be able to perform this function, and we have seen how various techniques can be used to facilitate this. Management accounting has, however, been criticised for its failure in this respect, and Johnson and Kaplan (1987) have argued that the role of management accounting has changed so that it is no longer relevant to managerial needs. In considering management accounting systems they state:

> Their original purpose of providing information to facilitate cost control and performance measurement in hierarchical organisations has been transformed to one of compiling costs for periodic financial statements.

While we will see, in our consideration of the various techniques of management accounting, that this is not entirely the case, and that management accounting does in fact facilitate the measurement of performance. It is important to recognise that a business manager, when using management accounting, operates within the broader environment of the organisation, and that accounting is used to satisfy other needs within the business. These other needs necessarily relate to financial accounting, and the relationship between costing, management accounting and financial accounting needs to be recognised, as does the role of accounting information and control systems within the organisation. It is also important to recognise that management accounting is subject to criticism and has limitations in its use. Thus each technique which a business manager might employ to help solve a problem gives both benefits and limitations, and we have explored both aspects of each of the techniques which we have considered. It is important for a manager to recognise limitations to any of the techniques which he/she might use to assist in the management of the business.

We will also see that accounting is presented as a quantitative subject which enables the analysis of facts relating to business decisions in order for rational decisions to be made. In fact this is not true and we have equally seen how the use of accounting information can affect individual behaviour within the firm and lead to either increasing or reducing the motivation of individual managers. The way in which control systems are designed and the way in which accounting information is used can therefore have a significant effect upon the performance of a business. It is important for business managers to recognise this and be aware of the effects of accounting upon themselves and others within the organisation. This awareness will help lead to better decision-making and subsequently to better performance by the manager.

Managers and business ethics

Business ethics is a subject of considerable importance to any organisation and accounting information has often been accused of providing an excuse for unethical behaviour. Indeed, this accusation has been extended to accountants and business managers generally who have been accused of behaving unethically in their search for profits to the exclusion of all else. The unethical ways in which accounting information has been used have been described in detail by Smith (1992) who describes the way in which new accounting techniques have been created with the sole purpose of boosting reported profits. These techniques have become known as creative accounting and have been the subject of much media attention. Smith's book, *Accounting for Growth*, makes interesting reading for any prospective business manager.

Other writers have, however, been concerned with highlighting the value of ethical behaviour and have claimed that this actually leads to better business performance. Thus McCoy (1985) considers that ethics need to be at the core of business behaviour and that effective business management is based upon ethical behaviour. He claims that this recognition, and acting accordingly, actually increases the performance of a business. The UK accounting bodies are also concerned with business ethics and all have a stance in this matter, and have incorporated a requirement for ethical behaviour into their codes of conduct. The subject of ethical behaviour amongst businesses has also had an effect upon auditing practice and upon the financial reporting of businesses.

Any manager operating in a business environment needs to be aware of the importance of ethical behaviour. Equally he/she will experience conflicts, in attempting to behave ethically, between different alternative courses of action, and may find conflicts between the firm's objectives and his/her own personal motivation and objectives. No ready solution to these conflicts is available but a manager should be aware that research has shown that ethical behaviour leads to better performance in the longer term, and so should be encouraged to act accordingly.

Organisation of the book

This book is concerned with various issues which managers are concerned with in the carrying out of their work. These can be classified into two types of issue:

- Problems concerned with whether or not to invest in a business. This requires an understanding of the nature of the business and how it has performed in the past. Financial accounting is concerned with assisting to inform this kind of problem.
- The problems which managers have to face in the performance of their duties and with the decisions which they need to take in order to be effective. Management accounting is a tool which is available to managers to help them to perform the tasks of their jobs better and to make better decisions.

The book is organised therefore around the problems which managers face and explains how the techniques of accounting can be used to assist. In particular, we will consider how accounting can assist but in a socially responsible way.

The remainder of the book is divided into three parts, as follows:

Part 1 considers the way in which financial information is reported externally and how that information can be used to evaluate business performance. This part is focused upon financial reporting.

Part 2 considers the way in which accounting information can be used within a business to help make decisions and monitor performance. This part focuses upon management accounting.

Part 3 explores a broader perspective on managing a business through considering stakeholder interests and the relationship between accounting and strategic management.

 ## Note

1 Reporting standards set out the way in which the transactions of a company should be recorded and reported upon.

 ## References

de Ste Croix, G.E.M. (1956). Greek and Roman accounting. In A.C. Littleton and B.S. Yamey (eds), *Studies in the History of Accounting*. London: Sweet and Maxwell.

Johnson, H.T. and Kaplan, R.S. (1987). *Relevance Lost: The Rise and Fall of Management Accounting*. Boston, MA: Harvard Business School Press.

Kaplan, R.S. (1986). *Cost Accounting for the 90's: The Challenge of Technological Change*. Proceedings, Montvale, NJ: National Association of Accountants.

McCoy, C.S. (1985). *Management of Values: The Ethical Difference in Corporate Policy and Performance*. Marshfield, MA: Pitman.

Robson, K. (1992). Accounting numbers as 'inscription': action at a distance and the development of accounting. *Accounting, Organizations and Society*, 17 (7), 685–708.

Smith, T. (1992). *Accounting for Growth*. London: Century Business.

 ## Additional questions

Question 1.1

List the main inputs for a firm. List the main outputs from the transformational process.

Question 1.2

Information is one of the key resources of any business manager. Distinguish between information and data and describe the key elements of information.

2
Reporting Financial Performance

Learning objectives

On completion of this chapter you should be able to:

- understand the basic principles of financial accounting and the way they underpin the preparation of financial statements;
- prepare a cash flow forecast;
- understand basic accounting concepts and conventions;
- interpret a profit and loss account and balance sheet;
- understand the reporting of socially responsible performance.

Introduction

All companies have a statutory duty to report upon their activity by means of annual accounts. Thus the Joint Stock Companies Act 1844 imposed upon firms the requirement to maintain accounts and to produce a balance sheet for shareholders. It was expected that such accounts would be published but this requirement to publish accounts was, however, repealed by the Joint Stock Companies Act 1856, with such accounts being required only for the internal purposes of the owners of the company. Nevertheless, the development of the limited company as a form of enterprise necessitated the development of corporate reporting as a means of communication between the managers of the company and its owners. This need became increasingly apparent with the increasing size of such enterprises and the concomitant divorcing of ownership from management of such enterprises. This in turn was one of the drivers which led to the development of accounting practice and the development of corporate reporting. Thus by 1890 such enterprises were being accounted for on the basis of their being 'going concerns' as one of the main accounting principles (Newman 1979), with accounting practice being based upon a separation of capital from income and profits from trading, both on the basis of a recognition of the divorcing of shareholding from management of the enterprise.

Thus by the start of the twentieth century it had been accepted that firms had a corporate identity which was distinct from that of their owners and that such firms embodied a presumption of immortality. Alongside this was the acceptance that control of the actions of the firm implied some liability for the effects of those actions and that the divorce of management from ownership necessitated some protection for the owners. This was achieved through the function of the audit of the activities of the firm and the Companies Act 1900 made compulsory the remuneration of such auditors. At the turn of the century it was generally accepted that accounting served the purpose of facilitating the relationship between managers and owners of a business, through its reporting function, but that the general public had no right to such information. Thus the Companies Act 1906 stated that there was no requirement for companies to produce financial statements, although the Companies (Consolidations) Act 1908 amended this to require the production of a profit and loss account and balance sheet. This was further amended by the Companies Act 1929 which required the production of these, together with a directors' report and an auditors' report for the AGM. Subsequent legislation has extended the reporting requirements of companies to the format seen today.

Such corporate reporting has, however, been extended in addition to satisfying legislative requirements. Thus the period up to the Second World War saw an increasing use of accounting information for analysis purposes but with an emphasis upon the income statement. This period also saw the extension of the directors' report to contain information about the company which was not to be found in the financial statements. This information was, however, primarily concerning the past actions of the company, as the emphasis in this period remained firmly upon the reporting of past actions as part of the relationship between the ownership and the management of the firm. It is only in the post-war period that this emphasis changed from backward looking to forward looking and from inward looking to outward looking. Gilmore and Willmott (1992) have argued that this was a reflection of the changing nature of such reporting to a focus upon investment decision-making and the need to attract investment into the company in this period of expansion. The emphasis remained firmly upon the needs of the company, however, and only the emphasis had changed from informing existing investors to attracting new investors.

The users of such corporate reports, although no longer only the shareholders of the company and its managers, were, however, still considered to be a restricted set of the population, having specialist knowledge of and interest in such reporting. Thus there was at that time a general acceptance that corporate reporting should be provided for the knowledgeable professional rather than the individual and in order to satisfy the needs of these professionals corporate reports became more extensive in content, with greater disclosure of financial and other information. No attention was paid to the development of the report itself, although it was recognised that the orientation of the report had changed and that increasing attention was being paid to the non-financial parts of the report such as the chairman's statement. Instead, attention was given to the form of accounting and the application of accounting principles and standards. This was reflected by the establishment of the Accounting Standards Steering Committee in 1969.[1] The primary focus for the accounting of organisations was financial accounting and this accounting was temporally divided, for reporting purposes, into annual periods to provide the subject matter of the annual report.

Recording the financial transactions undertaken by organisations and presenting intelligible monetary statements of income and expenditure and capital acquisitions are essential to good business management and also necessary for informing the various groups of people, both internal and external to the organisation, who have an interest in the business. These people will include, not just shareholders but also a wide range of other stakeholders who are interested in the company and its activities. These stakeholders will include creditors, suppliers, bankers, tax authorities and potential investors. They will also include employees and pensioners and possibly pressure groups and local society groups.

In this chapter you will be introduced to the main financial statements used by businesses, large and small. Financial statements are those reports of a business which detail its activity. They consist of the Balance Sheet, the Profit and Loss Account and the Cash Flow Statement. For publicly quoted companies they must be accompanied by notes explaining how the figures in them are made up. It is important to understand how to prepare a cash flow forecast, as cash is a key factor affecting all organisations, and so we will look at this in some detail. Preparing a profit and loss account, which is the statement organisations use to report their profits, or losses, for the year, and the balance sheet, which is a position statement at the end of the accounting period are, however, specialist jobs requiring a fair amount of technical skill. Consequently we will look at how these are produced and what their contents should be but we will not look in detail at actually preparing them. We will, however, examine the conventions applied in the preparation of these statements.

Cash flow statements

A cash flow statement shows what has happened to the company as far as income and expenditure are concerned. We will look at this firstly by means of the investigation of a simple business. Cash flow statements and cash flow forecasts are prepared using the same principles. Cash flow forecasts are produced as a guide to planning and are constructed at the beginning of the year. Large companies prepare cash flow statements, which are required to comply with accounting standards. In the UK the relevant standard is Financial Reporting Standard (FRS) Number 1. Financial Reporting Standards are produced by the accounting bodies to guide companies in how to account for activity in a uniform manner. The information must be presented in a specified format to ensure comparability between companies. Our focus, though, in this chapter will remain initially on the cash flow forecast, which is used by companies of all sizes to plan the movement of cash into and out of the business over the year. The format of cash flow forecasts is not governed by standards, and thus there is no specified format for them.

 ## Cash flow forecasts

Businesses prepare a number of financial statements each year and one of the most important is a cash flow forecast. When starting up a business the bank will want to know how cash will flow through the business and it is also important for the business to identify in advance if an overdraft is required. These are usually prepared for different time periods, from six months to one year. They may be prepared on a monthly or weekly basis depending on the organisation's needs. This is a statement for internal planning purposes and is not subject to the rules we will lay down later for the preparation of the profit and loss account and the balance sheet.

The following example shows the transactions for a new business. We will use this information to prepare a cash flow forecast and then move on and use the same information to prepare a profit and loss account and balance sheet. The detail provided in the example is intended to serve two purposes. We begin with the business looking forward, and trying to project its sales and costs in order to be able to forecast the cash coming into, and out of, the business. When we turn to a consideration of the profit and loss account and the balance sheet, which are backward-looking reporting statements, we assume that what happened was the same as that which was projected to happen. In this situation the cash flow forecast would turn out to be the same as the cash flow statement.

Smithson Ltd decides to set up a business buying and selling fashion clothes. This business is registered as a limited liability company and the following are the transactions for the year. Limited liability status is a legal mechanism, which allows investors to restrict their liability in case of company failure.

The business commences operations on 1 January 2000 by opening a separate bank account for the business and paying in £30 000 from the personal savings of the owners. In the first week the manager buys shop fittings for £8 000, and a small van for £10 000.

During the period from 1 January 2000 to 31 December 2000 the forecast level of transactions is as follows.

Sales of clothing are forecast as follows:

January to March	£15 000 per month
April to September	£22 000 per month
October to December	£25 000 per month

It is also assumed that cash payments are made for 80 per cent of sales, and that the remaining 20 per cent of sales are obtained on one month's credit, with settlement, therefore, taking place in the following month.

Purchases of stock are forecast as follows:

January	£30 000
February	£15 000
March	£8 000
April to September	£10 000 per month
October to December	£13 000 per month

For the first three months of the business all purchases of stock are assumed to have to be paid for in cash. Afterwards the owners of Smithson Ltd assume they will be able to negotiate the following terms with their suppliers, 50 per cent of purchases are on one month's credit with the remainder paid for in cash.

Other payments

Rent   £6 000 a year, payable quarterly in advance

This means that the payments are in four equal instalments and are paid at the start of each quarter of the year. The payments are therefore in January, April, July and October.

Light and heat   £5 200 a year, paid quarterly in arrears

This means that the payments are in four equal instalments and are paid at the end of each quarter of the year. The payments are therefore in March, June, September and December.

Advertising	£1 500 half paid in January the remainder in September
Wages	£42 000 a year, paid in equal monthly instalments.
General expenses	£400 per month
Printing postage and stationery	£200 per month
Telephone	£1 200 a year, paid quarterly in arrears

Let us assume that the last bill will be late in arriving. It is expected in December 2000, but will not arrive until January 2001. This means that when preparing the cash flow the last payment should not be entered as the money will not leave the bank account during the period the cash flow covers. This is a somewhat far-fetched assumption, unless we credit Smithson Ltd with an amazing gift of foresight. However, the assumption is made to highlight an important point, which is that you only enter transactions when cash moves, either in or out, of the bank account. You should also remember the way we are using the information in this example. We begin with Smithson Ltd projecting their sales and cost forecasts for the year ahead. However, if we consider a cash flow statement, drawn up at the end of the year, Smithson Ltd would know that the telephone bill did not arrive in December.

Preparation of the cash flow forecast

When preparing a cash flow forecast it is very important to know the payment terms for all transactions as these dictate when the transactions appear on the cash flow. The purpose of the statement is to track movements of cash through the bank account and it is therefore critical that entries are made only at the point of cash changing hands. We use cash here in the broadest sense as in practice many transactions will be paid by cheque, direct debit or electronic transfer. We will not consider customers making payment by credit card in the following scenario.

Cash flow forecasts are often prepared using spreadsheets as this facilitates planning uses. The business may have to consider the effect on its bank account of allowing customers a longer period to pay. By altering the receipt schedule on the spreadsheet one can see immediately if the business will have problems with such a proposal.

Cash flows are normally presented with the months running across the top and the detail running down the side. Based on the information in the example this will look as follows.

Notes on cash flow forecast

Here we provide some guidance on the figures in the cash flow forecast.

Receipts

Eighty per cent of monthly sales are paid in cash. Therefore, in January, where sales are forecast to be £15 000, cash sales will be £12 000. This appears in January's cash flow with the remaining £3000 of credit sales, which are settled a month in arrears, appearing in February. So, in February the cash coming into the bank account is the balance from January and 80 per cent of February's sales, which are again £12 000. You need to sit and work through this carefully until you are certain you understand the entries.

The £30 000 savings introduced by the owner need to be recorded in the bank account, and are entered in January, this being the month when the money is received into the bank account.

Payments

If you check back to the payment terms you will see that the first three months' purchases had to be paid for in cash. This changes in April, so be careful when completing the cash flow to split the payments between those for cash and those on credit.

The fittings and the van are purchased in January for cash, and so must be shown on the cash flow in that month.

Rent will be paid in four instalments, the first being January. Light and heat will be four instalments, the first being March. Advertising will be paid in two

Smithson Ltd
Cashflow forecast
For the year ended 31 December 2000

	Jan.	Feb.	Mar.	Apr.	May	June	July	Aug.	Sept.	Oct.	Nov.	Dec.	Total
Receipts													
Cash sales	12 000	12 000	12 000	17 600	17 600	17 600	17 600	17 600	17 600	20 000	20 000	20 000	201 600
Credit sales		3 000	3 000	3 000	4 400	4 400	4 400	4 400	4 400	4 400	5 000	5 000	45 400
Savings	30 000												30 000
	42 000	15 000	15 000	20 600	22 000	22 000	22 000	22 000	22 000	24 400	25 000	25 000	277 000
Payments													
Cash purchases	30 000	15 000	8 000	5 000	5 000	5 000	5 000	5 000	5 000	6 500	6 500	6 500	102 500
Credit purchases					5 000	5 000	5 000	5 000	5 000	5 000	6 500	6 500	43 000
Fittings	8 000												8 000
Van	10 000												10 000
Rent	1 500			1 500			1 500			1 500			6 000
Light and heat			1 300			1 300			1 300			1 300	5 200
Advertising	750								750				1 500
Wages	3 500	3 500	3 500	3 500	3 500	3 500	3 500	3 500	3 500	3 500	3 500	3 500	42 000
General Expenses	400	400	400	400	400	400	400	400	400	400	400	400	4 800
Printing postage	200	200	200	200	200	200	200	200	200	200	200	200	2 400
Telephone			300			300			300				900
	54 350	19 100	13 700	10 600	14 100	15 700	15 600	14 100	16 450	17 100	17 100	18 400	226 300
Opening balance	0	−12 350	−16 450	−15 150	−5 150	2 750	9 050	15 450	23 350	28 900	36 200	44 100	0
Receipts	42 000	15 000	15 000	20 600	22 000	22 000	22 000	22 000	22 000	24 400	25 000	25 000	277 000
Payments	54 350	19 100	13 700	10 600	14 100	15 700	15 600	14 100	16 450	17 100	17 100	18 400	226 300
Closing balance	−12 350	−16 450	−15 150	−5 150	2 750	9 050	15 450	23 350	28 900	36 200	44 100	50 700	50 700

instalments, the first being January. Wages are paid monthly. The wages for the year are £42 000, which means £3500 each month. General expenses are paid each month, as is printing, postage and stationary expenses. Telephone is paid in four instalments the first being March.

You will see from the cash flow that the receipts and payments for each month are totalled. At the bottom of each month is a section, which shows the total movement for that month.

The opening balance for January is nil, we add receipts (£42 000 in January) to this and subtract payments (January £54 350) to arrive at the month end position.

You will see that the business has spent more than it earned in the month of January and therefore we end up with an overdraft of £12 350.

The closing balance for January is the opening balance for February. The overdraft is treated as negative (−£12 350), the receipts for February (£15 000) are added to the opening balance and the payments (£19 100) are subtracted. The account is still in an overdraft position at the end of February (−£16 450).

This process is repeated for each month the cash flow covers.

The profit and loss account and the balance sheet

A concern with the cash flow statement is important because without cash a business cannot survive for long. However, companies exist not just to survive, but, amongst other things, to earn a return for their shareholders. Shareholders want to know how their investment is faring and what return they are making on that investment.

The balance sheet provides, for a particular moment in time, information on the wealth of a company, and on the forms in which this wealth is held. It is a snapshot of the company's financial position. If we were to compare the balance sheet of a company over the course of a year we would see how its stock of wealth had changed. The reason for this change can be found by considering the profit and loss account. This account provides information on the flow of wealth over a period. If the company has added to its stock of wealth it would be because it has made a profit over the period. We will return to the relationship between the profit and loss account and the balance sheet later in this chapter.

Both these statements are prepared under a set of rules to ensure consistency between all companies. These rules are known as concepts and conventions and we will look at the primary rules before continuing.

Recording financial transactions

Amongst the conventions used is the double aspect convention. This means that all transactions are entered twice, once as a debit and once as a credit. This is known as double-entry bookkeeping which is a founding principle of accounting. Most accounting systems are computer-based today and they operate by automatically generating one side of the entry. Transactions are in the main entered through the bank account with an identification code for the other side of the entry. The system then uses this information to generate the other side of the entry. Double-entry method was the way of ensuring accuracy in recording financial transactions in the period before computer packages became widely available. You will not be required to use this method to construct financial statements, but you should convince yourself of the equivalence of the double-entry method to the approach outlined in this chapter. The following example provides an indication of the double-entry approach.

Example

Let's take the January sales figure, which was £15 000 in total. If you remember £12 000 was received in cash in January and the remaining £3000 was received in February.

There are three distinct pieces of information here that the business needs to record.

Sales of £15 000   Cash received £12 000   Debtors £3000

The double entry record is:

Debit bank	£12 000
Credit sales	£15 000
Debit debtors	£3 000

When the debtors pay the cash in February, the following transactions will take place, which will result in the debtors being cancelled.

Credit debtors	£3000
Debit bank	£3000

Preparation of profit and loss account

The purpose of the profit and loss account is to report upon activity which has taken place during the year and thereby determine what profit has been made in an accounting period. It simply shows the total revenue generated during the period, and deducts from this the total expenses incurred in the production of this revenue. The profit and loss account is a statutory financial statement which records the activity of the business during an accounting period and the resulting profit or loss.

We are going to use a very simple example to demonstrate the basic principles, but you will notice later that large companies identify a number of profit figures on their statements. When comparing performance between companies it is important to be aware of the implications of the various profit figures. For the present we need to establish the 'gross profit'. Gross profit is the profit earned from selling goods, but before all expenses are taken into account.

Smithson Ltd
Profit and loss account
Year ended 31 December 2000

Sales		252 000
Opening stock	0	
Purchases	152 000	
Closing stock	20 800	
Cost of goods sold		131 200
Gross profit		120 800
Expenses		
Advertising	1 500	
Rent	6 000	
Light and heat	5 200	
Wages	42 000	
General expenses	4 800	
Telephone	1 200	
Printing postage	2 400	
Depreciation fittings	1 600	
Depreciation van	2 500	67 200
Operating profit		53 600
Taxation		12 300
Profit for the year		41 300

The above shows one format for the profit and loss account for the Smithson Ltd business. Another format is provided later in this chapter. There are a number of formats that can be adopted for drawing up the profit and loss account. The choice of a format will usually reflect the nature of the business the account is reporting on. There are prescribed formats that under UK company law must be used by limited liability companies in Britain for constructing a profit and loss account. Companies reporting in countries other than the UK will not, of course, be governed by these regulations, and hence the formats they adopt will differ from those in the UK. Similar requirements exist, however, in other countries.

Given the profit and loss account's focus on revenues and expenses, the first figure we seek to establish will be sales. The cash flow forecast shown earlier provides us with a sales figure for the year, but this is not appropriate for the profit and loss account. The profit and loss account needs to record all sales transactions for the year and the payment terms are irrelevant. If you refer back to the cash flow you will notice that 20 per cent of December sales are not recorded as the cash has not been received, but these must be identified as sales for the profit and loss account.

Sales as per cash flow forecast is £247 000 but there is £5000 outstanding for December. Therefore the sales figure for the profit and loss account is £252 000. This represents all sale transactions for the period the profit and loss account is covering.

We are applying the accruals and prudence concept in this approach. The accruals concept dictates that all transactions entered into in the financial year must be recorded. The prudence concept dictates that we cannot consider sales outside the period, i.e. we cannot look forward to January 2001 and bring in sales not yet completed.

Purchases

We need to treat purchases for resale in the same manner and take account of unpaid invoices at the end of the period.

Cash payments are £145 000 with outstanding invoices of £6500. Therefore the total transactions for the year are £152 000.

Stock

It is normal practice for businesses to have stock at the year-end. Valuing stock requires the company to look at all items of stock at the year-end and value each individually. There are different methods allowed for the valuation of stock to cover situations such as change of price during the year. You should refer back to the treatment of cost earlier to recall the discussion of damaged stock. Valuation of stock is a complex process and for simplicity sake we assume the value of the year-end stock at £20 800.

The stock figure must be subtracted from purchases to identify the 'cost of goods sold'. In our example this gives a figure of £131 200 and this is what it cost the company to purchase these goods that it later sold for £252 000.

The gross profit (£120 800) therefore is the difference between the sales figure (£252 000) and the cost of goods sold (£131 000).

All expenses are added together to arrive at operating costs on the profit and loss account. On the profit and loss account shown in p. 32 you can see that for most of the costs the total is the same as appears on the cash flow statement. The reason for this is that the full value of the expenses was paid in the year. The exception is telephone, where we assumed that the last bill for £300 did not arrive until the start of January. It could not be recorded on the cash flow as cash had not left the bank account, but this additional cost must be recorded on the profit and loss account as costs must be recorded on the profit and loss in the year in which they were incurred.

Depreciation

Depreciation is an accounting term. It is a recording in the accounts of a business that its assets wear out and will need to be replaced. When a business buys an item such as shop fittings or a motor vehicle, there is an expectation that these will be used by the business for a period in excess of one year. It is not considered acceptable to write off the cost in full in the year of acquisition. The rules governing the treatment of depreciation vary across countries. In the UK accounting rules set by the Accounting Standards Board allow a number of ways of calculating depreciation, but it is up to individual companies to decide a number of issues. The most important is how long will the asset be used for. Companies usually have policies to deal with this and for items such as fixtures and fittings a period of 4 to 5 years is often chosen. In our example we are going to assume that fittings have a useful life of 5 years and the van has a life of 4 years.

The simplest means of calculating depreciation is to write the cost off in equal instalments. This method is entitled straight-line depreciation. There are, however, other methods of calculating depreciation.

Therefore if we spread the cost of the fittings over a 5-year period we need to write off £1600 each year. The van is assumed to last 4 years and so we write off £2500 each year.

Again this highlights a difference between the cash flow and the profit and loss account. The cash flow recorded the full value of the items purchased as they were both paid for in cash. The profit and loss account is not concerned with cash, and depreciation is the means by which we write the assets off over their life.

Smithson Ltd
Profit and loss account
For the year ended 31 December 2000

Sales	252 000
Cost of goods sold	131 200
Gross profit	120 800
Operating expenses	67 200
Operating profit	53 600
Taxation	12 300
Profit for the year	41 300
Dividends	0
Retained profit	41 300

We now arrive at an operating profit on the profit and loss account and taxation must be deducted from this. We have assumed a figure of £12 300 here just to demonstrate where it appears on the profit and loss account. In reality this needs to be agreed with the taxation authorities. The taxation burden belongs to the company, as this is a limited company. It is not the tax liability of the owner.

Limited companies pay dividends to their shareholders. In this example in the first year of business none have been paid, the position is shown on the profit and loss account.

The balance sheet

The balance sheet is a position statement prepared at the end of the accounting period. It represents a list of balances, a snapshot of the business at the year-end. It is presented in a formal manner with strict use of definitions, which we need to look at before returning to our example. The balance sheet is a statutory financial statement recording the position of the business at the end of the accounting period. The balance sheet indicates, on the one hand, the assets of a business, and on the other it details the claims against the business. These claims are those of the owners of the business, capital, and the claims of outsiders, liabilities. Thus we get a balance sheet equation, which states that:

$$\text{Assets} = \text{Capital} + \text{Liabilities}$$

We need to look at each of these terms in detail.

Assets

These are items owned by the business, there are two categories of assets – fixed assets and current assets.

Fixed assets are items owned by the business with an expected life span of more than one year. These are items purchased for use in the business and not for the purpose of resale. An example is the fixtures and fittings used by Smithson Ltd.

Current assets are items owned by the business which are not held constant. Examples are stock, debtors and bank balances. Even though these headings will appear on the balance sheet each year, the constituents of them change. They are normally listed in the order of least liquidity. Liquidity is an accounting term for cash, so the order of appearance is stock, debtors and lastly cash. We have examples of all of these from the accounts of Smithson Ltd.

Liabilities

Liabilities are financial claims on the business by outsiders. They are again sub-divided into two categories – current liabilities and long-term liabilities.

Current liabilities are those that will be paid within one calendar year of the balance sheet date. An example of this is trade creditors. In our example creditors allow 30 days credit so the outstanding balance at the year-end will appear here.

Long-term liabilities are those which are paid in more than one year after the balance sheet date. An example of this would be a loan entered into for a 3-year period. The repayment date is more than one year after the date of the balance sheet and therefore this is classified as a long-term loan.

Capital

Capital is the net amount which has been invested in the business by its owners. It is defined as the difference between assets and liabilities. Essentially it is the cash invested by the owners, which in the case of a limited liability company is the share capital plus any profit not distributed at the end of the year.

The balance sheet equation allows us to see the link between the profit and loss account and the balance sheet.

Layout of the balance sheet

Smithson Ltd
Balance sheet
At 31 December 2000

Fixed assets (Note 1)			
Fittings			6 400
Van			7 500
			13 900
Current assets			
Stock		20 800	
Debtors		5 000	
Cash at bank		50 700	
		76 500	
Creditors: amounts falling due within one year			
Trade creditors		6 500	
Accruals		300	
Taxation		12 300	
		19 100	57 400
Net assets			71 300
Share capital			30 000
Profit for year			41 300
			71 300

Note 1 Fixed assets	Cost	Deprec.	Net book value
Fittings	8 000	1600	6400
Van	10 000	2500	7500

The format of this Smithson Ltd balance sheet corresponds to statutory requirements even though we are using a simple example.

Fixed Assets is always the first heading and the book value of assets is shown. This is the original cost less depreciation to date. In our example we purchased assets worth £18 000. We wrote off £4100 in the profit and loss account leaving a balance of £13 900 on the balance sheet.

Current assets and current liabilities are sub-totalled and the difference is referred to as working capital. We will see in Chapter 3 when we evaluate company performance how important this aspect of the balance sheet is.

Current assets: Our stock (£20 800) figure is taken from the profit and loss account. The debtors (£5000) represent the unpaid sales invoices for December.

The bank balance (£50 700) is taken from the cash flow forecast and is the closing balance for December.

Current liabilities: The creditor figure represents the unpaid invoices at the year-end of £6500. The accruals of £300 represent the unpaid telephone bill. The tax of £12 300, which we have entered on the profit and loss account, has not been paid at the year-end. Current assets minus current liabilities is referred to as working capital, and in the example it is equal to £57 400.

The next step is to add the fixed assets to working capital. Then subtract the long-term liabilities, which gives the figure for net assets. In our example we have no long-term liabilities.

The balance sheet, to this point, is termed the top half of the balance sheet.

The bottom half of the balance sheet is represented by the share capital invested by the owners and the undistributed profit.

In our example this is £30 000 invested by the owner and the remaining profit of £41 300.

Statutory accounts

The profit and loss account and balance sheet, together with the cash flow statement and notes which explain the various items in these accounts, constitute what is known as the statutory accounts of a company. These must be produced on an annual basis and are contained in what is known as the annual report of a company. The profit and loss account and balance sheet for a large company tend to be more complex than the example we have looked at but the principles remain the same. The following example is more like they actually appear and we will use this example in the next chapter.

Consolidated profit and loss account for the year ended	2002	2001
Currency	£ million	£ million
Turnover	3178.8	2976.0
Cost of sales	−2481.0	−2418.0
Gross profit	697.8	558.0
Operating expenses	−39.0	−22.0
Operating profit	658.8	536.0
Other costs/income	2.0	21.0
Profit before interest and taxation	660.8	557.0
Net interest receivable (payable)	−66.0	−66.0
Profit on ordinary activities before taxation	594.8	491.0
Tax on profit on ordinary activities	−178.4	−147.3
Profit on ordinary activities after taxation	416.4	343.7
Equity minority interests	−17.0	−20.0
Profit for the financial period	399.4	323.7
Dividends	−220.0	−202.0
Retained profit	179.4	121.7

Consolidated balance sheet	2002	2001
Currency	£ million	£ million
Fixed assets		
Intangible assets	1919.0	1721.0
Tangible assets	2351.0	2209.0
Investments	345.0	355.0
Total fixed assets	4615.0	4285.0
Current assets		
Stock	428.0	387.0
Debtors due within one year	552.0	496.0
Short-term investments	97.0	123.0
Cash at bank and in hand	175.0	134.0
Total current assets	1252.0	1140.0
Creditors: amounts falling due within one year	−1085.0	−989.0
Net current assets (liabilities)	167.0	151.0
Total assets less current liabilities	4782.0	4436.0
Creditors: amounts falling due after more than one year	−1077.0	−1061.0
Provisions for liabilities and charges	−398.0	−317.0
Net assets	3307.0	3058.0
Capital and reserves		
Called-up share capital	250.0	250.0
Share premium	550.0	519.0
Other reserves	109.0	109.0
Profit and loss account	2232.0	1977.0
Equity shareholders' funds	3141.0	2855.0
Minority interests	166.0	203.0
Total capital employed	3307.0	3058.0
Weighted average number of shares in issue in the period	1 057 000 000	1 047 000 000

The statutory accounts of a company will typically consist of 15–20 pages of an annual report whereas the full report will often consist of more than 50 pages. The remainder of the report will contain a report from the chairman and details outlining significant occurences during the year, together with an outline of plans for the future. A socially responsible organisation will include details of activity relating to social responsibility.

Traditional accounting, as reflected in the statutory accounts, is focused upon the actions of the organisation and upon reporting the effect of those actions upon the organisation and its performance. In doing so it ignores the effects of the organisation upon its external environment. A socially responsible organisation, however, recognises that the activities of an organisation impact upon the external environment, and all of its stakeholders, and realises that one of the roles of accounting is to report upon the impact of an organisation in this respect – in other words the accounting of organisations should be more outward looking.

The start of an outward-looking aspect to accounting can probably be identified in the immediate post-war period when organisations developed their reporting orientation towards the attraction of inward investment. This did not, however, herald a concern with the effect of the actions of the organisation upon its external environment. Such a suggestion probably first arose in the 1970s and a concern with a wider view of company performance is taken by some writers who evince concern with the social performance of a business, as a member of society at large. This concern was stated by Ackerman (1975) who argued that big business was recognising the need to adapt to a new social climate of community accountability but that the orientation of business to financial results was inhibiting social responsiveness. Indeed, at around the same time it was argued that companies were no longer the instruments of shareholders alone but existed within a society and so therefore had responsibilities to that society. Furthermore there was a general acceptance of a shift towards the greater accountability of companies to all stakeholders. Recognition of the rights of all stakeholders and the duty of a business to be accountable in this wider context therefore has been a relatively recent phenomenon and the economic view of accountability only to owners has only recently been subject to debate to any considerable extent.

It is apparent, however, that any actions which an organisation undertakes will have an effect not just upon the organisation itself but also upon the external environment of that organisation. In considering the effect of the organisation upon its external environment it must be recognised that this environment includes:

- the business environment in which the firm is operating;
- the local societal environment in which the organisation is located;
- and the wider global environment.

These effects of the organisation's activities can take many forms, such as:

- the utilisation of natural resources as a part of its production processes;
- the effects of competition between itself and other organisations in the same market;
- the enrichment of a local community through the creation of employment opportunities;
- transformation of the landscape due to raw material extraction or waste product storage;
- the distribution of wealth created within the firm to the owners of that firm (via dividends) and the workers of that firm (through wages) and the effect of this upon the welfare of individuals.

It can be seen therefore from these examples that an organisation can have a very significant effect upon its external environment and can actually change that environment through its activities. It can also be seen that these different effects can in some circumstances be viewed as beneficial and in other circumstances be viewed as detrimental to the environment. Indeed, the same actions can be viewed as beneficial by some people and detrimental by others and this is one of the problems with socially responsible behaviour – unlike accounting profit there is no accepted measure of performance in this respect. As such there is no universal acceptance as to which aspects of the activities of a firm are of importance and worthy of reporting upon.

Exactly how such socially responsible information can be quantified and incorporated into traditional company accounting is a matter of some debate. Current accounting practice, as enshrined within the Statements of Standard Accounting Practice (SSAPs) is essentially focused upon the firm as the subject for accounting. Thus SSAPs specifically exclude accounting for costs which have not (future costs) and possibly will not (contingent costs) be incurred by the firm. Even if accounting in such a manner were to be allowed in practice then the problems of how to quantify environmental impact would become of significance. In this respect it is argued that the accounting profession has a responsibility to address this issue and to develop a means of accounting which establishes a balance between accounting for profit and accounting for environmental impact. This accounting would be wider than the current practises regarding disclosure, which appear to be linked to a desire to create an appropriately environmentally conscious image rather than any true concern with environmental impact. Equally it is argued that ethical behaviour, corporate governance and social accounting are inextricably intertwined in determining the performance of a firm.

Generally speaking socially responsible corporate reporting involves greater disclosure concerning the activities of the corporation. It is generally accepted that the making of socially responsible decisions requires a multidisciplinary approach which needs the inclusion of non-accounting information as well as the development of new accounting techniques. Suggestions which have been made to address this problem include:

- social cost–benefit analysis and non-market valuation techniques;
- environmental management accounting, which is defined as a set of techniques concerned with the provision and interpretation of information to aid managerial decision-making and which takes into account effects upon the external environment;
- stakeholder accounting, which involves providing information which is deemed of significance to other stakeholders.

These techniques are proposed by different writers but all tend to fail to explain such techniques in a way which can be applied in practice by firms concerned with the effects of their actions upon the external environment.

At one level it can be argued that these individual members of society, whether members of environmental pressure groups or not, also may be stakeholders in the firm in other roles; for example they may well be customers, or potential customers, or suppliers or employees. As stakeholders may well have multiple roles in their interaction with an organisation it becomes impossible to separate out the reasons for an organisation desiring to increase the extent of its social reporting. It is also impossible to ascertain whether or not the firm is seeking to address a different audience, or merely seeking to address differing concerns of the same traditional audience, its owners or potential investors. Nevertheless, the extent of social reporting, in terms of the number of firms engaged in such reporting, has grown rapidly since 1990 and continues to grow.

Some writers argue that not only is there pressure for a general review of corporate reporting but there have been new types of accounting responding to this pressure. These include:

- the treatment of cash flow accounting;
- the distribution to different groups;
- the reporting of organisational activity in terms of value added.

An examination of the external reporting of organisations demonstrates an increasing recognition of the need to include social and environmental information. An increasing number of annual reports of companies include some information in this respect. One trend which is also apparent, however, is the tendency of companies to produce separate environmental reports. While these reports tend to contain much more detailed environmental information than is contained in the annual report, the implication of this trend is that such information is required by a separate constituency of stakeholders than the information contained in the annual report.

The discourse of corporate performance measurement suggests that social performance measurement and reporting is very different from traditional performance reporting, and that the use of accounting in such measurement and reporting is therefore very different. Furthermore it seems to be generally accepted that the concerns of the two forms of reporting are very different. Thus traditional corporate reporting is assumed to be for shareholders and be concerned only with the internal effects of the organisation's activities. Environmental reporting, on the other hand, is assumed to be for other stakeholders and to be concerned primarily, if not exclusively, with the effects of the organisation's activities on its external environment.

Although the annual report is produced to satisfy statutory requirements, and this requires the production of the accounting information contained in the report, it can be seen that this is only one purpose of producing the annual report (Crowther 2002). This report is actually produced for the whole audience who might read the text. One of the main parts of that audience consists of shareholders of the business, either actual or potential. For this audience the actual accounting information required for statutory purposes has some importance, but so too has the rest of the information contained in the report, and is given prominence. This other part of the report includes the social and environmental performance detail. Thus the accounting information required in order to satisfy statutory requirements tends to have been relegated to the back of the corporate report. Moreover the font used for the annual accounts is often smaller, and certainly never larger, than the font used in the rest of the text. Equally the use of colour is prevalent throughout the rest of the text but the accounting information is presented in single colour or at most two colours. The only financial information which is highlighted is that which is deemed important to the particular audience which the authors believe themselves to be addressing.

The production of environmental reports, which tend to detail socially responsible behaviour, is a recent phenomenon of corporate reporting. Even those companies which, in their annual report, mention their annual environmental report have only in fact produced a few such annual reports, even though the impression intended is of an extensive sequence. Other organisations produce periodic environmental reports which tend not to be tied into the annual statutory reporting cycle. Thus, for example, B&Q in 1995 produced an environmental report titled 'How Green is My Front Door?' which is quite plainly addressed to customers of the company. Increasingly, however, organisations are tending to produce environmental reports alongside the traditional annual report.

It appears, however, not to be universally accepted that an environmental report is actually required and research has shown that a minority (although increasing in number) actually produce an environmental report (Crowther 2000). This appears to differ from one industry to another.

The environmental reports which are produced tend to range in length between approximately 20 and 60 pages but this appears to be largely determined by the choice of layout and use of non-linguistic imagery rather than the textual content of the report. Some, such as Unilever and Wessex Water, are in the same format as the annual report and are clearly meant to be part of the same reporting. Others, such as Northumbrian Water, appear to be deliberately different through the use of unnecessarily poor quality recycled paper, presumably to reinforce the message about concern for the environment being translated into action. Still others such as Severn Trent and Anglian Water are different in form from the annual report without any discernible reason for this difference.

When looking at the actual content of the environmental reports themselves, these contain both image-building messages and actual reported measures of performance. It is considered, however, that these reported measures are not designed to enable an evaluation to take place but rather to create an impression of a rigorous scientific control and measurement of performance. This is because the measures actually selected for reporting have little meaning to anyone without the necessary detailed technical background in the area being reported upon for each specific measure. Thus when considering such environmental reports, it is not unusual to find:

- a variety of measures of activity and their effects;
- statements of achievements;
- reports upon activity;
- a variety of pictures to reinforce the impression of social responsibility.

There is, however, no common approach between companies.

Given the difficulties of evaluating socially responsible performance it might be expected that organisations would make reference to this difficulty as a means of obviating the need to report upon such environmental performance. This is not, however, the case and all organisations which produce environmental reports actually comment, to a greater or lesser extent, upon issues surrounding the organisational performance. This reporting of environmental performance does not segregate environmental performance from social performance, which tends to be subsumed within the reporting of environmental performance, and both together are considered to be aspects of environmental performance.

The actual language used in the reports to convey socially responsible activity is direct and is used to make statements of what the organisation has actually done, and moreover is going to do in the future. Examples include:

Our strategy is to support community activities in the immediate vicinity of our operations. Overseas we have recently made donations to two education charities in Belize to mark the transfer of the majority of shares in Belize Sugar to its employees. In the Philippines, we support an important conservation project on an island in the south of the island group. Like the earlier Programme for Belize (a rainforest conservation project), it enables supporters to 'own' a parcel of the land being conserved. (Tate & Lyle Annual Report 1995).

Kwik Save's commitment to the environment remains firm. As retailers we are well aware of our responsibilities to protect and maintain our environment and external recycling facilities available at a number of our larger stores include units for glass and bottles, paper, cans and textiles. In conjunction with Whizz-Kidz, Kwik Save participated in the Blue Peter Paperchain Appeal which resulted in over 200 tonnes of quality waste paper being collected through our stores. There are still 160 collecting skips in situ, continuing the appeal for the benefit of Whizz-Kidz and the environment. (Kwik Save Annual Report & Accounts 1995/96).

Every part of our business is concerned with protecting and improving the environment. For many companies this is only a peripheral part of their responsibility; for us, it is a core one. Each year we publish an objective assessment of our environmental performance to highlight our 'green' credentials. Anglian Water is the largest investor in environmental improvement in the region with a ten year £4bn programme aimed at improving the quality of drinking water, bathing waters, and waste water treatment systems. (Anglian Water Annual Report 1994).

As a major public company operating over some 8000 square miles in the centre of England, the company is conscious of its responsibilities to the communities it serves. Much of its community affairs programme is completely altruistic. (Severn Trent plc Annual report and accounts 1994/95).

> Large mining operations across the globe are properly accompanied by environmental and social obligations. Full acceptance of these responsibilities is essential to the well being of your company. The fact that we are a welcome partner to governments and other companies in various development areas across the world bears witness to our responsible approach. (RTZ Annual Report and Accounts 1992).

All companies tend to make some reference to their social and environmental activities and performance in their annual report, although details are not made explicit. When such details are made explicit this tends to be through the production of a separate environmental report. Such reports contain many details of social and environmental performance but because of the voluntary nature of such reporting the details reported upon vary greatly from one organisation to another. This is to some extent inevitable as the social and environmental concerns of different organisations will be different, as will the approaches adopted to dealing with them. This, however, has the disadvantage of eliminating the comparability aspect of studying such reports. What seems clear, however, is that an increasing number of companies recognise the importance of this aspect of performance and wish to report upon their actions in this respect.

Note

1 This subsequently metamorphosed into the Accounting Standards Board.

References

Ackerman, R.W. (1975). *The Social Challenge to Business.* Cambridge, MA: Harvard University Press.
Crowther, D. (2000). *Social and Environmental Accounting.* London: Pearson Education.
Crowther, D. (2002). *A Social Critique of Corporate Reporting.* Aldershot: Ashgate.
Gilmore, C.G. and Willmott, H. (1992). Company law and financial reporting: a sociological history of the UK experience. In M. Bromwich and A. Hopwood (eds). *Accounting and the Law.* Hemel Hempstead: Prentice-Hall, pp. 159–191.
Newman, M.S. (1979). Historical development of early accounting concepts and their relation to certain economic concepts. In E.N. Goffman (ed.). *Academy of Accounting Historians Working Paper Series Volume 1*, pp. 57–186.

Additional questions

Question 2.1

The Calculator Company Ltd has collected the following information to be used for the preparation of its budget for the next quarter:

Expected sales	10 000 units
Opening stock of finished goods	2 000 units
Closing stock of finished goods	2 000 units
Direct costs of production	
Labour	£30 000
Raw materials	£45 000
Overheads	£12 000
Fixed costs	£11 000
Selling price per unit	£15

All sales are for cash payable when the goods are supplied and all expenses are paid when incurred.

Prepare a cash flow forecast for the coming quarter.

Question 2.2

Williams Ltd produce children's games which they sell to the retail trade. The budgeted profit and loss figures for the company for the period July–December are as follows:

	Jul. (£'000)	Aug. (£'000)	Sept. (£'000)	Oct. (£'000)	Nov. (£'000)	Dec. (£'000)
Sales	80	120	200	240	320	400
Direct costs						
Materials	60	70	80	80	70	40
Labour	30	36	40	56	36	32
Overheads						
Production	32	38	44	48	36	24
Sales	12	12	20	30	30	40
Admin.	16	20	20	24	16	20

As management accountant for the company, you have been asked to prepare a cash flow forecast for the period October to December. You have been provided with the following information:

- wages are paid in the current month while suppliers of direct materials give two months credit;
- production overheads are paid in the month in which they occur and include depreciation of £10 000;
- 10 per cent of sales are cash sales, the remainder are credit sales, 90 per cent of which are paid one month in arrears with the remainder being paid the following month;
- administration overheads are paid one month in arrears;
- sales overheads include a sales commission of 10 per cent payable one month in arrears, the remaining sales overheads are paid in the current month;

- the cash balance for the company on 1 October was £16 000;
- a dividend of £50 000 is payable during October;
- a mortgage of company property will raise £100 000 in November, repayments of £5000 per month will begin in December;
- a new production machine costing £40 000 will be installed at the beginning of November, 10 per cent of the price is payable at that time with the remainder due three months later.

3

Analysing and Interpreting Company Accounts

Learning objectives

On completion of this chapter you should be able to:

- understand how to apply basic financial ratios to interpret financial statements;
- assess the financial condition and relative performance of firms;
- recognise the benefits of an integrated financial ratios approach to financial analysis;
- articulate criticisms of the reliability of ratio analysis for identifying corporate financial 'distress'.

Introduction

The interpretation of the information contained in the statutory reports of companies is an important management skill. In this chapter therefore we direct our attention to interpreting and analysing these financial statements in order to extract information which may be likely to assist management in their decision-making and financial judgements. Such analysis consists of first identifying important financial data (and where appropriate, non-financial data such as number of employees) and then relating these to one another and also to factors external to the firm. Typically, for firms we are interested in for one reason or another, we would wish to know how profitable they have been and what their potential earning capacity is.

The principal technique used for evaluating the performance and financial status of a firm is known as ratio analysis. Ratio analysis is the computation of indicators of financial performance; it involves taking financial information from the financial statements and making calculations which are likely to indicate business performance.

Note that accountants are not too strict about their use of the term ratios and many financial ratios are stated as percentages (i.e., the ratios are actually multiplied by 100). Financial ratios typically include profitability percentages, operational efficiency, liquidity ratios, debt and working capital ratios.

Analysing financial performance

The modern financial manager is likely to be required to provide information for management decision-making covering a vast array of activities which have financial implications, including decisions on sources of finance, project appraisal, dividend policy, working capital requirements and potential acquisitions and mergers. The financial manager is thus both concerned with providing information to aid management in its decision-making in the long term (for example, on debt and fixed assets) and in the short term (for example, on the availability of cash). However, when interpreting cost of sales and gross profit, especially for comparative analysis, we must be aware that there may be distortions arising from differential accounting methods (for example, in the application of alternative methods for valuing stocks and the fixed assets).

Financial ratio analysis is the main way in which a financial manager can understand financial statements. These statements cannot be understood, however, merely by calculating appropriate financial ratios. It is only by comparing ratios that this information can be evaluated. There are two main ways of making comparisons:

1 Comparing the analysis of the same company over time. It is in this way that any changes in the calculated ratios can be determined and this provides a basis for then considering the performance of the company and how this is changing over time.
2 Comparing the ratios of the company being analysed with those of a similar company. In this way we start to see how the company is performing in comparison with other firms in the same industry.

We also will need some more information about the company, the industry the company operates in and the general economic conditions in which it is operating in order to completely make sense of our analysis. We will return to this later but first we will undertake some financial ratio analysis.

In the examples that follow, financial ratios are defined and briefly discussed. In order to illustrate the application of financial ratios, the calculations

Consolidated profit and loss account for the year ended	2002	2001
Currency	£ million	£ million
Turnover	3178.8	2976.0
Cost of sales	−2481.0	−2418.0
Gross profit	697.8	558.0
Operating expenses	−39.0	−22.0
Operating profit	658.8	536.0
Other costs/income	2.0	21.0
Profit before interest and taxation	660.8	557.0
Net interest receivable (payable)	−66.0	−66.0
Profit on ordinary activities before taxation	594.8	491.0
Tax on profit on ordinary activities	−178.4	−147.3
Profit on ordinary activities after taxation	416.4	343.7
Equity minority interests	−17.0	−20.0
Profit for the financial period	399.4	323.7
Dividends	−220.0	−202.0
Retained profit	179.4	121.7

Consolidated balance sheet	2002	2001
Currency	£ million	£ million
Fixed assets		
Intangible assets	1919.0	1721.0
Tangible assets	2351.0	2209.0
Investments	345.0	355.0
Total fixed assets	4615.0	4285.0
Current assets		
Stock	428.0	387.0
Debtors due within one year	552.0	496.0
Short-term investments	97.0	123.0
Cash at bank and in hand	175.0	134.0
Total current assets	1252.0	1140.0
Creditors: amounts falling due within one year	−1085.0	−989.0
Net current assets (liabilities)	167.0	151.0
Total assets less current liabilities	4782.0	4436.0
Creditors: amounts falling due after more than one year	−1077.0	−1061.0
Provisions for liabilities and charges	−398.0	−317.0
Net assets	3307.0	3058.0
Capital and reserves		
Called-up share capital	250.0	250.0
Share premium	550.0	519.0
Other reserves	109.0	109.0
Profit and loss account	2232.0	1977.0
Equity shareholders' funds	3141.0	2855.0
Minority interests	166.0	203.0
Total capital employed	3307.0	3058.0
Weighted average number of shares in issue in the period	1 057 000 000	1 047 000 000

presented are based upon the profit and loss account and balance sheet shown in the last chapter. These are based upon a fictitious company but are very similar to what would actually be found in the financial statements of a real company. These statements are repeated here for ease of reference.

It is important that you understand what the annual reports of companies look like rather then just relying on the information contained in this book so it is suggested that you look at a variety of financial statements in order to get a feel for what they look like.

Fuller information about any company can be found in the annual report of that company. Every company is required to produce such an annual report each year and these are available for inspection in most public libraries. These reports contain the financial information as well as a lot of other information about the company and its plans for the future. In these reports financial statements are normally presented in a highly summarised format with notes attached to enable the reader to comprehend the basis of the figures. Many publicly owned companies (plc) comprise groups of subsidiaries and companies. There is a legal requirement in the UK for a company of this sort to prepare a separate set of accounts showing all the companies in the group. These are referred to as consolidated accounts.

Get hold of the annual report of any company and look at the information that it contains. Think about the way in which the information is presented. Does this information tell you anything about the company which is not provided by the financial information? The answer should be yes – there is a lot of information which is contained in the report which will give indications as to how the financial analysis should be interpreted. Examples include details of restructuring or expansion plans, indications of difficult trading period or factors affecting exporting or importing from particular parts of the world.

NB – If you cannot find any annual reports of companies in your local library then you can either write to a company and ask them to send you one or use the Internet to call up the report of a company – almost all companies produce their annual reports on the Internet as well as in published paper form.

Now let us turn our attention to the company which we will be using in this chapter to explain financial ratios. You will notice that this company has a consolidated profit and loss account and balance sheet which bring together the various transactions that all the different parts of the company involve themselves in. There are a number of special rules that govern the preparation of consolidated accounts. However, you do not need specialist knowledge of these rules to use these statements for analysis and interpretation purposes.

The financial ratio toolkit

There are a whole variety of financial ratios which can be used and accountants have the capability of creating new ones when they need to do so. It is not, however, necessary for us to understand all the ratios which can be used but only the most important ones. For this purpose therefore it is helpful if we can understand the main purpose of ratio analysis. We can best do this by describing the purpose of the different types of ratio and arriving at a classification of ratios.

We can therefore start by classifying ratios into four different types, depending upon what they tell us about a company. These four classes are:

1 Measures of profitability
2 Measures of efficiency
3 Measures of liquidity
4 Measures of risk.

Measures of profitability

Profitability (revenues less expenses over a reporting period) ratios measure how efficiently a firm appears to be using its fixed assets – the more efficiently a company uses its assets the greater the profit it can get from their use. The operating results are the most important for most private businesses and therefore it is the trading profit and loss account (or income statement) that is of primary importance in providing the data for measuring profitability. This provides the starting point for our ratio analysis.

Such ratios include return on the capital employed in the business, return on total assets and on net assets, return on equity (net profits available to ordinary shareholders divided by common equity), return on sales and asset turnover, and the earnings per share. Interpreting our calculations of financial ratios for profitability requires identifying the major factors we believe to be responsible for these changes. This usually requires us to extend our analysis to focus on management strategies to remedy or improve efficiency, productivity and thus profitability. Moreover, we can obtain some idea of how well different sections of a business have performed by making a closer study of the cost of goods sold, a form of analysis known as segmental analysis.

Return on capital employed (ROCE)

Return on capital employed measures the efficiency with which capital employed by the business has been utilised and is usually expressed as a percentage, that is, it is calculated by dividing profit by capital employed and multiplying by 100. Capital employed can be either total assets (i.e. fixed assets plus current assets) or net total assets (i.e. fixed assets plus current assets minus current liabilities). Using net total assets, for our example in the year 2002 we find:

$$\text{Return on capital employed} = \frac{\text{Profit for the financial period}}{\text{Net assets}}$$

$$= \frac{399.4}{4615.0 + 1252.0} = 6.8\%$$

The return on capital employed, as measured above, was 6.8 per cent for 2002 compared with (and 6 per cent for 2001) – a slight increase over the year. For all calculations there are two aspects which matter – how the ratio has changed over time and how it compares with what might be considered the norm for the industry in which the company is operating. Different industries have different norms and it is important to consider how the company being analysed is performing in comparison to industry norms.

Return on total assets

This is a similar ratio but is calculated by dividing the earnings before interest and taxation and exceptional items by average total assets for the period.

$$\text{Return total assets} = \frac{\text{Operating profit before interest paid, taxation and exceptional items}}{\text{Average total assets for the period}}$$

For our example the return on total assets (total fixed assets less depreciation + total current assets for 2001 and 2002 divided by 2) for 2002 is 11.7 per cent, calculated as follows:

$$= \frac{658.8}{(4615.0 + 1252.0 + 4285.0 + 1140.0)/2} = 11.7\%$$

Return on net total assets

It simply replaces average total assets with average net total assets in the denominator.

$$\text{Return total net total assets} = \frac{\text{Operating profit before interest paid, taxation and exceptional items}}{\text{Average net total assets for the period}}$$

The return on average net total assets (total fixed assets less depreciation + working capital divided by 2) for our example for 2002 was 14.3 per cent, as shown below.

$$= \frac{658.8}{(4615.0 + 167.0 + 4285.0 + 151.0)/2} = 14.3\%$$

Return on equity

This indicates the profitability of the firm in terms of the capital provided by the owners. It is calculated by dividing profit after interest and preference dividend but before tax by the average ordinary share capital, reserves and retained profit for the period.

$$\text{Return on equity} = \frac{\text{Profit after interest and preference dividends but before tax}}{\text{Ordinary share captial, reserves and retained profit for the period}}$$

Applying this ratio to our example we calculate the return on equity for the year 2002 to be 18.9 per cent as follows:

$$= \frac{594.8}{3141.0} = 18.9\%$$

All of these ratios provide a measure of how much return the shareholders are receiving (in terms of profit) from their investment and very often it does not matter which one of these we use. What is important is consistency. For our analysis to be meaningful it is important that we are comparing like with like. Thus it is crucial that we use the same measure and the same figures for our analysis over a period of years or between companies.

This leads us to a consideration of one of the problems with ratio analysis when we are seeking to compare different but similar companies in the same industry. This is that their accounts may not be prepared on the same basis. In this case it is necessary for us to make adjustments to the figures and we need to go to the notes which accompany the accounts (in the annual report) in order to get the information to make these adjustments.

Have another look at the annual report which you have previously looked at and turn to the notes to accompany the financial statements. (These are always shown towards the back of the report and follow the financial statements themselves.) See if this information helps you to understand the basis on which the figures in the report have been compiled.

The financial manager or analyst often calculates ratios that combine accounting and stock market data. Examples using market data include earnings per share (EPS), which is calculated by dividing earnings available to ordinary shareholders by the number of shares issued. Earnings per share indicates the amount of dividends available to ordinary shareholders.

Another ratio commonly used for this is known as the price-earnings ratio (P/E), which is the stock price divided by the EPS. The EPS and P/E ratio calculations are shown below.

$$\text{EPS} = \frac{\text{Earnings available to the ordinary shareholders}}{\text{Average total number of issued shares during the period capital}}$$

The higher the EPS the more profitable the company is and the more it is earning for its shareholders. Thus it is desirable to see a steadily increasing EPS for a company. We need to be careful when comparing different companies, however, as not all companies have shares of the same value. For instance, an EPS of 50p for a company whose shares are issued as £1 is less than an EPS of 30p for a company whose shares are issued as 50p.

$$P/E \ ratio = \frac{Average \ market \ price \ of \ the \ ordinary \ shares}{EPS}$$

The higher the P/E ratio the lower will an investor receive in terms of earnings for his investment. Thus we might expect that a low P/E ratio is desirable. This, however, depends upon the expectations of investors and these need to be considered in terms of expected future growth or the risk involved in making the investment. Thus a high P/E ratio may indicate that investors expect high dividend growth or that the security has low risk and therefore, investors are content with a low prospective return.

Dividend yield

It is simply the expected dividend as a proportion of the stock price.

$$Dividend \ yield = \frac{Dividend \ per \ share}{Share \ price}$$

Investors tend to look for companies with a steady expected growth in dividends: a volatile dividend trend is usually a negative signal to the stock market, resulting in a decline in the company's share price.

Market-to-book ratio

It is the ratio of stock price to book value per share.

$$Market-to-book \ ratio = \frac{Share \ price}{Book \ value \ per \ share}$$

Book value per share is just the shareholders' book equity (net worth) divided by the number of shares outstanding. Book equity equals common stock (i.e. ordinary shares) plus retained earnings – the net amount that the firm has received from stockholders or reinvested on their behalf.

Return on sales (RoS)

It is a measure which relates profits and sales revenue whilst *asset turnover* indicates the relationship between sales and capital employed. Profit to sales and sales to capital employed are usually expressed as percentages. Managers often measure the performance of a firm by the ratio of income to total assets. The net profit ratio and return on total assets ratio for our example accounts are given below:

$$\text{Return on sales} = \frac{\text{Profit}}{\text{Sales}}$$

$$= \frac{416.4}{3178.8}$$

$$= 12.9\%$$

$$\text{Return on total assets} = \frac{\text{Sales}}{\text{Average total assets}}$$

$$= \frac{3178.8}{(4615.0 + 1252.0 + 4285.0 + 1140.0)/2}$$

$$= 56.3\%$$

It can be seen that these two measures together represent a breaking down of the first measure which we considered – ROCE, as follows:

Return on capital employed = Return on sales × Return on total assets, i.e.

$$\frac{\text{Profit}}{\text{Assets}} = \frac{\text{Profit}}{\text{Sales}} \times \frac{\text{Sales}}{\text{Assets}}$$

Segmental analysis

Diversified firms complicate financial analysis using financial statements because it is important to separate and interpret the impact of individual business segments on the group as a whole. As different segments or divisions often experience varying rates of profitability, risk and growth opportunities, the analysis ought to be disaggregated into separate business segments sharing characteristics of variability, growth and risk.

Assessing risk and return is a major objective of financial statement analysis and this has led to the common practice, supported by regulatory agencies, of having established reporting requirements for industry segments, international activities, export sales and major customers. Analysis of companies operating across industry segments or geographic areas, which often have different rates of profitability, risk and growth, is aided by segment data. The data below show the operations and geographical disaggregation of Marks & Spencer plc Group's sales for the year 1997 as an example.

	Turnover (£m)	Operating profit (£m)	Operating assets (£m)
Operating activities:			
Retailing	7625.8	962.2	3243.6
Financial services	216.1	75.7	235.0
Total operating activities	7841.9	1037.9	3478.6

	Turnover (£m)	Operating profit (£m)	Operating assets (£m)
Geographical segments:			
UK	6565.6	946.5	2990.9
Europe (excluding UK)	551.5	37.7	324.9
The Americas	580.0	21.0	152.9
The Far East	144.8	32.7	9.9
Total operating activities	7841.9	1037.9	3478.6

Financial analysis of trends in sales by segments is useful in assessing profitability to establish the causes of differential growth. Profits can often be related to identifiable assets by segments and a comparison of capital expenditures to depreciation can help us to measure corporate growth. With disaggregated asset- and capital-employed values we may use this data to calculate return on capital employed by product and regional sub-division. However, in order to understand the profitability and performance of a firm in the recent past we should try to establish some 'benchmark' to compare the results of our financial ratios to other similar companies.

Measures of efficiency and effectiveness

As well as considering how well the shareholders' investment is being used in terms of the management of the fixed assets of the company it is also necessary to consider the management of the working capital of the company. This is achieved by a set of measures which are described as measures of efficiency.

Ratios related to specific resources such as stock, debtors and creditors and number of employees help to measure how well these resources have been managed over time (trends covering several preceding years are usually desirable). Considerable resources can be tied up in raw materials and work-in-progress and in unpaid credit sales. It is important that any stock- and credit-management inefficiencies are identified as soon as possible in order that remedial actions can be taken. Therefore, the relationships between sales and debtors and sales and stocks and work-in-progress often provide important clues for our evaluation of operating results and can be useful in predicting future company performance.

Let us look at these measures in more detail.

The *stock-turnover ratio* is calculated by dividing the cost of sales for the period by the stock at the end of the period (or the average stock level).

$$\text{Stock turnover} = \frac{\text{Cost of goods sold}}{\text{End of period stock}}$$

$$= \frac{2481.0}{428.0} = 5.8$$

This measure shows how quickly stock is sold – the higher the figure the more times it is turned over in a year. In this case the figure of 5.8 indicates that stock is turned over 5.8 times during the year and is therefore kept for just over two months on average before it is sold. This is an average figure, however, and the stock will comprise of fast selling lines as well as slower selling lines.

A high stock turnover is usually regarded as a sign of efficiency but care in interpretation is required as it could, for example, mean that the firm simply has inadequate working capital to build up stocks to the required level to meet production needs. Stock turnover will also vary greatly between industries. For example, a supermarket chain would expect stock to turnover much more quickly than would a manufacturer of electronic equipment. So a turnover figure of 5.8 would probably be good for the latter but very problematic for the former.

In most firms part of working capital is used to finance sales on credit, the balance of which appears as debtors in the current assets in the balance sheet. *Debtor turnover* and the *average collection period*, the amount of resources tied up in debtors and how efficiently the firm converts these credit sales into cash, are usually measured, respectively, by dividing sales by debtors, and the average collection period (in days) by dividing debtors by day's sales. Strictly speaking, these ratios should be based on credit sales for the period but we often do not have a breakdown of cash and credit sales and so the aggregate sales value is usually used as approximation of debtor turnover.

$$\text{Debtor trunover} = \frac{\text{Sales}}{\text{Debtors}}$$

$$= \frac{3178.8}{552.0} = 5.8$$

$$\text{Average collection period} = \frac{\text{Average debtors}}{\text{Average daily sales}}$$

$$= \frac{(552.0 + 496.0)/2}{3178.8/365} = 60 \text{ days}$$

A high ratio for debtor turnover would normally be considered efficient but could, for example, be caused by unduly restrictive credit sales. A low ratio for the average collection period would normally indicate an efficient credit management but could, for example, result from an unduly restrictive credit policy. Again this would vary according to industry as in some industries the terms of trade would expect long period of credit while others would not.

In a similar way to the above calculations for credit sales and debtors, the purchases of goods on credit can be used in conjunction with the creditors due, which appear in the current liabilities in the balance sheet, to calculate the *creditor turnover* and *credit payment period* taken by the firm. As with debtor turnover, purchases and creditors, the figures on the financial statements may not be disaggregated therefore precluding us from calculating a precise ratio and obliging us to make an approximate calculation using the aggregated values.

The creditor-turnover ratio is calculated by dividing the cash payments to suppliers during the period by the trade creditors at the end of the period and the creditor payment period by dividing 365 days by the creditor-turnover ratio.

Measures of liquidity

Liquidity is the availability of funds for ongoing operations. The availability of liquid funds to meet ongoing day-to-day cash requirements poses a problem for businesses of all types. Well-managed working capital is necessary not only for the organisation itself because outside agents, for example, analysts and bankers, will use measures of liquidity to assess a firm's future creditworthiness. A firm may become technically insolvent if it finds it is unable to meet its day-to-day cash creditors and as the data upon which liquidity ratios are based are constantly changing, care must be taken to ensure they are as up to date as possible and that the data is not, for some reason, atypical (in which case the results may be misleading). Liquidity ratios commonly used are the *current* and the *quick ratio*.

Current assets are those assets that the company expects to turn into cash in the near future whilst current liabilities are liabilities, which it expects to meet in the near future. The difference between the current assets and the current liabilities is known as *net working capital* and roughly measures the company's potential reservoir of cash. The *current ratio* or *working capital ratio* relates the current assets of an organisation to its current liabilities and is calculated by dividing current assets by current liabilities. For our example company the current ratio at the 2002 year-end was calculated as follows:

$$\text{Current ratio} = \frac{\text{Current assets}}{\text{Current liabilities}} = \frac{1252.0}{167.0} = 7.5$$

This is little changed from the previous year, which also has a current ratio of 7.5.

Changes in the current ratio can, however, be misleading. Suppose, for example, a company borrows a large sum from the bank and invests it in marketable securities. If nothing else changes, net working capital is unaffected but the current ratio changes. For this reason it might be preferable to net off the short-term investments and the short-term debt when calculating the current ratio.

The *quick ratio*, sometimes known as the *acid test ratio*, is similar to the current ratio but excludes those current assets from the numerator that may prove difficult to convert into cash quickly and is therefore a more severe test of an organisation's liquid position. It is calculated by dividing current assets minus stocks by current liabilities.

$$\text{Quick ratio} = \frac{\text{Cash + Marketable securities +}}{\text{Current liabilities}}$$

$$= \frac{175.0 + 97.0 + 552.0}{167.0} = 4.9$$

The normal expectation for the quick ratio is approximately 1. This is generally considered to be a sign of a healthy company. We can see therefore that the cash liquidity position of our example is very sound, indicating its ability to pay its day-to-day commitments. Firms with a quick ratio of much lower than 1 might be expected to run into financial difficulties and will certainly have cash flow problems. Firms with a quick ratio of much higher than one – as in our example – indicate that they are unnecessarily holding cash which might be put to better use.

Cash interest cover, cash dividend cover and cash debt cover are ratios that measure the ability of a firm to meet its charges and distribution commitments against income, over time (unlike the current and the quick ratios which measure liquidity at a single point in time). *Cash interest cover* divides interest paid into the net cash flow from operations and interest received.

$$\text{Cash interest cover} = \frac{\text{Net cash inflow from operations*}\text{ and interest received**}}{\text{Interest paid}}$$

*This amount will be found from the cash flow statement while **this amount needs to be taken from the notes to the accounts.

Cash dividend cover = net cash inflow after tax from operations – interest paid + interest received + dividends received from related companies/dividends paid.

$$\text{Cash dividend cover} = \frac{\begin{array}{c}\text{Net cash inflow after tax from operations} -\\ \text{Interest paid} + \text{Interest received} + \text{Dividends}\\ \text{received from related companies}\end{array}}{\text{Dividends paid}}$$

Again some of these figures will need to be taken from the notes and the cash flow statement.

Cash debt coverage is net cash inflow from operations after interest, tax and dividends divided by debt maturing within the next 12 months.

$$\text{Cash debt cover} = \frac{\begin{array}{c}\text{Net cash inflow from operations after}\\ \text{interest, tax and dividends}\end{array}}{\text{Debt maturing within the next 12 months}}$$

Again some of these figures will need to be taken from the notes and the cash flow statement.

Defensive interval measure

Instead of looking at a firm's liquid assets relative to its current liabilities, it may be useful to measure whether they are large relative to the firm's regular cash outgoings. One suggestion is the so-called defensive interval, which computes the amount of operating cash, outflows per day and relates it to the quick assets available.

$$\text{Interval measure} = \frac{\text{Cash + Marketable securities + Receivables}}{\text{Average daily operating cash outflows}}$$

Again some of these figures will need to be taken from the notes and the cash flow statement.

The interval measure indicates the number of days the company could survive at its present level of operating activity if no inflow of cash from sales or other sources took place.

Capital structure and financial risk

Capital structure is the relationship between shareholder funds and long-term debt. The long-term sources of finance for firms can be broken down into two basic categories: debt and equity. When a firm borrows money in the long term it creates *financial leverage* because each year the firm must pay the interest on its debt as a before-tax expense out of profits before the owners (shareholders in a company) can receive a dividend. Debt management ratios such as the debt ratio (total debt divided by total assets); interest cover which indicates the times interest earned is covered by earnings (operating profit divided by the annual cost of servicing debt); and long-term debt to equity (debt divided by total equity) help us to measure a firm's financial risk and, by comparing it with other similar firms in its industry, its relative overall risk (of being forced into liquidation). The most widely used ratio which measures the long-term capital structure is the debt to equity ratio.

$$\text{Long-term debt to equity ratio} = \frac{\text{Long-term loans + Preference shares}}{\text{Ordinary shareholders' funds}}$$

$$= \frac{1077.0}{3141.0} = 0.34$$

Capital gearing, interest dividend cover and total debt to total assets ratio are further ratios which help us to evaluate the financial risk of a company. Total debt to total assets ratio indicates the proportion of total assets financed by borrowed funds, both short and long term.

Total owing to total assets is a better indicator for unsecured lenders that the book value of the assets gives a comfortable surplus over the amount owing. All the amounts included in the short- and long-term liabilities are combined to form the total owing as follows:

$$\text{Total owing to total assets ratio} = \frac{\text{All creditors (less than one year)} + \text{Long-term liabilities}}{\text{Total assets}}$$

$$= \frac{1085.0 + 1077.0 + 398.0}{4615.0 + 1252.0} = 0.43\%$$

The total owing to total assets ratio indicates that 43 per cent of the business has been financed by third parties, some of whom require interest payments on their loans. However, there is still a very substantial surplus of book value of assets over the total amount owing to third parties.

Capital gearing focuses on the income position of the firm rather than on the capital structure and is a multiplier or factor which, when applied to variations in operating profits, indicates the disproportionate changes that would occur in profits available for the shareholders. The calculation for our example is given below.

$$\text{Capital gearing ratio} = \frac{\text{Profit on ordinary activities before interest} + \text{Interest received*}}{\text{Profit on ordinary activities before taxation}}$$

*This amount is taken from the notes to the accounts.

The capital gearing ratio indicates the proportionate change profit before tax in relation to a change in its profit before interest paid. If profit before interest is paid were to increase in the following year then the profits before tax will also rise.

Interest cover measures the ability of a company to meet its annual interest charges, and therefore the risk of it defaulting on its interest obligations. The ratio shows the number of times interest is covered by profits.

$$\text{Interest cover ratio} = \frac{\text{Profit before interest and tax}}{\text{Gross interest payable*}}$$

*This amount is taken from the notes to the accounts.

Similarly, dividend cover indicates the amount by which profits could fall before leading to a reduction in the current level of dividends. It is calculated as follows:

$$\text{Dividend cover ratio} = \frac{\text{Profits available for paying ordinary dividends}}{\text{Ordinary dividends}}$$

$$= \frac{399.4}{220.0} = 1.8$$

The dividend cover ratio is similar to the interest cover ratio in that it indicates the amount by which a company's profits could fall before the current level of dividend must be reduced. The dividend cover ratio is the reciprocal of the dividend payout ratio, the proportion of profits available to the equity owner paid out in dividends, but neither ratio measures the firm's ability to actually pay out in cash (the ability of a firm to pay out its dividend in cash is measured by the dividend cover ratio discussed above).

Applications of financial analysis

Being able to calculate the ratios we have looked at in this chapter is only the first part of financial analysis. It is the interpretation of these ratios which is crucial to the importance of the analysis. It is this interpretation which can give us useful information about the company and its financial health.

Ratio analysis, as we stated at the beginning of this chapter, is essentially a comparative process. Thus it is necessary when looking at a company to undertake this analysis over a period of years. Generally speaking 3 years is considered to be a necessary time period to give an indication of trends. What we are looking for is how these ratios are moving – either upwards or downwards – and what this might mean for the health of the company.

We also stated that it was necessary to have more information about the company, the industry the company operates in and the general economic conditions in which it is operating in order to completely make sense of our analysis. Thus in evaluating the health of a company the following information is also necessary:

- The nature of the company and its business; its plans for the future; and its past record. A company which is heavily involved in expansion or in major R&D projects, for example, might be expected to show a deteriorating position on many of its key ratios. This would not necessarily show that the company was running into problems but rather that it could be expected to capitalise in the future on its efforts in the present.
- The norms for the industry in which the company operates. Different industries have different levels of risk and different norms in terms of returns upon investment and capital employed. Equally different industries have different expectations in terms of profitability and dividend payments and different requirements for cash and working capital. What is important is how the company we are concerned with compares with other firms in its industry rather than with other firms in general.
- The state of the economy as a whole. In periods of recession companies can be expected to be less profitable and to have a deteriorating cash flow. While this is to be expected too great a change can mean a company which is running into difficulties. Similarly in times of expansion companies can be expected to have a deteriorating position with regard to working capital and again too great a change can mean a company which is running into difficulties.

We can see therefore that analysing a company using ratio analysis requires skill and judgement over and above an ability to calculate financial ratios. Fortunately there are always others who are analysing companies and willing to make their analysis public. They are chiefly such people as investment analysts who make a living on advising people which shares are a good buy at a particular price. We can use the work that these people have done to help us form our own opinions. Look also, for example, at the financial pages of a quality newspaper and see what is being said about this company in particular and the economy in general.

Analysing socially responsible performance

Financial performance comprises just one aspect of performance which we might wish to analyse. The other aspect of performance which is of interest is social responsibility. In this case, rather than having a variety of measures available, all of which are helpful for such analysis, there is in fact no measure which exists and is universally recognised as an appropriate measure. It is therefore necessary to consider what measures are available and their appropriateness for the purpose of this analysis.

In this context therefore it is important to recognise that, with the absence of any particular measure of socially responsible performance, there are a variety of measures which have a relationship with such performance but which do not necessarily fully reflect the extent of such performance. Such measures must therefore be considered to be merely surrogate measures for this dimension of performance, which provide some method of deriving a commonality in the evaluation of such performance.

From the annual statutory accounts there is only one measure which must be reported, and this is that of charitable donations. All, or virtually all, companies make charitable donations in the course of their operations and these donations need to be reported in the annual reports of those companies. It is not, however, necessary to report as to the purpose of such charitable donations or as to the recipients of such donations, except when a company wishes to make a virtue of a particular donation by mentioning it specifically in the script of the report. It is not therefore possible to identify whether a donation is for a social, a political or for an environmental purpose. Nevertheless it is reasonable to argue that the extent of charitable giving on the part of companies demonstrates the extent of concern with the external environment in one form or another. In other words it is argued that the greater the donations as a proportion of income, the greater the concern of the company with its external environment. While this concern is with the external environment in its widest definition it is also reasonable to argue that social and environmental issues are inevitably reflected in this concern and comprise the majority of such donations. Lacking any further information, therefore it seems reasonable to argue that the manifestation of such concern is proportionate to concern with other aspects of the external environment. On this basis therefore it seems reasonable to argue that the extent of charitable donations provides a proxy measure for the extent of concern with social and environmental issues and this is the reasoning behind including such a measure in this analysis.

Apart from this there is no need to report any particular figures and they are normally not therefore reported. So it becomes necessary to look elsewhere for an indication of socially responsible activity. One place to look is in the reports which accompany the formal statements. Each company has within its annual report a variety of statements concerning the importance of social/environmental issues to that company and concerning the performance of the company in terms of such issues. It is reasonable to argue that the more the text devoted to such issues, the greater their perceived importance to that company.

An increasing number of companies are producing environmental reports separately to the production of the annual report. Environmental reports differ from annual reports in that they are not statutorily obligated upon the companies. The production of an environmental report is therefore undertaken voluntarily by companies and such production, it is argued, is a reflection of the perceived importance of environmental issues to that company. Moreover, the size and frequency of production of such reports provide further evidence of their perceived importance. Such reports are normally described as environmental reports although they also demonstrate significant concern with social activity. Indeed, the term environmental generally seems to subsume the term social within its general meaning. There are three important issues to consider in the way in which companies decide to produce such reports:

1 whether a report is produced at all;
2 the frequency of production of such reports;
3 the size of such reports.

It is argued that a company which produces an annual environmental report places greater emphasis upon environmental issues than the one which only produces a periodic report. Such a company in turn places greater importance upon environmental issues than the one which does not produce such a report at all. Again it is argued that the number of pages contained in the report also provides a proxy measure of the importance attached to such issues.

Although producing an environmental report is important in its own right, of similar importance is the content of such a report. Some such reports are merely statements of perceived importance of the environment to the company while others report upon action being taken with regard to environmental issues. Indeed some, but by no means all, contain actual data measuring environmental impact and changes in such impact made by the companies as a result of their activities. This is an important feature of environmental reporting as, much as is the case for financial reporting, measurement enables comparisons to be made. One problem with such comparisons, however, is that the measures incorporated into the reports differ considerably from one company to another and so it is not a reasonable proposition to undertake a comparison of environmental impact between companies. Indeed, it is often not possible to compare the impact of a single company over time. It can be argued, however, that the inclusion of measured environmental importance in such reports is important in its own right and that the greater the number of reported measures the more the importance attached to the measurement of environmental impact.

Conclusions

In this chapter we have discussed how to calculate and interpret summary measures of a company's financial position and illustrate the methods for calculating financial ratios. Calculations of financial ratios can form the basis of a structured profile of a firm's past and present performance, which may help management in its strategic decision-making. A structured review of a firm's financial statements can also help different 'stakeholders' in the business (for example, bank managers considering lending to the firm, employees, creditors and investors) to assess either overall or more specific business performance. Such a review may be enhanced by making market comparisons using cross-sectional analysis and inter-firm comparisons, forecasting financial 'distress' using time series analysis, and devising models which are designed to predict the likelihood of bankruptcy or for equity share valuation.

Additional questions

Question 3.1

The following are summary financial statements for a 4-year period for a particular company.
(all figures are expressed as £'000)

Profit and loss account

	Year 4	Year 3	Year 2	Year 1
Turnover	11 098	10 984	11 213	10 997
Cost of sales	8 539	8 521	8 717	8 433
Gross profit	2 559	2 463	2 496	2 564
Other expenses	1 067	1 056	821	1 052
Operating profit	1 492	1 407	1 675	1 512
Tax	597	316	542	597
Net profit	895	1 091	1 133	915

Balance sheet

	Year 4		Year 3		Year 2		Year 1
Fixed assets		8 316		8 524		8 441		8 327
Stock	475		481		436		447	
Debtors	1187		1213		1014		1113	
Cash	554		704		567		683	
Current assets		2 216		2 398		2 017		2 243
Total assets		10 532		10 922		10 458		10 570
Current liabilities		2 509		2 298		1 882		2 240
Net assets		8 023		8 624		8 576		8 330
Long-term liabilities		2 247		3 000		2 863		2 828
Shareholder funds		5 776		5 624		5 713		5 502
Capital employed		8 023		8 624		8 576		8 330

Use these figures to perform a financial analysis of the company.

Question 3.2

Social responsibility is an increasingly important aspect of corporate perform-ance but assessing this is problematic. Explain why this is problematic and suggest ways in which socially responsible performance might be indicated.

4

Value Based Management

Learning objectives

After studying this chapter you should be able to:

- describe the principles upon which value based management (VBM) is based;
- understand the relationship between VBM and agency theory;
- describe the various techniques of VBM;
- critique VBM and its alternative, stakeholder theory;
- compare VBM with the traditional measurement of value.

Introduction

The managers of most companies recognise that their function is to serve the needs of the owners of that business – in other words their shareholders. Thus the concept of creating shareholder value, as an objective for the business, appears to be widely accepted within the business community. Indeed, the creation of value for shareholders is frequently seen to be one of the objectives of the company which is stated in its annual report. What is much less frequently stated, however, is the means by which the managers of the business ensure that such value is created; indeed the use of techniques as a quantified evaluation is less often found in practice.

The idea that the purpose of managing a business is to create value for the shareholders of that business is not, of course, a new idea; it is based upon agency theory. It has been commonly accepted that the arguments of agency theory are not subject to questioning. Agency theory suggests that the management of an organisation is undertaken on behalf of the owners of that organisation – in other words the shareholders of the organisation. Consequently the only concern surrounding the creation of value within an organisation is that it should accrue to the shareholders of that organisation, and that the purpose of the managers of the organisation is to find ways to increase that value. Thus the managers of a company are expected to manage on behalf of the shareholders in order to increase the value of the company for the benefit of shareholders. As a reward, of course, they can be expected to benefit from that value created by means of the executive reward scheme. Implicit within this view of the management of the firm is that society at large, and consequently all other stakeholders to the organisation, will also benefit as a result of managing the performance of the organisation in this manner. From this perspective therefore the concerns are focused upon how to manage performance for the shareholders and how to report upon that performance.

This view of an organisation has, however, been extensively challenged by many writers over the last 20 years; such writers argue that the way to maximise performance for society at large is to both manage on behalf of all stakeholders and ensure that the value thereby created is not appropriated by the shareholders but is distributed to all stakeholders. At the same time others argue that this debate is sterile and that organisations maximise value creation not by a concern with either shareholders or stakeholders but by focusing upon the operational objectives of the firm and assuming that value creation, and equitable distribution will thereby follow.

Adherents to each of these conflicting philosophies regarding the method of managing a business in order to secure maximum value creation have a tendency to adopt different perspectives on the management and evaluation of performance. Thus for one school of thought the correct way of managing and deciding upon priorities is assumed to be incorrect for the other schools of thought. Then for those concerned with managing on behalf of shareholders, one of the latest and most important techniques for doing so has become known as value based management. In this chapter we are going to look at this important technique in greater detail.

Value based management is a complex topic involving detailed calculations. So in this chapter we are going to restrict ourselves to understanding the principles upon which the technique is based and not get involved in any complex calculations. Suffice it to say that those in favour of the use of VBM argue that its use leads to better decision-making by the firm. For an example which illustrates the calculations involved and also shows how the use of VBM will lead to different decisions, see Crowther *et al.* (1998).

Creating value for shareholders

There has been a revival of interest in economic techniques to measure the value of a firm through the use of economic value added as a technique for measuring such value to shareholders. This technique, based upon the concept of economic value equating to total value, is founded upon the assumptions of classical liberal economic theory. Such techniques have been subject to criticism both from the point of view of the level of adjustment to published accounts needed to make the technique work and from the point of view of the validity of such techniques in actually measuring value in a meaningful context. Thus in this chapter we contrast this approach to managing the creation of value with more traditional techniques of measuring value created. We consider the merits of the respective techniques in explaining shareholder and managerial behaviour and the problems with using such techniques in considering the wider stakeholder concept of value.

Measuring value added for shareholders

The nature of the debate concerning the measurement and evaluation of corporate performance has broadened in recent years with the adoption of different perspectives and this has been reflected in the changing nature of corporate reporting. Thus there has been a shift from an economic view of corporate performance measurement to an informational perspective with a recognition of the social implications of an organisation's activities. This has resulted in a shift from treating financial figures as the foundation of corporate performance measurement to treating them as part of a broader range of measures. At the same time it has been argued that companies are no longer the instruments of shareholders alone but exist within society and so have responsibilities to that society.

The debate therefore seems to have moved away from the concerns of shareholders in the firm and away from the economic rationale for accounting towards a consideration of the wider stakeholder environment. At the same time, however, these concerns cannot be ignored and part of the debate has seen a return to economic values in assessing the performance of the firm. Thus some of the problems with accounting, such as the exclusion of risk and investment policies from the analysis, have been recognised and the concept of shareholder value and how this can be created and sustained has been addressed. Rappaport (1986) has developed a methodology of shareholder value, in which he argues that a shareholder value approach is the correct way of evaluating alternative company strategies, stating that the ultimate test of a corporate plan is whether it creates value for the shareholders, and that this is the sole method of evaluating performance. He identifies a conflict between the achievement of competitive advantage and creating shareholder value when he states:

> Increasingly, companies are becoming polarised into two camps: those who consider shareholder value the key to managing the company and those who put their faith in gaining competitive advantage. (p. 85)

but argues that both are based upon long-term productivity.

The return to a consideration of the importance of economic value to the theory of the firm therefore is based upon the assumption that maximising the value of a firm to its shareholders also maximises the value of that firm to society at large. Within the debate therefore the concept of shareholder value is frequently mentioned and there is acceptance of the need to account for shareholder value within the practitioner community. Indeed, the annual reports of companies regularly report the creating of value for shareholders and it is frequently cited as a corporate objective. What is less clear, however, from an examination of such annual reports is precisely what is meant by this creation of shareholder value, which often seems to be used in a nebulous manner to indicate some desirable but unidentifiable objective.

This, it is argued, is because the managers of a firm are preoccupied with other objectives such as growth in size, turnover, market share or accounting returns, which are more easily measured. The achievement of these objectives is also often correlated with managerial rewards but less so with increasing shareholder value. Indeed, agency theory can be used to demonstrate how following managerial interests can lead to higher rewards for those managers at the expense of a reduction in the value of the company.

Value based management

In recent years an alternative approach to managing an organisation has developed which is known as VBM. In comparison with stakeholder management, VBM techniques have the advantage that they propose the use of a single metric to measure performance as well as set objectives and reward executives, and therefore appear far simpler and more appealing. There is, however, more to the VBM approach to managing an organisation than mere simplicity. Although there seems to have been a move away from the concerns of shareholders of the firm and away from the economic rationale for accounting and towards a consideration of the wider stakeholder environment, this has not been universal. At the same time there has been a recognition that the concerns of shareholders cannot be ignored and another argument has seen a return to economic values in assessing the performance of the firm. Broadly speaking this approach is known as VBM – or alternatively shareholder value management. This approach is based upon a simple premise that the ultimate test of a corporate plan is whether it creates value for the shareholders, and that this is the sole method of evaluating performance.

This approach to managing an organisation is based upon the assumption that maximising the value of a firm to its shareholders also maximises the value of that firm to society at large. The concept of shareholder value as an objective appears to be widely accepted within the accounting community but its use as a quantified evaluation is less often found in practice. The central argument is based upon the inadequacy of traditional accounting and financial information to provide adequate information for corporate decision-making. Thus it is argued that problems arise from the use of accounting measures as a means of evaluating company performance. Many people consider how the use of earnings per share can be of doubtful value in achieving this end, both because of the different calculations used for the same accounting measure and because of the adoption of different accounting measures. Equally others argue that return on investment (ROI), return on assets (ROA) and return on equity (ROE) suffer from the same problem. The techniques of VBM are claimed to provide a solution to these problems through their different approach to using financial information for strategic decision-making.

If that is the case then the techniques are important to understand and so we must start by considering exactly what it is that we are considering. Perhaps the most succinct definition of VBM has been provided by Copeland *et al.* (1996) who state that it is:

an approach to management whereby the company's overall aspiration, analytical techniques and management processes are all aligned to help the company maximise its value by focusing on the key drivers of value.

This definition implies a different approach to management but concomitantly a differing use made of accounting information. Value based management therefore goes further than merely using accounting information differently as it also requires the application of appropriate measures of value to provide a 'shareholder value' perspective for all key internal planning and control systems – that is, strategic decision-making, resource allocation, performance measurement and control and managerial compensation. This is an important distinction between these techniques and other approaches to managing an organisation and this distinction, and the implications arising from it, needs to be clearly understood. An important, if not fundamental, feature of all VBM approaches is this alignment of objectives, measures and rewards intended to promote shareholder value creation at all levels of the business.

In addition VBM theoretically involves a shift away from the use of traditional accounting measures such as earnings per share and net profit, which are argued, by the proponents of VBM, to offer an unreliable guide to 'shareholder value creation'. In the place of such accounting numbers, a number of alternative measures have been proposed which are intended to provide a 'calculating machine consistent with the principles of economic income'. The use of VBM techniques does not remove any concern for accounting measures. Instead, it replaces a concern with such measures as earning per share with a concern for maximising the net present value of the company. This can be achieved by improving the economic returns achieved on existing assets employed and by seeking new investments giving positive net present values. A recent development in the quest for a tool to measure shareholder value has been the concept of economic value added,[1] which has been developed by Stewart as a better measure to assess corporate performance and the creation of shareholder value than conventional accounting measures. Indeed, Stewart states that:

Economic value added is an estimate, however simple or precise, of a business's true economic profit.

Economic value added is claimed to have a number of important advantages over traditional accounting measures, the chief one being that economic performance is only determined after the making of a risk-adjusted charge for the capital employed in the business. Critics, however, argue that while this may be theoretically sound, the need to make arbitrary adjustments to standard accounting numbers in order to put the technique into practice makes the technique of doubtful validity.

Mechanisms for calculating economic value added are described by Stewart (1991), who elaborates the standard adjustments needed to transform accounting information into an economic value added calculation. A definition of economic value added can be given simply as operating profits after tax less a charge for capital used to generate these profits. The residual from this calculation is the measure of economic value added and if positive demonstrates that the company has earned a greater return on its capital employed than the opportunity cost of the capital employed, and has hence added value to the company from the viewpoint of shareholders. Opportunity cost is defined in this context simply as the market cost of capital, appropriately weighted between equity and debt capital. If negative the opposite is the case and value has been lost.

Associated with economic value added is the measure market value added[2] which is defined by Stewart (1991) as the market value of the company (i.e. stock price $\times$ shares outstanding) minus the economic book value of the capital employed. Stewart argues that this measure is superior to just using market value as a means of assessing the value-creating performance of a company because market value can be increased simply by investing as much capital as possible, without consideration of the returns to be achieved from this investment. In theory, market value added should reflect the present value of expected future value added and thereby provides a measure of the expectation of shareholder value created. In practice this relationship is not as simple as this because of the factors affecting the operation of the market. It is therefore argued by proponents of this kind of shareholder value analysis technique that both measures need to be considered together in order to evaluate the value of the techniques of shareholder value analysis in assessing company performance. The two measures together are therefore taken as a representation of shareholder value.

There are a number of different approaches to VBM, each of which has been developed by a different firm of consultants – and we will look at these differences in this chapter. Whilst these alternative approaches to VBM share the essential characteristics described above, it should be recognised that there are differences between them, which relate mainly to the specific measures employed. Thus different approaches by different firms of consultants employ different measures of 'shareholder value creation'. For example, McTaggart et al. (1994) and Stewart favour a residual income type approach (economic profit and economic value added (EVA) respectively), whilst Rappaport advocates 'shareholder value added', and Madden promotes 'Cash Flow Return on Investment' (CFROI) as the preferred method of application. There has been much discussion on the merits of these different measures, particularly in terms of their relative accuracy and complexity, but in general there is much similarity in the techniques employed and the results obtained.

You will note that all of these writers have their own consultancies promoting their individual approaches to the management of shareholder value. Equally, you will note that these are primarily based in USA where these techniques were initially developed. Although they were initially used by firms in USA these techniques have gained widespread acceptance and are starting to be used by large companies throughout Europe, and increasingly throughout the rest of the world. Initially these techniques have been used primarily by large companies because of the cost of implementing the techniques, particularly when consultancy fees to these various consultancies are involved. Now, however, the techniques involved are becoming better understood and are starting to be implemented by many other companies also.

Advocates of VBM techniques have advanced strong claims on its behalf, the chief of which is that its use will lead to the creation of shareholder value. Thus McTaggart *et al.*, for example, claim that VBM will:

> . . . greatly improve the quality of decision-making, by improving the quality of the alternatives that management has to consider as well as building a bias for choosing and implementing the best available alternatives.

Stern Stewart (1995), meanwhile, claim that: 'The major benefit EVA firms can expect is a higher market value'. They also cite other significant benefits which will accrue from the use of the technique, stating that these are:

> . . . a common language for planning and managing, more accountability for delivering value, a greater concern for managing assets, a greater willingness to rationalise and redirect resources, better bridges to link operations and strategy with financial results, more collaborative long-term planning.

As a further example, Copeland *et al.* state that:

> . . . the management processes . . . provide decision-makers at all levels of the organisation with the right information and incentives to make value creating decisions.

These claims are extremely positive concerning the effects of VBM implementation within an organisation but it must be remembered that these claims have largely originated from the leading shareholder value consultants who arguably stand to gain the most from the widespread adoption of their preferred techniques. A recent survey by a variety of international firms of accountants and consultants has, however, provided some evidence in support of these claims and indicated that there is a growing interest in the techniques of VBM/shareholder value and a recognition of its importance. Moreover, these surveys have tended to show an increasing adoption of these techniques.

There are some problems with the adoption of these techniques in practice, however, and in how to apply them within a company. Key issues identified included the perceived complexity of the techniques, the need for cultural change to coincide with adoption of the techniques, implementation difficulties and perceived problems with the application in both corporate headquarters and particular types of business such as research and development-driven companies. One of the arguments of the consultants advocating these techniques is that they are not just a tally for strategic decision-making but also a way to manage a business and should be used at all stages in the business management process. In this respect similar international surveys have found that contrary to 'VBM theory' few companies have successfully applied 'full VBM' and also that profit-based measures are often used alongside shareholder value measures. The failure to apply 'full VBM' refers to companies in practice not applying VBM techniques consistently across all of the key internal planning and control systems: from decision-making through to managerial compensation.

In US, there has been a shift in recent years towards a more explicit shareholder value-oriented approach to corporate performance measurement, described variously as 'Value-Based Management' or 'Shareholder Value Management'. An increasing number of companies are reported to have adopted this approach, and it is receiving increasing interest in UK and Western Europe.[3]

The VBM concept which seems to have received most interest is the EVA approach, which has been advocated (Stewart 1991) as a better measure to assess corporate performance and the creation of shareholder value than conventional accounting measures. Economic value added is claimed to have a number of important advantages over traditional accounting measures, the chief one being that economic performance is only determined after the making of a risk-adjusted charge for the capital employed in the business. Critics, however, argue that while this may be theoretically sound, the need to make arbitrary adjustments to standard accounting numbers in order to put the technique into practice makes the technique of doubtful validity. The application of the technique and the adjustments needed were evaluated by Coates *et al.* (1995) who suggest that simplified calculations produce satisfactorily reliable results.

Management for stakeholders

The competing basis for managing performance in an organisation is based upon stakeholder management theory. A stakeholder approach to managing the performance of an organisation is based upon the idea that all stakeholders are important and their objectives need taking into consideration. Numerous definitions of a stakeholder have been provided by various people, but the following are perhaps the most common and easily understood:

- those groups without whose support the organisation would cease to exist;
- any group or individual who can affect or is affected by the achievement of the organisation's objectives.

A stakeholder approach to managing an organisation can be considered to exist when the management of that organisation considers the impact of its operations on its stakeholders before making its decision. Due to the diverse nature and conflicting needs of the relevant stakeholders it is necessary for this type of management to involve some form of tradeoff. This implies that all stakeholders are taken into consideration before any decision is made but in reality when stakeholder theory is used as a managerial tool it is specifically concerned with identifying which stakeholders are more important and as a result should receive a greater proportion of management's time.

It has been suggested that there are three reasons for the importance of stakeholder theory:

- The first is that it is an accurate description of how management works. This implies that all management is a form of stakeholder management where the interests of different stakeholders are actually considered.
- The second argues that it is more morally and ethically correct for organisations to consider wider needs than purely concentrating on the needs of one group, usually taken to be shareholders. Thus by adopting a stakeholder approach the objective of the firm is to become a more ethical and more socially responsible organisation.
- The third view suggests that the reason for managing your stakeholders is to create shareholder wealth. This view suggests that shareholder wealth can be created through the correct management of the other stakeholders and in this respect it is considered to have instrumental power.

The link between stakeholder performance and financial performance, its instrumental power, has been argued to exist for a number of reasons. Some suggest that a balance between the different stakeholder groups' interests is essential in ensuring that the organisation continues to be viable and achieves other performance goals. Others suggest that stakeholder management is a source of competitive advantage, as contracts between organisations and stakeholders will be on the basis of trust and co-operation and therefore less expense will be required in monitoring and enforcing such contracts. In a similar vein there have been numerous empirical studies performed attempting to find links between corporate social responsibility and financial performance.

An underlying assumption, which is not always explicitly recognised, is that an organisation should be operating for shareholders – that is, they should be shareholder wealth maximising. Therefore stakeholder management, or corporate social responsibility, is not an end in itself but is simply seen as a means for improving economic performance. A fundamental aspect of stakeholder theory, in any of its aspects, is that it attempts to identify numerous different factions within a society to whom an organisation may have some responsibility. It has been criticised for failing to satisfactorily identify these factions although some attempts have been made. Indeed, attempts have been made by stakeholder theorists to provide frameworks by which the relevant stakeholders of an organisation can be identified. One suggestion is that a stakeholder is relevant if it has invested something in the organisation and is therefore subject to some risk from that organisation's activities. These stakeholders can be separated these into two groups: the voluntary stakeholders, who choose to deal with an organisation, and the involuntary stakeholders, who do not choose to enter into – nor can they withdraw from – a relationship with the organisation.

Irrespective of which model is used, it is not controversial to suggest that there are some generic stakeholder groups that will be relevant to most organ- isations. Most people would recognise that the voluntary stakeholders include shareholders, investors, employees, managers, customers and suppliers, and each will require some value added otherwise they can withdraw their stake and choose not to invest in that organisation again. Equally, most people would accept that involuntary stakeholders such as individuals, communities, ecological environments, or future generations do not choose to deal with the organisation and therefore may need some form of protection may be through government legislation or regulation.

Stakeholder management has significant requirements for, often complex, information to meet the needs of the various stakeholders. It is extremely diffi- cult to manage on behalf of a variety of stakeholders if there is no measure- ment of how the organisation has performed for those stakeholders. Thus for each stakeholder identified it is necessary to have a performance measure by which the stakeholder performance can be considered. Due to the nature of the stakeholders, and their relationship with the organisation, this will not necessarily be easy, nor will it necessarily be possible in monetary terms. Therefore non-financial measures will be of great importance but this informa- tion is often considered more subjective than financial information. Therefore measures of customer satisfaction are sometimes based on surveys and some- times on statistical performance measures such as numbers of complaints or returns, or market share or customer retention. Recently there have been a number of multi-dimensional performance measurement frameworks that can be argued to have some level of stakeholder orientation.

Creating value

We have already noted that there is considerable debate concerning the extent to which a firm should be either shareholder- or stakeholder-oriented, yet there is little evidence of how firms themselves regard this issue, or indeed whether and how firms currently identify and manage the needs and interests of their various stakeholder communities. One of the perennial debates surrounding shareholder value techniques and their implementation concerns the effect of such techniques upon other stakeholders to an organisation. One strand of the debate suggests that the maximisation of shareholder value automatically maximises, as a corollary, the value created in a business for other stakeholders. An opposing strand of the debate, however, suggests that this shareholder value is not necessarily created but instead is merely maximised through an expropriation of value from other stakeholders to the business.

It has been argued therefore by different parties that each of the following mutually exclusive hypotheses holds true:

1 Value attributable to other stakeholders is sacrificed by companies in order to create higher levels of performance when judged in terms of stakeholder value.
2 Creating value for shareholders through the management process automatically creates value for other stakeholders.

For our purposes, there is little need to make this distinction and adopting the principles of VBM will resolve this issue. The creation of shareholder value, however, requires the management of the processes of the firm in an appropriate and consistent manner in order to achieve this end. This requires an understanding of the relationship between the various aspects of the management of that performance. In this respect it is possible to construct a three-part model to explore the relationship between the mission of the organisation, the techniques it employs in managing this mission and the outcomes in terms of reported performance. Such a model will look as shown in Figure 4.1.

In this book the view of the operation of the performance management system of an organisation is that the intention of a firm in terms of its stakeholder priorities and its own aspirations will affect the performance management systems of the firm as well as its actual performance. This can be modelled as shown in Figure 4.2.

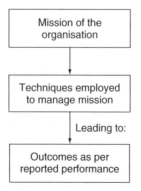

Figure 4.1 The relationship between mission and performance (from Crowther, D. 2002)

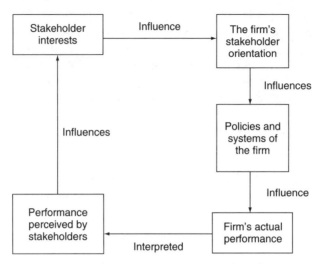

Figure 4.2 Operation of the performance management system (from Crowther, D. 2002)

The creation of value for shareholders therefore is generally considered to be the prime task of managers of a business. In general, when such value is created then it will accrue to the owners of the business – that is the shareholders – and either be returned to them in the form of dividends or will be invested in order to create further value in the future. Traditionally, therefore the question of whether or not value has been created – or how much value has been created – has been measured in accounting terms by such measures as earnings per share or return on capital employed. These measures give a calculation of the value which has been created by shareholders but it is argued by those who propose the techniques of VBM that they do not give a correct calculation. Moreover, they give a calculation after the event whereas VBM techniques also give a means of evaluating the strategies which might be adopted by the managers of a business in order to create this value. Thus VBM provides a means of managing a business and making decisions as well as a measure of what value has been created.

 Traditional measures of value created

Managers make use of a whole variety of financial ratios in order to understand and calculate the performance of a business. You will remember that these can be classified into four different types, depending upon what they tell us about a company. These four classes are:

1 Measures of profitability
2 Measures of efficiency

3 Measures of liquidity
4 Measures of risk.

In order to calculate the value which has been created for shareholder in a business, however, we need only concern ourselves with the first of these – measures of profitability. Profitability (revenues less expenses over a reporting period) ratios measure how efficiently a firm appears to be using its fixed assets – the more efficiently a company uses its assets the greater the profit it can get from their use and therefore the more the value created. The operating results are the most important for most private businesses and therefore it is the trading, profit and loss account (or income statement) that is of primary importance in providing the data for measuring profitability.

Such ratios include return on the capital employed in the business, return on total assets and on net assets, return on equity (net profits available to ordinary shareholders divided by common equity), return on sales and asset turnover, and the earnings per share. Interpreting calculations of financial ratios for profitability requires identifying the major factors we believe to be responsible for these changes. This usually requires us to extend our analysis to focus on management strategies to remedy or improve efficiency, productivity and thus profitability.

The basic technique of VBM

Traditionally, performance measurement and reward systems have been based on accounting numbers such as EPS and ROCE. A number of authors have criticised such measures for promoting a short-term focus for managerial actions. Rappaport (1986) argues that accounting profit fails to measure changes in the economic value of the firm, citing the following reasons:

- alternative accounting methods can be employed to give different figures;
- risk is excluded from the analysis;
- future investment requirements are excluded;
- the dividend policy in force is not considered;
- the time value of money is ignored.

Despite these limitations, there is a widespread belief in the UK and the US that share prices are driven by the capitalisation of a company's EPS at an appropriate price/earnings ratio multiple. A number of writers have described an apparent 'fixation' with EPS, and Rappaport (1986) states:

> In both corporate reports and the financial press, there is an obsessive fixation on earnings per share (EPS) as the scorecard of corporate performance.

The Accounting Standards Board has sought to reduce the emphasis placed on EPS, primarily through Financial Reporting Standard 3 (FRS 3), 'Reporting

Financial Performance', which required a number of changes to the presentation of the profit and loss account as well as the calculation of EPS and the definition of extraordinary items. Financial Reporting Standard 3 states:

> It is not possible to distil the performance of a complex organisation
> into a single measure. Undue significance, therefore, should not be
> placed on any one such measure which may purport to achieve this
> aim. (para. 52)

Soon after FRS 3 was published the Institute for Investment Management
and Research (IIMR) published guidance under which 'maintainable EPS'
could be calculated. The IIMR argued that this 'maintainable EPS' statistic was
the key indicator of corporate performance, providing further evidence of the
EPS fixation.

The popularity of share option schemes and profit-related bonus schemes
for top management, combined with the EPS fixation means that EPS is a
widely adopted performance measure in UK. However, Stewart (1991)
and Rappaport (1986) emphasise that there is only a limited relationship
between EPS and value creation by a company. Value based management
approaches, on the other hand, are claimed to offer a superior means of promoting wealth-creating corporate behaviour. According to Rappaport (1986)
it is widely accepted that the primary objective of the firm is to maximise
shareholder wealth. Indeed, finance theory has long assumed that this is the
case with, for example, Friedman (1970) suggests that a firm should seek to
maximise profits as to do anything else would be against the primary objective of the firm. Thus Brignall and Ballantine (1996) argue that shareholder
wealth is maximised 'by investing in all projects offering a positive Net Present Value (NPV)'. More recently, however, there has been increased interest
in a more explicit shareholder value-oriented approach to managing a business; such an approach has become more generally known as Value based
management or Shareholder Value Management.[4] This increased interest has
arisen not only within the academic discourse but also among practitioners
and business managers; this interest has been confirmed through recent survey evidence (Coopers and Lybrand 1996; Deloitte and Touche 1996; KPMG
1996, 1998; PA Consulting 1997).

Value based management has been defined as:

> an approach to management whereby the company's overall aspir-
> ation, analytical techniques and management processes are all
> aligned to help the company maximise its value by focusing on the key
> drivers of value. (Copeland *et al.* 1996, p. 96).

Put at its simplest then VBM can be defined as investing the capital of the
business in activities which earn a rate of return which exceeds the cost to the
business of its capital. This of course implies the undertaking of activity which
yields a positive NPV.

This implies a different approach to management but concomitantly a differing use made of accounting information. Value based management therefore goes further than merely using NPV for investment decisions as it also requires the application of appropriate measures of value to provide a 'shareholder value' perspective for all key internal planning and control systems: i.e. strategic decision-making, resource allocation, performance measurement and control and managerial compensation. An important, if not fundamental, feature of all VBM approaches is this alignment of objectives, measures and rewards intended to promote shareholder value creation at all levels of the business.

In addition, VBM theoretically involves a shift away from the use of traditional accounting measures such as EPS and net profit, which are argued, by the proponents of VBM, to offer an unreliable guide to shareholder value creation. In the place of such accounting numbers, a number of alternative measures have been proposed which are intended to provide a 'calculating machine consistent with the principles of economic income' (Bromwich 1998). The applications of VBM techniques do however still require that managers do seek to maximise the net present value of the company, through new investment in positive net present value opportunities and through improving the economic returns achieved on existing assets employed.

The different techniques in use

Value based management is widely perceived to be a relatively complex management approach given technical measurement issues surrounding the use of the metrics themselves and also related to the calculation and application of the cost of capital. As such we will not look in detail at any of the calculations involved but merely recognise that there are a number of different approaches used, indeed the different proponents of VBM use different approaches to the calculation of shareholder value. These are:

- Economic value added (EVA)
- Market value added (MVA)
- Total business returns (TBR)
- Cash flow return on investment (CFROI)
- Cash added value (CAV).

You will see reference to all of these in practice. Despite minor differences in their approach they are all similar in principle.

VBM and social responsibility

The techniques of VBM are based upon the idea of economic rationality and assume that the most rational economic decision is the one which should always be taken. Moreover, they are based upon the evaluation of alternative courses of action from the viewpoint of the firm. If a decision creates value when measured in this way then it should be undertaken. There is an automatic assumption that what benefits the firm will also benefit all of the stakeholders to the firm as well as benefiting society at large. This is based upon the 'trickle down theory' which argues that the creation of wealth in society will eventually permeate through all levels of society. There is absolutely no proof that this theory has any validity and a growing body of evidence which shows it to be false. Thus there is a danger that basing the decisions of the firm upon these principles can become merely exploitative of others. Social responsibility implies that other factors than economic wealth creation need to be taken into account whereas the techniques of VBM argue that these can be ignored – or will automatically be taken into account – through an economic calculation.

Conclusions

Most of the literature in the area of VBM has originated from the leading shareholder value consultants (e.g. Rappaport 1986; Stewart 1991; McTaggart *et al*. 1994; Copeland *et al*. 1996). This literature has focused on how shareholder value techniques should be applied according to each approach taken by the various consultants. An international survey of shareholder value management issues, conducted by Coopers and Lybrand in 1996, for example, found that in UK there is still great uncertainty on how to apply VBM principles throughout a company. Key issues identified included perceived complexity, the need for cultural change, implementation difficulties and the application in both corporate headquarters and particular types of business such as research and development-driven companies. Nevertheless this approach to financial management is popular in business and it is therefore important to gain an understanding of the principles under which the techniques operate.

Notes

1 The term Economic Value Added (EVA) is copyrighted as the property of Stern Stewart & Co.
2 The term Market Value Added is also copyrighted as the property of Stern Stewart & Co.
3 In this chapter the term VBM is used to encompass all the closely related concepts of value-based planning (VBP), shareholder value analysis (SVA), strategic value analysis and economic value added (EVA). Its approaches involve the application of the principles of discounted cash flow (DCF) analysis as used in the net present value (NPV) technique. Although theoretically consistent with NPV, the scope of VBM is much wider. Whereas the use of NPV has traditionally been associated primarily with capital

investment decisions only, VBM involves the use of DCF principles within an integrated financial system, covering strategic decision-making, performance measurement and reporting and also as the basis for managerial incentive schemes.

4 The terms 'Value based management' and 'Shareholder value management' are used interchangeably within the discourse. Although it is accepted that there are differences in technical application depending upon the approach favoured these are primarily ignored from our viewpoint.

References

Brignall, S. and Ballantine, J.A. (1996). *Interactions and trade-offs in multi-dimensional performance management*. Warwick Business School Research Bureau, No. 247.

Bromwich, M. (1998). Value based financial management systems; Editorial, *Management Accounting Research, Special Issue, 9*, 387–389.

Coates, J.B., Davies, M.L., Davis, E.W., Zafar, A. and Zwirlein, T. (1995). *Adopting performance measures that count: changing to a shareholder value focus*. Aston Business School Research Paper No. RP9510.

Coopers and Lybrand (1996). *International Survey of Shareholder Value Management Issues*. London.

Copeland, T., Koller, T., and Murrin, J. (1996). *Valuation: Measuring and Managing the Value of Companies*. New York: John Wiley & Sons.

Crowther, D. (2002). *Creating Shareholder Value*. London: Spiro.

Crowther, D., Davies, M.L. and Cooper, S.M. (1998). Evaluating corporate performance: a critique of economic value added. *Journal of Applied Accounting Research, 4 (2)*, 2–34.

Deloitte and Touche (1996). *Financial Management Survey 1996*. London.

Friedman, M. (1970). The social responsibility is to increase its profits. *The New York Times Magazine*, September, 32–33.

KPMG (1996). *Value Based Management: A Survey of European Industry*. Brussels.

KPMG (1998). *Value Based Management: The Growing Importance of Shareholder Value in Europe*. Brussels.

McTaggart, J.M., Kontes, P.W. and Manks, M.C. (1994). *The Value Imperative*. New York: Free Press.

PA Consulting (1997). *Managing for Shareholder Value*. London.

Rappaport, A. (1986). *Creating Shareholder Value*. New York: Free Press.

Stern Stewart & Co. (1995). *The EVA Company*. New York: Free Press.

Stewart, G.B. III (1991). *The Quest for Value: A Guide for Senior Managers*. New York: Harper Collins.

Further reading

Arnold, G. and Davies, M. (eds) (2000). *Value Based Management: Concepts and Application*. Chichester: John Wiley & Sons.

Cooper, S., Crowther, D., Davies, M. and Davis, E.W. (2001). *Shareholder or Stakeholder Value*. London: CIMA.

Crowther, D. (2002). *Creating Shareholder Value*. London: Spiro.

Additional questions

Question 4.1

Contrast the reasons for using VBM and the reasons for adopting stakeholder theory as bases for managing a business.

Question 4.2

What are the criticisms of accounting which led to the development of the VBM approach?

5

Introduction to Management Accounting

Learning objectives

After studying this chapter you should be able to:

- describe the purposes for which costs are classified;
- differentiate between fixed costs, variable costs and mixed costs;
- explain the limitations of cost classification for cost prediction purposes;
- classify costs appropriately for product costing purposes;
- identify an appropriate method to calculate the cost of any particular product;
- calculate product costs using appropriate methods.

Introduction

In the previous chapters we have looked at financial accounting in the context of external financial reporting. This is the public face of a company but accounting is also used extensively within a business. It is used for a number of reasons:

- Decision-making
- Performance measurement and management
- Resource allocation.

These uses of accounting are internal to the business and are collectively known as management accounting. In this chapter therefore, and for the remainder of this book, we turn to a consideration of some of the approaches and techniques of management accounting.

Management accounting as management support

Management accounting is concerned with the analysis and reporting of financial information for managers within a business in order to assist them in the performance of their jobs. The collection of this financial information is crucial to management accounting, and cost accounting has a large part to play in this. Other sources of information are, however, needed and not all information will be expressed in financial terms. Information regarding quantities of resources (in terms of physical units) may be important, as may qualitative information and so this too falls within the scope of management accounting.

Management accounting is essentially a part of management decision-making of use to all managers. It is used throughout the business rather than being focused within the finance department. Its use therefore is to help managers with decision-making in the following areas:

- *Planning*: what to produce and how best to meet the objectives of the organisation;
- *Control*: to ensure that the outcomes correspond to those planned;
- *Decision-making*: to decide between alternative courses of action by evaluating the consequences;
- *Measuring performance*: to decide if it matches the expectations set out in the plan and to take corrective action if not.

Management accounting information will be generated to a large extent by the accounting information system which a business possesses. As far as managers are concerned, this system is a means of collecting information and communicating it to them to aid their decision-making. The system therefore needs to have been developed to meet the requirements of the managers of the business, along with its other function of satisfying the financial accounting and reporting requirements of the business. These requirements will vary greatly according to the nature of the business and according to the role which each individual manager plays in that business. The information needs of a warehouse manager will naturally be greatly different to those of the manager of a sales force, while a manager in a hospital will have quite different information reporting needs to those of a manager within a textile company. These information needs will also be to some extent dependant upon the structure of the organisation, and the manager's place in that structure, and the culture of that organisation. Organisational structure and culture will tend to vary from one organisation to another, thus placing different demands upon the accounting information system.

The technology upon which an accounting information system is based will also vary greatly and will depend partly upon the size of the company. Nevertheless there are certain functions common to all such systems:

- *Information collection and recording*: This function ensures that the relevant information is identified and stored in a systematic way so that it can be used for the future.
- *Information analysis*: This function involves the interpretation of information and the sorting of it into such a form that it can be used to help the manager in the business.
- *Information reporting*: The relevant information needs to be communicated to managers in such a way that it enables them to use it to help make decisions. It is vital that information is reported in time to enable decisions to be made.

It is important to realise that a management accounting system is only a part, albeit an important part, of the management information system of an organisation. The precise form of the management information system will vary, depending on the size and complexity of the organisation in question, but all organisations will need to reassure themselves that their system is providing useful information. A socially responsible approach to management will make use of this accounting information just as much as any other approach, as accounting information is central to the management of any organisation. The kind of information which can be expected from a management accounting system includes information for:

- Scorekeeping
- Attention directing
- Problem solving.

Scorekeeping is an activity that lies at the heart of management accounting. Its objective is to provide the financial information that forms the basis for problem-solving and attention-directing aspects of management accounting. Scorekeeping's importance to management accounting is reflected in the fact that it is often referred to by the separate term cost accounting.

Corporate governance

We have mentioned before the notion of managers as the stewards of a company, and responsible to the owners of the company for its performance. An alternative conception of the relationship between managers and owners is to see managers as the 'elected government' of a company who are responsible to the 'electorate', shareholders. Corporate governance considers the nature of this relationship. There are four forces which determine the governance structure facing firms. These are:

1 the structure of company boards;
2 general societal pressures;
3 the regulatory and legal environment;
4 the pattern of ownership.

The impact of social pressure on companies can be seen in relation to corporate reporting on the social and environmental effects which we considered earlier. As concerns have grown about the impact of economic activity on the natural environment, some companies have taken to reporting on their environmental, as well as their financial, records. The role of the company board has also been the subject of debate in recent years; with for example, debates surrounding the role of boards in terms of the remuneration they award the senior managers of companies. These examples provide insights into some of the issues that have dominated the corporate governance literature in recent years.

The impact of these four pressures will vary between countries and, therefore, may account for differences in the way companies are managed in different countries. Indeed, some have argued that differences in governance systems affect not only company performance, but also national economic performance. We have already mentioned how variations in accounting regulations impact on the external reporting, through company accounts, in different countries. We could add to this the points raised in a previous chapter which explains how aspects of financial performance are often interpreted differently in various countries. The major differences relate to the sources of control that management are subjected to in these three countries. In Japan and Germany, for example, share ownership is relatively concentrated, with financial institutions, the main banks in Japan and the universal banks in Germany, participating closely in the running of companies. There also exist within these two countries widespread corporate cross-holdings, where companies own shares in each other. However, within Japan and Germany the extent of external control through the takeover process has been limited, although there are signs that this is becoming less true nowadays. In US, by contrast, external control is far more evident, and takeovers are seen as a major way of disciplining inefficient management. The two systems are often described as market-based, for the US, and relationship-based for Germany and Japan. One view is that the relationship-based system has advantages in that the closer relationship between managers and owners allows companies to maintain a longer-term perspective. Whereas the fear of takeover and the need to placate a diffuse group of shareholders cause managers in market-based systems to adopt a more short-term perspective, which is damaging for company performance. However, the debate regarding the relative merits of the two systems of governance is far from settled.

The objective of this section has been to make you aware of the dynamic nature of the financial environment in which companies operate. Management accounting, like other business functions, has had to respond and adapt to reflect the increasing complexity of business. Moreover, the challenges and pressures that have influenced the evolution of the finance function differ not only over time, but also as a consequence of the differing governance structures of countries. As we move to discuss some of the costing terms used by management accountants it is important to keep this in mind.

Stanley Brown is the transport manager of a food manufacturing company, based at its distribution centre, and he controls the operation of a fleet of vans. He needs to know the operating cost of the vehicles under his management in order to be able to calculate delivery costs to charge the company's customers for the products delivered.

His assistant has provided him with the following information in terms of cost per vehicle:

Purchase cost	£25 000
Expected sale value after 2 years	£7 000
Vehicle license per annum	£500
Insurance per annum	£500
Maintenance – each six-monthly service	£250
Replacement parts (per 1000 miles)	£75
Tyre replacement after 25 000 miles – 6 tyres @	£80 each
Average mileage per annum	30 000
Diesel fuel per gallon	£2.50
Average mpg	15

Stanley needs to classify this data in some way in order to be able to arrive at an estimated running cost per mile for his vehicles so that he can determine the cost of delivery to his customers.

The classification of costs

Although it may initially be thought that a cost to a business is simply that – a cost – in actual fact accountants spend a lot of time considering the nature of cost behaviour and attempting to arrive at a classification of costs which is appropriate to their purpose and to the needs of the business. If we look at the problem facing Stanley Brown we can see that he has information concerning the costs of his vehicles which he needs to classify, or organise, in some way in order to be able to work out the cost of delivery of goods to his customers. The information which he has been presented with will not enable him to do this until he has classified it in some way, and we need to consider how he might do this.

As we work through this book we shall look at various methods of classifying costs, that is grouping costs according to their meaning in a particular context, and we will investigate how these cost classifications can be used to help business managers solve some of the problems they face in managing a business. As a starting point, however, it is necessary to recognise that costs can be classified in a variety of ways, depending upon the purpose of the classification. Costs can be classified in the following ways:

- according to their behaviour;
- according to their relevance to the production of goods and services;
- according to the nature of the decision to be made.

We will look at these different classifications and see how they can help business decision-making. In this chapter we will consider the first of these methods of classification.

Cost classification according to behaviour

While business managers are concerned with what their costs have been in the past, they are naturally much more concerned with what their costs will be in the future. Cost prediction, the estimating of future costs, is therefore of crucial importance to business planning. In order to be able to predict costs it is necessary to be able to understand the behaviour of costs and how they will be affected by changes in methods of operation or levels of activity. The classification of costs according to their behaviour is therefore the basis of cost prediction and this is normally undertaken in relation to changes in the activity level, or output, of the firm. In this context costs can be classified into two types:

- Fixed costs
- Variable costs.

Fixed costs

A fixed cost is one which is not dependent upon the level of activity but which will be incurred on a recurring basis whatever the level of activity the firm undertakes. Thus for Stanley Brown the purchase cost of a van is a fixed cost which must be incurred whether or not the van is actually used.

Fixed costs are relevant to time periods rather than to activity levels and in terms of cost prediction the cost behaviour can be predicted into the future without regard to the expected activity level. Such costs are unchanged according to the level of activity and can be illustrated as shown in Figure 5.1.

Fixed costs are not, however, fixed indefinitely for all activity levels and at a certain point additional fixed costs will be incurred. Thus for Stanley Brown when the number of deliveries increases above a certain level an additional van will be required. This is known as a step change in fixed costs and can be illustrated as shown in Figure 5.2.

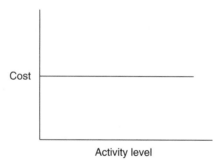

Figure 5.1 Fixed costs

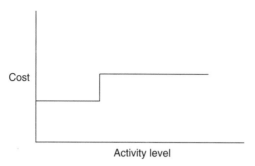

Figure 5.2 Stepped costs

Variable costs

A variable cost is one which is directly related to the level of activity of the firm and can be predicted to increase or decrease in direct proportion to an increase or decrease in the level of production. Thus for Stanley Brown diesel fuel can be considered to be a variable cost and a 10 per cent increase in the annual mileage of one of his vans can be expected to lead to a 10 per cent increase in the annual cost of diesel fuel. This can be illustrated as shown in Figure 5.3.

Variable costs therefore are related to the level of activity of the business and for cost prediction purposes cannot be estimated for the future without a consideration of the estimated level of activity, as any changes to this will lead to a change in cost. Although costs are predicted in total for a time period for variable costs it is useful to understand the cost behaviour in terms of unit cost – i.e. cost per unit produced, per 1000 units produced or per batch – or whatever unit is appropriate. For Stanley Brown an appropriate unit measure is cost per mile so variable costs such as tyre replacement can be predicted in terms of cost per mile.

This classification of costs into fixed and variable according to their behavioural characteristics is an essential preliminary to being able to undertake any

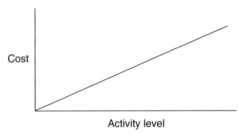

Figure 5.3 Variable costs

sort of cost prediction. For Stanley Brown therefore it is possible to classify his costs in this manner, as follows:

Fixed costs
   Purchase cost
   Vehicle license
   Insurance
   Maintenance

Variable costs
   Replacement parts
   Tyre replacement
   Diesel fuel

For cost prediction purposes it is necessary to convert these into costs per time period and in this case costs are considered on an annual basis as follows:

Fixed costs	£	£
Purchase of vehicle		
Purchase	25 000 –	
less resale value	7 000	
	18 000	
Cost per annum (over 2 years)		9 000
Vehicle license		500
Insurance		500
Maintenance (2 services @ £250 each)		500
Annual fixed cost		10 500

Variable costs	£
Replacement parts:	
£75 per 1000 miles – annual mileage 30 000	2 250
Tyres:	
£80 × 6 tyres every 25 000 miles – annual	
mileage 30 000 i.e. 80 × 6 × 30 000/25 000	576
Fuel:	
£2.50 per gallon @ 15 mpg – annual mileage 30 000	5 000
Annual variable cost	7 826

In order to be able to predict costs in the future for calculating delivery costs to customers Stanley Brown, having now classified costs appropriately, is able to calculate a cost per mile as follows:

	£
Fixed cost	10 500
Variable cost	7 826
Total cost	18 326
Cost per mile	
Fixed cost (10 500/30 000)	0.35
Variable cost (7826/30 000)	0.26
Total cost	0.61

Because Stanley has classified his costs into fixed and variable costs he is able to predict costs in the future at different levels of activity. The fixed costs will not change in total but if the average mileage changes they will change in terms of cost per mile. The variable costs on the other hand will change in total in direct proportion to the changed activity level but will remain the same in terms of unit cost per mile. Thus for example if each van is expected to travel 35 000 miles per annum in future instead of 30 000 miles costs can be predicted as follows:

	£
Fixed cost	10 500
Variable cost (£0.26 per mile × 35 000 miles)	9 100
Total cost	19 600
Cost per mile	
Fixed cost (10 500/35 000)	0.30
Variable cost	0.26
Total cost	0.56

Although this classification of costs forms the basis of cost prediction it needs to be recognised that this classification is not necessarily simple to achieve, nor is the prediction of cost based upon this classification as absolute as might be understood from the example. We will consider some of these difficulties in future chapters but for the moment the following problems with the classification of costs need to be understood:

Mixed costs

Not all costs can be classified as purely fixed or purely variable and many have an element of both fixed and variable costs. Examples include telephone charges or photocopy machine charges which have a fixed element of rent and a variable element depending upon usage. These costs are known as mixed

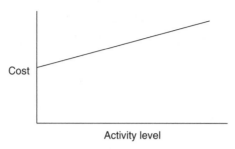

Figure 5.4 Mixed costs

costs or semi-fixed or semi-variable costs. Cost prediction must therefore recognise from these types of cost the nature of the behaviour of the cost and attempt to separate the two types of cost in order to predict future behaviour. This is often a difficult exercise and prediction is often made using statistical methods based upon an analysis of past cost behaviour. Such costs can be illustrated as shown in Figure 5.4.

Short- and long-term effects

The classification of costs into fixed and variable costs for prediction is basically only valid for short-term prediction – i.e. for the next time period or the next year. In the longer term all fixed costs can be regarded as variable and even long-term costs such as the factory costs themselves can be varied. Existing factories can be disposed of or new factories built given sufficient time and so even this type of cost is variable in the long term. In the long term there are also likely to be technological changes which will affect production methods or economic changes which may affect demand for a product. Cost prediction cannot therefore be made indefinitely into the future but only for fixed relatively short time periods.

Linearity

In predicting costs it is normally assumed that variable costs vary in direct proportion to changes in the level of activity, but in reality this may not be strictly true. Thus the assumption is made that a 10 per cent increase in output will result in a 10 per cent increase in variable costs and a 20 per cent increase in output will result in a 20 per cent increase in variable costs. The reality may, however, be a 12 per cent increase in costs for a 10 per cent increase in output and a 19 per cent increase for a 20 per cent increase in output. Cost behaviour is somewhat irregular, and even when regular the relationship may not actually be a linear relationship but may be a curvilinear one with costs changing predictably with changing activity levels but not in a linear manner. Nevertheless, while recognising this, it is often reasonable in predicting costs to make an assumption of linearity and calculate costs on this basis. For small changes in activity levels this may be sufficient and it may not be worth the effort of determining the exact nature of the cost behaviour.

The bigger the variation in activity level, however, the less precise such approximations are likely to be.

Relevant range

Both fixed and variable cost relationships only hold true within a specific range of activities, which is termed the relevant range, and outside this range the relationship no longer holds true. For example, with fixed costs an increase in the level of activity beyond a particular point may necessitate the introduction of a new production plant or an additional assembly line, hence causing an increase in the level of fixed costs. Fixed costs tend to increase in steps rather than gradually as the level of activity increases and these increases are known as 'stepped costs' in the production process. For variable costs the changes tend to be more gradual but, for example, an increase in activity may result in the need to recruit extra labour, or to work overtime at premium rates, or to introduce a shift working pattern. The effect of this is to change the unit cost of production beyond a particular level of activity and to move the variable cost behaviour into a different cost behaviour relationship. In predicting costs therefore it is necessary to recognise the relevant range within which particular cost behaviour applies.

Economics v. accounting

Economic theory suggests that costs behave in a predictable way, whatever the range of activity and that one cost function applies to all levels of activity. Economic theory further suggests that a cost function is not linear, but rather curvilinear. The difference between costs in accounting and in economics is considered in detail in Chapter 4.

Multiple causes of behaviour

It is often assumed that a variable cost is related to the level of production and varies directly with changes in the level of production. In reality variable costs may vary in relation to a number of different activities within the production process. Thus, for example, labour costs may vary according to the number of orders received, or the number of batches processed, or the number of times machines need to be reset for different production processes, or more likely to a combination of such reasons. It is an oversimplification to relate all variable costs to one activity measure, such as output, but one that is frequently assumed by manufacturing companies. Such an assumption, however, is often sufficient to classify costs for prediction purposes. At other times, however, the results from this may be misleading and it is for this reason that other methods of determining cost relationships have been developed. Activity-based costing is one such method which we will consider in greater detail in Chapter 8.

The objectives of cost classification

In order to consider how we might wish to classify the cost information which is available to us in a useful way it is a good starting point to consider the objectives which we have in mind for such a classification. Broadly speaking there are three reasons or objectives for wishing to classify costs, namely:

● stock valuation
● decision-making
● control.

The control of stock

A firm holds stock both as an essential part of its production process and as an essential part of its sales and distribution process. These stocks are, however, essentially different in nature. The first type is held for the firm's internal purposes in order to operate efficiently in a production environment while the second type is held for external purposes to meet demand from customers efficiently. It is therefore possible to categorise the types of stock which a firm holds into the following types:

Raw materials

These are purchased by a firm from its suppliers and are used in the manufacture of the products which the firm produces. The materials are all used in the manufacture of the products of the company and are held as stocks of raw materials until needed in the manufacturing process.

Work in progress

A product often goes through several processes in its manufacture. In between processes the product is in a part manufactured state and no longer consists of raw materials but is not yet a finished product. In terms of value the raw materials have had value added from the processes undertaken but do not yet have the value of a finished product. These items are known as work in progress which signifies that they need further processing in order to become a finished product. Work in progress is classified and valued separately from raw materials and the value attached is an attempt to estimate the value added from the production processes undertaken. Where a product undergoes several processes it can be expected that work in progress will consist of a variety of items at different stages of production.

Finished goods

Once production has been completed the product is finished and known as finished goods. These are then available for sale to customers. Finished goods are therefore held after completion until they can be sold.

Reason for holding stock

It can therefore be seen that the different types of stock held by a firm are different in nature and are held for different purposes. The reasons for holding stock are as follows:

Raw materials

1 *To ensure continuity in the production processes*: This is particularly important if the production process needs to operate at a particular level in order to operate efficiently. Thus some processes (e.g. in a chemical processing plant) need to operate continuously in order to be effective and there is a need to ensure that raw materials are in hand to enable this process to continue and to prevent disruption to the process.
2 *Seasonal availability*: Some raw materials are only available on a seasonal basis (especially natural products) and there is a need to obtain sufficient stocks to last from one season to the next.
3 *Bulk purchasing discounts*: For some materials it is possible to obtain substantial discounts from purchasing in bulk and this makes it attractive to the firm. This discount must be considered against the costs of holding stock in order to decide whether or not it is advantageous to the firm to take advantage of bulk purchasing discounts.

Work in progress

This type of stock is held because of the different nature and speed of the various production processes and acts as a buffer between the different processes in order to ensure the efficient operating of these various processes.

Finished goods

1 *To ensure sufficient goods to meet demand*: Most businesses do not manufacture goods to order but instead supply from stock in order to be able to supply within an acceptable time frame. For this type of business therefore it is essential to keep a supply of finished goods in stock in order to meet demand.
2 *Seasonal fluctuations*: The demand for some goods is seasonal with demand occurring mainly at a particular time of year. In order to maintain production processes, however, the firm will manufacture goods continuously throughout the year and the stock of finished goods will build up during

the year and be sold in the appropriate season. An example of this is toy manufacturing where the majority of goods are sold during the pre-Christmas season.

3 *Obsolete stock*: There is a danger when finished goods are held in stock until demanded by customers that this stock becomes obsolete and hence unsaleable. Although this is not a reason for holding stock, it is nevertheless one reason why stock may be held and a danger to be recognised in considering the extent of stockholding. In valuing stock therefore it is essential to bear this in mind and value stock at its sale value (if less than cost), revaluing when necessary. This will be considered further in the discussion of control procedures.

The cost of raw materials

While the purchase cost of raw materials is the main cost of the stock held by a firm, this is not the only cost involved with stock. In addition the following must be taken into account:

● costs of obtaining stock
● costs of holding stock

Additionally there are costs involved in not having materials to hand when needed and these are known as stockout costs.

The factors involved in these costs are as follows:

Costs of obtaining stock

Administration

Administrative effort is involved in obtaining stock and ensuring its delivery. This effort involves the ordering procedure, the checking procedure on its arrival and the payment procedure for the goods received. These procedures involve different people. For example a store clerk will order stocks, a storekeeper will physically check the goods on arrival, a stores clerk will certify bills for the stock for payment and an accounts clerk will arrange for the payment to be made. This segregation of duties is a normal feature of audit and control in a large business.

Transport

It is often necessary to arrange and pay separately for the transport of stock. This involves not just the delivery of raw materials from suppliers to the firm but also its transport around the manufacturing site. This also includes the transport of raw materials from where they are held in stock to the relevant production process and also the transport of work in progress from one process to the next.

Costs of holding stock

Storage costs

Goods held in stock need to be stored and therefore adequate storage space needs to be provided. The provision of storage space is a cost which the business must bear. Given that these materials are valuable it is necessary that storage space is secure enough to safeguard the stock. The storage space also needs to be appropriate to the type of stock held. Generally speaking the more valuable the stock is and the more prone it is to deterioration, the greater is the need for special storage facilities. This in turn adds to the cost of the stock.

Handling costs

The stores in which raw materials are kept need to be secure and records need to be kept of items received into stock and issued from stock. Thus there are handling costs of stock which involve not just physically moving stock but also the keeping of records. Depending upon the size of the stock kept this could involve one or more people being fully involved in storekeeping, thereby increasing the cost of stock. If stock is prone to deterioration then there is a need to ensure that the oldest stock is issued first and so the physical management of the stores becomes more time-consuming and costly. The principle of issuing the oldest stock first and ensuring that this cycle is maintained is known as stock rotation.

Insurance

As stock is valuable there is a need to insure it against loss and damage in the same way as other components of the firm will be insured.

Loss and deterioration

Although precaution will be taken by the firm to prevent the loss or deterioration of stock through the provision of adequate storage facilities there is nevertheless the possibility of the loss or deterioration of stock. Deterioration is of particular significance for the types of materials which deteriorate through ageing and care must be taken to ensure that the oldest items of a particular type are always issued before newer items. There is also the possibility that changes in the production process or range of goods manufactured could lead to particular items of stock becoming obsolete and no longer needed in the production process. The stock control procedures will need to identify stock which is no longer used and arrangements made for the disposal of such stock.

Interest on capital invested

The amount of stock held by a firm represents capital invested in the firm. This is part of the working capital of the firm. Such capital has a cost and one of the costs of stock therefore is the interest on capital invested in stock.

Stockout costs

We can see therefore that there are costs involved in holding stock in addition to the purchase cost of the stock itself but also that there are reasons for holding stock which are integral to the operating of the business. This might lead us to suppose that the firm should minimise its stockholding and this is, indeed, one of its objectives. It needs to be recognised, however, that there are also stockout costs – that is costs incurred by the firm because it does not have stock available to satisfy its production requirements. These costs can be identified as follows:

Loss of production

If a firm runs out of a particular item of stock this will halt the production process not just for the particular process for which this item is needed but also for all the processes in the manufacture of that particular product. Any such disruption to production can be costly and time-consuming to recover from. This is especially true in a continuous production environment where lack of an item of stock can lead to the closedown of the entire process and which can then take weeks to restart. This kind of process is relevant in oil refining, chemical production and ceramics.

Loss of future sales

Disruption to the production schedule from lack of stock will cause delays in production and this can lead to delays in the supply of goods to customers. It can, however, have a greater impact than this because it is possible that these delays can lead to a loss of goodwill from customers which will cause them to purchase goods from other suppliers in the future. Thus a stockout situation can cause not just a problem in the present but an effect into the future whereby orders which would have been received are lost to competitors because of the perceived unreliability of the firm amongst its customers.

Cost of urgent reorders

One way to recover from a stockout situation is to urgently reorder a quantity of the item concerned. Doing this, however, involves cost not just because the cost of purchase of a small quantity urgently will be higher – in fact an alternative supplier might be involved – but also in the ordering and handling costs of the stock ordered in this way.

Optimising stock levels

The control of stock therefore is an issue of some importance to a firm and the procedures used are known as stock control or inventory control. The objective of such control is to minimise the cost of stock while at the same time maximising its availability. Stock control therefore involves planning the need for particular items of stock, assessing its availability and ensuring that stock is available when required. It also involves at the same time ensuring that the level of stock is not higher than necessary. Controlling the cost of stock requires systems to ensure that the costs of obtaining and holding stock are minimised and that the level of stock held is the minimum necessary for the efficient functioning of the business. Various techniques have evolved for the controlling of stock levels and the following are of particular significance:

Economic order quantity (EOQ)

This technique involves calculating the level of stock for each item which needs to be held and calculating the size of order which needs to be placed for that item and the timing of the order. This can be calculated by the following formula:

$$EOQ = \sqrt{\frac{2DS}{I}}$$

where
D = demand per period for the stock item;
S = the cost of placing an order;
I = the cost of holding one unit of stock for one period.

   This calculation leads to ordering appropriate amounts at appropriate times to achieve maximum benefit to the company. Thus the costs of holding stock must be offset against the discounts which can be obtained from making large orders and the costs which the firm must bear if the stock of any items runs out. To do this it is necessary to calculate the rate of usage of the stock item and to know the time delay between ordering more of the item and its being delivered into stock. In theory it is then possible to reorder at a point in time which will ensure that new stock is delivered at the time when existing stock has just been completely used. In practice a safety margin is also needed to allow for irregularities in usage and delivery times and to ensure that the production schedule is not disrupted by a stock-out situation. This can be illustrated graphically as shown in Figure 5.5.

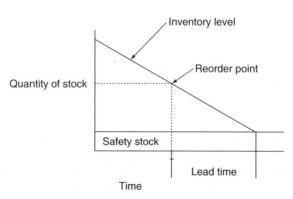

Figure 5.5 Calculation of reorder point for stock

Various techniques can be employed to arrive at a knowledge of future requirements of each item of stock, which will depend upon the scheduling of production for the future.

In addition to calculating when to order an item of stock it is also necessary to calculate how much to order at a particular time. In general the larger the size of any particular order the greater the discount which can be obtained. This needs to be offset, however, against the costs of holding stock described above. The firm will therefore need to calculate both of these and arrive at a calculation, by means of mathematical techniques, that will show the size of order which should be made for the best financial advantage to the company. The size and timing of such an order is known as the economic order quantity.

Just in time (JIT)

This technique has gained increasing importance in recent years and has been adopted by companies which have copied the techniques of Japanese manufacturing companies, in which the technique originated. The aim of the technique is to eliminate the need for the holding of stock altogether by ensuring that raw materials are delivered regularly in small quantities as they are needed in the manufacturing process. The raw materials are therefore not delivered into stock, but instead are delivered directly to the production department in which they are needed on a time scale which ensures that the production schedule can be met. The ordering process needs to be efficient, but more importantly delivery of raw materials from suppliers needs to be regular and on a time scale demanded by the company because buffer stocks do not exist to prevent disruption to production. These requirements of JIT tend to mean that companies have used the technique to reduce stock levels but have not gone as far as eliminating stores and the holding of stocks altogether. In practice, however, the British practice of stockholding can be contrasted with the Japanese practice insofar as the average Japanese stockholding is 3 days while the average British stockholding is 2 weeks usage quantity. From a socially responsible perspective, however, it should be noted that this technique reduces the level of stock held by a business but does not necessarily reduce the overall level of stock held as it is often held instead by the supplying business. This has the effect therefore of transferring costs from one business to another whereas a socially responsible business would value all stakeholders to the business and would be less likely to engage in this practice.

Inventory control procedures

We have seen the importance of control procedures, not just in ensuring that stock is ordered and held to meet requirements, but also in controlling the cost. An essential part of cost control is the recording of materials as they are received into stock and issued from stock to the production processes. These control procedures form part of the cost accounts of the firm and enable such information as product costing to be calculated, but they also form the control of the stock itself and the stock levels recorded can be checked by means of a physical stock check. There are a number of techniques which can be used for stock control and accounting but they are beyond the scope of this book.

Stock valuation

In order to value stock we need to be able to calculate its cost of production. This is important because it is crucial for a business to know whether or not it is operating profitably and to know whether or not each product made is being sold at a profit. Most companies manufacture more than one product and so need to know the costs of production for each product separately. This also applies to services industries and a company such as McDonald's will want to know the cost of production of a Big Mac separately from the cost of production of French Fries in order to know whether it is making a profit from producing and selling each of these products. An organisation following a socially responsible approach needs this information just as much as any other organisation as the foundation for the management of any business is based upon an understanding of costs and their behaviour.

Not all of the costs which a firm incurs are directly associated with the production of individual products. In the case of McDonald's its television advertising is concerned with all of its products from a sales point of view and not with production. Similarly, the heating and lighting of its individual restaurants is not for the production of individual products. We shall look at production costs in a later chapter but at this point it is important to be able to classify costs into two separate types for this purpose:

1 Product costs
2 Period costs.

Product costs

These are the costs associated with the actual production of the product itself. These will include the cost of raw materials involved in the production, the labour time involved in the production process, and a variety of other costs such as the cost of running machinery which is necessary to produce the finished goods.

Period costs

These are the costs incurred by the business which are not related to actual production but incurred because the company is in business. They are known as period costs because they are generally associated with a time period. For example, business rates are payable annually, telephone bills are payable quarterly and the managing director's salary is payable monthly. None of these costs can be considered to be directly attributable to the costs of producing any particular product.

If we look at the costs involved in running the vans which Stanley Brown is responsible for we can see that such items as insurance and vehicle license can be classified as period costs whereas costs such as tyre replacement and fuel costs can be classified as product costs – or in this case as service costs.

Decision-making

One of the prime functions of a business manager is the making of decisions and it is obvious that the best decisions are those that are based on the most accurate and meaningful information. As far as the classification of costs is concerned we can simply state at this point that some costs are affected by a decision and change depending upon that decision while some are not affected by the decision. We can therefore classify costs into the following two types:

1 *Relevant costs*: Those costs which change depending upon the decisions made or are incurred because a decision is made.
2 *Irrelevant costs*: Those costs which are not affected by the particular decision to be made.

Control

Controlling the operations of a business, or a part of a business, to ensure that objectives are met, is also a major part of the work of a manager, and Stanley Brown is responsible for the control of a fleet of vans to ensure that the objective of the delivery of the company's products to its customers is achieved. Part 4 of this book is devoted to considering the control of a business and the way in which accounting information can help the manager to achieve this. As far as the classification of costs is concerned it is important to recognise that some costs are within the control of the business, or a particular manager, and some are outside that control. Costs can therefore be classified into:

- controllable costs
- uncontrollable costs.

For Stanley Brown costs such as the vehicle license and the cost per gallon of fuel must be regarded as uncontrollable costs because he is unable to determine the cost of these items. Maintenance costs, however, can be considered a controllable cost because he can directly affect this cost and can even vary the time period over which the maintenance is undertaken.

Other methods of cost classification

Although the basic method of classifying costs for product costing and for the prediction of future costs is in relationship to the behaviour of those costs, there are other methods of classifying costs which are used and are of some importance to the business manager. These classifications can be considered to be sub-divisions of the cost classification system which are used to indicate the way in which the costs arise rather than indicating their behaviour. Three different classifications will be considered here, namely:

1 Direct and indirect costs
2 Prime cost and overheads
3 Departmental costs.

Direct and indirect costs

Direct costs are those which can be directly identified with a particular product or service which the business provides. These can be categorised into three distinct types:

- *Direct materials*: the raw materials which go into the product;
- *Direct labour*: the costs of labour which are directly involved in the production process;
- *Direct expenses*: expenses which are incurred specifically in the making of a particular product, such as royalties paid or hire of a particular piece of equipment.

Indirect costs are all those costs of materials, labour and expenses which are incurred in the production process but which cannot be identified with one particular product. Examples include the cost of foremen and maintenance staff in a business producing a range of different products or consumable materials used by machinery involved in the production process.

Prime cost and overheads

The total of all direct costs is known as prime cost and therefore:

Direct materials + Direct labour + Direct expenses = Prime cost

Indirect costs are also known as overheads, but overheads will also include not just production overheads as indirect costs but also other categories of overheads such as administration overheads and selling overheads. The total cost of a product therefore is the sum of the prime cost and overheads, thus:

Prime cost + Overheads = Total cost

The manufacturing cost of a product, however, is defined as the sum of the prime cost and production overheads, rather than all overheads, thus:

Prime cost + Production overheads = Manufacturing cost

The classification of cost by this method and the treatment of overheads will be considered in greater detail in the next chapter.

Departmental costs

Most businesses, and certainly all large businesses, are organised into departments, with each department being the responsibility of an individual manager. Costs are classified as attributable to a particular department to facilitate the control of those costs and to allocate responsibility for costs to a specific individual manager. The implications of this for control are considered later but at this point it should be understood that this classification of costs is for control purposes rather than for cost prediction purposes. Departments can be categorised into:

- Direct departments: which are those departments involved in the production process;
- Service departments: which perform functions for the business generally rather than for the production process.

Stanley Brown therefore is the manager of a service department which fulfils a service function to the business which is concerned with the production of food products. Other departments will be directly concerned with the manufacture of food products and these will be the direct departments. As Stanley is in charge of the transport department he controls the costs of that department and is responsible for its operations, but has no control over other costs of the business which will be the responsibility of other managers.

 ## Additional questions

Question 5.1

The Handtool Company Ltd produces screwdrivers. From the following information calculate the prime cost and total cost of its products:

	£
Direct labour	8000
Direct materials	
Steel	4000
Plastic	1800
Other	750
Factory rent	2500
Admin.	800
Insurance	350
Factory cleaning materials	75

Question 5.2

Classify the following into direct and indirect costs:
  floppy discs for the office computer
  steel used in product manufacture
  wages of machine operators
  wages of factory security guard
  patents royalties on product manufactured
  tools for maintenance mechanics
  painting of the factory gates
  tyre replacement on delivery vehicle
  telephone rental
  overtime payments for machine operators.

6

Cost–Volume–Profit (Break Even) Analysis

Learning objectives

When you have completed this chapter you should be able to:

- explain the relationship between profit, cost and production volume;
- calculate the break even point;
- understand and use the concept of contribution;
- identify the assumption underlying the analysis;
- solve C–V–P problems either graphically or algebraically;
- discuss the limitations of this type of analysis;
- identify business problems for which this type of analysis is useful.

Introduction

Any business, whether it be a manufacturing company, a service company or a charity, needs to understand the nature of its cost and revenues and the way in which these change as the volume of output or level of activity changes. This is necessary in order that the business manager can make operating decisions about the business and plan the level of production in the short term. A technique which examines the relationship between changes in volume and changes in total cost and total revenue is that of cost–volume–profit analysis (C–V–P). This technique is also known as break even analysis. It is intended to be a guide for a business manager for short-term decision-making and planning by considering the effects of business decisions on these three interrelated aspects of cost, profit and volume. The kinds of short-term decisions which can be helped by an understanding of the C–V–P relationship for a business include pricing decisions, planned levels of output, shift working patterns and special order acceptance/rejection decisions.

In the last chapter we introduced some of the basic cost concepts used by management accountants. In this chapter we are going to extend the use of these concepts to consider how they can be used to assist managers in their decision-making role. The focus of our attention will be on the relationship between the total cost of production, the volume of sales, and the profit made. This C–V–P relationship can provide useful insights into a number of areas, and we give examples of some of these later in this chapter. Cost–Volume–Profit analysis is an important tool in short-term management decision-making. It studies the relationship between costs and profit when the volume of production varies.

Knowing the level of sales that will cover costs provides managers with a number of useful insights. Once total sales revenue has equalled total costs, the organisation is said to be operating at break even level. At this level of activity the business is making neither a profit nor a loss: it is simply covering its costs.

Cost–Volume–Profit analysis can be described as a marginal costing technique. We will consider a comparison of the marginal costing technique with alternatives, such as absorption costing and activity-based costing, in Chapter 8, rather than here. Here we concentrate upon the application of management accounting, so we discuss applications before we consider, in full, all the various costing techniques adopted by management accountants. However, you should be reassured that C–V–P analysis requires an understanding of fixed and variable costs, and these concepts have been explained in the previous chapter.

You may tend to think that every time the volume of sales (i.e. number sold) increases so do the profits, but this is not always so. It all depends on how the costs and sales revenue will be affected by the number of items sold. You might also imagine that higher prices will lead to higher profits, but again this is not always the case because if demand falls away sharply sales revenues could turn out to be less than that before sales prices were increased. It all depends on how the costs, the number of sales and the prices charged per unit interrelate.

The understanding and the use of the concept known as break even analysis will assist the exploration of this important triangular relationship. Break even analysis being the process of finding the sales volume point, expressed either in units or in revenue, where total costs are exactly equal to total revenue. At this point, the break even point, profit is zero.

Let us look at the following scenario:

Holidays for Children is a registered charity which runs a holiday home for disadvantaged children. This home is situated on the east coast in the holiday resort of Anytown. The home is let to local authorities for the provision of holidays for visiting parties of children in care. The home is open during the summer season for 30 weeks each year.

Each visiting party of children is accompanied by its own housemother who supervises the children throughout their holiday. The home accommodates up to 16 guests and is let for at least 6 people at a time. The charge made is £100 per person and the same charge is applied to both adults and children.

The weekly costs per guest incurred by Holidays for Children are:

	£
Food	18
Electricity	4
Domestic cleaning	6
Use of minibus	15

Seasonal staff supervise and carry out all necessary duties at the home at a cost of £12 000 for the 30-week season. This provides sufficient staffing for 6–10 guests but if 11 or more guests are to be accommodated additional staff are required at a cost of £200 per week. Such additional staff need to be recruited for the whole 30-week season.

Rent of the property amounts to £2500 per annum and the garden of the home is maintained by the council's recreation department which charges a nominal fee of £1500 per annum.

The chief executive of the charity is concerned about the viability of this home and has asked Fred Davis, a member of the accounts team, to provide a report to him showing the level of occupancy needed for the home to cover its costs

A socially responsible approach to this kind of business would indicate that this charity would want to provide as many holidays for children as possible. It should therefore be interested in ensuring that the home is occupied by groups of children for each of the 30 weeks of the holiday season. This assumption is, however, overly simplistic because a charity, like every other organisation, must ensure its financial viability in order that it can continue to fulfil its mission in the future. Thus, this type of organisation needs to know its operating costs and break even point just as much as a profit-seeking organisation.

Break even analysis

We will use this example to highlight aspects of break even analysis, and the way in which the break even point can be calculated. However, we begin with some insights derived from the definition of the break even point introduced in the previous section. Here the break even point was defined as the sales volume where total costs is equal to total revenue.

In the previous chapter we discussed a variety of possible ways in which costs could be classified. However, as we have already pointed out, C–V–P analysis uses a cost classification where costs are classified as either fixed or variable costs. If you are unsure of the distinction between fixed and variable you should refer back to the previous chapter. There you will see that fixed costs are those costs that do not vary with the level of sales, whereas variable costs do vary as sales change.

The use of C–V–P analysis

Firstly, C–V–P analysis provides insights into the level of sales at which total revenues equal costs, and where profit, is consequently, zero. It also highlights the importance of the concept of contribution. The practical application of this concept can be seen in a variety of situations.

For example, holiday companies who are prepared to offer trips, during low points in the season, at very substantial discounts. These companies, with a range of fixed costs such as head office expenses to cover, will search for business at low prices as long as the price paid by the customer is sufficient to cover variable costs and thus make a contribution. Their variable costs will include the cost of flights and hotel accommodation for tourists. However, the airlines and the hotels used by holiday companies are also likely to be prepared to cut their prices during off-peak periods. They too are likely to have a cost structure where fixed costs are a significant proportion of total costs. Thus, they will be prepared to accept lower prices, as long as contribution is still positive, and so the variable costs of holiday companies will be lower in low season providing them with even further incentives to discount holidays.

That companies where fixed costs are a significant proportion of total costs should exhibit a greater propensity to cut prices to encourage sales in periods of low demand is one insight provided by C–V–P analysis, but there are others. Those that will be discussed in this chapter are as follows:

- Profit targets
- Sensitivity analysis
- Reviewing multiple products
- Assessing financial risk.

We will consider each in turn.

Profit targets

Whilst breaking even is of interest to all companies, in order to survive a company must make a profit and will often have a target level of profit that it wishes to earn from a particular project. The break even formula can be amended to show the requirement that in addition to covering fixed costs a specified level of profits is also required. Thus:

$$\text{Unit sales to earn target profit} = \frac{\text{Total fixed costs} + \text{Target profit}}{\text{Contribution per unit}}$$

The graphical approach to C–V–P analysis

The graphical approach to C–V–P analysis provides a simple overview of the relationships for a business and illustrates the effects which decisions will have on these relationships. It is not, however, suitable when precise figures are required and for this an algebraic solution is required. The graph drawn is known as a break even chart and looks as shown in Figure 6.1.

From this chart it can be seen that up to the level of output b the firm is operating at a loss and for levels of output in excess of b the firm is operating at a profit. This point is known as the break even point – that is the point at which neither a loss nor a profit is being made.

Point c represents the planned level of activity and at this point the expected profit level is represented by e − d. The difference between the planned level of activity and the break even level of activity (i.e. c − b) is known as the margin of safety and represents the amount by which actual output may fall short of that planned without a loss being incurred. The margin of safety is expressed as a percentage of sales, and can be expressed either in terms of number of units or in terms of revenue.

It can be seen from the graphs that the margin of safety is dependent upon the respective proportions of fixed and variable costs that are involved in producing a product and that the higher the level of fixed costs in relation to variable costs, the lower the margin of safety at any given sales level.

It is important for a business manager to understand the concept of margin of safety and how it can vary from one business to another as it is an

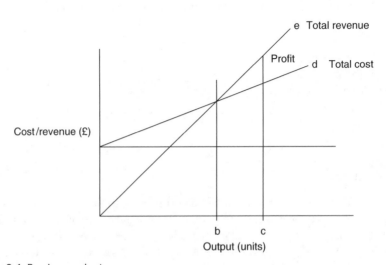

Figure 6.1 Break even chart

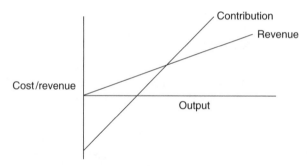

Figure 6.2 Contribution break even chart

important part of understanding budgeting and planning and the effect of shortfalls against budgeted activity can have upon the profitability of the business.

An alternative form of break even chart is known as the contribution break even chart which looks as shown in Figure 6.2.

From this it is possible to establish the contribution made by the product which is given by the following formula:

$$\text{Contribution} = \text{Sales} - \text{Variable costs}$$

The revenue therefore can be seen to contribute firstly to the fixed costs of the business and then to profit, once the fixed costs are covered. This approach is of particular relevance when a marginal costing approach is used (see Chapter 8).

It is possible for Fred Davis to use this graphical approach to C–V–P analysis to understand the nature of the cost – occupancy relationship for the Holidays for Children holiday home.

The cost and income relationships are calculated as follows:

No. of guests	Income (£ p.a.)	Fixed costs (£ p.a.)	Variable costs (£ p.a.)	Total costs (£ p.a.)	Net revenue (£ p.a.)
6	18 000	16 000	7 740	23 740	(5740)
7	21 000	16 000	9 030	25 030	(4030)
8	24 000	16 000	10 320	26 320	(2320)
9	27 000	16 000	11 610	27 610	(610)
10	30 000	16 000	12 900	28 900	1100
11	33 000	22 000	14 190	36 190	(3190)
12	36 000	22 000	15 480	37 480	(1480)
13	39 000	22 000	16 770	38 770	230
14	42 000	22 000	18 060	40 060	1940
15	45 000	22 000	19 350	41 350	3650
16	48 000	22 000	20 640	42 640	7360

Calculations

Income

100 per week × 30 weeks × no. of guests

Fixed costs

up to 10 guests: 12 000 + 2500 + 1500

over 10 guests: 12 000 + 2500 + 1500 + (200 per week × 30 weeks)

Variable cost

(18 + 4 + 6 + 15) × 30 weeks × no. of guests

From this a break even graph can be produced as shown in Figure 6.3.

From this graph it can be seen that, due to the stepped nature of the fixed costs, there are two break even points for the holiday home. These are at approximately 9 and 13 guests per week. For more precise figures an algebraic solution is required.

The algebraic solution of C–V–P analysis

The algebraic approach enables the precise calculation of figures for break even point, profit and contribution margin at any level of activity, and the margin of safety. These can be obtained using the following formulae:

$$\text{Break even point (in terms of revenue)} = \frac{f}{(p - v)/p}$$

$$\text{Break even point (in terms of number of units)} = \frac{f}{p - v}$$

$$\text{Profit} = y(p - v) - f$$

$$\text{Contribution margin ratio} = \frac{p - v}{p}$$

$$\text{Margin of safety} = \frac{\text{Planned sales} - \text{Break even point sales}}{\text{Break even point sales}} \times 100\%$$

where

y = units produced and sold;

p = price per unit;

v = variable cost per unit;

f = total fixed cost.

For Holidays for Children therefore the calculation of the break even point (BEP) for the holiday home is as follows:

For fixed cost of £16 000 p.a.

$$\text{BEP} = \frac{f}{p - v}$$

$$= \frac{16\,000}{(100 \times 30 - 43 \times 30)}$$

$$= 9.36 \text{ guests}$$

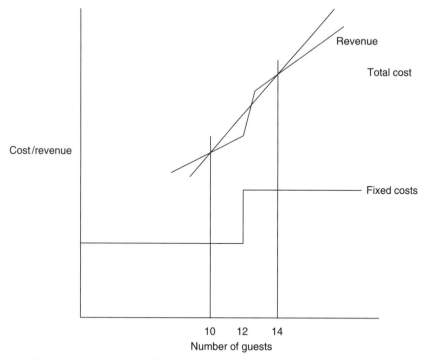

Figure 6.3 Break even chart for holiday home

Therefore 10 guests represents the break even point (as part guests do not exist). *For fixed costs of £22 000 p.a.*

$$\text{BEP} = \frac{f}{p - v}$$

$$= \frac{22\ 000}{(100 \times 30 - 43 \times 30)}$$

$$= 12.87\ \text{guests}$$

Therefore 13 guests represents the break even point (as part guests do not exist).

This shows that for the holiday home, to break even each week of the season it needs to attract 10 guests (9 or 11 would result in a loss) or 13–15 guests. In order to break even over the season, average occupancy needs to be considered and for this the average occupancy would need to be between 9.36 and 10 (with a maximum of 10 in any one week) or over 12.87 per week. An understanding of this C–V–P relationship would therefore enable the council to plan its occupancy levels for the holiday home for the forthcoming season.

It can also be seen that this understanding of the C–V–P relationship for a business would help any manager to understand the implications of any decisions made in the business regarding selling price, costs or volume.

Margin of safety

In assessing the viability of the holiday home it is useful to be able not just to calculate the average occupancy needed per week but also to be able to assess the scope for failing to meet this average occupancy before a loss is incurred. This is known as the margin of safety and is the difference between the break even level of sales and the expected level of sales. The margin of safety is expressed as a percentage and can be calculated from the following formula:

$$\text{Margin of safety} = \frac{\text{Expected sales} - \text{Break even sales}}{\text{Break even sales}} \times 100\%$$

This can be calculated in terms of sales value or in terms of number of units.

For Holidays for Children the margin of safety for the holiday home would be as follows:

Occupancy up to 10 people

$$\text{Margin of safety} = \frac{\text{Expexted sales} - \text{Break even sales}}{\text{Break even sales}} \times 100\%$$

$$= \frac{10 - 9.36 \times 100\%}{10}$$

$$= 7.6\%$$

Occupancy of more than 10 people

$$\text{Margin of safety} = \frac{\text{Expected sales} - \text{Break even sales}}{\text{Break even sales}} \times 100\%$$

$$= \frac{16 - 12.87}{16} \times 100\%$$

$$= 19.6\%$$

This shows that a small margin of safety exists for occupancy of up to 10 people between the level of occupancy which makes a profit and the level of occupancy which causes additional costs to be incurred and the home to make a loss. For occupancy of more than 10 people a higher margin of safety exists between the break even point and the maximum occupancy of the home. The margin of safety is an indication of how much an estimate of levels of sales

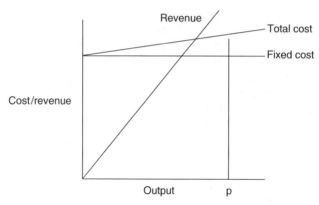

Figure 6.4 Margin of safety

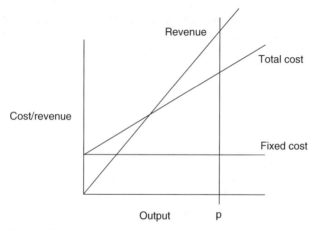

Figure 6.5 Margin of safety

(in this case of occupancy) can vary before the operation ceases to make a profit and starts to make a loss. The smaller the margin of safety, the closer the possibility of making a loss.

Margin of safety is related to the relative proportions of fixed and variable costs which a firm incurs. In general terms the higher the proportion of fixed costs for a given level of sales, the smaller the margin of safety. This can be illustrated graphically as shown in Figures 6.4 and 6.5, where at output p, the margin of safety is the difference between the total line and the total cost line.

Sensitivity analysis

Earlier we considered the level of sales that was required to achieve a particular profit target. If estimated sales are thought to be greater than the level of sales needed to make the target then a business can be reasonably confident that it will achieve its required level of profits. The concept of a margin of safety highlights the vulnerability of profits to changes in demand.

Sensitivity analysis considers the changes in the range of factors that impact on the C–V–P relationship. This analysis can reflect uncertainty regarding one or other of the key variables, such as selling price, fixed costs or variable costs. As such it can be thought of as a variation of the margin of safety concept. Here the vulnerability of profits to changes in the contribution, or in fixed costs, replaces the focus on the impact of fluctuations in demand.

Alternatively, sensitivity analysis can be used to consider alternative business ideas.

Multiple products

If a firm manufactures and sells a range of products then C–V–P analysis needs to be amended to reflect this. Of course, most firms sell more than one product and many will sell the same product at different prices depending on the distribution channel used. When there is more than one product on sale, the weighted average contribution is calculated using the percentage of total sales accounted for by each product as the relevant weight.

The assumptions of C–V–P analysis

As stated earlier, C–V–P analysis is a mathematical technique devised to explain the relationship between costs, profit and level of activity, and the technique is open to both graphical and algebraic solutions. As a mathematical technique, there are several assumptions which are made about the behaviour of costs and revenue as the level of activity changes. We will consider the limitations to this technique caused by these assumptions later in the chapter but first we must consider the nature of these assumptions.

Costs

It is assumed that all costs can be readily divided into fixed and variable costs although we have seen previously that this is by no means a simple process. For fixed costs it is assumed that these costs remain constant over the different levels of activity which are under consideration. For variable costs it is assumed that these vary with the changing level of activity but that they remain constant per unit of output. It is therefore assumed that for both fixed and variable costs there is a linear relationship between the total cost level and the total activity level as illustrated in Figures 6.6 and 6.7.

The technique therefore assumes that efficiency and productivity remain constant and do not vary in accordance with the level of activity. This assumption is at variance with economic theory which suggests that returns to scale (i.e. economies of scale) will reduce unit costs up to a certain level before diminishing returns than cause an increase in unit costs. The technique further assumes that the behaviour of costs can be explained in terms of the single variable of changing level of activity.

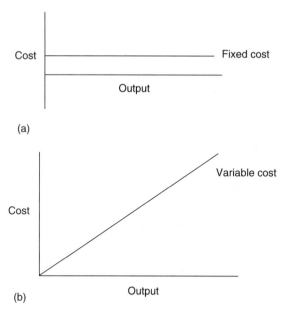

(a)

(b)

Figure 6.6 (a) Relationship between cost and output for fixed cost; (b) Relationship between cost and output for variable cost

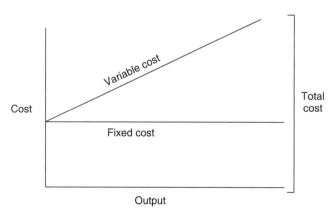

Figure 6.7 Relationship between cost and output

Revenue

It is assumed that revenue per unit remains constant and that there is therefore a linear relationship between total revenue and total output as shown in Figure 6.8.

Relevant range

These assumptions of the linearity of the relationship between costs and revenue and output do not hold true whatever the level of activity which the business undertakes. Nevertheless it is reasonable to assume that these

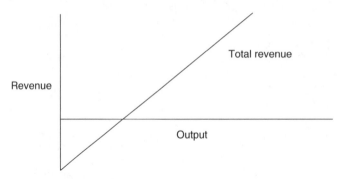

Figure 6.8 Relationship between total revenue and total output

relationships hold true within a certain range of activity and this range is known as the relevant range. This range may be quite small in terms of the possible levels of activity of a business but nevertheless sufficient for a firm to understand the C–V–P relationship for its business and to consider changes to its activity level in the short term.

Short term

These assumptions are based upon the situation as it exists within the business at the time in which the analysis is undertaken, and the analysis therefore assumes that these relationships will hold constant in the future. In the long run, however, these relationships do not hold true and such factors as economic conditions or competition can affect the revenue – volume relationship. Similarly technological changes or economic conditions can affect the cost–volume relationship. This analysis therefore is only appropriate for short-term decision-making (i.e. within the next year) rather than for long-term planning.

Constant sales mix

If a business makes a variety of products within its business then a change in the mix by varying the respective proportions of each product will of necessity change the total revenue function and probably also the variable cost function. C–V–P analysis assumes therefore either a single product or a constant sales mix.

   These assumptions may seem unnecessarily restrictive and to diminish the value of C–V–P analysis, but these assumptions are made to ensure linear relationships which it is possible to solve algebraically. It is possible to relax all these assumptions and explore the C–V–P relationships which exist in a business in this situation. Many businesses do indeed use this technique in this manner to do so but this requires complicated mathematical techniques of modelling which are outside the scope of this module. The use of PCs, however, means that in a business a manager who understands the principles explained here concerning C–V–P analysis can build a computer model which enables him/her to explore these relationships as they exist within the business in which he/she is employed.

Assessing financial risk

All firms operate under conditions of uncertainty and there is an element of risk attached to all planning and decision-making. This risk and uncertainty has a cost to it for a business, which will expect rewards commensurate with the risks which are being undertaken. Cost–Volume–Profit analysis ignores these elements and assumes that the future, in terms of returns and costs associated with different activity levels, is perfectly predictable.

We have seen that managerial decision-making involves deciding between alternative courses of action. Managers do this by forecasting the outcomes from each of the alternatives available to them and then deciding upon the appropriate course of action to follow. Thus decision-making involves forecasting the future effects of a present decision and there is therefore an element of uncertainty involved in the forecast, and a level of risk attached to any decision made. A manager's job is to reduce the level of risk and uncertainty involved in decision-making in order that the forecasting of outcomes provides as reliable basis as possible for making the decision.

The theoretical distinction is normally made between risk and uncertainty, and the two are defined as follows:

Risk

This term is used to apply to a situation where there are several possible outcomes but past experience, or research, enables statistical evidence to be produced which enables the prediction of possible outcomes.

Uncertainty

This term is used to apply to a situation where there is no evidence to enable the possible outcomes to be predicted.

In decision-making it is desirable to reduce uncertainty surrounding the decision and thus enable the forecasting of outcomes to be more reliable. This suggests that the more information that is available, the more likely the uncertainty surrounding a decision to be reduced. Information therefore has a value, as we have seen previously. There is also a cost involved in obtaining that information, and to be of benefit the value of the information obtained must exceed the costs of obtaining it. Later in this chapter we will look at ways of quantifying this value of information in order to decide whether or not it is beneficial to obtain additional information.

Reducing uncertainty, however, can be achieved not just through the acquiring of additional information. It can also be achieved through the quantification of existing information, and the converting of it into expected outcomes. This is achieved through the use of statistical techniques based upon probability theory.

Probability and expected values

The likelihood of an event occurring is known as its probability, and this is expressed in decimal form with a value ranging between 0 and 1. A value of 0 indicates that an event will not occur while a value of 1 indicates a certainty that the event will occur. Probabilities range between these two absolutes and thus a probability of 0.2 indicates that an event is expected to occur on 2 occasions out of 10. When a range of possible outcomes exists and a probability can be assigned to each of them then the sum of the probabilities for all possible outcomes must equal 1. This is because one of the possible outcomes must occur.

When a range of possible outcomes exists for an event it is possible to construct a probability distribution showing the range of outcomes with their associated probabilities. When making managerial decisions therefore this is one way of reducing uncertainty, through evaluating the likelihood of each outcome occurring and constructing a probability distribution. For business decisions it must be recognised that this is a subjective process based upon a manager's past experience, his/her expert knowledge of the subject area, and his/her assessment of the current and future situation. Probabilities assigned in this way are unlikely to be absolutely correct and different managers may well assign different probabilities to the same event. This means that any predictions based upon these subjective probabilities are prone to error but nevertheless this provides a basis for managers to forecast future outcomes which are likely to be more accurate than using intuition alone.

Probability distributions enable the calculation of the expected outcome of an event. This outcome is known as the expected value of the decision. Thus:

The expected value = The sum of the weighted possible outcomes arrived at by means of the probability distribution

Calculating the expected value of a decision provides a means of reducing uncertainty through the quantification of the possible outcomes, and so this can help in the decision-making process. Using expected values, however, has the problem of ignoring the range of alternatives and of ignoring any skewness in the probability distribution. It assumes that the representation of the outcomes as a single figure is sufficient for decision-making. The range of the probability distribution obviously affects the reliability of the expected value and a widely ranged distribution is likely to make the expected value less reliable than for a narrowly ranged distribution. In order to take this effect into account it is often helpful to undertake some kind of sensitivity analysis. It is also useful to look at the best and the worst case positions in relation to the break even position in order to use managerial judgement in assessing likely levels of risk. Thus decision will tend to be made not just upon the accounting analysis but also using the expertise gained from actually operating in a managerial position.

Sensitivity analysis, which we have considered earlier, is an attempt to measure how wrong the expected value calculated can be before an alternative decision would be preferable.

Attitudes to risk

In practice, statistical techniques for evaluating alternatives can help to reduce uncertainty but they cannot eliminate the risk associated with any particular decision. The decision is therefore ultimately dependant upon managerial judgement, and people make decisions based upon their attitude to risk. In terms of their attitude to risk, people can be classified into three types:

Risk seeking

A risk seeker is a person who will value a positive outcome more highly than a negative outcome. When faced with two equal possibilities of a profit or a loss arising from a particular decision, a risk seeking person will choose to proceed because of the possibility of profit.

Risk averse

A risk averter would value the negative outcome more highly than the positive and in the same situation would choose not to proceed because of the possibility of a loss.

Risk neutral

A risk neutral person would value both outcomes equally and would be indifferent about whether to proceed or not in this situation.

Different people have different attitudes to risk and this influences their decision-making and how they value possible outcomes. Research has shown, however, that for important business decisions, such as capital expenditure appraisal, managers tend to be risk averse in their decision-making. They therefore tend to choose decisions which might have lower expected values than other decisions but which have less risk associated with them. Managers of a business have responsibilities to the owners of that business (i.e. the shareholders) and one of these responsibilities is to act as stewards of that business and to maintain the value of the business and its future viability. This duty will tend to lead managers towards less risky decisions, which they are making on behalf of the owners of the business, than they may perhaps make on their own behalf.

The assessment of risk is the same for a socially responsible organisation as it is for any other. Equally people's attitudes to risk do not change because they are following a socially responsible philosophy. What might change, however, is the kind of decision which may be made after analysis. The kind of analysis we have looked at in this chapter is used to inform decisions but the decision itself is made by a manager, using his/her judgement. It is at this point that any concern for social responsibility becomes apparent as any decision made will be based not just upon financial analysis but also according to the objectives of the organisation. For example, a socially responsible organisation such as Holidays for Children will not be seeking to maximise profit but will rather be seeking to maximise the utilisation of their holiday home subject to the overriding criterion of needing to at least break even.

 ## Advantages and shortcomings of using the concept of C–V–P analysis

Whilst C–V–P is widely used, like many decision-making models there are shortcomings and disadvantages. As is so often the case, the weaknesses of this analytical and decision-making tool lie in the assumptions upon which the model is based. We have already considered that there are a number of assumptions which need to be made to make use of C–V–P analysis. The technique has, however, a number of applications in practice:

Pricing decisions

Changing the price of a product would change the total revenue function of the business and this would affect the break even point and the margin of safety. These factors need to be considered along with market-based factors such as the demand for the product.

Sales mix decisions

Altering the sales mix in a multi-product environment would tend to alter the total revenue function of the business and also the variable cost function (and hence the total cost function). This would affect the break even point and margin of safety but by explaining the effects of different sales mixes it is possible to consider their effect on the profitability of the business and this will facilitate decisions regarding the sales mix.

Production capacity planning

We have seen that the cost and revenue relationships do not apply indefinitely but only within the relevant range. As activity is expanded it will eventually be constrained by a shortage of one of the factors of production (e.g. machine hours, factory space or skilled labour) and this factor is known as the limiting factor. While this limitation can be overcome in the long term, in the short term maximum profits can be made by maximising the contribution per unit of the limiting factor. The limiting factor is the major constraint on organisational activity. We will discuss this in greater detail in Chapter 10. Here we will merely state that C–V–P analysis can facilitate an understanding of the effects upon profit of the limiting factor.

Profit planning

Cost–Volume–Profit analysis provides an understanding of profit in relation to output levels and the way in which profit changes as the level of activity changes. The technique can therefore help in planning profit by planning the level of activity for the next period and also in revising profit plans if the actual activity level varies from that which has been planned.

Problems with C–V–P analysis

Despite the widespread use of C–V–P analysis there are a variety of problems with using this technique, stemming from the assumptions made, which limit its effectiveness as a technique to help a business manager. These are as follows:

Relevant range

The assumptions of C–V–P analysis concerning linearity mean that the value of the analysis is restricted to the relevant range of activity. This range is the current level of activity plus or minus a certain amount (perhaps 20 per cent). While this might be appropriate for a business looking for a small change in its level of activity it means that the technique is inappropriate for a firm seeking to change its activity level considerably – perhaps a firm planning a rapid expansion programme. It also has the problem that it is difficult to determine exactly what is the relevant range within which the assumptions made actually do apply.

Short term

The assumptions of the technique mean that it is appropriate for short-term decisions regarding production, pricing, etc. Firms normally plan for the long term, however, and wish to ensure that any short-term decisions also fit with the longer-term planning. The assumptions of C–V–P analysis mean that there are difficulties in reconciling decision made from this analysis with any long-term planning.

Perfect knowledge

There is an assumption that the firm has perfect knowledge of the behaviour of its cost and revenue functions. In practice this is not the case, and this reduces the reliability of any analysis undertaken using this technique.

Perfect market

It is assumed that a perfect market exists and that the firm therefore accepts the price determined by the market. In reality a firm can significantly affect market prices through its actions and this cannot be ignored in pricing and production decisions.

Technological change

Changing technology and production methods are a continuing feature of modern business and these changes cause continuous changes in the cost function of a firm. C–V–P analysis ignores this and assumes that current production methods (and hence costs of production) will remain unchanged in the future. This makes the analysis less reliable the further into the future it is projected.

Market change

In addition to changes within the firm due to technology the market itself is constantly changing and is affected not just by the actions of the firm but also by the actions of its competitors as well as by economic conditions, consumer preference and taste and product developments. Cost–Volume–Profit analysis assumes that the market will remain unchanged.

Comparison of economic theory and the accounting approach

Economic theory suggests that the total cost function and the total revenue function of a firm are both curvilinear (as shown in Figure 6.9) rather than linear as assumed by the accountant's model of C–V–P analysis.

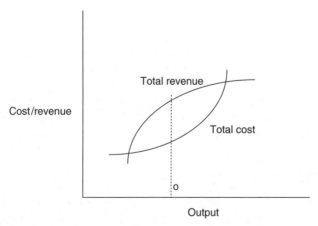

Figure 6.9 Cost and revenue in economic theory

This means that in the economist's model there are two break even points with the optimal level of activity being at point o between the two points. The economist's model, however, attempts to predict the behaviour of costs and revenues over the whole possible range of activity rather than the smaller range of the accountant's model (i.e. the relevant range). Economic theory attempts to produce a model which is designed to enable prediction to be made about the behaviour of market variables (i.e. price, output, etc.) whereas the accountant's model of C–V–P relationships merely attempts to provide assistance to business managers for short-term decision-making within a particular firm. The two alternative views of C–V–P relationships therefore should not be considered to be competing but merely to be showing different approaches to differing aspects of the same situation.

Conclusion

Cost–Volume–Profit analysis is a technique which can be used by business managers to help understand the relationship between costs, revenue and level of activity for a particular business. It is designed to help in short-term decision-making within the firm and we have seen how this can be the case. Nevertheless there are limitations to the value of C–V–P analysis which we have also considered, and a business manager needs to be aware not just of how the technique can help in decision-making but also of these limitations in order to be able to make best use of the technique in helping manage the business.

Additional questions

Question 6.1

Gardening Ltd manufactures garden ornaments which they supply to garden centres. Their results for the past 12 months have been as follows:

	£'000	£'000
Sales (1 00 000 units)		5000
Direct materials	1000	
Direct labour	1300	
Variable production overheads	750	
Variable selling and distribution overheads	450	
Fixed production overheads	700	
Fixed selling and distribution overheads	200	4400
Net profit		600

Required:

(1) Calculate the contribution per unit and break even level of production.
(2) The company is considering the purchase of new manufacturing equipment which will have the following effect:

fixed production costs will increase by £200 000 per annum;
direct labour costs will reduce by £3 per unit;
variable production overheads will decrease by 50p per unit.

(a) If the price is maintained what effect will this have on profit?
(b) If it is desired that profits should remain at the present level what price will need to be set for the product if sales volume is unaffected?

(3) If advertising expenditure were to be increased by £250 000, it is believed that the price could be increased by 6 per cent without affecting sales volume. What effect would this have on the profits of Gardening Ltd?
(4) If the current price is increased by 10 per cent it is believed that sales volume would reduce by 5 per cent. What effect would this have on net profit?

Question 6.2

Alpha Production Ltd produces a single product which sells for £10 per unit. Variable costs amount to £8 per unit. If the break even point in terms of sales revenue is £350 000, calculate the amount of fixed costs which the company incurs.

If the fixed costs incurred were reduced to £50 000, but sales revenue remained unchanged calculate the new break even point and the margin of safety from operating at this level of sales.

Question 6.3

Caring Products Ltd sold 180 000 units of its product last year at a price of £20 each, out of a total production of 20 000 units, the capacity of the plant. Variable costs of production amount to £14 (£10 for manufacturing and £3 for selling). Fixed costs amounted to £500 000 for manufacturing costs and £292 000 for administrative costs, and were incurred evenly throughout the year.

Calculate the following:

profit for the year;
break even point in terms of units and sales value;
margin of safety at which the company is operating.

If labour costs amount to 50 per cent of variable costs and 20 per cent of fixed costs, calculate the changed break even point if wages are increased by 10 per cent.

Question 6.4

Ryan Co. Ltd produces a single product, an electric mixer. Currently the mixer is selling at £20 per unit and has a variable cost of production of £14. Fixed costs are £65 000 and the company sold 20 000 units in the last year.

The sales director believes that sales can be increased significantly by reducing the price of the mixer. She has proposed three alternatives, which are to reduce the price by 5, 10 and 15 per cent respectively.

She has asked you, as the management accountant, to evaluate her proposals and calculate the margin of safety under which the company would be operating at current volumes and the alternative price levels for the product. She has also asked you to calculate how many extra sales would be required at each price level in order to maintain existing levels of profit.

7

Allocation and Apportionment of Costs

Learning objectives

After studying this chapter you should be able to:

- explain the purpose of product costing;
- distinguish between direct and indirect costs;
- allocate costs to departments appropriately and allocate service department costs to production departments;
- calculate overhead absorption rates using suitable bases;
- explain the difference in principle with socially responsible costing;
- explain the consequences of using different measures of capacity;
- explain the difference between the main costing methods used in industry;
- identify an appropriate method to calculate the cost of any particular product or service;
- calculate product costs using appropriate methods;
- critically evaluate costing methods in the light of modern production methods.

Introduction

Being able to calculate the cost of a product or service is fundamental to all operational decisions made within an organisation. The ability to calculate these requires accounting so that the costs of a business are ultimately charged to these products or services. We have seen how the behaviour of costs helps to determine the future level of costs for a business, and we now turn to an examination of the method of determining the costs of production for a product which a company manufactures. We have seen how the costs incurred by a firm can be divided into those costs directly associated with the production of a particular product and those which are concerned with the operating of the business. In order for it to be worthwhile for a business to produce a product, the price at which it can sell the product must at least equal the cost of its production. If not the business would be better off by not producing the product and by concentrating its efforts on the production of other items. (There are exceptions to this which we will consider in later chapters.) This leads us, however, to a consideration of why the establishment of the cost of production of a product is so important to a business, and how this can help a manager of the business.

Joan Palfreyman is the cost accountant of the company, Walker Ltd, which produces high quality domestic kitchen units. It sells these units directly to individual customers and the products are made to order.

The company is organised into five departments, three of which are involved in the production of the units – machining department, assembly department and finishing department – and two departments which support the production departments – maintenance department and stores.

The company has received an order from a customer for a particular set of kitchen units and Joan has been asked to calculate the cost of production of the units. Bill Wilson, the production manager, has estimated that the following materials and time will be involved in the production of each unit:

Materials	£500
Labour – machining department	5 hours
Labour – assembly department	3 hours
Labour – finishing department	2 hours

Joan has already worked out the budget for Walker Ltd for the coming month and has the following information in front of her:

	Machining (£'000)	Assembly (£'000)	Finishing (£'000)	Maintenance (£'000)	Stores (£'000)	Total (£'000)
Direct materials	20 000	2000	2000			24 000
Direct labour	5 000	6000	3000			14 000
Indirect materials	2 000	1000	1000	500	1500	6 000
Indirect labour	2 000	2000	1000	3000	1000	9 000
Power	3 000	2000	3000	500	200	8 700
Rent and rates						6 000
Administration						4 200
Machine insurance						500

Her assistant, John Woods, has also provided her with the following additional information:

	Machining	Assembly	Finishing	Maintenance	Stores	Total
Floor area (sq. mtrs)	10 000	8000	5000	1000	6000	30 000
Machine hours ('000)	1 500	300	200			2 000
Direct labour hours ('000)	1 000	1400	600			3 000
No. of employees	1 000	1200	600			2 800
Value of machinery	2 500	1500	1000			5 000

Direct material only is issued from stores.

Joan knows that she needs to use this information in order to calculate the cost of production of the kitchen units ordered.

The value of product costing

In a company which manufactures a variety of products such as Walker Ltd, the ability to determine the cost of production for each type of product is essential to enable the managers of the business to be able to plan the business and its activities. Knowledge of the cost of production of a product is necessary to determine a price for the product as it is essential that the price exceeds the cost of production. Generally speaking the price for a product must exceed its manufacturing cost so that it will contribute towards the general costs of the business and towards the profit made by the business. If this is not the case then the firm may well be better off by not making the product and concentrating instead upon the manufacture of other products. The resources of a business are finite and there is a limit to how much it is able to produce. One reason for product costing therefore is to enable the allocation of the scarce resources of the business in the way which is most advantageous to it. Thus Walker Ltd needs to know whether it should make the kinds of units ordered by this particular customer and sell them at the agreed price, or whether it would be better off to stop making these units and concentrate upon other kinds of kitchen furniture.

If a calculation of the costs of production of individual products within the product range is not undertaken then it is possible that the company is operating profitably because some of its products are highly profitable and some are being produced at a loss. This would be disguised by the overall profitability of the business but some products would be subsidising others. This is known as cross-subsidy. In practice not all products are equally profitable and some will be more profitable than others. Statistical techniques have been employed in businesses making many different products which show that generally speaking 20 per cent of the product range generates 80 per cent of the profit of the business. This is known as the Pareto Rule (after the inventor of this statistical technique) and is commonly known as the 80/20 rule.

Businesses are constantly seeking to improve their production methods and to expand capacity, or to produce goods at a lower cost. To do so generally involves some capital investment, and we will look at this in detail in Chapter 11. In deciding whether or not to invest, however, the business naturally wants to undertake investment which is most beneficial to it. It makes sense for the business to concentrate its investment in the areas of production from which it will derive the most benefit. Product costing will help it to decide which areas these are.

The basic reasons why product costing is important therefore can be summarised as follows:

- to help make pricing decisions;
- to allocate scarce resources;
- to help make decisions concerning investment.

The components of the cost of production

We have seen in the last chapter that the cost of a product is made up of direct and indirect costs and that these can be broken down as follows:

- Direct costs
  Materials
  Labour
- Indirect costs
  Overheads.

The total direct costs of materials and labour will equal the prime cost of the product.

We will now look at each of these in turn and consider the way in which these are accumulated in order to determine the cost of a product.

Materials

We have seen previously how materials can be categorised into direct materials, which go directly into producing the product, and indirect materials, which help the production process but do not go into the product. For Walker

Ltd direct materials would include wood, paint and laminates while indirect materials would include such things as saw blades and sanding discs. All these raw materials are held in stock to be used as needed. Materials can be held centrally in a stores, such as the direct materials for Walker Ltd, and this needs a control and issuing procedure. Alternatively they can be allocated directly to a production department to be used as needed. This is the case with the indirect materials of Walker Ltd. We will look at the costing implications of this in more details later but the decision will be made to a large extent on the value of the materials in relation to the cost of the products being made. Thus saw blades are low cost items and are used frequently in the machining department, but probably nowhere else, and so it is not worth the expense to the company of having a formal control and issuing procedure for these items.

One feature of manufacturing which is of increasing importance at the present time, and which affects the treatment of stocks and of raw materials used in the production process, is JIT, which endeavours to eliminate stocks of raw materials entirely. The aim of this approach is to ensure that the ordering procedure enables materials to be ordered and delivered just in time for when they are needed rather than being delivered in advance and held in stock. This system, together with Materials Requirements Planning systems (MRP), is changing the nature of stock control, and therefore product costing.

At this point, however, if we consider Walker Ltd we can see that the direct materials are delivered into stock and are issued as required to each of the production departments and charged to those departments as part of the costs of production. Indirect materials, however, are delivered directly to the individual departments and form part of the costs of those departments. This is reflected in the budget which Joan Palfreyman has worked out for the company as follows:

	Machining (£'000)	Assembly (£'000)	Finishing (£'000)	Maintenance (£'000)	Stores (£'000)	Total (£'000)
Direct materials	20 000	2000	2000			24 000
Indirect materials	2 000	1000	1000	500	1500	6 000

Labour

Labour costs also can be categorised into direct labour costs and indirect labour costs. For Walker Ltd the direct labour costs are charged directly to the production department and consist of the costs of the people working in those departments directly involved in the production process. Thus direct labour costs can only occur in a production department and the labour costs of support departments are considered to be indirect labour costs because they do not directly relate to the production of any particular product. Indirect labour costs can, however, be incurred in both production and service departments, and this is the case for Walker Ltd. In the stores and maintenance departments the indirect labour costs will be all the staff of the departments – storekeepers, engineers, repair staff, etc. In the production departments the indirect labour costs will be made up of those people who do not directly participate in the production process – foremen and supervisory staff, wages clerks, ordering clerks and other administrative staff. In some businesses supervisory staff are involved in the production process and so would form part of the direct labour costs. Whether or not this is the case it is normally dependent upon the processes involved and upon the job specification of the individual supervisor concerned.

The budget for Walker Ltd can be seen therefore as follows:

	Machining (£'000)	Assembly (£'000)	Finishing (£'000)	Maintenance (£'000)	Stores (£'000)	Total (£'000)
Direct labour	5000	6000	3000			14 000
Indirect labour	2000	2000	1000	3000	1000	9 000

Labour costs can be classified into the direct costs of labour and the indirect costs of labour regardless of whether or not they are considered to be direct or indirect labour, and it is important to distinguish between these two classifications. The direct costs of labour are the wages, salaries, bonuses and overtime paid to the people themselves. The indirect costs of labour are such things as employers' national insurance and pension contributions, sick pay and the costs of calculating and operating the payroll system. This distinction is important as far as financial accounting is concerned but to the business manager the indirect and direct costs of labour are unimportant and it is just the total cost of labour which is of concern. This is the figure which is used in product costing, classified into direct and indirect labour.

When overtime is worked by members of the labour force this is often paid at a premium rate. Also when shift working is in operation some shifts attract a premium rate. Thus the cost of labour varies according to its timing. It therefore costs more to manufacture a product when overtime is being worked than it does during normal time. It is not, however, reasonable to suggest that the cost of production of any individual product depends upon when it is manufactured, although there are exceptions to this in special cases which will be considered in later chapters. The precise time of manufacture depends upon the production scheduling process and what is important for calculating labour cost is the average cost of labour. Labour rates are therefore calculated as an average of the total cost of labour divided by the total productive hours worked, regardless of the rate paid for any particular time period or to any particular person. Thus from the information Joan Palfreyman has she is able to calculate the average cost of direct labour in each of the production departments and express this as a direct labour hour rate which can be used in establishing the costs of production for any particular product. This calculation is as follows:

	Machining (£'000)	Assembly (£'000)	Finishing (£'000)	Total (£'000)
Direct labour	5000	6000	3000	14 000
Direct labour hours ('000)	1000	1400	600	3 000
Direct labour hour rate	5.00	4.29	5.00	

Overheads

All materials and labour expenditure, as well as all other expenditure which cannot be directly identified with the product itself is classed as indirect expenditure and in total this is known as overhead. Overheads can be considered in total but it is more usual to separate them into categories according to the function which has caused the overhead to be incurred. Thus production, selling, distribution and administration are common categories of overhead, in a traditional manufacturing environment. In the case of Walker Ltd, however, the categories of overhead will be production overhead and administration overhead.

Some overheads comprise expenditure which is attributable directly to specific departments, and for Walker Ltd indirect materials, indirect labour and power can be attributable directly to the respective departments. Other expenditure however, such as rent and rates and administration is incurred in total and is not readily related to any specific department. In order to determine product cost, however, it is necessary that all expenditure be allocated to a particular department, whether it be a production department or a service department. Thus all centrally incurred expenditure for Walker Ltd which Joan Palfreyman has budgeted for she must allocate to one of the five departments of the company. Part of her task is to allocate this expenditure in some way and to find a reasonable basis for her allocation. For example, rent and rates expenditure is obviously incurred in part by each of the five departments and therefore needs to be charged partly to each department. This process of splitting common costs over individual departments is known as apportionment and the means of dividing up the common costs is known as the basis of apportionment.

The apportionment of expenditure

The objective of cost accounting is ultimately to be able to calculate the cost of production of individual products or services which a firm provides. Classifying costs is the starting point for this exercise, but it is necessary to go on from this to be able to charge the indirect costs (i.e. overheads) of production to individual products. This process is known as apportionment. The steps which need to be undertaken to arrive at this apportionment procedure are summarised in Figure 7.1.

One of the skills of a cost accountant, such as Joan Palfreyman, is to find a basis of apportionment for each type of cost she comes across, which is a reasonable representation of the way in which the cost arises. Departmental managers are naturally interested in these bases and are keen to ensure that the costs of their department are not higher than they need to be because of a basis of apportionment which disadvantages their department for the benefit of another department. Thus the apportionment of cost is a matter of particular interest in a business.

The basis of apportionment of a cost can be anything which is a reasonable representation of the way in which a cost is incurred. Obviously, however, a certain limited range of bases are common, but this does not mean that a different basis should not be considered and used, if appropriate to the circumstances. If we look at the expenses which Joan has to allocate to the five

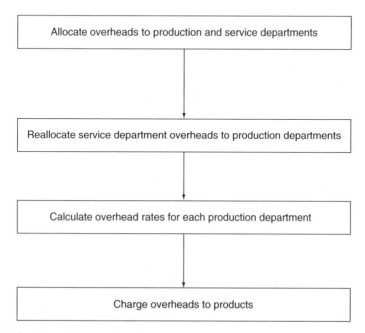

Figure 7.1 Overhead allocation procedure

departments of Walker Ltd we can see illustrations of the way in which suitable bases are identified and used.

Rent and rates

Rent and rates are incurred for the existence and use of a building and its size. Size in this context is often considered to equate to floor area and this is a common basis of apportionment. In some circumstances volume may be more appropriate and therefore used for apportioning costs. In this case, however, floor area is considered appropriate and the rent and rates charge would thus be related to the floor area occupied by each department and apportioned as follows:

	Machining (£'000)	Assembly (£'000)	Finishing (£'000)	Maintenance (£'000)	Stores (£'000)	Total (£'000)
Rent and rates						6 000
Floor area (sq. mtrs)	10 000	8000	5000	1000	6000	30 000
Departmental apportionment	2 000	1600	1000	200	1200	6 000

Administration

Administration expenses are generally incurred because of the existence of employees in the business, and relate to those employees and their management. At least this is one of the causes of the expenditure, and it is reasonable therefore to suggest that a department incurs administration expenditure in relation to its size in terms of number of employees. Alternative bases which could be considered would be number of orders received or computing hours involved for each department, or any other reasonable basis. In this case number of employees seems to be a reasonable basis for apportionment of administration expenses and can be calculated as follows:

	Machining (£'000)	Assembly (£'000)	Finishing (£'000)	Maintenance (£'000)	Stores (£'000)	Total (£'000)
Administration						4200
No. of employees	1000	1200	600			2800
Departmental apportionment	1500	1800	900			4200

Machine insurance

This expenditure is obviously related to the machinery itself and more specifically to the value of that machinery. Thus machinery value provides a suitable basis for apportionment, and can be calculated as follows:

	Machining (£'000)	Assembly (£'000)	Finishing (£'000)	Maintenance (£'000)	Stores (£'000)	Total (£'000)
Machine insurance						500
Value of machinery	2500	1500	1000			5000
Departmental apportionment	250	150	100			500

Once all expenses have been apportioned over then departments, the cost of operation for each department can be calculated. For Walker Ltd the cost of each of the five departments is calculated as follows:

	Machining (£'000)	Assembly (£'000)	Finishing (£'000)	Maintenance (£'000)	Stores (£'000)	Total (£'000)
Indirect materials	2 000	1000	1000	500	1500	6 000
Indirect labour	2 000	2000	1000	3000	1000	9 000
Power	3 000	2000	3000	500	200	8 700
Rent and rates	2 000	1600	1000	200	1200	6 000
Administration	1 500	1800	900			4 200
Machine insurance	250	150	100			500
Total cost	10 750	8550	7000	4200	3900	34 400

Relating departmental costs to production

The overhead costs of production departments can be directly related to the cost of production of the goods produced. The costs of support departments are equally related to the cost of production but cannot be directly related. It is, however, necessary to include them in the costing of products as they are part of the cost of production. It is necessary therefore to find a way in which to do so.

The way in which this is done is to reallocate the service department costs to the production departments using a suitable basis for doing so which reflects the service provided by each service department to the production departments.

Thus Joan Palfreyman needs to reallocate the costs of the maintenance and stores departments to the three production departments using a suitable basis. She can do this as follows:

Maintenance department

This department is concerned with the maintenance of the machinery used by the three production departments. The level of maintenance required by machinery can be expected to be proportional to the usage of that machinery. The number of machine hours used by each department can therefore be considered as a suitable basis for apportionment. This department's costs can therefore be reallocated as follows:

	Machining (£'000)	Assembly (£'000)	Finishing (£'000)	Maintenance (£'000)	Stores (£'000)	Total (£'000)
Total cost	10 750	8550	7000	4200	3900	34 400
Machine hours ('000)	1 500	300	200			2 000
Reallocated cost	3 250	630	420	(4200)		

Stores department

The stores department handles the stores and issues the direct materials to the three production departments. The activity of this department is therefore related to the volume of materials used by each department. In this case the volume of materials is expressed in terms of value rather than by physical volume, and this provides a basis for reallocating the costs of the stores department. The calculation is as follows:

	Machining (£'000)	Assembly (£'000)	Finishing (£'000)	Maintenance (£'000)	Stores (£'000)	Total (£'000)
Total cost	10 750	8550	7000	4200	3900	34 400
Direct materials	20 000	2000	2000			24 000
Reallocated cost	3 250	325	325		(3900)	

Once the costs of the service departments have been reallocated to the production departments, the total costs of those production departments, in terms of overhead costs involved in production can be ascertained. These are as follows:

	Machining (£'000)	Assembly (£'000)	Finishing (£'000)	Maintenance (£'000)	Stores (£'000)	Total (£'000)
Total cost	10 750	8550	7000	4200	3900	34 400
Reallocated cost (maintenance)	3 150	630	420	(4200)		
Reallocated cost (stores)	3 250	325	325		(3900)	
Total cost	17 150	9505	7745			34 400

Calculating overhead recovery rates

It is now possible to calculate the cost of production for each individual product which Walker Ltd makes within its range.

Overhead costs are part of the costs of production of each department and Joan Palfreyman needs to find a way of relating these costs to the actual production. The way in which this is done is to calculate an overhead recovery rate related to one of the direct costs of production. Again any suitable basis can be used but the two most common bases are:

1 Direct labour hour rate
2 Direct machine hour rate.

Labour and machine time are the chief components of any product in a manufacturing environment and this is the reason why they are used as the bases for recovering overheads. This has the result of spreading the overheads over the greatest individual direct cost, and the one selected tends to be the greater of the two in any particular process. In a service industry labour cost tends to be the greatest direct cost in providing a service and so overhead again tends to be apportioned according to direct labour hours.

Each of these two bases relates to the number of hours of each factor of production which goes into the product. For Walker Ltd the cost of production of the kitchen units which it manufactures is more directly related to the labour involved in their manufacture, particularly for the assembly and finishing departments. This therefore is the basis which Joan has selected for the recovery of overheads. The calculation is as follows:

$$\text{Overhead rates} = \frac{\text{Total cost}}{\text{Total direct labour hours}}$$

i.e.

$$\text{Machining: } \frac{17\ 150}{1000} = \text{£17.15 per hour}$$

$$\text{Assembly: } \frac{9505}{1400} = \text{£6.79 per hour}$$

$$\text{Finishing: } \frac{7745}{600} = \text{£12.91 per hour}$$

If machine hours were used instead the following overhead rates would be calculated:

$$\text{Overhead rates} = \frac{\text{total cost}}{\text{total machine hours}}$$

i.e.

$$\text{Machining: } \frac{17\ 150}{1500} = \text{£11.43 per hour}$$

$$\text{Assembly: } \frac{9505}{300} = \text{£31.68 per hour}$$

$$\text{Finishing: } \frac{7745}{200} = \text{£38.72 per hour}$$

The total cost of production for these products therefore consists of the direct materials used in the product and the direct labour and overheads used in the product. Total costs can therefore be expressed as

Total cost = Direct materials + Direct labour (rate)

The calculation of the direct labour rate is arrived at by totalling the labour cost per hour and the overhead recovery rate, i.e.

Direct labour charging rate = Labour rate + Overhead rate

The calculation for each of the three departments of Walker Ltd, using the direct labour hour rate, therefore is as follows:

Charging rates

Machining: £5.00 + £17.15 = £22.15
Assembly: £4.29 + £6.79 = £11.08
Finishing: £5.00 + £12.91 = £17.91

Capacity measurement

It should be noted that overhead recovery rates are calculated from the budgets prepared at the start of the period and are therefore based upon expected levels of activity. In setting the budget for the level of activity expected for a period it is necessary to estimate activity levels and this is dependent upon an assessment of capacity. Capacity can be considered to be the level of activity which the company can undertake in the period but this can be expressed in a variety of ways:

- *Maximum capacity*: the maximum level of activity which can be undertaken;
- *Maximum practical capacity*: the maximum practical level of activity which can be undertaken taking into account the needs of retooling, maintenance, etc.;
- *Normal capacity*: the level of activity normally achieved allowing for the above and downtime, sickness, etc.

It can be seen that these three measures will each give a different measurement of capacity and so a different level of activity expected. This will result in different overhead recovery rates being charged and so different costs of production being calculated. The basis of capacity measurement is therefore important in the determination of the cost of production of a product.

Additionally the fact that the recovery rates are based upon budgets means that the actual costs are likely to be different and so the true costs of production will be different to those calculated in advance. The actual costs will be known only after the event and so it is necessary to calculate the actual costs based upon budgets so that the business can plan its operations. The implications of the difference between budget activity and cost and those actually arising are considered in detail in subsequent chapters.

 ## Calculation of the cost of a product

Once the indirect costs of production have been ascertained and a basis for adding them to the product cost has been arrived at, it is possible to combine these costs with the direct costs in order to arrive at the cost of production of a product. Thus Joan Palfreyman is able to calculate the cost of production of the units which have been ordered by the customer. The calculation is as follows:

Direct materials	£500
Direct labour – machining department	5 hours
Direct labour – assembly department	3 hours
Direct labour – finishing department	2 hours

Calculation of cost:

	£
Direct materials	500
Machining cost – 5 hours × £22.15	110.75
Assembly cost – 3 hours × £11.08	33.24
Finishing cost – 2 hours × £17.91	35.82
Cost of production	679.81

Socially responsible cost allocation

An important function of socially responsible accounting is to highlight environmental costs and bring the appropriate information to the decision-makers within the organisation. If these costs are identified separately then it becomes possible to consider ways of avoiding or reducing these costs and thereby bringing about an improvement in environmental quality. One of the problems of cost allocation is that a large part of the costs of a business (and this applies particularly to environmental costs) are collected together into an overhead pool and important environmental data can thereby be lost to the sight of the decision-makers.

The implementation of socially responsible accounting would necessitate the treatment of some of these overhead costs differently. Thus environmental costs would be pulled out of the general overhead pool and allocated to the appropriate cost centre which caused them to be incurred. This means that they would be allocated directly to the product, service or process which caused them to be incurred. In this respect, therefore environmental accounting is similar to activity-based costing in that more costs will be treated as direct costs rather than as a part of the general overhead cost. The allocation of environmental costs to the product, service or process which generates them highlights these costs. This can provide a motivation to the managers concerned to find alternatives which can have the effect of lowering the cost of the product, profit or service and thereby increasing profitability as well as enhancing environmental quality.

Socially responsible accounting can also affect product costing in a more direct way. This is brought about through the different treatment of environmental costs rather than their being lost in the general overhead pool. Under traditional costing overheads are treated in one of the following ways:

- They are allocated to a particular (often volume-based and arbitrary) basis to all products which pass through the process concerned. If overhead costs are allocated incorrectly then this means that one product is bearing an overhead allocation greater than is warranted while another product is bearing an allocation which is less than is warranted. The effect of this is that product costing is less accurate than is possible and this may affect both pricing and profitability. It can also affect both decision-making and resource allocation.

- They are collected into the general pool of overheads and not allocated to any particular product. If costs are not allocated to products then they will not be reflected in the product cost and hence the price. As a consequence the true cost of production is unknown to managers and there is insufficient information available to these managers to enable them to seek ways of reducing these costs.

If environmental costs are not identified separately and attached to the products, services or processes which cause them then there is a danger that either, or both, of these situations will arise. It is thus important to identify environmental costs and to separate them from the general overhead cost pool and to treat them appropriately. This is important not just to increase the accuracy of product costing but also because it can act as a focus for cost reduction activity through the way in which these costs are revealed to the managers concerned. This would therefore require that the cost allocation system within the firm is changed to take account of such costs in a different manner.

This can be illustrated diagrammatically as shown in Figure 7.2, using hazardous waste product and its associated costs as an example.

Under this approach the cost of hazardous waste are allocated to all products whether or not they originate in the production of these products. Using environmental accounting these costs would be treated differently and allocated only to the product which caused them to be incurred. Thus if Product A was the only product involving hazardous waste then the treatment would be as shown in Figure 7.3.

Thus the costs of dealing with the hazardous waste, which only relates to Product A, would be charged directly to this product. This would have the effect of increasing the cost of this product while reducing the costs of the other products which had previously borne part of the cost of the hazardous waste. Thus the cost of each product would be different but would more accurately

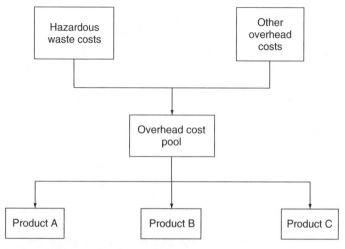

Figure 7.2 The traditional cost allocation approach

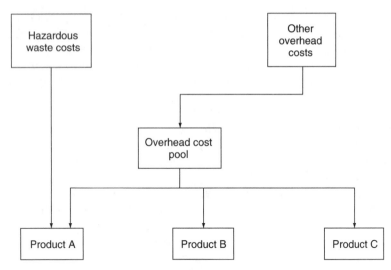

Figure 7.3 The environmental accounting approach

reflect the true cost involved in its manufacture. This more accurate costing may well be significant for pricing and decision-making purposes.

Once the effect of the costs of hazardous waste and their effects upon product costs have been recognised then an investigation may reveal that a different process or treatment may be possible which will reduce these costs. This is one potential benefit of environmental accounting. Alternatively, investigation may well reveal that the hazardous waste may well be subject to a treatment which will render it saleable. In this case environmental accounting would suggest that this waste and the sales resulting from further treatment should be treated as a by-product of Product A and accounted for in the conventional by-product costing manner as shown in Figure 7.4.

Thus socially responsible accounting will identify all the costs and benefits associated with any environmentally related issue. This can not just result in more accurate product costing, with associated better decisions regarding pricing and resource allocation, but also highlight the scope for both cost reduction and increased income generation. All of these can result in increased profitability but can also help with the community relationships and with the image of the company.

In summary, therefore the allocation of costs under environmental accounting can create many potential benefits to the business. Such cost allocation involves the following stages:

- identify environmental costs;
- quantify such costs;
- allocate such costs to the responsible process, product or service;
- consider scope for alternative treatments, cost reductions or income generation opportunities;

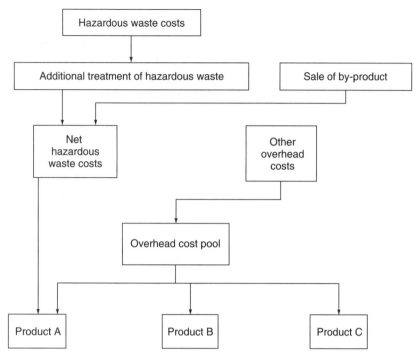

Figure 7.4 The environmental accounting approach to by-products

- identify any additional income which might arise from the process;
- allocate all costs and benefits to the responsible process, product or service.

Different costing systems

Although the basic principles of costing relating to the classification, allocation, apportionment and absorption of costs are common to all types of manufacturing there are nevertheless differences in the way in which products are manufactured or processed. It is for this reason that different methods of costing have been developed which are designed to suit the particular production methods of an individual firm. The main costing methods used by industry are:

- Job costing
- Batch costing
- Contract costing
- Process costing.

Each of these costing methods provides a basis upon which costs can be classified and absorbed into product costs, and so each can be considered to be a variant of absorption costing. The principle difference between them is the way in which cost accumulation is related to the operating methods of the business.

Joseph Gibson is the cost accountant of Jones & Andrews Ltd, a company which provides building repairs and maintenance service. The company operates a job costing system in order to identify the cost and profit for each job carried out. Several jobs tend to be in progress at any particular time. One such job is number 3152, for the repair of a local office block. This job was completed totally during the quarter.

Joseph has the task of preparing a statement of costs associated with this job and the resulting profit arising from its completion. He has collected the following information concerning the job:

Issues of the main material, cement, were 960 kilos and issues of all other materials were costed at £2120. Of the total materials issued to the job, wastage cost £38 and materials used for rectification work cost £36. Materials are issued from stores to the job as required.

The hours of direct personnel working on the job were 494, including 35 hours of overtime, 14 hours of idle time and 8 hours spent on rectification work. Overtime is worked as necessary to meet the general requirements of the business and is paid at a premium of 30 per cent over the basic rate. The basic rate for direct personnel is £6 per hour.

Joseph has also collected the following information concerning all work carried out during the quarter:

The opening stock of cement was 3225 kilos valued at £5822. Purchases during the month were 3600 kilos at £1.81 per kilo and 3800 kilos at £1.82 per kilo. Issues from stores amounted to 7160 kilos for all jobs, including 60 kilos which were subsequently wasted and 340 kilos which were used for rectification work. Raw materials are priced at the end of the period using a weighted average basis.

Other materials issued to jobs were costed at £19 396, including £228 wastage and £197 for rectification.

Direct personnel were paid at basic rate for 3660 hours with a further 310 hours paid at overtime rate. These hours include 81 hours of idle time and 38 hours spent on rectification work.

Other costs incurred during the period were:

	£
Supervisory labour	3760
Depreciation on plant	590
Cleaning materials	67
Telephone and stationery	281
Rent and rates	969
Vehicle running costs	318
Other administration	716

Overheads are absorbed into job costs at the end of each quarter at an actual rate per direct labour hour. Idle time, wastage and rectification work, after the completion of jobs, are normal features of the business. The company policy is that idle time is not expected to exceed 2 per cent of total hours, wastage is not expected to exceed 1 per cent of the costs of materials issued to a job and rectification costs are not expected to exceed 1.5 per cent of direct costs. Such costs are not charged as direct costs of individual jobs.

The price for the job was £11 000.

Joseph knows that he is expected to produce a costing and profitability statement for job number 3152 and to comment upon the amount of idle time and rectification work associated with the job.

Job costing

Job costing is used where the nature of the business is such that each individual job is separate and individual in nature. This type of costing is used by a firm which makes products to order (e.g. a specialist iron foundry) and is particularly suitable for a building contractor working on individual repairs and maintenance contracts, such as Jones & Andrews Ltd. The main purpose of job costing is to enable a firm to establish the profit (or loss) made on each individual job and to provide a valuation of work in progress for each job in the process of completion.

Job costing can be illustrated as shown in Figure 7.5.

Job costing is undertaken by creating an individual job cost card for each job and so job number 3152 would be one such job cost card. This card (a computer record most probably now, although originally a card) would contain details of the following:

- *Direct labour costs*: including time based and piecework costs;
- *Direct materials costs*: based on stores issued and special purchases;
- *Direct expenses*: expenses incurred specifically for that particular job, e.g. tool hire.

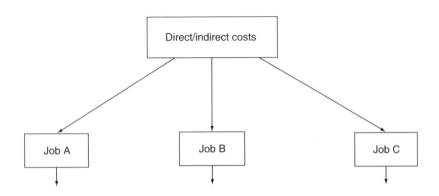

Figure 7.5 Job costing

For job 3152 the following details would be entered:
    Job card   job 3152

Direct labour hours
    Standard rate* $496 - 35 - 14 - 8 = 439$
    Overtime rate   38
    * Direct labour hours at standard rate = total hours − (overtime + idle time
                                                        + rectification time)

Direct labour cost
    Standard rate $439 \times 6.00 = 2634$
    Overtime rate $35 \times 7.80 = 273$

    Total cost   2907

Direct materials
    Cement   960 kilos @ $1.81^* = 1738$
    Other materials $= 2120$
    Less wastage   38
    Less rectification   36

    Total cost   3784

*Price calculation
    3225 in stock $= 5594$
    3600 @ $1.81 = 6516$
    3800 @ $1.82 = 6916$
    total 10 625 @ cost 19 254
    average price – 1.81

Using these details the production overheads would be added to the job by means of the calculation of an overhead recovery rate. For job 3152 this calculation would be as follows:

Calculation of overhead recovery rate
Overhead costs incurred:

	£
Supervisory labour	3760
Depreciation on plant	590
Cleaning materials	67
Telephone and stationery	281
Rent and rates	964
Vehicle running costs	318
Other administration	716
Total costs	6696

Direct labour hours:
    $3660 + 310 - 81 - 38 = 3851$

Overhead recovery rate:
$$\frac{6696}{3851} = 1.74 \text{ per direct labour hour}$$

A job is normally valued at works cost until it is completed and it is at this point that administration and selling expenses are added to the job cost, as a percentage of works cost. Until this point the job represents work in progress and the total of all the job cost cards represents the total value of work in progress.

Once the job is finished all costs can be accumulated and the total cost of the job computed. For job 3152 a statement of costs would be as follows:

Direct labour	2907
Direct materials	3784
Prime cost	6691
Overheads [1.74 × (437 + 35)]	821
Total cost	7512

From this it is possible for Joseph Gibson to produce a costing and profitability statement for job 3152 which would be as follows:

Profitability statement for job no. 3152

	£
Revenue	11 000
Cost	7 512
Profit	3 488

Joseph Gibson also needs to comment on the amount of idle time and rectification work associated with the job and in a job costing environment it is normal to consider such performance data for each individual job. Idle time is defined as the amount of time spent between jobs in not performing any function. Rectification work is caused by faulty initial work; in a manufacturing environment this may well result in scrap products but in this environment it requires time to be spent in reworking the initial work to an acceptable standard.

Joseph Gibson's calculations and comments would be as follows:

	Job 3152	All jobs
Idle time	2.83% (14/494)	2.04% (81/3970)
Wastage	1.00% (38/3784)	0.87% $\dfrac{*60 \times 1.81 + 228}{19\ 254 + 19\ 396}$
Rectification work	1.57% $\dfrac{8 \times 6 + 36}{6679}$	1.65% $\dfrac{**[(38 \times 6) + (340 \times 1.81) + 197]}{[19\ 254 + 19\ 396 + (3660 \times 6.00) + (310 \times 7.80)]}$

* Materials wastage: cement 60 kilos × £1.81; total cement cost £19 254; other £228; total cost £19 396.

** Labour – rectification work 38 hrs @ £6.00 per hour – total cost 3660 hrs @ 36.00 + 310 hrs @ £7.80.

Cement – rectification work 340 kilos @ £1.81 – total cost £19 254 (calculated previously). Other materials – rectification work £197 – total cost £19 396.

For job 3152 performance was below expectation as far as idle time and rectification work was concerned but met the target for wastage. For all jobs completed during the quarter performance was below expectation as far as idle time was concerned but exceeded expectations as far as wastage and rectification work were concerned. Performance for job 3152 was below the average for all three measures.

Batch costing

This is a variation of job costing which is appropriate when a quantity of identical items are produced together as a batch. In this case the batch would be treated as a job and costs accumulated for the batch. When the batch has been completed the total costs of the batch would be divided by the number of successfully completed items in the batch to provide the cost per unit. This method of costing therefore simplifies the production costing by enabling all units completed together to be costed together, rather than attempting to cost each item individually. Batch costing is commonly used in a variety of industries such as engineering components and clothing.

Contract costing

Contract costing also is a variation of job costing but which is usually adopted for work which is of long-term duration, based at a particular site, and undertaken as an individual contract to meet the particular requirements of the customer. As such it is a method of costing which is employed within the construction industry for major projects such as the construction of a housing estate, office block, new motor way or railway.

This type of costing differs from job costing in that as the project takes place on a self-contained site more costs can be identified as direct costs and therefore charged to the contract. Thus costs such as those for telephones on site, supervision and site vehicle and planning salaries can be identified as specific to the contract and treated as a direct costs rather than as overheads as in a job costing environment. Also because of the lengthy nature of a typical contract, extending over several years, and the value involved in a contract it is normal for the contractor to receive payments at stages throughout the project (known as stage payments or progress payments) and to estimate a profit made on work completed to date. This estimation of profit made year by year is necessary to avoid undue fluctuations in the profit of the firm. Interim payments are generally made on the certification by an architect or surveyor of work completed to date and will be to a formula agreed between the customer and the contractor which allows for some retention by the customer (a percentage of value of work certificated as completed) which will be paid upon completion of the whole contract. These contracts normally include a time scale for completion of the work, details of when payments will be made upon completion of agreed stages of the work, and what penalties or forfeitures will be required for unsatisfactory work or unsatisfactory completion times. Profits taken during the course of the contract will need to be conservative to allow for unforeseen difficulties and costs, and there tend to be industry norms which suggest the amount of profit to be taken in stages throughout the contract.

Process costing

Process costing is appropriate in an industry where the product in course of manufacture follows a series of sequential processes and the transfer from one process to another is frequently automatic. Examples of such automatic sequential processing industries include brewing, oil refining, food processing and glass making. In this type of manufacturing process it is not possible to divide the product into discrete units (i.e. jobs or batches) and process costing therefore is concerned with collecting the total costs of each process and averaging these costs over the total throughput of the process. Throughput in this environment will also include work in progress, and partly completed products will be treated as equivalent units of completed products. Thus 100 gallons of beer which is 80 per cent completed as far as processing is concerned will be treated as 80 gallons equivalent of fully completed beer.

In this environment the cost of the output of one process is charged as the raw material input of the next process and cost is added process by process throughout production until the product is fully complete. The cost of production of each unit therefore is an accumulation of the average cost of each process through which the product has passed.

Process costing can be illustrated as shown in Figure 7.6.

With many processes in this type of production environment it is common that the quantity of output, in terms of weight or volume, is less than the quantity of the raw materials input. There is therefore a norm for the quantity

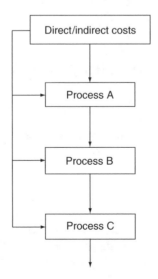

Figure 7.6 Process costing

of finished product which can be expected from any specific quantity of raw materials. Losses in materials can be expected from such factors as evaporation, imperfect use of raw materials or shrinkage. When differences such as this arise there are three possibilities.

1 *Normal process losses*: the losses are as expected in this type of process;
2 *Abnormal process losses*: the losses are greater than expected in this type of process;
3 *Abnormal process gains*: the losses are less than expected in this type of process.

When there are normal losses in the production process these are treated as overheads and the costs are spread over the good production. Abnormal losses or gains, however, are excluded from such routine reporting. These abnormal items are treated as separate items in the process account. Such abnormal gains or losses would be of interest to the manager of the process and would be the subject of investigation for possible problems in the same way that the performance data for Jones & Andrews Ltd in a job costing environment is subject to investigation.

It is normal in a manufacturing environment that part of the direct materials issued into production end up as scrap. Examples include offcuts of wood, cloth or metal. In some cases this scrap has a realisable value and when sold the revenue can be used to reduce the overall cost of production, rather than to reduce the cost of individual products. In other cases a business must pay for the disposal of scrap (e.g. toxic material) and this will increase the overall cost of production. The small value of scrap means that a business will treat scrap in this way rather than accounting separately for it.

Although losses in the production process are treated as overheads, and a certain proportion of loss is expected, this represents wastage and inefficiency in the production process.

The treatment of joint products

Joint products are those which undergo the same processing together as one product for part of their processing. At some point in the manufacturing process these products are split and processed separately until completed and at this split off point they become separately identified products. An example of joint products can be found in the oil refining industry where crude oil is refined as a product but at certain points the product is split and treated separately to become aviation fuel, petrol, kerosene, etc.

For costing purposes it is normal to treat all costs together for a joint process and to treat costs separately for each product from the split off point, at which the products can be identified as distinct products. Common costs – i.e. those incurred during the joint processing – are then apportioned to the individual products to arrive at a total cost of production for each product. Two alternative methods are used for apportioning joint costs and these are:

1 Physical unit basis: where costs are apportioned in proportion to the weight or volume of each of the products produced;
2 Sales value basis: where costs are apportioned according to the sales value of each of the products produced.

These alternative methods of apportioning joint costs are based upon the accounting conventions of the firm concerned rather than on any underlying rationale, but it can be understood that the two alternatives can produce significantly different costs of production for the joint products concerned. The cost apportionment mechanism therefore needs to be understood by the business manager as these costs can affect product profitability and business decisions associated with pricing and investment.

The treatment of by-products

A by-product is one which is produced incidentally during the course of manufacture of the main product and tends to have relatively little sales value. Examples are spent yeast from the brewing industry (sold for use in animal food production) and sawdust and bark from the timber processing industry. As these products tend to have relatively little value compared with the main products being produced and arise as a result of that processing rather than being specifically manufactured in their own right it is not normal to cost the production separately from the cost of production of the main product. The normal method of costing therefore is to cost the production of the main product and to credit against this the net realisable value of the by-product, thereby effectively reducing the total cost of production of the main product.

Although by-products are incidental to the production of the main product it sometimes happens that the by-products become desirable products in their

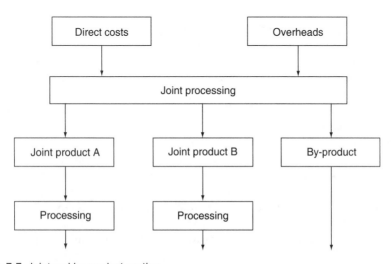

Figure 7.7 Joint and by-product costing

own right and hence have high value. If this happens then the product will need to cease being treated as a by-product and the two products will be treated a joint products. It is therefore important for managers to pay due regard to the by-products of their firm and to look for market opportunities for these products where they can add value to the production process and add to the profitability of the firm.

Joint and by-product processing can be illustrated as shown in Figure 7.7.

Costing in a service environment

These costing techniques have been developed within a production environment and have tended to be considered less relevant to a service environment. In a service environment, however, the processes which the firm undergoes in the provision of their service can be considered similar to production processes. The difference is that generally a service has no value until it is complete and delivered to the customer. There is thus no question of value attached to work in progress. Thus in a restaurant, for example, a meal has no value until it is supplied to a customer and any not supplied will be wasted. Similarly the work of a travel agent has no value until a holiday can be provided to a customer.

Until the service is complete therefore no value is attached to it, although costs are incurred. It is thus possible to accumulate costs for the various parts of the firm involved in the provision of the service. Thus for a restaurant the cost of cooking meals can be accumulated, as can the costs of serving meals and the costs of cleaning up afterwards. Thus a restaurant could be treated as a form of job costing as far as cost accumulation is concerned, while process costing might be more appropriate for a travel agency.

These costing methods we have considered represent methods of accumulating costs and so can be equally appropriate to service businesses.

An appraisal of product costing

Costing systems such as described above are widely used in industry. Such methods of costing however were developed during the early part of this century to deal with product costing in the typical factory which existed then. Over the time since these techniques were developed the typical production environment has changed significantly and this has led to a questioning of the appropriateness of these methods of product costing.

The techniques of product costing were designed for the type of environment which existed at that time. This was an environment in which:

- The direct costs of production (i.e. materials and labour) formed a very high proportion of the total cost.
- The support functions were few in number and overheads were therefore relatively low.

- The production environment was one of low levels of mechanisation.
- Larger runs of standardised products were manufactured.
- There was a slow rate of change in terms of production methods and product development.

In such an environment the apportioning of overheads to products in proportion to direct costs seemed a reasonable costing basis and the method of apportionment and the development of suitable bases made little difference to the overall cost of production of any product. Costing methods were therefore relatively uncontroversial and provided merely a means of accumulating costs.

In a modern environment cost patterns have changed significantly. The features of a modern production environment are:

- Direct costs, particularly labour in a highly automated environment, form a much lower proportion of the total cost of production.
- Overheads, however, form a much higher proportion of total costs.
- There has been a growth in the cost and extent of service functions needed to support the efficient production of high quality products and to market them to customers.

Examples of these new functions include product design, machine tool setting using CNC (computer numerically controlled) machines, data processing, O&M (organisation and methods), production control and scheduling. The significant feature of these new types of overhead is that they do not vary according to production volume but tend to vary over the long term according to the range and complexity of products manufactured, rather than according to volume. This factor, together with the increased automation of production processes, has tended to mean that a much higher proportion of production overheads are fixed rather than variable.

The basis of apportionment of overheads is therefore a significant factor to a modern business and of much more importance than when these costing methods were developed. One effect of the changing nature of overheads and their changing importance in terms of the proportion of total cost has been that these traditional costing methods, based upon apportioning overheads based upon volume, have tended to overstate the production cost of high volume products while understating the production costs of low volume products. This can have a significant effect upon product profitability and upon the decisions made by business manager based upon product costing. A recognition of this type of problem has led to the discussion, amongst accountants and business managers, of the suitability of these costing methods to a modern business and to the development of new costing techniques which attempt to address these problems. The most successful of these new techniques of costing has been activity-based costing which is considered in Chapter 8.

A further change in business which is concerned with product costing has been the increasing use of costing data, not just to provide information about the production costs of products, but also to provide data for performance measurement, such as the data produced by Joseph Gibson of Jones & Andrews Ltd regarding idle time and rectification work. The increasing use of this data for performance measurement has called into question the appropriateness of costing data, particularly by people such as Johnson and Kaplan, who suggest that the changing use of this data means that decisions are made within the business based upon inappropriate data. The changing use of this data has had implications for the behaviour of business managers and for decisions taken within a firm.

Conclusions

Understanding the allocation and apportionment of costs is fundamental to all management accounting and therefore forms the basis for all decision-making using accounting information. In this chapter we have considered the various issues involved and have seen how the allocation of costs might change if a socially responsible approach is adopted. The way in which the calculated costs change under this approach illustrates one important fact concerning cost allocation and apportionment and the subsequent calculation of the cost of products or services, namely that this is not an exact science but rather an attempt to arrive at a reasonable basis for decision-making.

Further reading

Johnson, H.T. and Kaplan, R.S. *Relevance Lost: The Rise and Fall of Management Accounting.* Boston, MA: Harward Business School Press.
Sizer, J. (any edition). *An Insight Into Management Accounting.* Chapter 3. Penguin.

Additional questions

Question 7.1

Although one of the main functions of cost accounting is the determination of product costs, in a situation in which joint products are produced the treatment of joint process and the resulting apportionment of their costs depend upon the method of apportionment selected. This makes the product costs difficult to define absolutely and prevents managers from making decisions about the future of the products based upon certainty of information. This problem is exacerbated when a by-product is involved. Discuss.

Question 7.2

Total Engineering Co. makes brackets which are fitted into motor vehicles. It manufactures these brackets in batches of 400. Batch number 36 was produced and machined at the rate of 20 per hour but 50 brackets failed to pass the final inspection. Of these 20 were scrapped, and the scrap value credited to the batch cost account. The remaining brackets were considered to be rectifiable and rectification work took 10 hours.

Data for batch 36 is as follows:

	£
Raw materials per bracket	2.40
Scrap value per bracket	0.80
Hourly rate of machine operators	6.80
Machine overhead rate (per running hour)	2.50
Setting up cost of machine – normal –	32.00
rectification	36.00

Calculate:
(a) the cost per unit of units actually produced;
(b) the cost of defective work.

Question 7.3

Calculate four different overhead absorption rates based on the following data:

Total overheads for the period	£25 800
Units produce in the period	1 075
Labour hours for the period	2 600
Direct materials for the period	£12 800
Direct wages for the period	£7 200

Question 7.4

Warburton Ltd produces several products which pass through two production departments in its factory. These two departments are concerned with cutting and finishing. The company also has two service departments, maintenance and canteen.

Service department costs are allocated as follows:

Maintenance:	
Cutting	75%
Finishing	20%
Canteen	5%

Canteen:

Cutting	60%
Finishing	30%
Maintenance	10%

During the period just ended actual overheads were as follows:

	£
Cutting	71 500
Finishing	47 300
Maintenance	25 100
Canteen	24 300

Allocate all overheads in order to calculate the overheads absorbed by the production departments.

8
Costing

Learning objectives

After studying this chapter you should be able to:

- explain the purpose of absorption costing and marginal costing;
- explain the meaning and treatment of over- and under-recoveries of costs;
- calculate a product cost using absorption costing, marginal costing or activity-based costing;
- describe how activity-based costing differs from traditional costing;
- explain the meaning of cost drivers and identify appropriate cost drivers;
- discuss the advantages and disadvantages of the various forms of costing;
- calculate product costs using activity-based costing.

Introduction

We have seen that overheads form part of the cost of production of a product but that they cannot be directly identified with any particular product. Instead they are general costs associated with the production process and therefore cannot be directly charged as a cost of production in the same way that direct costs can be. We have seen that it is, however, necessary to charge overheads as a cost of production in order that the full cost of a product can be calculated. The way in which this is done is to spread the overheads over a cost unit by a process which is known as overhead recovery or overhead absorption.

As part of its product range the Office Furniture Company manufactures and sells one design of free standing coat rack for use in offices. Jill Reeves, the management accountant of the company, has been asked to prepare an income statement for the company's operations for the past year and a projected income statement for the forthcoming year. She has collected the following information:

Direct cost of manufacture	£8.00 per unit
Fixed costs incurred last year	£50 000
Projected fixed cost for next year	£51 000
Sales price	£15.00 per unit
Selling expenses for last year	£3 000
Projected selling expenses for next year	£3 200
Administration expenses associated with production (each year)	£1 400

Bill Johnson, the production manager, has confirmed to her that fixed factory overhead is based upon an estimated activity level of 20 000 units in each year. He also has provided her with the following sales and production data:

	Actual last year (units)	Estimated next year (units)
Opening stock of finished goods	1 000	6 000
Production	22 000	18 000
Sales	17 000	22 000
Closing stock	6 000	2 000

Jill Reeves knows that she has all the information she needs to produce the required income statements, and so needs to produce these statements for the forthcoming board meeting.

The absorption of overheads

Overhead absorption is normally done by calculating the overhead absorption rate which is based upon an estimate of overhead costs for the period and an estimate of the level of activity during the period. Dividing the costs by the activity level therefore provides an overhead recovery rate and this is the rate at which overheads are recovered during the period depending upon the production achieved during the period. For Office Furniture Company therefore the calculation of the overhead absorption rate for each year is as follows:

	Last year	Next year
Projected fixed costs divided by	£60 000*	£51 000
Expected production level equals	20 000	18 000 (units)
Overhead rate	£3.00	£2.83 per unit

* Projected costs = 20 000 units × £3.00

This rate will be added to the direct costs of manufacture to arrive at a calculation of the total costs of manufacture. Thus for Office Furniture Company we can see that the cost of manufacture of the coat rack will change for next year as compared with last year due to the changed overhead absorption rate. The comparison is as follows:

	This year (£ per unit)	Next year (£ per unit)
Direct cost	8.00	8.00
Overheads absorbed	3.00	2.83
Production cost	11.00	10.83

We can therefore see that the overhead absorption rate is based upon estimates, both of future costs and of future activity levels. It can be expected therefore that the actual overhead absorption rate, calculated by using actual costs and actual activity will be different from the predetermined rate used, and comparison of estimated and actual overhead absorption rates for Office Furniture Company for this year is as follows:

	Estimate	Actual
Fixed costs	£60 000*	£50 000
Production (units)	20 000	22 000
Overhead recovery rate (per unit) (i.e. costs/production)	£3.00	£2.27

* Estimated fixed costs are calculated as number of production units × overhead recovery rate.

For Office Furniture Company therefore we can see that the costs of manufacture of goods charged in the accounts has been higher than it actually should have been based upon actual costs. Thus more overheads have been recovered through the overhead absorption rate than were actually incurred. This has resulted in what is known as an over-recovery of overheads and the accounts need to be adjusted to reflect the actual cost. The treatment of over-recoveries and under-recoveries (i.e. the opposite) will be considered later in this chapter.

This over-recovery of overheads does, however, illustrate one problem with the treatment of overheads in this manner. This is that the calculation of the overhead absorption rate is based upon estimates of both cost and activity level. These estimates are made based largely upon past and current performance, adjusted for known factors, and so a firm is using past data to predict future performance. Using such estimates of costs can obviously affect the performance of the firm and affect its decision-making regarding such things as price setting, investment and the product mix. There is a danger using this method that these decisions are made upon inaccurate data as the true cost of production is known only after the event – at the end of the period. Office Furniture Company makes this calculation at the end of its year but most manufacturing companies, particularly those in which this information is crucial to decision-making, will operate overhead absorption rates on a month by month basis, recalculating as necessary in the light of actual data.

We can see therefore that the calculation of the overhead absorption rate is crucial to a firm and it needs to get this rate as close to the actual as possible. This rate is of significance to business managers in all areas of the firm who will be making decisions, such as product mix, pricing or sales forecasting, based upon the cost of manufacture of the product. It is important therefore that these managers understand the basis of product costing as used in their firm and the possible consequences of using this method of treating overheads.

Absorption costing

This procedure by which overheads are absorbed into the costs of production of a product is known as absorption costing. The procedure operates through the calculation of an overhead absorption rate, which we considered in the last chapter. You will remember that it can be explained as shown in Figure 8.1.

The total overheads absorbed in this manner include:

- *Fixed costs*: i.e. those costs which are not dependent upon the level of activity of the firm, such as rent or supervisory salaries.
- *Variable costs*: i.e. those which vary roughly in proportion to the level of activity undertaken such as power or consumables for machines.

Absorption costing therefore has implications as far as stock valuation and performance measurement are concerned. The weakness of absorption costing in these respects has been recognised and has been the subject of criticism by both accountants and business managers. These weaknesses are considered later in this chapter. An alternative method of costing exists which excludes fixed costs from the absorption process and charges them in total against the results of the period. This method is known as marginal costing and will be considered later. A more modern method of costing has been developed which is activity-based costing and this also will be considered later.

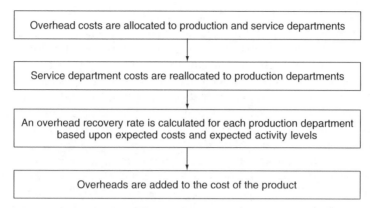

Figure 8.1 Steps in the absorption costing process

Absorption costing by its very nature implies that indirect costs are related to products in proportion to the time consumed in their manufacture. Thus the most common bases for absorbing overheads are either direct labour hours or direct machine hours. Each provides a basis for allocation based upon time taken in the manufacture of the product. In an environment in which a range of products is manufactured, however, it has been argued that this time basis does not accurately reflect the way in which costs are incurred. It is for this reason that the development of activity-based costing has taken place and it is argued that this method of costing provides a more accurate representation of the cost of manufacture of individual products within a range.

A variation of absorption costing is the technique known as standard costing. In this technique standards are set for activities which basically are predetermined estimates of costs and activities based upon what the firm expects to achieve in normal operating conditions. Performance is therefore evaluated against these standards.

The treatment of over- and under-recovery of costs

We have seen how the use of absorption costing can lead to an over-recovery or an under-recovery of indirect costs because of the need to estimate both costs and levels of activity at the start of the accounting period. In the case of Office Furniture Company this has led to an over-recovery of costs in the last year amounting to £16 000. Thus statement of overheads incurred and absorbed can be given as follows:

	£
Overheads absorbed (£3.00 per unit × 22 000 units)	66 000
Overheads incurred	50 000
Over-absorption of overheads	16 000

The result of this is that more cost has been charged to the accounts than has actually been incurred and the manufacturing account for the company for the last year shows a higher cost of production for the goods produced than has actually been incurred. This also means that the cost of production of each coat rack as shown in the accounts is higher than it actually was and so the valuation of stock (which is shown as cost of production) is higher than it should be because of this over-recovery of overheads. We can therefore see that stock valuation for a firm is affected by the overhead recovery rate and this is another problem with absorption costing.

It is necessary that the accounts of a firm reflect the actual cost incurred by that firm relating to the period in question. The fact that there has been an over-statement of cost in the manufacturing of coat racks by Office Furniture Company due to the over-recovery of overheads therefore means that there needs to be an adjustment in the accounts. This is needed to ensure that the accounts reflect the actual costs of manufacture. The way in which this adjustment is effected is to consider the over- or under-recovery of overheads in total as a period cost and to show the net figure as an entry in the profit and loss account. This can be illustrated for Office Furniture Company by examining the income statement which Joseph Gibson has been asked to prepare for the company which parallels the profit and loss account. This statement will appear as follows:

Office Furniture Company
Income statement

	This year (actual) (£)	(£)	Next year (estimated) (£)	(£)
Sales		255 000		330 000
Less cost of goods sold				
Opening stock	11 000		66 000	
Production	242 000		195 000	
Cost of goods available	253 000		261 000	
Less closing stock	66 000	187 000	21 660	239 340
Gross profit		68 000		90 660
Less period costs				
Administration costs	1 400		1 400	
Selling costs	3 000		3 200	
Over-absorption of overheads	(16 000)	(11 600)		4 600
Net profit		79 600		86 060

Absorption costing in a multi-product environment

Most manufacturing companies produce more than one product and in such an environment there is a need to absorb overheads over the whole range of products. This is done in exactly the same way as Office Furniture Company absorbs overheads. In other words whatever basis is chosen for the absorption of any particular overhead this is applied throughout the product range. Thus, for example, if overheads were to be absorbed on the basis of direct labour hours then an overhead absorption rate would be calculated and this would be applied to all products, based upon the number of direct labour hours which went into the production of each individual product.

Absorption costing in service industries

In service industries absorption costing is used for the recovery of overheads in much the same way as it is used in manufacturing industry. In this case there are no products produced but instead services are provided. These can be equated, however, to products and overhead absorption rates calculated and applied in a similar manner.

Reasons for using absorption costing

We have seen that there are a variety of problems in a firm using absorption costing which is important for the business manager to be aware of. Given the existence of these problems and the existence of the other methods of costing which have been mentioned it might be thought that absorption costing should not be used by a firm and that another method would be preferable. Unfortunately these other costing methods too have their disadvantages as well as advantages. Also there exist some compelling arguments for using absorption costing, as well as some problems in its use. The advantages and disadvantages of absorption costing therefore need to be recognised and these can be considered to be the following:

Advantages of absorption costing

SSAP9 (stocks and work in progress). The Accounting Standards Committee, which consists of members of the UK accounting bodies, has issued a set of Statements of Standard Accounting Practice (SSAPs) which UK companies are required to adhere to in completing their accounts. This particular statement (SSAP9) requires that costs and revenues are matched in the period in which the revenue arises rather than in the period in which the costs are incurred. It also recommends that stock valuation must include all the production over-heads which are incurred in the normal course of business even if such costs are time-related (i.e. fixed in nature). These production overheads must be based upon normal activity levels. This SSAP therefore has the effect of requir-ing that absorption costing be used by a firm as far as the production of its final accounts is concerned and thus provides the reason for the widespread use of absorption costing in industry. The value of marginal costing therefore as an alternative method of costing is relegated to purely internal use within the firm.

Reducing profit fluctuations

Where production levels are fairly constant but sales fluctuate absorption costing has the effect of reducing fluctuations in net profit. Similarly where stock building is an essential part of the operating of the firm (e.g. whisky maturing) absorption costing is both necessary and desirable in order to include fixed costs in the stock valuation. Otherwise the accounts of the business would show a series of losses which would be followed by a very large profit when the stock was eventually sold.

Ensures all costs are covered

The inclusion of fixed costs in the cost of production recognises that these are an essential part of the cost of producing the product and that the assets represented by these costs are an essential part of the production process. Failure to recognise this could lead to pricing decisions, particularly in an environment in which a variety of products are manufactured, which did not ensure that all the costs of production were covered in the prices charged for the various products.

Avoids cost separation

The split between fixed and variable costs is often arbitrary and many costs are mixed, containing an element of both fixed and variable costs. The use of absorption costing in charging all production overheads to product cost simplifies the accounting procedures and reduces argument by eliminating the need to split costs into fixed and variable and to split mixed costs into their fixed and variable components. This has the effect of reducing subjectivity in the cost allocation process.

Creates an awareness of resources used

Fixed costs are a significant proportion of the costs of a business and without the buildings, machinery, etc. which cause the fixed costs to be incurred the product could not be manufactured. The inclusion of fixed costs in the production overhead and therefore in the production cost and stock valuation provides a signal to managers in the business that these items are utilised in the manufacture of the product, thereby reminding them that the resources used include more than those represented by the variable costs. It therefore provides a reminder to those managers not involved in the production process of all the resources that are used in production and need to be considered in the planning of the business.

SSAP2 *(accounting policies).* This statement requires the implementation of the accruals concept of accounting by requiring that costs be charged to the accounts in the time period to which they relate rather than in the time period in which they are incurred. As fixed costs are an essential part of the cost of production of a product of the firm this statement therefore implies that these costs should be accrued during production and charged when stock is sold. This SSAP has therefore been interpreted as requiring the use of absorption costing by a manufacturing company.

Reveals inefficient use of resources

As the full cost of overheads is charged to production in each period using the overhead absorption rate, this implies that the lower the level of activity in any area of the business, the higher the overhead absorption rate. Consideration of this rate therefore and examination of changes to the rate over time, or by comparing the actual rate calculated at the end of the period with the estimated rate calculated at the beginning of the period will indicate to the managers of the business where activity levels are not as planned or costs are not as expected. This can indicate problems in production and can also indicate where the resources of the business are not being used as efficiently as possible. The search for the most efficient means of production possible will cause managers to seek to drive this overhead absorption rate down to as low a level as possible. Absorption costing therefore provides a means of indicating possible inefficiencies in the use of resources within the business.

Disadvantages of absorption costing

Profit varies with production

Using absorption costing costs are charged to production and incorporated within the stock valuation and this occurs whether or not the product is actually sold. It is therefore possible to make a profit as far as the books of the business are concerned merely by producing for stock and it is possible to increase profits merely by increasing the level of production even if the level of sales does not increase and this increased production is represented only by increased stock holding of finished goods. In some businesses with irregular sales patterns (e.g. toy manufacturing) or long production cycles (e.g. forestry and timber production) this technique can be used to even out profit fluctuations. It must be recognised, however, that for all businesses using absorption costing, profits are to some extent dependent upon production levels and a business manager needs to ensure that profits are related to sales rather than to production by concerning him or herself with stock levels as well as production levels and sales levels.

Allocation is arbitrary

The apportionment of fixed costs to departments and ultimately to the product itself is frequently on an arbitrary basis as no reasonable basis exists for such apportionment. Thus in a firm such as Office Furniture Company the salary of Joseph Gibson can be readily charged to the cost of production of the sole product. If several products were made, however, there is no correct basis of apportioning his salary which is essentially indivisible in nature. Any apportionment which will need to be made therefore will be on the basis of an allocation which is by its nature arbitrary. The need to apportion all costs leads to the need to find a basis for each allocation and the resources of the business are used in determining a suitable basis for the allocation of each cost type. These bases of allocation can also be a source of tension within an organisation as each departmental manager seeks to reduce the allocation made to his/her department by arguing about the suitability of any basis of allocation for that particular cost. Absorption costing therefore can consume the time not just of the accountants in the business but also of the managers of the business and can lead to increased cost and an inefficient use of managerial time

We have seen therefore that there are problems in the use of absorption costing within a business but also that there are compelling reasons why it should be used. It is therefore used in one form or another throughout manufacturing industry, and throughout service industries. We have also seen that the use of this costing method has implications for the business which affect not just the accountants within the business but also the managers of the business whether or not they are involved in the production process. It can be seen therefore that it is important to business managers to understand the principles of the costing system used by the business in which they are employed and the effects which this might have upon their areas of responsibility. We have seen, however, that there are problems in using absorption costing, and so we will consider some alternative methods of costing which a business might use.

Costing a product

Traditional methods of costing are based upon the assumption that costs are related to the volume of production of each of the products made by a business. Thus costs are absorbed in relation to volume and it is assumed that all costs are related to a product in this manner. There is a tendency, using this traditional method of product costing, that the costs of production of high volume products are overstated while the cost of low volume products is understated. This is because economies of scale in the production process are not recognised in traditional methods of costing, which assume that volume is the sole determinant of cost. It has also been argued that not all overhead costs relate in equal proportions to the volume of production of each product and that the costs of production are therefore not as accurately calculated as is desirable. This has obvious implications for a business where pricing decisions are based to some extent upon the calculated costs of production of each product in the range.

We have also seen how changes in manufacturing techniques have tended to result in a smaller proportion of the cost of manufacture of a product being attributable to direct costs and a correspondingly greater proportion being attributable to overhead costs. Any inequality in overhead cost apportionment using absorption costing is therefore exaggerated in a modern production environment. It is for this reason therefore that more attention has been given to the way in which overhead costs arise in relation to the manufacture of a product. This investigation has led to the development of activity-based costing (ABC) which seeks to allocate overhead costs to products on a more realistic basis than that of production volume.

Sunanda Singh is the management accountant of Reid Manufacturing Ltd, a small company which manufactures industrial batteries. The managing director has become aware of activity-based costing as a technique which more accurately reflects the cost of manufacture of products. He considers that this information may be of significance to the company in setting its prices for its products. He has therefore asked Sunanda to prepare a comparative statement of product costs using traditional absorption costing and activity based costing.

Reid Manufacturing Ltd makes four different types of batteries: X432; X467; Y145; Z359.

Sunanda has collected the following information which she needs for her comparative analysis of product costing:

Product	Volume (units)	Material cost per unit (£)	Direct labour per unit (hours)	Machine time per unit (hours)	Labour cost per unit (£)
X432	600	6	0.5	0.4	4
X467	6000	5	0.5	0.2	4
Y145	700	18	1.5	1.0	12
Z359	8000	20	2.0	1.2	16

Factory overheads recovered over machine hours: £35 220
Set-up costs: £4096
Cost of ordering materials: £2304
Material handling costs: £6440
Administration for spare parts: £10.024

These overhead costs are currently absorbed by products on the basis of machine hours at a rate of £4.95 per hour.

Sunanda has investigated the production activities of the company for the last period. Her investigations have revealed the following:

	X432	X467	Y145	Z359
Number of set-ups required	2	5	2	7
Number of materials orders	1	5	2	4
Number of times materials were handled	2	8	4	9
Number of spare parts required	1	6	2	5

Sunanda knows that she has all the information she needs to complete her analysis of product costs using the two methods.

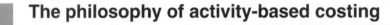

The philosophy of activity-based costing

Activity-based costing is based upon the philosophy that costs arise when an activity is performed rather than when a product is produced. Thus for example costs are incurred every time a machine set-up takes place and therefore a product which takes seven machine set-ups is more costly to produce than one which requires only one machine set-up. Activity-based costing attempts to reflect this cost difference in the product costing by identifying those activities in the production process which cause cost to be incurred.

These activities are known as cost drivers and for Reid Manufacturing Ltd, Sunanda Singh has identified the following activities as causing costs to be incurred in the battery manufacturing process:

● machine set-up
● ordering of materials
● handling of materials
● administration of spare parts.

The key concept of ABC is to focus attention upon the factors which cause costs to be incurred – i.e. which drive costs and are hence known as cost drivers. A cost driver can be defined as an activity or transaction which is a significant determinant of cost.

There are no simple rules for identifying cost drivers and these depend upon the individual business and the way in which it operates. R.S. Kaplan, one of the main proponents of ABC, suggests that the best approach is to identify those resources which constitute a significant proportion of the cost of a product and to determine their cost behaviour.

In order for ABC to be of value to a business in determining product costing it is necessary for the cost drivers selected to be a realistic representation of the way in which costs are incurred in the production process. In other words the product costs produced from the use of ABC are only as realistic as the cost drivers identified as contributing to costs. It is necessary therefore that the production process is understood in detail when the cost drivers are selected and the managers of the production process must therefore be involved to a large extent in defining the ABC system in order for it to be of value in better identifying the cost of production of individual products within the product range.

The steps in activity-based costing

In order to develop an ABC system the following steps need to be undertaken:

1 Identify the main activities undertaken in the organisation which relate to the production process. Such activities can include materials ordering and handling, machining, and assembly.

2 Identify the factors which determine the cost of an activity. These are known as cost drivers and include such things as number of purchase orders made, number of machine set-ups, and number of times materials are handled.

3 Collect the costs of each activity in a cost pool. This cost pool is equivalent to a cost centre in a conventional absorption costing system.

4 Estimate an appropriate cost absorption rate for each cost driver based upon estimated costs and estimated usage. This is the application rate for the cost driver.

5 Use the application rate for each use of the cost driver in order to apply activity costs to the products being produced.

This can be summarised in Figure 8.2.

The principles of ABC can be seen in Figure 8.3.

This can be compared with the principles of conventional product costing which are illustrated in Figure 8.4.

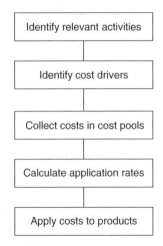

Figure 8.2 Attributing costs using ABC

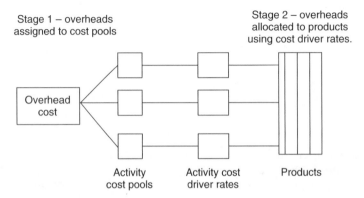

Figure 8.3 Activity-based costing

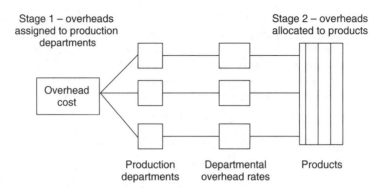

Stage 1 – overheads
assigned to production
departments

Stage 2 – overheads
allocated to products

Overhead
cost

Production
departments

Departmental
overhead rates

Products

Figure 8.4 Absorption costing

The calculation of product costs using ABC

Once the cost drivers have been identified in the manufacturing process the next step in the calculation of product costs is to calculate the cost driver application rates. For Reid Manufacturing Ltd these can be calculated as follows:

Machine-related cost driver (factory overheads)
(i.e. using the same basis as for the absorption costing system)
  Cost of factory overheads: £35 220
  Number of machine hours: 600×0.4 (X432)
                                             $+6000 \times 0.2$ (X467)
                                             $+700 \times 1$ (Y145)
                                             $+8000 \times 1.2$ (Z359)
                                             $= 11\ 740$

  Cost per machine hour $= \dfrac{35\ 220}{11\ 740} = £3.00$

Set-up cost driver
  Cost of machine set-ups: £4096
  Number of set-ups: 2 (X432) + 5 (X467) + 2 (Y145) + 7 (Z359) = 16
  Cost per set-up $= \dfrac{4096}{16} = £256$

Materials order cost driver
  Cost of ordering materials: £2304
  Number of orders: 1 (X432) + 5 (X467) + 2 (Y145) + 4 (Z359) = 12
  Cost per set-up $= \dfrac{2304}{12} = £192$

Materials handling cost driver
  Cost of handling materials: £6440
  Number of handlings: 2 (X432) + 8 (X467) + 4 (Y145) + 9 (Z359) = 23
  Cost per set-up $= \dfrac{6440}{23} = £280$

Spare parts cost driver

Cost of administering spare parts: £10 024

Number of orders: 1 (X432) + 6 (X467) + 2 (Y145) + 5 (Z359) = 14

$$\text{Cost per set-up} = \frac{10\ 024}{14} = £716$$

These application rates are then used to apply the costs of each of the activities to the products being produced and for Reid Manufacturing Ltd these would be applied as follows:

Machine-related overhead cost per unit of output (number of hours × cost per hour)

X432: 0.4 × 3.00 = £1.20
X467: 0.2 × 3.00 = £0.60
Y145: 1 × 3.00 = £3.00
Z359: 1.2 × 3.00 = £3.60

Set-up cost per unit of output (number of set-ups × cost per set-up)/number of units produced

$$\text{X432: } \frac{(2 \times 256)}{600} = £0.85$$

$$\text{X467: } \frac{(5 \times 256)}{6000} = £0.21$$

$$\text{Y145: } \frac{(2 \times 256)}{700} = £0.73$$

$$\text{Z359: } \frac{(7 \times 256)}{8000} = £0.22$$

Materials ordering cost per unit of output (number of orders × cost per order)/number of units produced

$$\text{X432: } \frac{(1 \times 192)}{600} = £0.32$$

$$\text{X467: } \frac{(5 \times 192)}{6000} = £0.16$$

$$\text{Y145: } \frac{(2 \times 192)}{700} = £0.55$$

$$\text{Z359: } \frac{(4 \times 192)}{8000} = £0.10$$

Materials handling cost per unit of output (number of handlings × cost per handling)/ number of units produced

$$\text{X432: } \frac{(2 \times 280)}{600} = £0.93$$

$$\text{X467: } \frac{(8 \times 280)}{6000} = £0.37$$

$$\text{Y145: } \frac{(4 \times 280)}{700} = £1.60$$

$$\text{Z359: } \frac{(9 \times 280)}{8000} = £0.37$$

Spare parts admin. cost per unit of output (number of spare parts $\times$ cost per part)/number of units produced

$$X432: \frac{(1 \times 716)}{600} = £1.19$$

$$X467: \frac{(6 \times 716)}{6000} = £0.72$$

$$Y145: \frac{(2 \times 716)}{700} = £2.05$$

$$Z359: \frac{(45 \times 716)}{8000} = £0.45$$

It is then possible to calculate the total overhead cost for each product as follows:

	X432 (£)	X467 (£)	Y145 (£)	Z359 (£)
Overhead costs				
Factory overheads	1.20	0.60	3.00	3.60
Set-up costs	0.85	0.21	0.73	0.22
Material ordering costs	0.32	0.16	0.55	0.10
Material handling costs	0.93	0.37	1.60	0.37
Spare parts costs	1.19	0.72	2.05	0.45
Total overhead cost	4.49	2.06	7.93	4.74

Also, the total cost of production for each of the four products which Reid manufacturing Ltd produces can be calculated as follows:

	X432 (£)	X467 (£)	Y145 (£)	Z359 (£)
Product cost				
Direct materials	6.00	5.00	18.00	20.00
Direct labour costs	4.00	4.00	12.00	16.00
Total overhead cost	4.49	2.06	7.93	4.74
Total product cost	14.49	11.06	37.93	40.74

A traditional absorption costing approach would produce product costs as follows:

Overhead cost per unit of output (number of hours $\times$ cost per hour)

    X432: $0.4 \times 4.95 = £1.98$
    X467: $0.2 \times 4.95 = £0.99$
    Y145: $1 \times 4.95 = £4.95$
    Z359: $1.2 \times 4.95 = £5.94$

	X432 (£)	X467 (£)	Y145 (£)	Z359 (£)
Product cost				
Direct materials	6.00	5.00	18.00	20.00
Direct labour costs	4.00	4.00	12.00	16.00
Total overhead cost	1.98	0.99	4.95	5.94
Total product cost	11.98	9.99	34.95	41.94

It is therefore possible for Sunanda Singh to produce a statement comparing the cost of production using ABC and absorption costing and her statement would be as follows:

	X432 (£)	X467 (£)	Y145 (£)	Z359 (£)
Product cost				
Absorption costing	11.98	9.99	34.95	41.94
Activity-based costing	14.49	11.06	37.93	40.74
Difference	+2.51	+1.07	+2.98	−1.20

Here + means that ABC leads to an increased product cost and − means that ABC leads to a reduced product cost.

It can be seen that the two product costing systems produce very different costs for the four products and this can have a significant impact upon the business and upon the prices charged for each of the products. It can therefore be seen that the product costing system used by a company is not merely an impartial reporting mechanism but can significantly shape the performance of the business and can affect the prices charged for the various products, the quantities sold based upon these prices, and ultimately the viability of producing some of the products in the product range.

Activity-based costing in service organisations

This discussion of ABC has been set in a manufacturing environment but its use is equally appropriate in a service environment. The principle of linking costs to activities in the service process would assist in providing more accurate costs of individual services just as much as providing costs of individual products in a manufacturing environment. Thus ABC has been used successfully in service industries such as banking, where cost drivers can be related to the volume of activity on a customer's account rather than to the number of accounts which a person possesses or the size of any particular balance.

 ## The variable–fixed cost dichotomy

The traditional method of cost classification is to divide costs into variable costs and fixed costs. Variable costs are those which vary with the volume of production and include direct costs. Fixed costs are those which are not dependant upon the production volume and this includes the majority of overhead costs. Activity-based costing, however, attributes costs to activities and this requires a different classification of costs. This different classification is needed because some overhead costs are related to production volumes while other overhead costs are related to the production process. There is a need, when using ABC, to consider not just whether costs are variable but also why they may vary. Kaplan therefore has proposed classifying costs into the following three categories:

Short-term variable costs

These costs do vary with production volumes, such as power costs which are directly related to machine hours used. It is suggested that such costs are traced to product cost using production-volume-related cost drivers, such as machine hours or direct labour hours, in the manner of traditional absorption costing. In most organisations only a relatively small proportion of overhead costs will be classified as short-term variable costs.

Long-term variable costs

These costs do not vary in accordance with production volume but rather with other measures of activity. Examples would include stock purchasing and handling, machine set-up costs, and general support activities. Such costs can be regarded as fixed in the short term but variable in the longer term, depending upon the range and complexity of products manufactured and changes in product mix or production methods. In traditional costing systems such costs would be regarded as fixed and recovered through a general overhead recovery rate. With ABC, however, they are regarded as variable and can be recovered through the transaction-based cost drivers identified within the system. These costs are likely to include the majority of overhead costs, particularly in an advanced manufacturing technology environment.

Fixed costs

Such costs do not vary with any activity indicator and are therefore classified as fixed. They would include such things as directors' salaries and it is suggested that these costs will form a relatively small proportion of total costs.

Activity-based costing therefore requires that costs be looked at differently to the way in which they are viewed in traditional costing systems. It has the advantage that a much greater proportion of overheads can be regarded as variable, rather than fixed, and allocated to product costs in relation to how they are incurred. This is particularly important in a modern production environment and is one of the main reasons why it is claimed that ABC enables more accurate product costings to be calculated.

 # The advantages of activity-based costing

The following can be considered to be the main advantages of ABC:

Better product costing

It enables more overheads to be traced to product costs and provides a more realistic assessment of how costs are incurred. It therefore leads to more realistic product costing, particularly in a modern manufacturing environment where support costs comprise a high proportion of total costs.

Control of costs

Activity-based costing recognises that it is activities which cause costs to arise rather than production volume. It therefore focuses attention on the real nature of cost behaviour. This makes it possible to control costs better, by controlling the activities which cause costs. This therefore will lead to better use of managerial time.

Supports cost reduction efforts

It also enables the recognition of the value added by the various activities in the production process by comparing costs with benefits. It therefore facilitates the identification of non-value-adding activities which can therefore be reduced in scope, as part of the cost reduction efforts of the management process, thereby leading to a better use of managerial time. This can also lead to job redesign as the activities which do not add value are eliminated and workers are able to concentrate their efforts on the value-adding parts of the firm's activities. A recognition of the value added by certain functions can also increase motivation for those performing those functions, who will realise that the value of their work is recognised by the firm.

Facilitates performance measurement

It provides a variety of measures of performance which includes financial measures, such as the cost driver application rates, as well as non-financial measures, such as transaction volumes. These measures together give a better means for managers to measure and evaluate performance than do the measures provided by traditional costing systems.

Facilitates strategic decisions

More realistic product costs enable the managers of a business to make strategic decisions based upon better information. Such decisions will include not just pricing decisions and investment decisions but also decisions involving product mix changes and introducing or discontinuing products. Competitiveness with other businesses making similar products is also better able to be evaluated for all of the products in the range on an individual product basis.

 # The disadvantages of activity-based costing

Activity-based costing, however, also has some disadvantages in comparison with traditional costing systems, which can be summarised as follows:

Costly to operate

The need to collect costs in a variety of cost pools and to operate a variety of cost driver application rates is more complex to administer than a simple overhead absorption rate. Thus ABC is inevitably more expensive to operate than traditional costing systems.

Use of managerial time

Activity-based costing requires the selection of appropriate cost drivers and realistic product costing is dependant upon the selection of these cost drivers. Such cost drivers are pertinent only to an individual company and therefore managerial effort is required to identify these cost drivers. This identification of appropriate cost drivers requires a detailed knowledge of the production processes and a constant review of operations to ensure that relevant and realistic cost drivers continue to be used. This managerial effort can be offset against the reduction in managerial time spent in controlling costs and activities but nevertheless represents a change in emphasis for managers of the business rather than a reduction in managerial effort.

Based on historical cost

Like all costing systems, ABC is based upon historical costs and activities and these may not represent a sound basis for planning future activity. It therefore has the disadvantage of a historical base which limits its appropriateness to an manufacturing environment in the same way as more traditional costing systems. This has a tendency to negate one of the claimed advantages of ABC in its appropriateness for such environments.

Activity-based costing is one of a range of accounting techniques which have been developed in order to provide a better basis for controlling a business operating in a modern manufacturing environment. We have seen that it addresses some of the problems discussed previously concerning product costing and decision-making but we have also seen that it has limitations. The heavy investment of time involved in setting up such a system is perhaps one reason why it has not been universally adopted by businesses. The costs of running such a system make it only practical for larger multi-product businesses but its limitations for an manufacturing environment tend to preclude it from being adopted by such businesses.

It is perhaps for these reasons that its adoption is more widespread in the USA, where it was developed as a technique, than in the rest of the world where it remains something of a rarity. Nevertheless as a costing system it does offer advantages to a business manager who understands the principles underlying it and is sufficiently widespread in use for a business manager to need to understand it as a method of product costing.

An alternative form of costing

We have looked in detail at the costing of products and services and the way in which these costs are built up through the activities of the firm. We have seen that both direct costs and indirect costs form part of the cost of a product or service. Indirect costs include all the fixed costs of the firm and, as these too form part of the cost of production, these also are included in the product or service cost and are charged to the cost of the product or service in the form of overheads. We have identified the basic method of product costing as absorption costing and have seen that this method of costing enables us to value stock at its full cost of production and to calculate the profit of the business which is derived from its trading. This costing method also enables the firm to satisfy its legal reporting requirements and comply with accounting conventions as specified in the appropriate SSAP.

When we have looked at the internal operations of a business, however, we have seen that the use of absorption costing causes problems within the firm by the way in which costs are allocated to the various products or services. This allocation is often arbitrary and so it has been argued that the costs of production do not necessarily represent the true cost of delivering a particular service or producing a particular product. We have seen examples, particularly through the use of ABC, whereby the allocation of costs to products in a different way results in quite different product costings. Given this problem of identifying the costs of a product or service therefore it is difficult for a firm to plan efficiently for its operations, decide upon the optimum mix of products or services to deliver, to price those products or services in accordance with market conditions. This problem also makes it difficult for a firm to decide upon the allocation of its resources in such a way that the use of any additional resources available to the business can be utilised to best effect in terms of performance improvement.

It is for these reasons that a firm uses a different method of costing when considering its internal reporting and the making of operational and investment decisions, while continuing to use absorption costing for stock valuation and profit accounting purposes. This different method of costing is known as marginal costing, or alternatively as variable costing or direct costing. As decisions are made on the basis of marginal costing it is important that business managers understand the principles of this method of costing, its benefits and limitations, and can distinguish between the use of costs for decision-making and the use of costs for stock valuation and reporting. In this chapter we will therefore also consider the principles of marginal costing in detail.

Franklin Technology Ltd is a manufacturer of high technology electronic components. The products manufactured, due to the pace of technological development in this area, have a short product life cycle. The average life of a product is one year. Competition amongst manufacturers in this industry is intense leading to very high marketing costs. The technological nature of the products also makes the development costs of a product substantial.

The company has just developed a new product for the market which has the following cost profile:

	£	£
Direct costs		
Materials	123	
Labour	28	
Expenses	57	208
Absorbed manufacturing overheads		
Fixed	40	
Variable	30	70
		278
Absorbed non-manufacturing overheads		
General administrative costs	37	
Development costs	240	
Marketing costs	110	387
Total product cost		665

The absorbed non-manufacturing costs and fixed manufacturing costs have been arrived at by dividing the total costs in each category by the total number of products planned to be produced during the year.

The board of Franklin Technology Ltd are concerned that they cannot launch this product onto the market at a price which will enable the product cost to be covered due to the competitive nature of the market for this product. They have therefore asked David Smith, the management accountant, to investigate the product costs calculated to see if this cost is correct.

Marginal costing defined

Marginal costing is concerned with the marginal cost of production of an extra unit of the product or service. Marginal cost can be defined as the sum of the additional or incremental costs which are incurred as a result of production and distribution of one extra unit.

As it is not practical to identify the marginal cost of one extra unit of production in this manner in a normal production environment the technique focuses upon the variable cost of production, hence the term variable costing as an alternative.

Thus:

$$\text{Marginal cost} = \text{Variable cost}$$

Marginal costing is concerned with all the costs that are incurred in the production process, both direct and indirect costs, just as absorption costing and ABC are. In Chapter 3, however, we distinguished between product costs and period costs. Marginal costing considers fixed costs to be period costs, which continue to be incurred whatever be the level of production. Marginal costing tries to measure the relative impact of changes in production levels upon a business and therefore is only concerned with variable costs as far as product costs calculations are concerned. Thus:

$$\text{Marginal cost} = \text{Direct labour cost} + \text{Direct materials cost} + \text{Direct expenses} + \text{Variable overheads}$$

For Franklin Technology Ltd therefore the marginal cost of the new product can be calculated as follows:

	£	£
Direct costs		
Materials	123	
Labour	28	
Expenses	57	208
Absorbed manufacturing overheads		
Variable		30
Marginal cost		238

Marginal costing therefore traces all variable costs to products or services and treats all fixed costs, both manufacturing and non-manufacturing, as period costs rather than as overheads. We have considered previously (Chapter 3), however, that fixed costs are only fixed within a particular range, and we will consider in detail the relationship between costs and production volume in Chapter 10. It therefore follows that in certain circumstances the marginal cost of changes to production might involve additional fixed costs. We will consider this further in Chapter 12 when we consider the relevant costs for making any particular decision.

Figure 8.5 explains the marginal costing approach.

A comparison of marginal costing with absorption costing can be seen from Figures 8.6 and 8.7.

Marginal costing is defined by CIMA as follows:

> the accounting system in which variable costs are charged to cost units and fixed costs of the period are written off in full against the aggregate contribution. Its special value is in decision making.

The term contribution in this definition is calculated as the difference between selling price and marginal cost, and is the contribution made by the unit of production towards fixed costs and profit. Thus:

$$\text{Contribution} = \text{Selling price} - \text{Marginal cost}$$

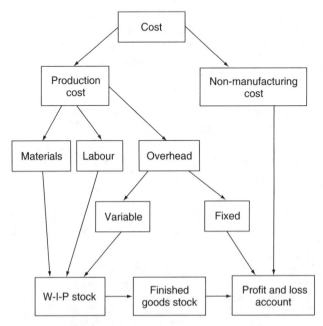

Figure 8.5 Cost accumulation using marginal costing

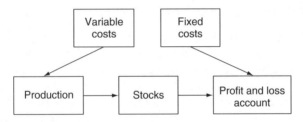

Figure 8.6 Marginal costing

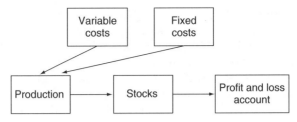

Figure 8.7 Absorption costing

and the relationship between marginal cost and profit can be explained thus:

$$\text{Selling price} - \text{Marginal cost} = \text{Contribution}$$

and

$$\text{Contribution} - \text{Fixed cost} = \text{Profit}$$

Because marginal costing makes use of variable costs as the equivalent of marginal costs and bases product or service costs on average variable cost, three important assumptions are made in the calculations. These are:

- *Linearity*: It is assumed that all costs have a linear relationship with production volume so that the variable cost of each unit is identical with that of each other unit.
- *No step costs*: It is assumed that no step costs exist in the variable costs of production so that the linear relationship exists throughout the range of activity under consideration.
- *Relevant range*: It is assumed that the relationship between costs and production holds throughout the range under consideration and so the analysis is restricted to the relevant range.

In subsequent chapters we will examine the effects of these assumptions not being true as far as decision-making is concerned but for now we will assume that these assumptions remain true.

The theoretical argument for marginal costing

The principal difference between absorption costing and marginal costing is in the treatment of fixed costs. In absorption costing they are treated as product costs whereas in marginal costing they are treated as period costs. The argument for treating fixed costs as product costs is based upon the revenue production concept while the argument for treating them as period costs is based upon the cost obviation concept. These two concepts can be explained as follows:

Revenue production concept

This concept distinguishes the costs of producing stock between assets and expenses by defining an asset in terms of its ability to contribute towards the production of revenue in the future. All costs which cannot contribute in this way are defined as expenses. These expenses should be matched against the revenue obtained when the stock is sold, and therefore included in the stock valuation as part of the production costs. Fixed costs of a firm must be classified as expenses according to this definition because they do not contribute towards future revenue production. This concept therefore implies that absorption costing must be used.

Cost obviation concept

This concept defines assets differently and identifies an asset in terms of its potential to save future costs. Thus Horngren and Sorter state:

> If the total future cost of an enterprise will be decreased because of the presence of a given cost, the cost is relevant to the future and is an asset.

Using this definition it can be seen that stock is defined as an asset because it saves future costs. On the other hand the fixed costs of a business will not save costs in the future and will need to be incurred again in future periods. This implies that fixed costs should not be included in stock valuation but should be treated as period costs. Thus marginal costing should be used.

It can be seen therefore that theoretical arguments exist for the use of both absorption costing and marginal costing, but in practical terms absorption costing must be used by a firm in valuing stock in order to comply with the appropriate SSAP. Any use of marginal costing therefore is restricted to the internal reporting of a firm. For it to be used in addition to absorption costing it must fulfil a function which justifies its use as an additional costing method.

The advantages of marginal costing

In making decisions the use of marginal costing can be seen to give the following advantages to business managers who need to make those decisions:

Avoids arbitrary apportionment of fixed costs

Under marginal costing fixed costs are treated as a whole and charged to revenue rather than being absorbed into product costs. The absorption of fixed costs into product costs involves, as we have seen, some arbitrary allocations of those costs to products. These allocations can cause argument and conflict within the firm between different managers and can also lead to different product costs depending upon how the costs are allocated. Marginal costing, however, only charges variable costs to products and these are inevitably directly attributable to those products. Marginal costing splits costs into fixed and variable, and enables projections to be made, which are dependent upon this split and therefore provides information relevant to decision-making.

Avoids the need for determining suitable bases

For fixed costs to be charged to products or services there needs to be a suitable basis for absorbing each of these costs into the various products or services. This requires the development of a basis for each type of fixed cost incurred and which is based upon an approximation of the relationship of this cost to the various products. This is a time-consuming operation which can be subject to much argument and revision, and needs to be followed by calculation to apportion the cost for allocation purposes. We can see that this takes time and effort for absorption costing and even more so for ABC. This involves managerial time and the time of accountants in activities which do not add to the overall performance of the organisation. Marginal costing avoids this and is much simpler to operate.

Avoids the time element of fixed cost

Fixed costs are incurred due to the passage of time and do not relate to the level of activity of the firm. Thus salaries are incurred monthly, rates annually and telephone charges quarterly regardless of the level of activity of the period concerned, and regardless of when a product is made or when it is sold. Under absorption costing the overhead charge for fixed costs is dependent on the level of activity and so production costs increase when the level of activity decreases, and vice versa. These overhead charges do not, however, represent changes in the level of costs of the business. Also these fixed costs need to be incurred with the passage of time and absorption costing absorbs these costs into stock costs and recovers these costs when the product is sold, even in a future time period when the fixed costs are being incurred again for that period. These costs, however, relate to the firm in the period in which they are incurred, and are incurred due to the existence of the firm in that period. It can therefore be argued that it is logical to write them off to revenue in that period and marginal costing does so.

Restricts costs to controllable costs

Variable costs of production are controllable within the production process whereas fixed costs are not. Thus using marginal costing as a means of measuring production costs restricts the costs of production to those which are controllable by the managers responsible for production. The costs which are not controllable by them are treated as period costs. This helps the managers concerned with their planning and also enables responsibility to be restricted to those costs which can be influenced by the managers concerned. This in turn helps the firm and its managers to measure and evaluate the performance of particular operations within the firm.

Profits not dependent upon production levels

We have seen in that when absorption costing is used profit is dependent upon the level of sales and also the level of production. Thus when absorption costing is used profit can be earned in any particular period merely by producing more goods which are not sold but instead increase stock levels. This is because the fixed costs are absorbed into stock valuation and only charged to revenue when the stock is sold. Conversely when sales increase and this increased demand is satisfied by a reduction in stock levels, the profit earned does not increase in relation to the increased sales volume. Thus profit levels of the firm can be distorted by changing stock levels. When marginal costing is used, however, profit is entirely dependent upon the level of sales achieved and varies in accordance with these sales.

No under- or over-absorption of overheads

Under- or over-absorption of costs is due to the absorption of fixed costs into product costs. The overhead absorption rate is set based upon expected levels of costs and expected levels of activity. When the actual costs or activity level differ from the planned level this will result in an under- or over-absorption of these costs. Marginal costing, by contrast, is based entirely upon variable costs and so this situation cannot arise. Thus marginal costing avoids this complication and makes the accounting simpler to operate and to understand.

Cash flow comparisons

Profit is dependent upon the accounting method used, as we have seen, and does not necessarily relate to cash flow. Cash flow is dependent upon the level of sales achieved and the level of costs incurred in any particular time period. Marginal costing accounts for costs on the basis of those actually incurred and therefore marginal costing provides a closer approximation to the cash flow position of the firm than does absorption costing. Cash flow is important to a business and is more directly relevant to a firm's success and short-term survival than is its measurement of profit over the short term. A method of costing which approximates to the cash flow position of the firm has benefits therefore for planning future operations.

Helps pricing decisions

We have seen how changing the method of absorbing costs can influence the product costings and hence the prices set by the firm. Marginal costing determines the variable costs of producing a product or delivering a service, and any price set needs to at least cover the variable costs of production in order for it to be worthwhile for the firm to produce the product. The price need not, however, cover the full cost of the product in order for the firm to benefit from producing the product. Marginal costing determines the contribution made by a product towards fixed costs and profit, and this provides the basis for deciding whether a product is worth producing or not. Generally speaking a product is worth producing by a firm if its selling price exceeds its marginal cost and it therefore makes a contribution, provided no better alternative use for the resources employed in producing the product exists. Maximising the total contribution from the product mix can be seen as the way for a firm to maximise its profit.

The disadvantages of marginal costing

We have already seen that marginal costing cannot be used by a firm for its external reporting and stock valuation because of its failure to comply with SSAP9 and so one disadvantage of a firm using marginal costing in its decision-making is that it still needs to have an absorption costing system. This therefore necessitates a firm operating two costing systems, absorption costing for its external reporting and marginal costing for its decision-making. The use of IT in business, however, means that this is not an insuperable problem and computers make it realistic to operate two costing systems. There are, however, other disadvantages in using marginal costing:

Pricing may not cover total costs

While it may be advantageous for a firm to produce a product if its selling price exceeds its marginal cost and it thereby makes a contribution to fixed costs, this only applies to individual products and only in the short term. Within the total product mix of the firm it is necessary that the contributions from all the products at least cover the total fixed costs as well as each product covering its individual variable costs, because otherwise the firm will not be making a profit and will in fact be operating at a loss. While a firm can survive in the short term by operating at a loss, in order to do so it is utilising some of its net value (i.e. capital) in order to do so. Many firms do manage to survive in this manner for some time, particularly in a period of recession. The long-term survival of a business, however, is dependent upon it making a profit, and so decisions made based upon marginal costs need to ensure that over the whole product range and in the long term this leads to the firm making a profit.

Distorts revenue when stocks fluctuate

Although we have seen that marginal costing can eliminate profit fluctuations based upon stock level changes and production level changes, this can be a disadvantage for some businesses. For example, a manufacturer of seasonal goods will produce those goods throughout the year but only sell them at a particular time of year. Such a manufacturer will wish to ensure that the profit earned will be spread over the various periods of the accounting year. A marginal costing approach would show the firm making a loss throughout the year until the season in which the sales were made even though an overall profit would eventually be made from the production and sale of such products. This profit needs to be spread throughout the year in order to more truly represent the operating positions of the company and prevent excessive fluctuations in profit. This problem would be even more severe if the production cycle ran throughout more than one year. Absorption costing on the other hand can take into account these irregular production and sales patterns and reflect a more steady profit for the business and hence provides a better reflection of the actual operating situation of the business.

Understates the importance of fixed costs

Marginal costing separates fixed costs from the production process and charges them as period costs, thereby implying that the fixed costs are not relevant to the production process. In a modern manufacturing environment, however, fixed costs form an increasing part of production costs and in no situation can a firm produce products or deliver a service without incurring some fixed costs, such as the costs of buildings or plant and equipment. The exclusion of such fixed costs from a decision-making context based upon marginal costing ignores the importance of these fixed costs to the decision and can mean that the implications of any decision, as far as fixed costs are concerned, are ignored in the making of that decision. It is thus unwise to assume that fixed costs are not related to production but are merely time-based costs, and marginal costing tends to give this impression. Techniques such as ABC have also addressed this problem and sought to define costs differently.

Product costing for Franklin Technology Ltd

Franklin Technology Ltd has calculated the cost of production of its new product by using absorption costing. If we analyse its cost of production we can see that it is made up as follows:

	£	%
Direct costs	208	31
Absorbed manufacturing overheads		
Fixed	40	6
Variable	30	5
Absorbed non-manufacturing overheads		
General administrative costs	37	5
Development costs	240	36
Marketing costs	110	17
Total product cost	665	100

The company is concerned that its cost of production is higher than the market price for the product and so it cannot be sold profitable. However, if we consider the components of this cost of production we can see the following:

- The marginal cost of producing this new product is £238 (i.e. direct costs of £208 + variable overheads of £30) and so any price which could be charged for the product in excess of this amount would mean that the product would make a contribution towards fixed costs and profit, even if that price was below the calculated full cost of production of £665. It may therefore be worthwhile for Franklin Technology Ltd to produce and sell this product at a price exceeding marginal cost if no alternative use is available for the resources of the company. We will consider further the implications of alternative uses for resources when making decisions in Chapter 13.
- Fixed manufacturing costs and general administrative costs are costs which need to be incurred for the operating of the business, regardless of whether or not this product is manufactured. The basis of apportionment has been arrived at entirely based upon the planned level of production for the year and this may well not be the most appropriate basis for apportionment for all costs included under these headings. Thus the problem of allocation of costs is a feature of the costing method used, which would be eliminated by the use of marginal costing. We have considered previously the effect of using a different basis of apportionment and how this could result in a different cost of production. In the case of this product 12 per cent of the calculated cost of production of this new product is caused by these overheads and so a recalculation based upon different bases may make a significant difference to the cost of the product.
- Development costs account for 36 per cent of the total product cost but this calculated cost of £240 has again been arrived at by spreading the total development costs over the total planned production. It is probable that the development costs differ between products quite considerably and it would be reasonable to suggest that development costs be identified specifically to individual products. We do not, however, know what effect this would have upon the calculated cost of this particular product. Also this particular product has been developed already and so the development costs of this

product have already been incurred. We will consider the significance of this for decision-making in detail in Chapters 12 and 13.

- Marketing costs account for 17 per cent of the total product cost and again this has been calculated by spreading total marketing costs over the total planned production, and the marketing costs may well be different for different products. Indeed if this product does not go into production because it cannot be sold profitably there will be no marketing costs for it and the costs will need to be absorbed by the other products made by Franklin Technology Ltd. The marketing costs have been treated by the company as fixed costs but in reality some costs will be fixed, such as staff costs, while others will be variable, such as advertising. The variable costs can be attributed to particular products and treated as part of the marginal cost of that product.

We can see therefore the problems that arise from using absorption costing by Franklin Technology Ltd and how this gives them no basis upon which to make a decision about whether or not to launch this particular product. Using marginal costing, as calculated but revised to take into account the variable marketing costs, would provide the company with a basis from which to make this decision.

The relative merits of absorption and marginal costing

You will have noticed that the advantages of marginal costing are roughly the same as the disadvantages of absorption costing and vice versa, and thus neither method of costing is superior to the other in all circumstances. We have seen that certain SSAPs have the effect of requiring the use of absorption costing in the production of published accounts, although absorption costing can be modified through the use of ABC to give more accurate product costs. Nevertheless there still remains a place for marginal costing in business. Indeed marginal costing is of particular relevance to a business manager in planning the activities of the business, measuring performance and appraising projects. At this point we should understand that a business manager needs to understand the principles of all the differing methods of arriving at product costs which we have considered so far but that marginal costing is a technique which has been developed specifically for decision-making.

Social responsibility and costing

We saw in the last chapter how costs might be attributed to products in a way which makes clear environmental effects. In general terms social responsibility in the context of costing would require the clear identification of costs on the basis that the more clearly costs are identified and related to particular products or services, or to particular aspects of the production process, the more possible it is for managers to make appropriate decisions.

Further reading

Emmanuel, C., Otley, D. and Merchant, K. (1992). *Accounting for Management Control*. London: Chapman & Hall.
Sizer, J. (any edition). *An Insight Into Management Accounting*. Penguin.

Additional questions

Question 8.1

A company manufactures a single product with the following variable costs per unit:

Direct materials	£6.00
Direct labour	£7.50
Manufacturing overheads	£2.40

The selling price of the product is £35.00 per unit. Fixed manufacturing costs are expected to be £1 240 000 for the period. Fixed non-manufacturing costs are expected to be £765 000. Fixed manufacturing costs can be analysed as follows:

Production depts		Maintenance dept.	Stores dept.
1	2		
360 000	470 000	240 000	170 000

Stores department costs are related to materials issued. Issues are as follows:

Production dept. 1	35%
Production dept. 2	50%
Maintenance dept.	15%

40 per cent of the maintenance department costs are labour-related and the remaining 60 per cent are machine-related. Normal production department activity is:

	Direct labour (hours)	Machine (hours)	Production (units)
Dept. 1	90 000	3600	150 000
Dept. 2	120 000	3400	150 000

Fixed manufacturing overheads are absorbed on a per unit of production basis for each production department, based on normal activity.

Prepare a profit statement for the period using the full cost absorption costing system as described above, and showing each element of cost separately. Costs for the period were as per expectation, except for additional expenditure of £20 000 on fixed manufacturing overheads in production department 1. Production and sales were 146 000 and 144 000 respectively for the period.

Prepare a profit statement for the period using marginal costing principles instead.

Question 8.2

Galbraith Manufacturing Co. Ltd manufactures a single product with the following variable costs per unit:

Direct materials	£6.00
Direct labour	£6.50
Manufacturing overheads	£3.00

The selling price of the product is £40.00 per unit.

Fixed manufacturing costs are expected to amount to £1 265 000 for the period. Fixed non-manufacturing costs are expected to be £920 000. Fixed manufacturing costs can be analysed as follows:

Production depts		Service dept. (£)	General factory overheads (£)
1 (£)	2 (£)		
360 000	455 000	220 000	230 000

General factory costs represent space costs (e.g. lighting, heating and rent). Space utilisation is as follows:

Production dept. 1	45%
Production dept. 2	35%
Service dept.	20%

Service department costs are related to labour activity (50 per cent) and to machine activity (50 per cent). Normal production department activity is as follows:

	Direct labour (hours)	Machine (hours)	Production (units)
Dept. 1	70 000	3200	150 000
Dept. 2	110 000	2600	150 000

Fixed manufacturing overheads are absorbed at a predetermined rate per unit of production for each production department, based upon normal activity levels. The company operates a full absorption costing system.

Actual costs were as per expectations except for additional expenditure of £25 000 on fixed manufacturing overheads in department 1. Actual production level achieved and level of sales were 146 000 units.

Prepare a profit statement for the period.

Question 8.3

Hall Products Ltd makes three main products and uses basically similar equipment and production methods for each. At present a traditional absorption costing system is used by the company but the managing director is interested in the use of activity-based costing. She has therefore asked you, as management accountant, to evaluate the two methods of product costing by calculating the unit cost of each of the three products the company makes using both traditional and activity-based costing methods.

The following information is available to you:

	Product A	Product B	Product C
Labour hours per unit	0.5	1	1.3
Machine hours per unit	1	1.5	2.5
Materials cost per unit (£)	17	12	20
Annual volume (units)	1000	1500	6000

Production overheads are absorbed on the basis of machine hours at a rate of £24 per machine hour. Direct labour is paid at a rate of £8 per hour.

Analysis of production overheads has shown that they can be classified as follows:

Machining costs	35%
Set-up costs	30%
Materials handling costs	15%
Inspection costs	20%

Activities in respect of these classifications relate to the total production volume and have been established as follows:

	Product A	Product B	Product C
Number of set-ups	100	120	350
Number of materials movements	15	12	65
Number of inspections	100	240	500

9

Budgeting

Learning objectives

After studying this chapter you should be able to:

- explain the purpose of budgeting;
- describe the components of a budget;
- calculate the cash implication of a budget;
- discuss the purposes of budgetary control;
- discuss the implications of budgeting for managerial behaviour;
- describe the purposes of an operational control system;
- explain the impact of the budgeting process on managerial behaviour;
- discuss managerial behaviour in terms of motivation theories.

The function of management accounting

We have seen that management accounting can be used by the managers of a business in order to help them plan and control the operating of that business. Accounting can be seen to be the language of business, and using the language of accounting it is possible to translate operational problems and decisions into plans which are precise in nature. It is also possible to monitor those plans as they are put into effect and to control the business. Accounting can be used to measure not just the performance of the business but also the performance of individual departments, activities and even managers. The precise nature of the quantitative information given by accounting makes the evaluation of performance a relatively straightforward exercise. We have also seen that the communication of the plans for the business, and the subsequent performance of the business in terms of meeting the plan, is helped by the use of accounting. One of the main purposes of accounting information therefore is to aid communication throughout the organisation, as well as enabling the planning and control of the operations involved in the activity of the business. Another purpose of accounting information which is achieved through the budgeting and reporting system is to encourage goal congruence amongst the managers of the organisation. The techniques which we have investigated can be seen to be helpful to a business manager in understanding these functions of management.

Management accounting therefore is an important tool for business management and we have seen examples of how it can be used to achieve the following purposes:

● achieve operational control of the business;
● influence managerial behaviour and facilitate goal congruence;
● provide motivation to managers;
● measure and evaluate performance;
● plan the future of the business;
● facilitate decision-making.

We have also considered how the way in which accounting information, particularly management accounting information, is used can have an effect upon performance of the business and upon the behaviour of individual managers within the business. Additionally we have seen that some of the techniques of management accounting have problems associated with them and need to be understood within the context in which they are being used in order to be effective tools for managers. One of the contexts within which these techniques are used is that of the people themselves involved in the management process, as all organisations operate through people. We now need therefore to look in detail at the effect which the use of accounting for control and performance measurement purposes might have upon the people involved in the managing and operating of a business.

The budget planning process

The budgeting process is essentially a planning process for the operational activities of the firm. In terms of individual managers we have also seen that the budgeting process provides not just a means of communicating to them the plan for the business but also a means whereby the plan is translated into individual targets for managers to achieve in running that part of the business for which they are responsible. Research by Ronen and Livingstone (1975) has shown that managerial involvement in the budgeting process, through participation in the development of the budget, leads to higher motivation for managers to achieve the budget targets set. Thus involvement in the setting of targets leads to 'ownership' of those targets by the managers concerned and this in turn leads to a higher motivation towards the achievement of those targets. Similarly research by Rockness (1977) has shown that the setting of a budget which is difficult to achieve will result in better performance than the setting of one which is relatively easy to achieve.

Thus participation in the budgeting process will lead to better performance by managers and hence to better performance by the firm itself. In order to achieve this improved performance, however, managers must also believe that they are in a position to affect the achievement of the budget targets which have been set through the actions which they are able to take. Participation in the budgeting process must therefore be coupled with the responsibility for achieving the targets set and the autonomy to make decisions which will affect the achievement of those targets. Only if all these conditions exist will a manager feel that he/she actually owns the budget for that part of the business for which he/she is responsible and have the motivation to act accordingly. A socially responsible approach would of course recognise that managers are one of the stakeholders of the business who must be motivated not just for socially responsible behaviour by the business but also for the benefit of the business itself.

Alongside participation in the budgeting process therefore goes the responsibility for achieving the targets set in the process. The measurement of performance of individual managers must therefore reflect this and performance needs to be measured, not in terms of the operations for which the manager is responsible as reflected in the target level of performance set, but rather in terms of the operations which the manager can influence through the decisions made. In a modern company with highly interdependent processes this can become problematical. In a production environment, for example, the performance of one production process is dependent upon the performance of other processes in the production cycle. If a manager depends upon the receipt of components from another process in the cycle in order to manage the completion of the processing which is his/her responsibility then problems in that component production process can affect the performance of that manager in a way in which he/she cannot influence. Similarly in a service industry, such as a restaurant, the performance of the restaurant manager, in terms of customer throughput and satisfaction, is dependent upon the performance of the kitchen staff.

Performance measurement systems attempt to recognise these problems through a system of responsibility accounting but in an integrated business it is not easy to achieve this separation of performance accountability. Nevertheless the fact that individual performance can be influenced by factors outside the control of a manager can have a demotivational effect. The performance evaluation and reward systems need to recognise this and allow for it as far as possible. Failure to do so can lead to conflict between managers and a consequent waste of managerial effort and reduction in company performance.

One of the consequences of the introduction of conflict into the operational processes of a firm feeds back into the budgeting process and the way in which managers behave during the budget preparation cycle. This is that managers will attempt to introduce slack into the budget so that the elimination of that slack during the management of operations will help them achieve their targets whatever operational circumstances present themselves. Research by Williamson (1964) has emphasised that managers are motivated by the desire to achieve two sets of goals – the goals of the firm and their own personal goals. He suggests that personal goals can best be met by the introduction of slack into budgets which will help them achieve the targets by which their own performance will be evaluated. Schiff and Lewin (1970) have found evidence that managers create slack in the budget through both overstating costs and understating revenues. While the existence of slack in the plan for the company may help managers to achieve their personal goals it does not help the company to maximise its performance. This needs to be achieved through the elimination of slack, for which motivation of managers needs to be directed towards the maximisation of company performance through the promotion of goal congruence.

One further problem with budgeting which is brought about by senior managers involving themselves in the budgeting process by means of arbitrating between competing requirements for resources is that managers have a tendency to use the budgeting process as a means of bidding for resources for their own area of responsibility. Thus managers will overstate their requirement for resources in the expectation that senior management will allow less than is stated to be required and reduce the budgets accordingly. This tendency is also brought about by the competitive nature of managers and the fact that, in many firms, the control of a larger budget is perceived to increase the status of a manager relative to his fellow managers.

This is a dysfunctional consequence of budgeting which wastes managerial time but more importantly can lead to the allocation of resources being less than optimal. This happens if budgets are scaled down arbitrarily because the true need for resources for each manager's area of responsibility is hidden within his/her overstatement of a need for resources. Thus some managers may be allocated insufficient resources to maximise performance while others may still have slack within their budgets. This problem is brought about by the fact that the resources of the firm are scarce and insufficient to meet all needs when coupled with the desire of individual managers to achieve personal goals. Again the promotion of goal-congruent behaviour is needed to address this problem. One approach which has been introduced by firms to address this problem is the use of zero-based budgeting whereby managers need to justify their need for resources afresh for each budgeting cycle.

Influencing managerial behaviour

One of the most important functions of the accounting control system is to promote goal congruence within the organisation. The effect of goal congruence is that managers of the organisation seek, through their actions, to achieve the goals of the organisation. While it must be accepted that managers have their own personal goals, the control system of the organisation should seek to ensure that these personal managerial goals do not conflict with corporate goals. Ideally a manager, in seeking to achieve his/her personal goals, should at the same time be seeking to achieve the goals of the firm because these coincide. The budgeting system is an important mechanism for promoting goal congruence but the performance measurement system, by which managerial performance is evaluated against the targets derived from the budgeting system, is the most important vehicle for promoting goal congruence. Goal congruence can be encouraged within a firm by the reward structures for managerial performance and by the participatory involvement of managers in the planning stages of budgeting. In order to consider the effectiveness of these methods of encouraging goal congruence it is, however, necessary to consider motivational theory.

The expectancy theory of motivation was developed by Lawler (1973) and states that a person will be motivated to undertake a task by a combination of his/her expectation that he/she will be able to complete the task and the value which he/she personally attaches to the completion of that task. In other words the more important the task is to a person the greater the effort which will be put into its completion provided that the person considers that it is possible to complete the task. This theory of motivation therefore suggests that managers should set targets which are attainable but more importantly they should be involved in the setting of these targets (i.e. they should be involved in the budgeting process) and be given the responsibility for achieving these targets, with their rewards being linked to successful completion.

Herzberg (1966), on the other hand, divides the factors affecting motivation into two groups – hygiene factors and motivational factors. Hygiene factors are such things as working conditions, relationships with colleagues and superiors, and salary. His research showed that while dissatisfaction with these factors would demotivate a person at work and improvement in these factors would not provide a motivational force for a person. Motivation is provided by a different set of factors which include responsibility, recognition and a sense of achievement. Herzberg's theory therefore suggests that involvement in the planning process and responsibility for meeting targets together with the autonomy to influence the way in which these targets are met are important motivating forces while the rewards (financial rather than in terms of recognition) are less important, and need only be sufficient to prevent demotivation. This therefore implies that managers are not motivated primarily by money, and the rewards offered to managers need to take this into account. Thus while linking reward structures to performance is a part of the process of motivating a manager and encouraging goal congruence, it is actually the challenge set for that manager in terms of responsibility and autonomy which provides a motivating force when coupled with the recognition of the achievements made. Both of these motivation theories are based upon McGregor's Theory Y behaviour and provide insight into the way an organisation and its accounting information system should be structured in order to provide the maximum incentive for managerial performance.

In designing accounting control, budgeting and performance measurement systems it is important to design systems which address the motivational needs of managers as well as encouraging them to seek to achieve corporate objectives. It is necessary, however, to recognise that people are fallible and can make mistakes and fail to achieve targets. The feedback on performance which is provided is therefore a necessary part of the control system as it can provide information, not just to the individual manager but also to his/her superiors, at an early stage that a problem exists and targets may not be met. This enables corrective action to be taken at an early stage. If managers are involved in the target-setting process and are encouraged to set challenging targets for themselves then it is inevitable that some of those targets will not be achieved. If managers are punished for failure to achieve targets then this will provide a powerful demotivator for managers, who will be reluctant to agree to targets which are difficult to achieve. Overall company performance will thereby be reduced. It is important therefore that managers are rewarded, either financially or through recognition, for success but not penalised for failure, other than by the absence of rewards.

If the accounting control systems of a company are designed and managed properly, with due recognition of the individual needs of managers, as far as motivation and the achievement of personal goals are concerned, then these systems will provide an environment in which managers will be encouraged to maximise not just their individual performance but also corporate performance. Failure to recognise the behavioural implications of accounting control systems will, however, lead to dysfunctional behaviour, demotivation and conflict. It is imperative therefore that business managers are aware of these behavioural factors involved in accounting and take them into account when making decisions regarding the management of a business.

The essential nature of budgeting

Industrial Dies plc is a company which manufactures a variety of industrial chemicals using a standardised process which takes one month to complete for each product. Each production batch is started at the commencement of a period and transferred to finished goods at the end of the period. The cost structure of production, based upon current selling price, is:

	%	%
Sales price		100
Variable costs		
Raw materials	35	
Other variable costs	40	
Total variable costs (used for stock valuation)		75
Contribution		25

Activity levels are constant throughout the year and annual sales, which are made entirely on credit, amount to £30 million. The company is now planning to expand in order to increase sales volume by 50 per cent and unit sales price by 10 per cent. This expansion would not affect the fixed costs of £600 000 per month (which includes £120 000 for depreciation of plant). Variable cost per unit will not be affected by this expansion or by the price increase planned.

The current end of period working capital position is:

	£'000	£'000
Raw materials	750	
Work in progress	1600	
Finished goods	1875	4225
Debtors		2500
Cash		800
		7525
Creditors		875
Net working capital		6650

In order to facilitate the planned expansion the following operating conditions are expected:

● The average period of credit allowed to customers will be increased from one month to two, effective immediately.
● Suppliers will continue to be paid on monthly terms.
● Stocks of raw materials and finished goods will continue to be sufficient for one month's production and sales.
● There will be no changes to production periods and other variable costs will continue to be paid in the month of production.
● Increased production will commence in two month's time, necessitating increased raw materials purchasing the previous month.
● The planned price increase will take place in one month's time.
● Sales volume is expected to increase by 50 per cent in three months time.

The managing director has asked Angela Jones, the management accountant, to prepare a budget for the planned expansion, detailing the cash flow implications of the plan, the working capital requirements and the expected increase in profit resulting.

A budget for a business can simply be described as a plan for the future activity of that business. A budget, however, is specific in that this plan is quantified in financial terms in order to calculate the financial implications of that plan. We can see therefore that budgeting can help the planning process of the business by enabling the evaluation of the financial implications of the proposed activities of that business. We can see also that it can be used to compare alternative proposals for future activity and to evaluate them in terms of their respective financial implications. This comparison needs to be in terms of not just the financial result but also the achievement of the objectives of the business and the extent of its socially responsible behaviour. Thus we can again see that the role of accounting is to help make the decisions necessary to run a business, based upon informed evaluations.

A budget takes into account all the activities of the business. This includes not just its normal operations, which we have discussed previously in terms of production levels and product costing, but also possible changes in its operations. These changes can include capital investment, changing methods of operation and changing conditions of trading. Such a change is the case for Industrial Dies plc.

Budgeting is concerned with both short-term and long-term planning. Short-term planning focuses upon the next period, and is usually on a year by year basis. This plan is normally referred to as the budget, and comprises a detailed plan (in financial terms) of all the activities of the business. This budget is the subject matter of this chapter. Budgets are, however, produced for long-term planning and these are part of the Corporate Plan. Long-term budgets are, by their nature, less accurate than the annual budget and hence tend to be completed in less detail. The annual budget can be regarded as one stage in the fulfilment of the Corporate Plan.

Preparing budgets

A complete budget addresses all the activities of the organisation in detail, and in order to prepare such a budget it is necessary to start by compiling budgets for each activity which is undertaken within the organisation. This will normally be done at a departmental level and so each production department will start by forecasting its planned level of activity and calculating the financial effect of this planned activity level. Similarly each service department will produce a budget of the planned costs for its activities. Some costs are incurred centrally, such as rent and rates or telephone costs, and this budget calculation for these expenses will normally be carried out centrally by the accounts department. By combining all these cost budgets of the various departments and activity centres a budget for the total cost of the organisation can be built up.

The budget does not, however, consist just of the costs incurred by the business in its operations and it will be necessary to forecast also the revenue expected from its activities. This will consist of sales of the product or service provided by the business and the sales department will therefore also need to prepare a budget based upon the expected sales of the various products or services, based upon expected price levels. Indeed the sales budget is often considered to be the most important part of the budget and hence the first to

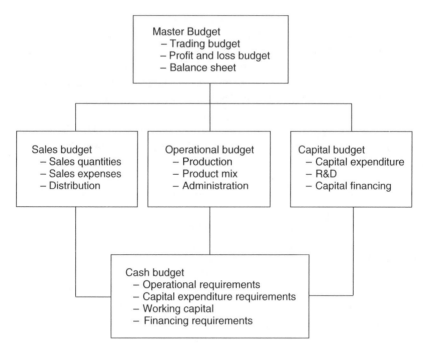

Figure 9.1 The Master Budget

be completed. The reason for this is that the firm will seek to produce the goods which it expects to sell rather than attempting to sell whatever the production budget suggests it can produce. The emphasis therefore is upon the market and the needs of the customer, rather than the needs of the firm. Combining this sales budget with the cost budget will enable a budget of all operational activity to be produced. This will, in turn, be combined with the budget for such items as capital expenditure and R&D to enable the overall budget, known as the Master Budget, to be produced.

The components of the Master Budget can be illustrated as shown in Figure 9.1.

Co-ordination and responsibility

The final budget needs to be feasible and this requires co-ordination. Thus it is essential that the production budget and the sales budget are related so that the planned level of sales matches the planned level of production, unless changes in stock level are planned. Similarly planned production, or purchase, of components must match the planned level and mix of final products and the planned activity level in each production department must be co-ordinated to ensure an achievable flow of production through the various departments. The budget therefore needs to be feasible in terms of it being possible to meet the various planned levels of activity but it must also be achievable in that the planned requirements for raw materials, labour and machine time can be met. Equally the planned level of sales and planned price levels need to meet expectations as far as market conditions are concerned.

We can see therefore that co-ordination is a requirement in the budgeting process in order to ensure that a feasible and achievable budget is produced. The production of this budget requires communication among all the people concerned in its production as well as co-operation in ensuring that a co-ordinated final budget is produced which is both realistic and feasible. The final version of the budget will only be arrived at after much discussion and revision of individual budgets in order to arrive at a satisfactorily feasible budget. In order to make this process effective it is necessary to have an overall budget co-ordinator (i.e. a nominated senior person) but also to assign responsibility for the production of each individual budget. It is normal to give this responsibility for the production of each individual budget to the manager who will be responsible for the achievement of that budget in actual operating conditions. This is known as responsibility budgeting.

Although negotiation is required in the budgeting process there is also a requirement that the budget be completed. This may mean that a budget is imposed upon certain people and this can have a demotivating effect upon the people concerned. An imposed budget is an example of a top-down method of budgeting while negotiating is an example of a bottom-up method of budget construction.

In preparing the budget it is normal to find that one particular factor provides an overriding limit to the activities of the organisation. This factor could be the production capacity of the plant, the availability of labour or raw materials, or the level of demand for the final product or service. This factor constrains the overall planning involved in the budgeting process and is known as the principle budget factor, or limiting factor. It is essential that this factor is identified so that the various budgets can be developed with due regard for this limitation.

It is possible for more than one limiting factor to exist and if this is the case then the budgeting process becomes more complicated and mathematical techniques are often used to plan optimal levels of activity. This is often the case in manufacturing environments where production is constrained by manufacturing limitations, or bottlenecks, in several processes. Limiting factors exist at a particular time and can be expected to change or be removed over the longer period. Indeed one of the functions of the long-term Corporate Plan is to address such issues as limiting factors and the action to be taken to remove them.

Working capital budgeting

A feasible budget needs to consider not just the production and sales levels to be achieved by the business but also the requirements of the business in terms of the working capital which will be required to put the plan into effect.

These requirements need to be considered not just for the start and end of the budget period but on a continual basis throughout the period. For example, a seasonal goods manufacturer, such as a toy manufacturer which sells most of its products in the pre-Christmas trading period, may start and finish its budget year with relatively low stock levels, but during the year will have a large build up of stock which is all sold off at one particular time of year according to its trading cycle. Such a trading pattern has obvious implications as far as working capital budgeting is concerned. The budget process needs to recognise this trading pattern and ensure that sufficient working capital exists throughout the year to finance this stock build-up and ensure that the budget remains feasible.

Although working capital includes stock and debtors (less creditors), which must all be budgeted for and managed, the primary concern of working capital budgeting is the cash situation of the organisation. The preparation of a cash budget therefore is an essential part of the budgeting process, and it is important to distinguish between profit arising from the activities of the firm and cash. Many firms may be operating profitably but suffer from a shortage of cash at particular periods. In fact a shortage of cash is the principal reason for the failure of seemingly profitable companies. The preparation of a cash budget is therefore a key part of the budgeting process.

It is not sufficient for a cash budget to be prepared in terms of the total requirements for the budget period, as what is important is to ensure that sufficient cash is available continuously throughout the year to meet the requirements of the business. Equally, however, at certain times of year a surplus of cash may exist within the business and if the budget makes this apparent it is possible for the business to make productive use of this cash rather than having a surplus sitting in its bank account. Thus a cash budget needs to be prepared month by month (or possibly even more frequently if a critical situation exists) in order to identify the maximum cash needs of the business during the period of the budget and to be able to plan to ensure that this cash is available when required. Businesses which fail are much more likely to do so because of a cash shortage than because they are trading unprofitably, and so cash management is a crucial part of business management. The cash budget therefore has a key role to play in the management of a business.

The cash budget is important for all organisations but is of particular importance if trading is seasonal, such as for a toy manufacturer, a major capital investment plan is being undertaken, or there is a major revision to trading conditions. The latter is the case as far as Industrial Dies plc is concerned.

In the case of Industrial Dies plc, the production budget could be produced merely by scaling up the current budget, as the cost structure of its operations remains unchanged. Also the sales budget can be calculated in a similar manner. The major changes from the planned expansion are in the terms of trade, which will affect working capital requirements, and in the cash flow of the company. Angela Jones therefore needs to recalculate the company's working capital requirements and the cash requirements stemming from these changes. A calculation of the changed working capital requirements would be as follows:

$$\text{Monthly sales} = \text{£30 million} \times \frac{1.5}{12} = \text{£3 750 000}$$

	£'000
Raw materials (one month) (3.75 million × 35%)	1 312
Work in progress (assume 50% increase for sales vol.)	2 400
Finished goods (one month) (3.75 million × 70%)	2 812
(i.e. at cost of production)	
Debtors (two months) (3.75 million × 2)	7 500
	14 024
Less creditors (one month's raw materials)	1 312
	12 712
Current working capital	6 650
Increased working capital requirement	6 062

This shows a significant increase in working capital requirements, and this will need to be financed. The increased cash from sales can be used to finance this increased working capital requirement but the timing of the cash flow changes is also important, as this will have implications as far as the cash requirements of the company are concerned.

A calculation of the cash implications of the expansion plans is therefore needed and a cash budget on a month by month basis will indicate the implications for cash flow of the plan. A cash budget for the next six months would be as follows:

	Month					
	1 (£'000)	2 (£'000)	3 (£'000)	4 (£'000)	5 (£'000)	6 (£'000)
Sales	2500	2500	2500	3750	3750	3750
Cash from sales	2500	–	2500	2500	2500	3750
Expenditure						
Raw materials	750	750	1312	1312	1312	1312
Variable costs	1000	1000	1000	1500	1500	1500
Fixed costs	480	480	480	480	480	480
Total expenditure	2230	2230	2792	3292	3292	3292
Net cash flow	270	(2230)	(292)	(792)	(792)	458
Opening cash balance	800	1070	(1160)	(1352)	(2144)	(2936)
Closing cash balance	1070	(1160)	(1352)	(2144)	(2936)	(2478)

This cash budget shows a net cash outflow during months 2–5 and even taking into account the cash in hand at the start of the expansion period it can be seen that there is a need for extra cash from month 2 onwards to finance the expansion of the business. Equally it can be seen that this need for extra cash is temporary in nature and the increased sales will generate sufficient cash in the longer term. The monthly cash flow will be generating a surplus from month 6 onwards but if we complete the cash budget for the next six months then we can see that the company will not be in surplus until month 12.

	Month					
	7 (£'000)	8 (£'000)	9 (£'000)	10 (£'000)	11 (£'000)	12 (£'000)
Sales	3750	3750	3750	3750	3750	3750
Cash from sales	3750	3750	3750	3750	3750	3750
Expenditure						
Raw materials	1312	1312	1312	1312	1312	1312
Variable costs	1500	1500	1500	1500	1500	1500
Fixed costs	480	480	480	480	480	480
Total expenditure	3292	3292	3292	3292	3292	3292
Net cash flow	458	458	458	458	458	458
Opening cash balance	(2478)	(2020)	(1562)	(1104)	(646)	(182)
Closing cash balance	(2020)	(1562)	(1104)	(646)	(182)	276

The preparation of a cash budget therefore reveals the need for extra cash in the short term to finance the expansion of the business whereas it can be seen that from the end of month 12 this need has disappeared. The preparation of an annual budget would not reveal this shortage of cash during the year as it has disappeared by the end of the year. Recognising this need for cash in the short term is crucial to the successful implementation of the expansion plans, however, for Industrial Dies plc. This illustrates the importance of the cash budget to the planning of operations for a business. Once it has been identified this need for cash will require to be satisfied and arrangements made for the availability of this extra cash. In the case of a large established company such as Industrial Dies plc a short-term need for cash, such as this, can often be best satisfied by means of a bank overdraft. A newer or less well-established company may find the source of extra cash more problematical however, especially if this need is for a longer period. Nevertheless the recognition of the need is the first step in the process of seeking such a cash inflow.

Relating cash budgets to profit

Cash budgets detail the expected cash inflows and outflows of a trading period whereas the profit expected during the period will depend upon normal accounting conventions. These include the separation of capital and revenue transactions, taking account of the accruals concept, and including relevant non-cash items such as depreciation. The cash budget and the budgeted profit for a period will never coincide therefore. This can be illustrated by considering the budgeted profit for Industrial Dies plc for the next year, which can be calculated as follows:

| | Month | | | | | |
	1 (£'000)	2 (£'000)	3 (£'000)	4 (£'000)	5 (£'000)	6 (£'000)
Sales less	2500	2500	2500	3750	3750	3750
Variable costs (70%)	1875	1875	1875	2812	2812	2812
Fixed costs	600	600	600	600	600	600
Profit	25	25	25	338	338	338

Comparison of operating profit and cash budget is as follows:

| | Month | | | | | |
	1 (£'000)	2 (£'000)	3 (£'000)	4 (£'000)	5 (£'000)	6 (£'000)
Net cash flow	270	(2230)	(292)	(792)	(792)	458
Profit	25	25	25	338	338	338

Approaches to budgeting

The value of budgeting as a planning tool is very much dependant upon the way in which budgeting is undertaken within the organisation. Obviously the more accurate the calculation of costs dependant upon activity levels is, the more accurate the budget is likely to be and hence the more useful it will be as a planning tool. This is particularly true if alternative courses of action are to be compared and evaluated. To be effective therefore this implies that all the activities of the organisation need to be re-evaluated at the start of the budgeting process, and only planned for inclusion if they can be justified in terms of business needs. This approach is known as zero-based budgeting (ZBB), which is defined by CIMA as follows:

> A method of budgeting whereby all activities are re-evaluated each time a budget is formulated. Each functional budget starts with the assumption that the function does not exist and is a zero cost. Increments of cost are compared with increments of benefit, culminating in the planning maximum benefit for a given budgeted cost.

While this is the ideal situation for budgeting it is time-consuming to produce budgets in this manner. Thus ZBB tends not to be used on a continuing basis but rather is used periodically to ensure that the resources asked for by managers are really required. In other words managers are expected to justify their need for resources periodically rather than on an ongoing basis in each budget cycle. Thus approach is used particularly in times of financial constraint, such as during a recession.

In reality managers will normally prepare budgets by considering current costs and activity levels and adjusting these into the future for known, or expected, variations in costs or levels of activity. This approach is known as incremental budgeting. Managers also tend to view the budgeting process as a mechanism for bidding for resources rather than as a planning process for optimising future production activities. They therefore have a tendency to overstate their resource requirements. The budgeting process therefore has other issues than planning incorporated into it and budgeting systems can have dysfunctional consequences for the organisation.

Budgetary control

We have seen how budgeting is an essential part of the planning process of a business, but budgets also form an essential part of the control process. This is known as budgetary control. The control of a particular budget is normally the responsibility of the manager in charge of the department concerned and responsible for the achievement of that part of the organisation's plan. Although this tends to be the responsibility of such individual managers the involvement of the members of the accounting department is required. These people tend to prepare the reports for budgetary control which report on actual performance against the plan, and have the technical expertise to assist managers in understanding and controlling their budgets. Indeed formal procedures, such as budget committees, may exist to formalise such arrangements. Responsibility accounting, the subject of the next chapter, is a system of accounting whereby costs and revenues are analysed into areas of personal responsibility so that the performance of budget holders can be evaluated in financial terms. In order to do this it is necessary to divide costs into controllable and non-controllable items, as follows:

- *Controllable costs*: These are items over which the manager has significant influence and against which it is possible to evaluate his/her performance.
- *Non-controllable costs*: These are items relevant to a particular department or budget head but outside the control of the manager responsible. It is therefore not possible to judge managerial performance in terms of these costs although it is important to remember that these costs are controllable by someone in the organisation. Non-controllable in this context merely means therefore as far as a particular budget holder is concerned.

Figure 9.2 The feedback loop

Budgetary control therefore provides a means of measuring and evaluating performance for each individual activity within the business as a means of controlling the overall performance of the business. This control is in terms of measuring performance against the initial plan (i.e. budget) and in terms of assigning responsibility for the achievement of that plan to individuals within the business. The principle of comparing budgeted costs and activity against the actual can be extended to all areas of the business. One mechanism for such control is in terms of flexible budgets by which the initial budget is altered to provide 'target costs' for the actual level of activity achieved. Thus control is exercised in terms of budgeted activity levels and budgeted costs and also in terms of revised budgeted costs (i.e. flexed budgets) for actual activity levels.

Budgetary control therefore forms an essential part of the feedback loop by which an organisation can evaluate performance against the plan (i.e. budget) and alter operations if necessary to ensure future achievement of the objectives of the plan.

The feedback loop in this context can be illustrated as shown in Figure 9.2.

Benefits and problems associated with budgeting

Budgeting can therefore be seen to be an essential part of the planning and control processes within an organisation. As such it has the following benefits:

- It provides a formal way in which the objectives of the organisation and its long-term plan can be translated into specific plans and tasks, providing clear guidelines to managers regarding current operations.
- It facilitates the comparison and selection between alternative courses of action and their evaluation.
- It provides a means of communicating organisational plans to all members of the organisation.
- Constraints upon production capability are highlighted (the limiting factor(s)).
- Preparing budgets provides an opportunity to review operations and revise if necessary.

- Performance at all levels of the organisation can be measured and evaluated against an accepted yardstick of the budgeted plan.

Budgeting, however, also has the following problems associated with it:

- As a planning tool budgeting is only as good as the calculations made and limitations on managerial calculation affect this.
- The budgeting process can be viewed as a competitive bidding for funds rather than as a planning process.
- The existence of detailed budgets can cause inflexibility and a resistance to adapting to changed business circumstances.
- Variations require explanation and this may use managerial time ineffectively if these explanations do not help future performance.
- Control through budgets can only be exercised by an 'after the event' comparison of actuals with budgets and this may be of little help as a guide to current operations.

Conclusions

The budget is a crucial tool for any business and no manager can escape the exposure to the use of these budgets as a tool for managing the business. Often, however, a manager only sees a part of the budget with which he/she is concerned whereas it is important to see the complete budget in order to understand how his/her contribution is being made to the overall performance of the organisation. Thus one of the important uses of the budget is as a communication tool to enable all within the organisation understand the plan for the organisation. A socially responsible approach would ensure that this communication happens.

The planning aspect of budgeting, however, is concerned with the matching of the available resources of the organisation with its intended activities – in order to meet the objectives of the organisation. Although the budget is expressed in financial terms the objectives will not necessarily be, particularly those concerned with social responsibility. These objectives, however, need to be converted into financial terms in order to be incorporated into the budget and more particularly to enable the other main function of the budget to be fulfilled – namely, to manage performance towards the achievement of the budgetary targets.

References

Herzberg, F. (1966). *Work and the Nature of Man*. London: Staples Press.
Lawler, E.E. (1973). *Motivation in Work Organizations*. New York: Wadswaorth.
Rockness, H.O. (1977). Expectancy theory in a budgetary setting: an experimental examination. *The Accounting Review*, 52, 893–903.

Ronen, J. and Livingstone, J.L. (1975). An expectancy theory approach to the motivational impact of budgets. *The Accounting Review*, 50, 671–685.

Schiff, M. and Lewin, A.Y. (1970). The impact of people on budgets. *The Accounting Review*, 45, 259–268.

Williamson, O.E. (1964). *The Economics of Discretionary Behaviour*. London: Prentice-Hall.

 ## Further reading

Emmanuel, C., Otley, D. and Merchant, K. (1992). *Accounting for Management Control*. London: Chapman & Hall.

McGregor, D. (1960). *The Human Side of Enterprise*. London: McGraw-Hill.

Sizer, J. (any edition). *An Insight into Management Accounting*. Harmondsworth: Penguin.

 ## Additional questions

Question 9.1

The Calculator Company Ltd has collected the following information to be used for the preparation of its budget for the next quarter:

Expected sales	10 000 units
Opening stock of finished goods	2 000 units
Closing stock of finished goods	2 000 units
Direct costs of production	
Labour	£30 000
Raw materials	£45 000
Overheads	£12 000
Fixed costs	£11 000
Selling price per unit	£15

All sales are for cash payable when the goods are supplied and all expenses are paid when incurred.

Prepare a cash budget for the coming quarter.

Question 9.2

The Carousel Co. Ltd is due to commence operations next month. Production costs of its single product are as follows:

Raw materials	£4.00 per unit
Direct labour	£2.00 per unit
Variable overhead	£0.40 per unit
Fixed factory costs (including £2000 depreciation)	£10 000 per month
Selling and admin. expenses (including £500 depreciation)	£3 000 per month

The selling price of the product has been set at £10.00 and it is expected that 75 per cent of sales will be for cash, with the cash being collected at the time of the sale. The remaining sales will be on credit and be paid in the month following the sale.

Stocks of raw materials will be maintained at one month's requirements and all expenses will be paid in the month incurred. There is no opening stock.

Production and sales have been estimated for the first four months of operations as follows:

	Production (units)	*Sales* (units)
Month 1	10 000	6 000
Month 2	10 000	8 000
Month 3	12 000	11 000
Month 4	12 000	12 000

Calculate the working capital requirements of the company in each of its first three months of operations.

Question 9.3

Budgeting is an essential part of the planning and control system of any organisation, and as such has many benefits to the organisation. There are, however, problems associated with budgeting which need to be recognised by the managers of any organisation. Identify the benefits and drawbacks of budgeting to an organisation.

10

The Management of Performance

Learning objectives

After studying this chapter you should be able to:

- explain the purpose of performance measurement and the associated problems;
- describe and use a variety of performance measurement techniques;
- critically evaluate agency theory in the context of managerial motivation;
- evaluate the role of accounting in the management of performance.

Introduction

We have looked at the need for operational control of a business and seen how management accounting forms a part of the control system of a business. For control systems to be effective they need to have a reporting mechanism built into them so that current performance can be evaluated, and corrective action taken if necessary to prevent deviations from the plan. Thus an important part of the control mechanism is feedback. This can be illustrated as shown in Figure 10.1.

Feedback is necessary so that individual managers can be informed of how the business is performing in relation to the planned level of performance and in order to indicate what corrective action needs to be taken in order to correct deviations from the plan. Thus individual managers need feedback on the performance of that part of the business for which they are responsible. Accounting information from the accounting control system, in the form of reports on current performance, is an important part of the feedback. This feedback needs to be frequent and regular but also needs to be timely so that the feedback is

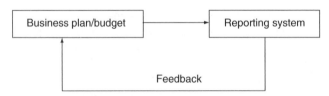

Figure 10.1 The control system

received as soon after the action as possible. This is important in order to ensure that the feedback can be related to the actual decisions made and to ensure that any corrective action can be speedily taken. Detailed feedback given long after the event is of little value in the operations of a business.

We have previously considered how accounting information can be used to help managers control that part of the business for which they are responsible. It is not sufficient, however, for each individual manager to ensure the optimum performance of his/her area of responsibility because this will not in itself necessarily lead to the optimisation of overall company performance. For optimum performance for the company, managers need to be aware of what the company's objectives are and how their own performance in the particular area for which they are responsible fits into the overall company plan. Equally the feedback on current performance needs to detail not just the performance of their own particular area but also the performance of the company as a whole. This will help managerial performance by enabling managers to assess their performance individually in terms of the overall company performance, and also help them to feel more involved in company performance. It also facilitates synergy as managers can see how certain action which they might take can influence company performance even if it does not necessarily improve their individual performance. Thus a team approach to management leads to better performance than does an individualistic approach.

The control of the performance of a business needs to be considered in terms of the people who are involved in that business and behavioural scientists have investigated in detail the factors that lead to improved performance in people. McGregor (1960) in his book, *The Human Side of Enterprise*, stated:

> Every managerial decision has behavioural consequences. Successful management depends – not alone, but significantly – upon the ability to predict and control human behaviour.

McGregor argued that managers' behaviour towards others was influenced by their assumptions regarding human nature. He separated these assumptions into two categories – Theory X and Theory Y. Theory X is based upon the assumption that people dislike work and will avoid it if at all possible, and that they have little ambition, want to avoid responsibility and be directed. Theory X therefore assumes that people need to be controlled and directed in order to get them to put effort into the achievement of organisational objectives.

This theory therefore requires strict control systems which report upon performance, particularly deviations from planned performance, not just to the person him or herself but also to his/her supervisor for corrective action. Theory Y on the other hand assumes that people are conscientious and committed, and capable of self-direction to meet the objectives of the company if committed to them. This theory leads to a greater co-operation in working and is based upon gaining commitment through an understanding of corporate goals.

Emery and Thorsrud (1963) identify six criteria which a job needs to have in order to maintain the interest of an employee. Such a job must:

- be reasonably demanding in terms other than sheer endurance, yet provide a certain amount of variety;
- allow the person to learn as he/she works;
- give the person an area of decision-making or responsibility which can be considered to be his/her own;
- increase the person's respect for the task he/she is undertaking;
- have a meaningful relationship with outside life;
- hold out some sort of desirable future, and not just in terms of promotion, because not everyone can be promoted.

The management of a business therefore needs to take into account the needs of the people working in that business, and this must be reflected in the control system of that business. Specifically this needs to be reflected in the setting of targets, the recognition of achievements and the reward structure for the level of performance achieved.

Setting of targets. The targets set for managers need to be achievable but research has shown that targets which are difficult to achieve and which stretch managers have a higher motivational effect than those which are relatively easy to achieve. On the other hand targets which are too difficult to achieve are felt to be unreasonable and therefore lead to a loss of motivation. Targets are set in the budgeting process, which we will consider later, but it is important to recognise here that research has also shown that people tend to set harder targets for themselves than those which are set for them by others. This suggests the need for managerial involvement in the budgeting process.

Recognising achievements. Recognition of achievements has a powerful motivational effect not only for the person recognised but also for others who are aware of the recognition given. It is for this reason that firms have tended to introduce achievement recognition systems such as the award of merit certificates, distinctions, 'manager of the month' schemes, and prizes for the best performance.

Rewarding performance. The reward structure for managers needs to be related to their performance in such a way that managers can relate their rewards directly to their performance. This performance, however, needs to be measured in such a way that individual managerial performance can be directly translated into company performance. Reward systems normally operate in the form of bonuses and the payment of a bonus can be related either to the individual manager meeting or exceeding his/her target level of performance or to the performance of the company as a whole. The first method aims to maximise individual performance while the second method aims to maximise company performance and stresses the fact that each individual is contributing towards company performance. There is merit in both methods of reward and it is for this reason that managerial rewards and payment tend to be linked to both, with a bonus payable partly for individual performance and partly for company performance.

The operational control systems of a business need to recognise the problems associated with setting standards of performance which are realistic and allow for the revision of standards on a regular basis. The systems also need to recognise that business circumstances can change, and that the economic and competitive climate can also change, thereby making these standards inappropriate. The control systems therefore need to be flexible and need to encourage maximum performance rather than merely the achievement of the standards set. This is particularly important in a modern business environment where the emphasis is upon quality and level of service rather than merely the control of the costs identified within the accounting system.

Stakeholder perspectives on performance

While few would argue with the claim that a business is an entity insofar as it is perceived to act as a whole towards the fulfilment of the particular objectives which it has, it is in reality a composite entity which consists of an association of individuals each working towards a commonalty of shared purpose. The actuality is different to this in that the common purpose is often not clearly identified and articulated and that the individuals are not necessarily working totally towards that common purpose, particularly when this purpose conflicts with or diverges from their individual motivations and objectives. This is particularly apparent when these individuals are considered within the context of the stakeholder community because the different stakeholder groupings have different desires and different motivations, which are often in conflict with those of other stakeholders. These conflicts need to be resolved in some fashion in order for the business to function and it is obvious that, as businesses do actually function, they end up being resolved by some means.

Just as the functioning of an organisation, however, can be seen to be a composite of its various constituents, so too does this reflect upon the performance of the business and the multiple facets of that performance. It is clear that the determination of good performance is dependent upon the perspective from which that performance is being considered and that what one stakeholder grouping might consider to be good performance may very well be considered by another grouping to be poor performance (Child 1984). The evaluation of performance therefore for a business depends not just upon the identification of adequate means of measuring that performance but also upon the determination of what good performance actually consists of. Just as the determination of standards of performance depends upon the perspective from which it is being evaluated, so too does the measurement of that performance, which needs suitably relevant measures to evaluate performance, not absolutely as this has no meaning, but within the context in which it is being evaluated. From an external perspective therefore a very different evaluation of performance might arise, but moreover a very different measurement of performance, implying a very different use of accounting in that measurement process, might arise.

The measurement of stakeholder performance is perhaps even more problematic than the measurement of financial performance. Objective measures of stakeholder performance are not reported in the annual reports of companies and therefore we have chosen to consider the subjective measures included within the 'Britain's Most Admired Companies' surveys annually published in *Management Today*. These measures provide a reputation rating, as gathered from 'rivals' perceptions, in nine categories and these measures are also added to provide a total score. The nine categories are:

- quality of management;
- quality of goods and services;
- capacity to innovate;
- quality of marketing;
- ability to retain top talent;
- community and environmental responsibility;
- financial soundness;
- value as long-term investment;
- and use of corporate assets.

These ratings have previously been used by academics especially in the environmental field, for a recent example see Toms (2000). As Toms notes, the use of such ratings is met by 'scepticism in some quarters' but the market does appear to value them. The 'Britain's Most Admired Companies' articles report on the ratings of 260 large UK companies in 26 different sectors each year. Due to the subjective nature of the scoring it is difficult to predict whether there would be an industry effect although it would appear that this is less likely. Also it is only the largest 260 companies that are included in these surveys and therefore no separate size effect test has been undertaken. The companies reported on are not necessarily the same for each year although there is a lot of overlap.

In considering the various stakeholders it is important to recognise that determining performance for each is problematic because there is not the certainty of financial information to measure performance. It is necessary therefore to use proxy measures which can be considered to give a representative indication of performance. Companies will tend to develop their own proxy measures of factors which they believe are important for their own stakeholders, examples include:

- quality of goods and services as a proxy measure of customer performance;
- the ability to retain top talent as a measure of employee performance;
- community and environmental responsibility for environmental performance.

One additional factor of concern to many companies is the capacity to innovate. Although it cannot strictly be considered as representing a concern with stakeholders we will consider it here because it is not subject to financial measurement. Let us look at the most important stakeholders in greater detail.

Customers

The quality of goods and services that a company has can be considered as a proxy for customer performance. What this measure appears to neglect is any reference to price or value for money but it will still provide information on an important and significant component of customer satisfaction.

Employees

The ability to retain top talent can be considered as a proxy for employee satisfaction, which relates back to our consideration of reward systems in the preceding chapter. Again this measure is not a perfect match and only considers 'top talent' rather than the whole workforce, although it is potentially true that the companies that score well in this respect have a different attitude to employees. Possibly for some companies such measures as days lost due to industrial action might be more important. Others might consider health and safety measures to be more important.

The environment

The environment, although not considered important by as many companies as consumers and employees, has been identified as important by a significant number of companies. This practitioner interest is certainly reflected by a very considerable academic interest over the last 20 years.

The capacity to innovate

It was decided to consider this rating here because of the importance placed upon innovation in Kaplan and Norton's 'Balanced Scorecard'. They 'recommend that managers define a complete internal-process value chain that starts with the innovation process' (Kaplan and Norton 1996: 82). This is not to say that innovation is the whole of the internal process, rather only the start.

The balanced scorecard

One factor of importance to all organisations, which comes from its control system, is the factor of performance measurement and evaluation. To evaluate performance it is necessary to measure performance and Churchman (1967) states that measurement needs the following components:

- language to express results;
- specification of objects to which the results will apply;
- standardisation for transferability between organisations or over time; and
- accuracy and control to permit evaluation.

Accounting information inevitably has a role to play in the evaluation of performance but Govindarajan (1984) suggests that a strong fit between environmental uncertainty and performance evaluation style is associated with higher business unit performance, and the higher the level of environmental uncertainty, the more subjective the approach to evaluation. As long ago as 1956, Ridgway considered the dysfunctional aspects of performance measurement and suggested that the use of purely quantitative measures of performance led to undesirable consequences for organisational performance (Ridgway 1956).

Various investigations have been undertaken into the actual practice of organisations concerning performance measurement and evaluation. Thus Fitzgerald et al. (1991) considered service businesses and suggested that business unit performance needs to be measured in relation to the objectives identified in the planning process. A variety of measures were used and were linked to the competitive environment, the service type, business strategy and the motivation and reward structure. Davis et al. (1992) considered multinational companies and found that a variety of financial and non-financial measures were in use, linked to organisational culture, but suggested that these measures could result in risk-minimising behaviour and short-term decision-making rather than optimal behaviour. Jackson (1986) considered the public sector and identified difficulties in setting measures appropriate to consumer needs but sufficiently standardised to be implemented. It therefore appears that a variety of performance measures are used and that there is widespread recognition of the need to link these to the strategy of the organisation and to the needs of the stakeholder community. It is also recognised that this is a difficult process which has not necessarily been adequately addressed.

Considerations of the role of accounting in the control of business operations therefore can be seen to be concerned with both the appropriateness of the use of accounting for such control and the appropriateness of particular techniques in the control process. Actual practice, however, recognises that accounting in isolation is insufficient for the control of business operations and that the context in which accounting is used is also important to the effectiveness of its use. Indeed the context determines just how accounting information is used, either within the organisation or externally to that organisation. There is a general recognition in the discourse that accounting and people are inseparable in any consideration of organisational decision-making and performance, with each affecting the other. There is, however, an implicit assumption of agency theory insofar as it is assumed that all managers in a firm are seeking to maximise benefit for the owners of the business and the discourse need only be concerned with how best to achieve this. This discourse is broadened by a consideration by the firm of its wider stakeholder community, in terms of issues of accountability.

There is considerable doubt therefore concerning the value of planning as a formal process for strategic management. The question of evaluating strategic performance is equally subject to debate and Chakravarthy (1986) suggests that traditional measures of performance based upon profitability are inadequate for evaluating strategic performance. He argues that, rather than using conventional financially based measures, alternative measures should be used, and suggests composite measures. He also suggests that rather than the conventional perspective of market-based evaluation of performance, alternative perspectives are needed which recognise the need to satisfy multiple stakeholders. Kimberley *et al.* (1983) also make this point and argue that traditional measures do not necessarily even measure some aspects of performance and can certainly lead to inadequate and misleading evaluations of performance. They state that:

> Traditional perspectives on performance tend to ignore the fact that organisations also perform in other, less observable arenas. Their performance in these arenas may in some cases be more powerful shapers of future possibilities than how they measure up on traditional criteria. And, paradoxically competence in the less observable arenas may be interpreted as incompetence by those whose judgements are based solely on traditional criteria. Particularly in the case of organisations serving the interests of more than one group where power is not highly skewed and orientations diverge, the ability to develop and maintain a variety of relationships in the context of diverse and perhaps contradictory pressure is critical yet not necessarily visible to the external observer. (p. 251)

It appears therefore that it is difficult to identify the determinants of the level of performance of an organisation and this point is made by Child (1974, 1975) who examines both the universality theory and the contingency theory of organisational behaviour and finds support for both theories. Kay (1993) considers organisational performance in terms of added value and suggests measures such as comparison of historic and current costs, measurement of shareholder value and cash flow, and capital costs and the equivalence of financial measures of performance. He argues that strategy involves identifying a firm's distinctive capabilities and applying them to appropriate markets. He also argues that strategy concerns the relationship between the firm and its competitors, customers and suppliers and that strategic management therefore needs an external focus rather than the internal focus of a planning model.

Stacey (1991) on the other hand argues that business organisations are feedback mechanisms and that parameters in the performance feedback mechanism need to take account of instability as well as stability, irregularity and random shocks, adapting to as well as shaping customer requirements, and an awareness that small changes escalate over time. He argues that rather than the traditional mechanistic, organic or power models of an organisation what is needed is the scientific chaos model. This model, he claims, recognises the following factors: complex patterns of behaviour, extreme sensitivity to change, hidden patterns, chaos is essential to innovation, and innovation emerges at critical points in the life cycle of the organisation. The implications of this model for strategic planning are that: long-term financial models are of little value, probabilistic models only help in the short term, long-term forecasts and simulations are impossible, long-term plans make no contribution to the business, and short interval control is vital. This model would seem to imply a total refutation of the value of planning and while it is true that plans become less reliable the further into the future they are projected this does not necessarily equate with their being valueless. Nevertheless a recognition of the existence of unpredictable events and behaviours is important and this seems to be the real value of chaos theory to organisational management and planning.

In a similar vein Dermer (1988) defines organisational order as a sustained pattern of behaviours and beliefs, and argues in favour of a pluralistic model of the organisation. He identifies the key elements of this model as leadership (i.e. management), citizenship (i.e. the various stakeholders), institutions (the formal and informal patterns of relating) and ideologies (the patterns of belief). He argues that the system of control for such an organisation consists of four components: managerially imposed regulations; self-regulatory activities; co-operation sufficient to permit commonalty rather than goal attainment; and a fit which implies accommodation among the various interest groups.

A different perspective upon performance evaluation has been proposed by Kaplan and Norton (1992) with the development of their balanced scorecard approach. They argue that traditional measurement systems in organisation are based upon the finance function and so have a control bias, but that the balanced scorecard puts strategy and vision at the centre. They identify four components of the balanced scorecard, each of equal importance, and each having associated goals and measures. The four components are:

1 *Financial perspective*: how does the firm look to shareholders;
2 *Customer perspective*: how do customers perceive the firm;
3 *Internal business perspective*: what must the firm excel at;
4 *Innovation and learning perspective*: can the firm continue to improve and create value.

Kaplan and Norton (1993) state that measurement is an integral part of strategy, stating

> Today's managers recognise the impact that measures have on performance. But they rarely think of measurement as an essential part of their strategy. For example, executives may introduce new strategies and innovative operating processes intended to achieve breakthrough performance, then continue to use the same short-term financial indicators they have used for decades, measures like return on investment, sales growth, and operating income. (p. 135)

and

> Effective measurement, however, must be an integral part of the management process. (p. 136)

They maintain that the balanced scorecard is a way of evaluating performance which recognises all the factors affecting performance and it is certainly true that an external perspective, in the shape of customers, is included in this framework. The framework they propose looks as in Figure 10.2. The scorecard enables companies to balance their short-run and long-run goals. It also highlights where results have been achieved by tradeoff of other objectives.

The scorecard uses four perspectives from which to view the firm. These are:

1 *Financial*: How the company is perceived by the shareholders?
2 *Customers*: How the company is perceived by its customers?
3 *Internal*: What must the company excel at (e.g. core competencies)?
4 *Innovation and learning*: How can future value be created?

Each business that adopts the approach develops its own purpose-built scorecard that reflects its 'mission, strategy, technology and culture'. The strength of the system is that it measures the success in achieving the strategies cascaded down by top management. There is often a divergence between mission statements, strategies and performance measures. The scorecard offers a mechanism to avoid this divergence. The scorecard could, for example, take a

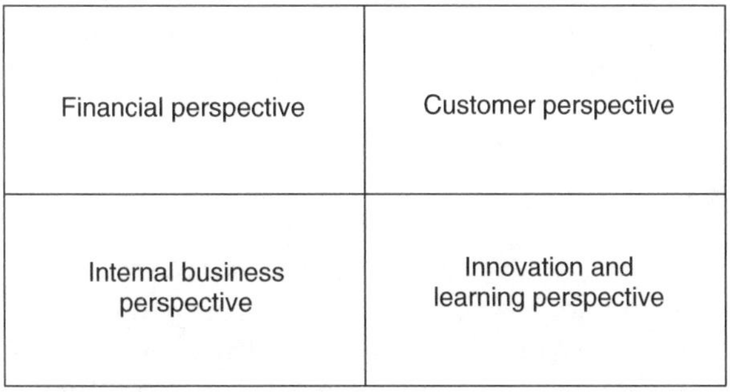

Financial perspective	Customer perspective
Internal business perspective	Innovation and learning perspective

Figure 10.2 The balanced scorecard

mission statement that has a customer focus and convert generally stated goals into specific objectives and then develop associated performance measures. In this example the measurement system may seek an interface with the customer's management information system. If the customer has a system for capturing data that assesses its suppliers, the firm could attempt to capture this information to enable it to judge its performance through the customer's eyes.

The balanced scorecard system, it is claimed, actually balances the competing needs of an organisation. In its original form (1992) the balanced scorecard was credited with the ability to 'allow managers to look at the business from four important perspectives'. The technique is claimed to focus upon the needs of the stakeholders of a business. Thus shareholders and customers are two specific stakeholders that are mentioned within the balanced scorecard. The focus upon innovation and learning however, and upon continuous improvement would also indicate the need for employee development and supplier relations should be incorporated within the internal-business-process perspective. In fact each business is expected to design and adopt its own scorecard to meet its own needs. Kaplan and Norton (1996) explicitly state that they 'don't think that all stakeholders are entitled to a position on a business unit's scorecard. The scorecard outcomes and performance drivers should measure those factors that create competitive advantage and breakthroughs for an organization'. The overarching objective of the balanced scorecard is to achieve both short-term and long-term financial success and is actually competing with other more explicitly shareholder-value-based approaches as a method to enable businesses to achieve this.

The measurement of performance

The measurement of performance is central to any consideration of performance evaluation and this resolves into two areas for consideration, namely why measure and what to measure. Measurement theory states that measurement is essentially a comparative process, and comparison provides the purpose for measurement. Measurement enables the comparison of the constituents of performance in the following areas:

- temporally by enabling the comparison of one time period with another;
- geographically by enabling the comparison of one business, sector or nation with another;
- strategically by enabling alternative courses of action and their projected consequences to be compared.

Performance itself is not absolute but rather comparative and it is essential in evaluating performance to be able to assess comparatively in the nature of 'better than expected', 'worse than the competition', etc. It is not possible to assess performance in other than these terms and so a quantitative approach to performance evaluation is essential even if some aspects of performance are qualitative in nature. It is necessary therefore that measurement is a constituent of performance evaluation and so it becomes necessary to determine what should be measured in order to evaluate performance. It is essential therefore to select appropriate measures for the purpose of the evaluation. It is argued, however, that appropriate measures cannot be selected until the purpose of evaluation has been determined. It is therefore again demonstrated that the foundation of performance measurement is the identification of the reasons for the evaluation of performance, and this must now be considered. It is clear from the evaluation of the literature, and a consideration of actual practice, that the evaluation of performance takes place for several reasons. Each of these reasons exists in isolation from the other reasons, and so can be examined separately.

Evaluation for control

In order to exercise control in the business environment it is necessary for the manager of the business to have information concerning the activities of that business. In order to determine whether or not the business, or that part of the business which is the concern of a particular manager, is operating as expected it is necessary in the first place that there is a plan for the activities of the business. It is also necessary that there be a means of evaluating the performance of the business in achieving the objectives of the plan. Evaluation is therefore necessary for the control of the business in order to measure and assess performance against the plan and to have a means of assessing any changes in control necessary to correct any deviations from that plan. The measures used for this purpose need to be appropriate and meaningful for the context in which they are used, and management accounting in particular has been developed for the control of the internal processes and activities of a business, as well as for the evaluation of internal opportunities for gain. The quantitative nature of accounting makes the comparative measurement of performance a relatively simple process and it has been suggested by Cherns (1978) that measurement equates with control. This proposition is overly simplistic but it is certainly the case that measurement facilitates evaluation, thereby enabling control to be exercised.

Evaluation for strategy formulation

Evaluation for control purposes is concerned primarily with past data and its present implications. Evaluation for strategy formulation purposes, however, has a future orientation, based upon the present, and, while taking into account past data, is rather concerned with predictions for the future. A business, in developing its strategy, is faced with a range of alternatives from which it must select those most appropriate to its current circumstances and constraints, future objectives and environmental stance. In order to select appropriate strategies it must have a means of evaluating these strategic alternatives in whatever terms it deems appropriate and relevant. The criteria for evaluating possible strategies are diverse and pertinent individually to each business. The process of evaluation however, through measurement and prediction, is common to all. Measurement can be seen to be the core of this evaluation and appropriate measures are needed. There is no reason to suppose that measures developed for control purposes will be appropriate for strategy formulation purposes, and measures used must be appropriate for the purpose to which they are put. Indeed they need to be developed for this purpose if they do not exist. To evaluate performance on any other basis is to negate the process by a failure to recognise the purpose of the evaluation.

Evaluation for accountability

Increasingly the external environment within which a business operates has changed and continues to change. While this affects both the strategy formulation and control purposes of performance evaluation it is of particular pertinence to the accountability purpose of evaluation. The increasing power and concern of all stakeholders within the wider stakeholder community of a business and the way in which their respective power continues to change have led to an increasing demand for the business to be accountable to them. This means that organisations have increasingly tended to adopt a stakeholder approach to performance evaluation rather than merely the much narrower traditional ownership approach. This has caused the recognition of the need for a different approach to performance measurement along the lines suggested by Eccles (1991). There is increasing concern with accountability therefore, rather than simply with accounting, with a greater emphasis upon social and environmental accounting, and with organisational accountability to its employees (Panozzo 1996). The need for suitable measures to evaluate performance in this wider context necessitates the adoption of new measures of performance, which are not necessarily appropriate for other evaluation purposes. Such measures are not necessarily always accounting-based and indeed are not necessarily even quantitative, although such measures need to facilitate comparison. At the same time, however, the needs of ownership accountability cannot be neglected. Accountability therefore is an area of performance which is increasing in importance and changing in nature thereby reflecting a changing need for the development of measures suitable for the evaluation of performance.

The reporting of performance

The evaluation of performance depends not just upon the appropriate measurement of performance but also upon the reporting of that performance. It is inevitable that each person or stakeholder grouping interested in the evaluation of the performance of an organisation needs a report, in some form, of the organisation's performance in order to undertake evaluation. It can be seen that the informational needs of different groups will differ considerably, depending upon their respective interests and concerns. The internal control needs, the needs of the owners, the needs of investors and potential investors, and the needs of the community as a stakeholder will all differ from each other and this poses a problem for the reporting of performance. In order to meet the reporting needs of the diverse stakeholder community it is necessary first to identify those needs, and this necessitates a consideration of the perspective of each stakeholder and a consideration of the interests in evaluation of the organisation's performance which is of importance to each stakeholder. These will be different between different groupings, which will therefore increase the reporting needs which the organisation must address.

The need for new measures to evaluate performance has to be set within the context of a changing external environment. Thus organisations are increasingly being concerned with a holistic approach (whereby the needs of the whole stakeholder community are considered), together with such issues as soft systems, culture and the establishment of competencies, as well as with accountability. This has led to the need to evaluate performance against a set of diverse and often conflicting criteria which have led to the development of measures to evaluate performance for quite different purposes. These performance evaluation needs have a tendency to lead to the creation of tensions within the organisational performance measurement system as organisations have sought to evaluate performance against conflicting criteria. This in turn has led to tensions within the operational systems of an organisation, as organisations have sought to meet often incompatible needs.

Agency theory suggests that the management of an organisation is undertaken on behalf of the owners of that organisation, in other words the shareholders. Consequently the management of value created by the organisation is only pertinent insofar as that value accrues to the shareholders of the firm. Implicit within this view of the management of the firm is that society at large, and consequently all other stakeholders to the organisation, will also benefit as a result of managing the performance of the organisation in this manner. From this perspective therefore the concerns are focused upon how to manage performance for the shareholders and how to report upon that performance (Myners 1998).

This view of an organisation has, however, been extensively challenged by many writers, who argue that the way to maximise performance for society at large is to both manage on behalf of all stakeholders and ensure that the value thereby created is not appropriated by the shareholders but is distributed to all stakeholders. Others such as Kay (1998) argue that this debate is sterile and that organisations maximise value creation not by a concern with either shareholders or stakeholders but by focusing upon the operational objectives of the firm and assuming that value creation, and equitable distribution will thereby follow.

Adherents to each of these conflicting philosophies regarding the method of managing a business in order to secure maximum value creation have a tendency to adopt different perspectives on the evaluation of performance. Thus good performance for one school of thought is assumed to be poor performance for another school of thought. Performance maximising philosophies are thus polarised in the discourse and this leads to a polarisation of performance reporting.

The evaluation of performance

A variety of measures exist to measure performance evaluatively, and while these have been criticised in their efficiency by some writers, it is nevertheless true that such measures have a role in this function. The efficiency of measures of performance can only be determined, however, by considering their use in the measurement of performance when the purpose of that measurement has been determined. It seems reasonable to argue that different purposes need different measures and that perhaps some, but by no means all, measures are universal in addressing all needs. Measurements derive their meaning, however, from the use to which they are applied, and mismeasurement by using measures incorrectly causes conflict and misunderstanding. Once a framework has been developed which identifies and addresses needs and purposes of evaluation it is then possible to consider the efficiency and effectiveness of existing measures and identify deficiencies in the measurement system. It is then possible to develop and implement new measures which are appropriate to the purposes identified.

It can readily be seen that the differing needs of different parties in the evaluation process cause tensions within the organisation as it seeks to meet its internal control, strategy formulation and accountability functions and produce a reporting structure to meet these needs. While the basic information required to satisfy these needs is the same, or at least derives from the same source data, the way in which it is analysed and used is different, which can lead to conflict within the organisation. Such conflict is exacerbated when a measure is adapted for one need but only at the expense of a deterioration in its appropriateness for another purpose. Part of the semiotic of corporate reporting, however, is that managers have the ability to manage information provision in such a way that all stakeholders can be satisfied both with the information received and with the performance of the organisation.

One factor of importance in performance evaluation is the concept of the sustainability of performance. It is therefore important for all stakeholders to be able to ascertain, or at least project, not just current performance but its implications for the future. Performance evaluation must therefore necessarily have a future orientation for all evaluations. The appropriate measures developed through this proposed framework are likely to facilitate a better projection of the sustainability of performance levels and the future impact of current performance. This is because the addressing of the needs of all stakeholders is likely to reveal factors which will impact upon future performance and which might not be considered if a more traditional approach was taken towards performance evaluation. An example might be the degree to which raw materials from renewable resources have become significant to many industries recently but were not considered at all until recently by any stakeholders of an organisation other than community and environmental pressure groups.

Accounting and other measurements

Traditionally performance has been measured in accounting terms using the annual report as the reporting mechanism for external reporting and management accounting reports for internal reporting. To some extent this has been determined by legal requirements and to some extent by the easily quantitative nature of accounting information. It has been increasingly argued, however, that accounting information does not provide a full picture of the performance of an organisation, and does not necessarily provide an accurate picture for those areas in which it does not report performance. One problem with accounting is that it lends itself to comparative analysis and has tended to be used for control purposes to track performance against budget. The purpose of doing so is to highlight problem areas for corrective action rather than to highlight areas of significance. Its use therefore has been essentially defensive rather than strategic. This use has been highlighted by Drucker (1985: 36–37) who argues that strategic opportunities for organisational benefit are missed because accounting information is used defensively. He states:

> Far more often, the unexpected success is simply not seen at all. Nobody pays any attention to it. Hence nobody exploits it . . . One reason for this blindness to the unexpected success is that our existing reporting systems do not as a rule report it, let alone clamour for management attention. Practically every company . . . has a monthly or quarterly report. The first sheet lists the areas in which performance is below expectations: it lists the problems and the shortfalls. At the meetings of the management group . . . everybody therefore focuses on the problem areas. No one even looks at the areas where the company has done better than expected. And if the unexpected success is not quantitative but qualitative . . . the figures will not even show the unexpected success as a rule.

This illustrates that the evaluation of performance is dependant not just upon the perspective of those evaluating performance but also upon the measurement and reporting system. It also illustrates the danger of accepting the presentation of accounting information as truth, rather than as interpretation of the situation. The increasing dissatisfaction with accounting as the sole means of measuring performance has led to the use of other measures in addition to accounting measures. Such measures include qualitative measures as well as quantitative measures. The development of new measures of performance has largely therefore, in recent times, taken place outside the arena of accounting and has reflected the increasing concerns of both organisations and society with such issues as quality and environmental impact. There is a need, however, to view accounting and other quantitative and qualitative measures not as separate systems for measuring performance but as parts of an integrated system, and attention has turned to this.

At the same time the means by which an organisation has reported upon performance have undergone considerable change (Eccles 1991) and the extent of disclosure of performance has changed from an emphasis upon minimisation to one of maximisation of disclosure. This is reflected in changes to corporate reports but also in the publication of environmental impact reports and the increasing use of press releases and general informative publicity. It is possible to track these changes over time to reveal changes in the extent of disclosure and also changes in the parties to whom disclosure is made. This arguably reflects a change from an ownership-reporting stance to one of a stakeholder stance.

The role of performance measurement

We commence our review by identifying the role of performance measurement and the context in which, it operates in the organisation. Nowadays, it is common for firms to adopt a mission statement. These statements explain the firm's raison d'être. They define purpose, scope, and boundaries, and should accord with the desires of the major stakeholders of the firm. By their nature, however, mission statements are very broad and generalised and this may cause a problem for managers attempting to understand how they can contribute to the success of the mission. To overcome this problem mission statements need to be made more specific. The firm will achieve this firstly, through the adoption of goals that assist it in moving towards its mission: the quantification of these goals establishes specific objectives. Secondly, the firm will develop a strategy that will determine the actions needed to achieve its stated objectives. Once the company has embarked upon its strategy it will need a system to assess regularly its success in implementing that strategy. This is where performance measures feature. Performance measurement provides this assessment system. Coates *et al.* (1993) state that performance measures serve the following purposes:

- directing and motivating managers to adopt goal congruent actions;
- to indicate the effectiveness of current strategies;
- providing a control mechanism for comparison of actual v. target performance;
- to provide a basis of remuneration, promotion and incentives.

They note, however, that often there is a difference between the definition of the overriding purpose given in the mission statement and the performance measures adopted to judge success. Thus, whilst marketing imperatives figure dominantly in mission statements few companies use measures that specifically assess market success. Instead, financial performance measures are commonly adopted.

Performance measures adopted by traditional management accounting emphasise efficiency and cost reduction as the route to greater profitability. Most companies use the level of profits earned as a measure of performance. Whilst the level of profit is important, on its own it is poor indicator of performance. Instead, profit adequacy requires expression in relation to the amount of capital resource utilised in the generation of that profit. The most common method of achieving this evaluation is through the measure of return on capital employed (ROCE). This is determined by the result of the firm's or division's net earnings before tax (NEBT) divided by the capital employed in the economic unit. Thus:

$$\text{ROCE} = \frac{\text{NEBT}}{\text{Capital employed}}$$

The widespread use of ROCE reflects the fact that the measure has many positive features. Specifically, it uses routinely collected accounting data, and as such it benefits from having low data collection cost and having the objectivity that is inherent in financial accounting numbers. In addition, ROCE makes possible performance comparisons across divisions of different size and business activity.

However, ROCE does suffer from several weaknesses which are well documented by Dearden (1969). For example, without specific adjustment, ROCE fails to recognise the effect of price changes. Thus, whilst profits relate to the current review period the asset base may be valued at costs incurred several decades ago. Apart from the technical weaknesses inherent in the measure, ROCE may also lead to dysfunctional manager behaviour. This dysfunctionality may manifest itself in a number of ways. It will be apparent that the achievement of an improved ROCE is possible by either increasing profits or reducing the level of asset employment. Managers may consider the manipulation of either, or both, of these variables to improve local short-term divisional results. This manipulation may, however, be detrimental to the long-term well-being of the overall company. We will illustrate this with two examples.

Firstly, managers may decline to invest in worthwhile projects. Traditional financial theory suggests that a company should adopt new projects that yield a positive NPV after being discounted at the firm's cost of capital. However, if the cost of capital is below the division's current ROCE, it is possible for an adopted project to yield a positive NPV whilst lowering the ROCE. In these circumstances managers, judged on ROCE performance, may be reluctant to embark upon a project which whilst beneficial for the company leads to a deterioration of its own ROCE.

Secondly, managers may decline to incur discretionary expenditure. Such actions, whilst enhancing short-term results, may cause damage to the longer-term well-being of the company. Within this category of discretionary expenditure are the costs of employee training and development, research and development, advertising expenditure and plant and building maintenance.

Managers can decide to reduce, or in some cases eliminate, discretionary expenditure in the short term with little apparent disadvantage. In the longer term, however, this expenditure creates the intangible assets that provide the company with its competitive advantage.

We may question why ROCE, introduced in the 1920s by the Du Pont organisation and successfully applied by many organisations for several decades since, has now run into problems in its application. Johnson and Kaplan offer six possible reasons:

1 there is currently greater pressure for good short-term results than prevailed several decades ago;
2 in the past managers were promoted less frequently and as such had to live with their decisions over longer periods;
3 decisions were more transparent in the smaller organisations of the past;
4 nowadays businesses are frequently run by managers with limited experience of the associated technology;
5 bonus and incentive schemes are commonly linked to accounting measures;
6 changes in the competitive, global macroeconomic and technological environments render traditional measures inappropriate.

To overcome the dysfunctional behaviour of rejecting projects that have positive NPVs but which result in returns below the current ROCE, some companies have adopted residual income as a performance measure. This approach was first introduced by the General Electric Company around the turn of the Second World War. Interestingly, the concept did not appear in management accounting literature, however, until the 1960s.

Residual income is determined by deducting a charge for the cost of capital from the NEBT. Using residual income as a performance measure overcomes the problem of the rejection of positive NPV projects. This is clear since a project that yields a positive NPV will be able to absorb a charge for the cost of capital and still increase residual value. An additional positive feature residual income has over ROCE is that it is possible to apply different costs of capital to projects with varying degrees of risk. The concept is, therefore, in accord with the risk–reward tradeoff adopted by the capital asset pricing model. Residual income thus has the ability to recognise different risk profiles whereas ROCE has no such ability. Residual income does have a downside, however, compared with ROCE in that it does not recognise the impact of size on an economic unit. It is clearly easier for a large division to earn a given residual income than for a smaller division. To overcome this problem companies often specify absolute target levels of residual income for their divisional companies.

Modern financial theory holds that the objective of the firm is shareholder wealth maximisation. It might appear appropriate, therefore, to utilise a performance measure with the capability to assess success in satisfying this objective. The firm achieves this firstly by evaluating strategic options to determine which of the available strategies should maximise shareholder wealth. The evaluation process utilises discounted cash flow (DCF) techniques in the evaluation of individual investment projects. The shareholder wealth maximisation (SWM) model, however, utilises DCF techniques to evaluate the strategies of the whole firm rather than simply those of individual projects. The firm then adopts those strategies that the evaluation process suggests will maximise the NPV of the firm as a whole. The pursuance of NPV-maximising strategies should in turn maximise the firm's share price and hence the wealth of its shareholders.

The ordinary share price is usually taken as a proxy for SWM. The theory holds that the share price represents the future dividend flow and capital gains enjoyed by ownership of the share. Implicit in this model is that the stock market is efficient. Accordingly, the share price is always correct, encompasses all risk and reward expectations and quickly incorporates new information. The market should thus correctly evaluate the NPV-maximising strategies adopted by the firm and the share price should reflect the maximising strategies. The evaluation of strategies using DCF techniques is, however, difficult in practice. It assumes that strategy formulation is a rational planned process whereas modern strategic theory suggests that in a complex and rapidly changing environment strategy is more likely to emerge through 'logical incrementalism' (Quinn 1980). The strategic planning process involves the firm positioning itself to take advantage of opportunities as they emerge rather than the pre-planned process assumed by Ansoff (1988). The incrementalist view holds that managers will not commit the firm to particular strategies at the outset, but instead will wait for a clearer picture to emerge as strategic options unfold. Thus, we can observe that the SWM model is actually attempting to evaluate options and the DCF model is unsuitable for option evaluation.

A number of features should be apparent from the foregoing. Firstly, performance measurement systems can influence the behaviour of managers. We have also seen that many of the traditional measures can cause dysfunctional behaviour. By contrast, an effective performance measurement system should have a positive impact on behaviour. Secondly, businesses operate in a dynamic environment typified by: global competition, mass customisation, shortened product life cycles, total quality management and continuous improvement. An effective performance management system should be capable of assessing the various imperatives critical to success in this dynamic setting. Clearly, simple financial measures cannot on their own convey how a firm is performing across this multitude of variables. In addition, financial measures suffer from being backwards focused. They indicate how well the firm has done, but do not address the firm's position to be successful in the future. Supplementary measures are, therefore, needed to assess how the firm is managing the factors that are critical to the future success of the firm.

Multi-dimensional performance management

Probably the best known of the multi-dimensional performance measurement frameworks is the *balanced scorecard* . Another example is the *service profit chain* which specifically considers three stakeholders – namely employees, customers and shareholders. Again this model specifically considers the first two stake-holders as means to achieving superior financial results. Thus it is argued that satisfied and motivated employees are essential if service quality is to be of a high standard and hence customers are to be satisfied. Further it is then argued that satisfied customers provide the base for superior financial results. Both of these models acknowledge the needs of stakeholder groups and thus deem it necessary to measure performance for these groups but still target financial performance as the ultimate goal.

A stakeholder-managed organisation therefore attempts to consider the diverse and conflicting interests of its stakeholders and balance these inter-ests equitably. The motivations for organisations to use stakeholder manage-ment maybe in order to improve financial performance or social or ethical performance, howsoever these may be measured. In order to be able to adequately manage stakeholder interests it is necessary to measure the organisation's performance to these stakeholders and this can prove compli-cated and time-consuming.

Agency theory

It is important to recognise that management accounting has traditionally emphasised a normative concern for defining 'best practice'. Under this approach, the firm is assumed to exist for the benefit of its owners who are assumed to be solely interested in the maximisation of their wealth. Man-agers, on the other hand, are the decision-makers in an organisation and they are implicitly assumed to automatically act in the best interests of owners, either because they are also the owners or because they share the same inter-ests. In other words, managers are assumed to make the same decisions that owners would make, irrespective of the effect on their personal interests. In this context, according to Fox (1984), the main problems of decision-making relate to:

1 the timing of cash flows;
2 the estimation of risk;
3 the effects of resource constraints;
4 the cost of information.

Managers are, therefore, assumed to assess objectively alternative actions, and always select the option favoured by the owners of the firm. The manage-ment accountant, therefore, is then concerned with providing the 'right' infor-mation combined with the 'right' decision model which will help the manager make the 'right' decision. An obvious criticism of this approach, however, is that it fails to recognise that managers may not share the same interests as owners, and that this is likely to impact upon real-world decision-making. Agency theory attempts to address this problem, by providing a more realistic representation of decision-making.

Agency theory therefore recognises that people are unlikely to ignore their own self-interest in making decisions; in other words people do not behave altruistically. It is a relatively new approach to analysing decision-making which provides a framework within which the political and behavioural aspects of decision-making can be considered as part of the decision-making process. The theory is therefore positive rather than normative as it seeks to understand and explain what happens in practice rather than seeking to prescribe what ought to happen. It recognises that the manager is an agent of the owners of the firm, whose actions the management accounting system seeks to influence.

An agency relationship exists whenever one party, the principal (P), hires another party, the agent (A), to perform some task. This applies to many superior – subordinate relationships in business and elsewhere, and in a management accounting context, agency relationships can be seen to exist between shareholders and directors, between directors and managers (including divisional managers), and between managers and other employees. In this chapter, we will concentrate on the relationship between the owners of the firm and its managers – in other words the owner–manager principal–agent relationship.

Under agency theory both P and A are assumed to be rational economic persons: in other words they know what they are doing and they act consistently and rationally. They are both assumed to be motivated by self-interest alone, although the theory recognises that they possess different preferences, beliefs and information. Both wish to maximise their own 'utility' (the value or benefit they place on any economic good they receive). P and A may also have different attitudes to risk, an issue to which we return later. Agency theory is concerned with the design of effective contracts between the P and A, which specify the combination of incentives, risk-sharing and information system which maximise the utility of P subject to the constraints imposed by ensuring that A's self-interest will also be served through his/her actions. Thus agency theory provides a means of establishing a contract between the principal and the agent which will lead to optimal performance by the agent on behalf of the principal. This can be depicted as shown in Figure 10.3.

Focusing on the shareholder–manager agency relationship, the key elements of agency theory will now be examined.

The owners of the firm provide capital to the firm, and are assumed to be interested solely in the returns to be derived from their use of capital in the firm – in other words the expected monetary value of their investment. Managers,

Figure 10.3 Optimal contracts: balancing risk, incentives and choice of information system

on the other hand, derive utility not only from their wealth provided through their employment in the firm, but also from their leisure time, when they are not employed by the firm. Thus managers derive utility from all their activities, whether or not these activities are associated with the firm by which they are employed. It is important to appreciate this distinction between 'utility' and 'monetary wealth' in this context, as utility applies to well-being in general rather than simply to wealth.

While it is certainly true that managers derive utility from additional wealth, it must be recognised that this is unlikely to be in the form of a linear relationship whereby each increment to wealth results in the same addition to utility. Managers will derive greater incremental utility from additions to wealth from lower levels of wealth, but as wealth increases the extra amount of utility gained from each unit in addition to wealth will diminish. In other words, the utility which managers derive from wealth is subject to decreasing marginal returns.

For example, a manager who is paid £100 000 per annum derives greater utility from the first £10 000 of pay than that which takes his pay from £90 000 to £100 000. At higher levels of pay, non-financial factors associated with employment such as status, job-related pressure and so on take on greater significance.

The manager's utility function in relation to income received from employment is shown in Figure 10.4.

In addition however, managers are assumed to value their own leisure time, which means that they attach disutility to effort. The extra utility which is derived from higher levels of compensation is offest, therefore, by the negative utility which is derived from any extra effort required of the manager to achieve that higher level of compensation. The term 'leisure' in this context is defined as the opposite of any effort that increases the expected value of the firm to its owners. It includes the manager's consumption of so-called 'perquisites' (commonly known as perks), which are benefits relating to the job such as company cars, lavish offices and so on. The consumption of such perquisites diverts the owners' capital away from

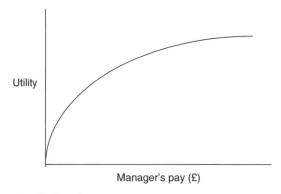

Figure 10.4 Manager's utility function

what the owners would regard as desirable productive investments into the manager's own consumption.

Therefore, to summarise, the owners supply capital to the firm and hire managers to act on their behalf. Managers allocate their time at work between productive effort and leisure ('shirking'), and also allocate the firm's resources between productive investments and the consumption of perquisites.

An intuitive solution to the above situation would be for owners to simply monitor the actions of managers to reduce shirking and the over-consumption of perquisites. This, however, can be extremely difficult in practice. There are several reasons why this monitoring is difficult in practice. Firstly, the tasks undertaken by managers are generally considered to be relatively complex and consequently not well understood by the owners who are not involved in the detailed running of the business. Secondly, the decisions made by managers are taken in an uncertain environment, which makes it difficult for owners to judge the appropriateness of managerial actions in any particular set of circumstances. Finally, and perhaps most importantly, information is not evenly distributed between managers and owners. This problem is known as 'information asymmetry' and has two separate, though related elements: moral hazard and adverse selection.

Moral hazard

Moral hazard arises where it is difficult or costly for owners to observe or infer the amount of effort exerted by managers. In such a situation, there is an inevitable temptation for managers to avoid working to the terms of the agreed employment contract, since owners are unable to assess the 'true picture'. Managers may also have the incentive as well as the means to conceal the 'true picture' by misrepresenting the actual outcomes reported to the owners. Accounting provides one such means for misrepresentation through its ability to represent outcomes from any course of action in more than one way – a point which we will return to in subsequent chapters.

Adverse selection

Whereas moral hazard relates to the 'post-decision' consequences of information asymmetry, adverse selection is concerned with the 'pre-decision' situation. Since all the information that is available to the manager at the time a decision is made is not also available to the owner, the owner cannot be sure that the manager made the right decision in the circumstances. In addition, the manager has no incentive to reveal what he/she knows since this will then make it easier for the principal to properly assess his/her actions in the future. This is known as 'information impactedness'.

The existence of 'information asymmetry' means that for owners to obtain relevant information concerning the manager's effort, they must either rely on the communications received from the managers themselves or incur monitoring costs. An example of monitoring costs would include the annual audit of the firm's financial statements; indeed such auditing of financial statements was instituted as a means of safeguarding such investments in firms made by those who had no part in the operational activity of the firm. In the context of the agency relationship between top management and divisional management, such monitoring costs would include the cost of employing head office staff to monitor the performance of divisions. One approach to this problem is to get managers to commit to acting in the best interests of the owners, but in this situation the owners will incur a bonding cost to effect this relationship. Even in this situation, however, since managers may not share the same beliefs and preferences as the owner, there may still be a 'residual loss'.

Information asymmetry can be depicted as shown in Figure 10.5.

Agency theory, as applied in practice, is concerned with the design of employment contracts which reduce shirking and the consumption of perquisites, so that instead of acting in their own interests managers act more in the interests of the owners of the firm. Solutions to agency problems are often described as 'second-best'. This is due to the conflicting implications of the incentive-effect and the risk-sharing aspects of the agency relationship. These should be inter-related as shown in Figure 10.6.

On the one hand, the optimal contract should achieve optimal risk-sharing. As the owner is able to hold a diversified portfolio of shares, it is usually assumed that he is risk-neutral and will not take risk into account in deciding between one course of action and another. The manager, on the other hand, clearly cannot diversify his job, and is more likely to be risk-averse and hence to make risk-minimising decisions. In this situation therefore optimal risk-sharing would imply that the owner of the firm should bear the most risk, since the manager will require compensation for risk-bearing, whereas the owner will not. A flat fee paid to the manager irrespective of performance achieves this, since the manager's salary is shielded from the uncertainty which affects expected outcomes. Such a flat fee as remuneration for the

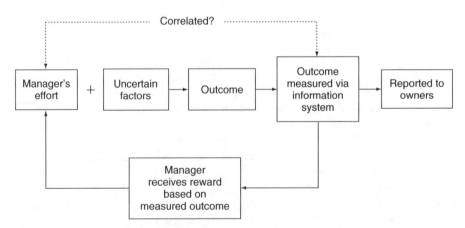

Figure 10.5 Information asymmetry

Figure 10.6 Interrelations between the incentive-effect and the risk-sharing aspects

manager's effort, however, provides no incentive for the manager to exert optimum effort. Due to the fact that the manager's effort cannot realistically be observed, only if the manager's income is linked to performance will the manager be motivated to contribute more effort. This, in turn, exposes the manager to risk. A double-edged sword is evident. The more a manager's income is dependent upon performance, the greater will be the incentive effect, yet at the same time, the sharing of risk becomes increasingly sub-optimal. The 'first-best' solution would be to pay a flat fee to reward 'conscientious' managers who do exert optimum effort. Such a 'first-best' solution is not viable, however, since it is not realistically possible to judge whether or not a manager has acted 'conscientiously' in any particular set of circumstances.

The implications of agency theory for management accounting

There are four ways in which this theory has implications as far as management accounting is concerned, as follows:

The decision-making process

Management accounting is concerned with the provision of information which aids decision-making. Agency theory throws new light on how this process works in practice, which in itself, is of benefit to management accounting.

The design of new accounting information systems

Agency theory also provides an improved awareness of the impact of new information systems on the behaviour of managers which could potentially lead to an improvement in their design.

From an agency theory perspective, accounting information is required for two purposes. Firstly, at the pre-decision stage, information is required by the agent (and principal) about the expected state of the world as an aid to decision-making. Secondly, at the post-decision stage, information is required concerning the outcome achieved, as an aid to performance evaluation. Post-decision information has received the most attention in the literature. It has been demonstrated that any information about the agent's effort, even if it is partial or only partially accurate, has positive value to the principal, and can never give rise to a Pareto-inferior result, providing the information can be obtained at no cost.

Turning to pre-decision information, extra information made available to the agent after the contract has been agreed but before effort has been expended could make the principal worse off, since, although on the one hand the agent is better informed, on the other, the agent is relieved of some of the uncertainty concerning the outcome which may reduce his motivation.

Participation in budgeting

Agency theory also provides insights into the effect of participation in the setting of budgets and standards. Traditionally the potential creation of budgetary slack has been seen as a potential downside of participation, but there was little to explain why this should arise, except perhaps because some managers were more cynical and devious than others. Agency theory, however, predicts that managers will engage in the budget setting process in a rational manner, with the aim being to maximise their own expected utility. Budgetary slack is therefore an entirely logical outcome given the existence of asymmetric pre-decision information. The implication of this is that there may be a need for better information for the principal.

Responsibility accounting systems

Responsibility accounting is, arguably, one of the major themes of the traditional 'textbook' approach to management accounting. The principle behind this system is that the evaluation of the performance of a manager should be based only on those factors under his control. Agency theory takes a different perspective. If the principal is risk-neutral, then the performance-related reward is for motivational reasons only, and in that case may be linked to areas over which the manager may exert influence. If, however, the principal is risk-averse then the manager should not be shielded from the effects of uncertainty and should, therefore, bear at least some of the risks associated with the possible outcomes of decisions. Otherwise, the manager will behave as if he was risk-neutral, which may not result in the maximisation of the principal's utility.

Conclusions

Accounting information is widely used for the management of performance within an organisation. This is because of the way it can be used to measure that performance. Equally, of course, accounting information is widely recognised as being insufficient to give an accurate picture of the performance of the organisation. This is especially true if a socially responsible approach is adopted and it is for this reason that a variety of other measures have been adopted by organisations. Techniques such as the balanced scorecard attempt to give a rounded picture of an organisation and recognise the importance of the various stakeholders to the organisation.

At the same time the management of the performance of the organisation is in the hands of its managers, who are responsible for seeking to ensure that performance is in accordance with the objectives of the organisation. The budget, which we discussed in the last chapter, is one of the major ways of achieving this. Managers are very often rewarded according to how well they achieve the objectives of their organisation, as reflected in the budgetary plan and agency theory provides a basis for establishing a reward structure which provides appropriate incentives.

References

Ansoff, H.I. (1988). *Corporate Strategy*. London: Pelican.

Chakravarthy, B.S. (1986). Measuring strategic performance. *Strategic Management Journal*, 7, 437–458.

Cherns, A.B. (1978). Alienation and accountancy. *Accounting, Organizations and Society*, 3 (2), 105–114.

Child, J. (1974). Managerial and organisational factors associated with company performance – part 1. *Journal of Management Studies*, 11, 73–189.

Child, J. (1975). Managerial and organisational factors associated with company performance – part 2. *Journal of Management Studies*, 12, 12–27.

Child, J. (1984). *Organisation: A Guide to Problems and Practice*. London: Harper & Row.

Churchman, C.W. (1967). Why measure. In C.W. Chuchman and P. Ratoosh (eds), *Measurement: Definition and Theories*. London: Wiley, pp. 83–94.

Coates, J.B., Davis, E.W., Longden, S.G., Stacey, R.J. and Emmanuel, C. (1993). *Corporate Performance Evaluation in Multinationals*. London: CIMA.

Davis, E.W., Coates, J.B., Emmanuel, C.R., Longden, S.G. and Stacey, R.J. (1992). Multinational companies performance measurement systems: international perspectives. *Management Accounting Research*, 3, 102–124.

Dearden, J. (1969). The case against ROI control. *Harvard Business Review*, 47 (3), 124–135.

Dermer, J. (1988). Control and organisational order. *Accounting, Organizations and Society*, 13 (1), 25–36.

Drucker, P.F. (1985). *Innovation and Entrepreneurship*. Oxford: Butterworth-Heinemann.

Eccles, R.G. (1991). The performance evaluation manifesto. *Harvard Business Review*, 69 (1), 131–137.

Emery, F.E. and Thorsrud, E. (1963). *Form and Content in Industrial Democracy*. London: Tavistock.

Fitzgerald, L., Johnston, R., Brignall, S., Silvestro, R. and Voss, C. (1991). *Performance Measurement in Service Businesses*. London: CIMA.

Fox, R.E. (1984). Main bottleneck on the factory floor? *Management Review*, November, 55–61.

Govindarajan, V. (1984). Appropriateness of accounting data in performance evaluation: an empirical examination of environmental uncertainty as an intervening variable. *Accounting, Organizations and Society*, 9 (2), 125–135.

Jackson, P. (1986). Performance measurement and value for money in the public sector. In *Research in Action – Performance Measurement*; ICAS & CIPFA Conference proceedings, London.

Kaplan, R.S. and Norton, D.P. (1992). The balanced scorecard – measures that drive performance. *Harvard Business Review*, Jan./Feb., 71–79.

Kaplan, R.S. and Norton, D.P. (1993). Putting the balanced scorecard to work. *Harvard Business Review, Sept./Oct.*, 134–147.

Kaplan, R.S. and Norton, D.P. (1996). Using the Balanced Scorecard as a strategic management system, *Harvard Business Review*, Jan./Feb., 75–85.

Kay, J. (1993). *Foundations of Corporate Success*. Oxford: OUP.

Kay, J. (1998). Good business. *Prospect, 28 (March)*, 25–29.

Kimberley, J., Norling, R. and Weiss, J.A. (1983). Pondering the performance puzzle: effectiveness in interorganisational settings. In R.H. Hall and R.E. Quinn (eds), *Organisational Theory and Public Practice*. Beverly Hills: Sage, pp. 249–264.

McGregor, D. (1960). *The Human Side of Enterprise*. London: McGraw-Hill.

Myners, P. (1998). Improving performance reporting to the market. In A. Carey and J. Sancto (eds), *Performance Measurement in the Digital Age*. London: ICAEW, pp. 27–33.

Panozzo, F. (1996). Accountability and identity: accounting and the democratic organization. In R. Munro and J. Mouritsen (eds), *Accountability*. London: International Thomson.

Quinn, J.B. (1980). *Strategies for Change*. Irwin.

Ridgway, W.F. (1956). Dysfunctional consequences of performance measurement. *Administrative Sciences Quarterly, 1 (2)*, 240–247.

Stacey, R.D. (1991). *The Chaos Frontier*. Oxford: Butterworth-Heinemann.

Toms, J.S. (2000). *Environmental Management, Environmental Accounting and Financial Performance*. London: CIMA.

Additional questions

Question 10.1

Your manager has called you into her office and says to you:
'I have worked out the budgets for next year. This is what you are responsible for:'

	£
Direct materials	200 000
Direct labour (12 people)	125 000
Allocated machine costs	
Operating expenses	80 000
Depreciation	24 000
Allocated production overheads	35 120
Allocated admin. expenses	12 346
	476 466

Budgeted production: 125 000 units

She continues: 'It is a tough budget to achieve but I am sure you will do your best.'

You know that your performance will be assessed on how you perform in relation to this budget and that your bonus is dependant upon you achieving this budget.

Outline the likely problems caused by this approach to budgeting and the essential features of a budgeting system which aims to maximise organisational and individual performance.

Question 10.2

Greenfield Consulting is a management consulting firm with offices in several major cities. The managers of the various offices have been complaining continually about the difficulty they have in meeting the targets set for them by the senior management of the firm. These targets are set in the budgeting process and include targets for both cost containment and for income generation. The office managers argue that it is difficult to motivate their staff to achieve the targets set, that this causes problems when bonus payments are not received, and is a cause of general demotivation among staff.

The senior management has listened to these complaints and has asked you to prepare a report outlining the cause of the problems and possible solutions.

11
Investment Appraisal

After studying this chapter you should be able to:

- outline the differences between capital expenditure decision and short-term decisions;
- describe the main methods of evaluating investment proposals;
- evaluate capital investment proposals using any of these methods;
- describe the other factors needed to be considered in any evaluation;
- outline the features of life cycle costing;
- describe the main ways of allocating resources.

Introduction

The most significant decisions which a company will make are normally concerned with capital investment. This need not necessarily be the case, however, and other significant decisions are concerned with such things as diversification or with product or market development. In the vast majority of cases, however, we are concerned with investment decisions – essentially decisions concerned with the longer term. Acquisition decisions can be considered in the same light as a capital investment decision as these are basically the same – capital investment through the acquisition of resources rather than through the internal generation and development of those resources. In both cases funding must be found to finance the investment. Consequently they can be evaluated in a similar manner.

Probably the most significant decisions therefore which a company makes are those concerned with capital investment. These are significant not just because of the significant cost effects of these decisions, nor because of the effect which such decisions have upon the operational performance of the business. Rather they are especially significant because of the long time frame upon which the decision must be made. A capital investment decision must be evaluated over a number of years in order to reach a conclusion as to whether or not the investment can be justified and obviously this requires a projection into the future of the expected costs and benefits associated with the decision. Equally obviously the further into the future those projections are made, the more uncertainty is attached to the validity of those projections. This is not just because the future effects within the business become less certain but also because the external environment also becomes less certain. This external environment will be affected by the general economic climate and by changes in fashion or technology. It will also be affected by the actions of competitors.

At its simplest, however, it is possible to determine whether or not a possible investment will create value for shareholders by using the techniques of appraisal which we will consider in this chapter. Although this may sound relatively simple the reality is of course more complex. Obviously every significant decision is evaluated according to a range of criteria – whatever might be important to an individual company or to a particular decision. Here, although we are primarily concerned with the analysis that supports the company's decision evaluation system, we are equally concerned with considering the other factors which need to be taken into consideration.

Most companies take other considerations into account when making investment decisions. Only some, however, state that they take into account either strategic or stakeholder or social responsibility issues. This can be taken to mean that this is done formally in some companies and less formally in others but will be done to some extent in all companies. It is important to remember that accounting evaluations are important to decision-making but by themselves cannot be used to make all important decisions. Thus managerial judgement is an important part of the decision-making process for these kinds of decisions (as it is for all decisions). Thus in reality the techniques used for appraisal are supplemented, or even overridden, by the use of such judgement. This of course can be expected to be the same in all companies whatever their preferred use of techniques and illustrates that the making of significant, and long term, decisions for a company is a complex process which can only partly be explained in terms of the techniques adopted.

We will explore the issues and techniques involved in investment appraisal by looking at the following scenario:

Dogfood plc is a quoted company manufacturing pet foods. It currently has funding to undertake some capital investment in its manufacturing process. Two alternatives have been identified:

Option 1

This is to build a canning plant at a cost of £3 500 000. It is expected that this plant will have a useful life of 10 years, after which it will have no residual value

It is expected that this equipment will generate additional sales revenue of £2 350 000 per annum. Variable costs of production amount to 60 per cent of total sales revenue and this proportion will be unchanged if this new equipment is purchased.

Option 2

This is to install energy recovery equipment which will cost £800 000. This equipment will have a life expectancy of 5 years, after which it will have no residual value.

Estimated benefits from this option are as follows:

	Reduced energy cost (£'000)	Reduced direct labour cost (£'000)	Increased raw materials cost (£'000)
Year 1	385	50	25
Year 2	275	35	25
Year 3	190	30	20
Year 4	145	25	20
Year 5	80	20	20

The company depreciates its plant using a straight-line basis and charges depreciation at the end of each year. It normally uses a discount rate of 12 per cent, as the basis for evaluation of capital investment projects.

The managing director is keen to show the social and environmental awareness of the company and therefore favours the energy recovery equipment project.

Capital investment decision-making

As we have already considered, capital investment decisions are basically long term in their nature. The expenditure incurred in making capital investment may be incurred over a short period of time, such as any investment in new equipment, or may be incurred over a longer period of time, such as if a new factory is to be built. The distinguishing feature of capital investment decisions, however, is the time scale over which the benefits can be expected to accrue, and this takes place over an extended period of time running into years. Thus capital investment decisions involve incurring costs in the present and immediate future in the expectation of accruing benefits in the future. Analysing such decisions therefore requires not just a calculation of the costs and benefits arising from the decision but also an evaluation based upon time scales and taking into account when costs will be incurred and benefits can be expected to accrue.

An example of a particularly long-term investment is the decision to build the Channel Tunnel. Evaluating this proposal involved calculating the costs of the investment, which were spread over several years, and then calculating the revenue, which was expected to arise over an even longer period. With such a long time scale to consider there is obviously an element of risk attached to investing in this project, which will need to be considered in any evaluation. We will, however, consider methods of evaluating such an investment proposal in this tutorial. These methods remain the same whatever the size of the investment and whatever the expected time scale involved.

Another factor which influences business decisions regarding capital investment is the effect of tax regulations upon the decision. These regulations can affect such decisions because the extent to which capital allowances are given and the timing of the tax payments on costs incurred can make a significant difference to a business in deciding when and how to undertake capital investment. The effect of taxation on such decisions is a complex subject which is outside the scope of this book – and in any case the precise rules affecting tax change on a regular basis. We shall therefore ignore the effects of taxation in our consideration of capital investment decisions.

Cost of capital and capital investment decisions

Money is a scarce resource and the owners of capital, be they shareholders or long-term lenders, require a return commensurate with the risks involved. The return which investors seek will affect the firm's cost of capital and the return which any new investment project must earn in order to meet investor's expectations.

The cost of capital will vary from one company to another. It is determined by the return which investors expect to earn from the company given its financial and economic risk and other macroeconomic factors such as the level of current and forecasted interest rates and investor's expectations of the future prospects for corporate earnings.

Investment decisions have the most profound effects on a firm's future survival and success. In order for a business to stay competitive, and ahead of the game, it must invest in a wide range of tangible and intangible assets. Investment decisions are central to the firm, and firms have to consider what are often large proposals for capital expenditure with the greatest care. Sub-optimal investment decisions could damage the firm's long-term viability and therefore it is crucial that there is a logical and practical way of assessing capital investment projects.

In order for management to make good investment decisions they must be able to either find assets which are currently undervalued, invent new products or realise that an existing service could be radically altered thereby bringing new benefits to consumers and higher returns to the owners. It is these types of decisions which will enhance the value of the firm. Wealth can only be created if the future benefits exceed the cost of owning the asset that is expected to generate more benefits.

Investment decision revolve around three main actions:

1 the identification of alternative investment opportunities which are open to the firm;
2 the projection of how much needs to be spend on each alternative;
3 the decision concerning how should each be financed.

Capital structure and the cost of capital

Before we embark on the exploration of the process of investment appraisal it is imperative that you know the meaning of capital structure and how to apply the concept of opportunity cost in calculating the weighted average cost of capital (WACC) for a firm.

Capital structure

As we saw in Chapter 2, for a business, there are two basic sources of capital:

1 *Equity*: capital provided by shareholders who are the owners of the business; this takes the form of share capital;
2 *Debt*: capital provided by long-term lenders who do not own the business (i.e. they are long-term creditors of the business); this takes the form of loan capital.

Each of these sources of capital has different advantages and disadvantages but in general a firm will make use of both forms of capital. The word gearing is used to define the capital structure of a firm. Companies can often chose how they will raise the additional capital they need. If they decide to raise more money by issuing additional shares, they are said to be increasing their equity capital while, if they chose to borrow the money, they are said to be increasing their debt capital. Whilst investors, be they shareholders or long-term creditors, can share the risk in any proportion they choose, the firm's opportunity cost of capital is always the required rate of return required by an investor for investing in a project with a given level of risk.

The choice of the proportions of equity and debt is dictated by the following considerations:

● *Cost*: the cost of raising and servicing the capital;
● *Control*: which is given to equity holders or lenders.

Cost of capital

Any additional capital raised will have to be paid for and so the business must be able to generate a return from its capital employed which exceeds its cost. The cost of capital is the cost of funds raised to finance a project/investment and is a function of the dividend payments and/or interest charges which will need to be incurred. The difference is that while dividend payments are the servicing cost of equity capital, interest charges are the servicing cost of debt capital.

The combination of these two is the cost of capital. Most companies express the cost of capital as a WACC. This means that the cost of servicing each component of the capital structure is aggregated in proportion to their proportions of the total capital employed. This is then used as the minimum return expected on any new investment. In accounting terms this minimum return is referred to as the hurdle rate.

Let us see what is meant by WACC by means of the following example:

Dogfood plc uses capital of £7 million. This is made up of the following:

- Long-term loans with a book value of £3 million. This debt incurs an interest rate of 11 per cent.
- Equity capital (i.e. shares) with a market value of £4 million. This equity has a cost of 12.75 per cent, which is the average return to shareholders in the form of dividends. This average rate is the rate which shareholders expect to receive in the form of dividends. Normally returns to shareholders will be expected to be higher than that to debtors because of the higher risk involved.

The calculation of the WACC is as follows:

$$\text{Cost of debt} = 0.11 \times 3\ 000\ 000 = 330\ 000$$
$$\text{Cost of equity} = 0.1275 \times 4\ 000\ 000 = 510\ 000$$
$$\text{WACC} = \frac{360\ 000 + 675\ 000}{3\ 000\ 000 + 4\ 000\ 000} = 12.0\%$$

From the above example we can see how a company can reduce its overall cost of capital by mixing the amount of equity capital and debt capital in its capital structure. The WACC is relatively easy to calculate and is therefore widely used by businesses. However, it has come in for some criticisms from academics. There are two main reasons why a firm should not use its historical cost of capital as shown in the balance sheet when evaluating the desired return from a new investment. Firstly, the cost of capital may have risen if investors require higher, returns than previously for financing such investments. This is why the firm's cost of capital as shown in the balance sheet should not be used to calculate the firm's cost of capital for investment purposes. Secondly, the new project may expose the business to a different level of risk than its existing projects and, if this is the case investors will demand a higher rate of return to compensate them for the extra risk. Finally, management must remember that an investment will only increase shareholder wealth if it can earn the return which investors expect from financing this type of investment.

Opportunity cost

The opportunity cost rate may be defined as the rate of return on the next best alternative investment of equal risk. A firm can use its opportunity cost rate as the basis for discounting future cash flows to obtain their present values (PVs) (see below). Every business investment decision has an opportunity cost attached to it and this is really the true cost of any investment decision. In order that the WACC reflects opportunity cost, the components of the capital structure should be valued at market values wherever this is practicable before calculating the cost of servicing each separate component and aggregating them, i.e. we want to obtain an estimate of the opportunity WACC.

Capital budgeting

All businesses need to incur capital expenditure at some time, whether it is a small plumber buying a new van, a manufacturer purchasing new equipment, or a retailer building a new hypermarket. Capital investment in a business is essential both to replace existing assets as they become worn out (and fully depreciated) and to provide additional assets in order to improve the performance of the business. This improved performance can be in terms of reduced costs of production, increased quality, increased output or changes in the product mix. It is important therefore that capital expenditure proposals are considered in the context of the objectives of the organisation and its long-term plan in order to ensure that any proposed expenditure helps the business to achieve its objectives.

Whatever the size of a business capital investment will represent significant activity by the business and will involve committing a significant proportion of the resources of the business to the investment. It is also likely that the investment, once committed to, will be irreversible, or at least the costs of changing the decision will be substantial. As each investment decision is so important to the business in terms of the resources involved, making capital investment decisions is very important to the business and a detailed analysis of costs and benefits is needed before a decision is made. Although each such decision is an individual decision, and made on its own merits, the consequences of the decision can impact upon the business in areas other than those with which the investment is concerned.

We have seen previously that a business operates in an environment of scarce resources and that there are competing uses for those resources. This is equally true of the resources available for capital investment and a business is likely to have a variety of proposals for capital expenditure, all of which will improve the performance of the business. The available resources, however, are unlikely to be sufficient to undertake all possible investments which will improve performance, and so some form of selection is needed in order to decide which to undertake and which to defer or cancel. One effect of a capital expenditure decision therefore is that it excludes the possibility of undertaking alternative investments.

Capital investment naturally involves expenditure and this needs to be incorporated into the budgeting process (see Chapter 9) in order to be able to calculate the effects of the expenditure on the cash flow of the business. This expenditure also needs to be financed through cash inflows and these can be either through raising finance externally (i.e. borrowings or share issues) or internally through using the profits generated from the firm's trading activities or cash generated from the sale of other assets. In practice a combination of externally raised funds and internally generated funds may well be used but budgeting for the capital expenditure is necessary in order to plan for the extent of the commitment involved and for its timing.

Life cycle costing

All capital investment decisions involve expenditure in the acquisition of the assets concerned, but they also involve a commitment to future expenditure in using those assets. In order to plan capital investment effectively it is important to recognise this and to incorporate both acquisition and operating costs into the evaluation. Thus, for example, an asset which has a high acquisition cost but low operating costs may be more effective for a business than one which has a low acquisition cost but high operating costs. An evaluation of capital investment based solely on acquisition costs will not take this into account and the most effective decision may not be made.

Evaluating capital investment decision in this manner is known as life cycle costing, or terotechnology. It is defined by CIMA as:

> The practice of obtaining over their life-times, the best use of physical assets at the lowest cost to the entity. This is achieved through a combination of management, financial, engineering and other disciplines.

The costs incurred over the full life cycle of an asset are the following:

- *Acquisition costs*: e.g. research and development, purchase price, installation and testing;
- *Operating costs*: e.g. maintenance, energy, spares, training;
- *Ongoing capital costs*: e.g. equipment upgrades, modifications;
- *Disposal costs*: e.g. demolition, salvage, site reclamation.

Life cycle costing takes into account all of these costs associated with an asset in the evaluating of capital expenditure proposals. It is sound financial planning to take all potential future costs into account; it also reflects a concern with social responsibility. Such costs as those associated with disposal may well be unknown in the present, and indeed may be found to become more significant as time progresses: examples would be those associated with the use of asbestos or with nuclear electricity generation. A failure to take these costs into account may well make a project seems attractive in the present but this is in effect a transfer of costs into the future. One of the features of corporate social responsibility is to take into account the long term as well as the short term, and one of the features of the present is that companies are now being faced with costs associated with decisions made in the past which were not then taken into account.

Allocating scarce resources between capital investment proposals

Given that a firm will have insufficient resources to undertake all the capital investment options available to it, there is a need to identify those which are the most important for it to undertake. This involves an evaluation of the costs and benefits of each option in order to determine its attractiveness, and there are a variety of techniques for doing this which we will examine later. First, however, we need to recognise that there are constraints on capital investment which might exist for a firm, and which provide a mechanism for an initial screening of capital investment proposals. These are:

Capital rationing

Capital rationing exists when there is an absolute limit to the amount of capital expenditure which can be undertaken by a business in any particular period of time. This limit may be imposed through outside constraints, such as the inability to raise funds through the financial markets, and this is known as hard capital rationing. Alternatively this limit may be imposed internally within the company, and this is known as soft capital rationing. This limit may be determined by the finite borrowing limit available to the business. Alternatively this limit may be externally imposed. Externally imposed limits tend to be a feature of public services in the UK whereby maximum levels of capital expenditure are set by the central government. The existence of a limited supply of capital for investment means that a business must select between the alternatives available to it. In doing so the business will select those alternatives which give the best returns to the business. This therefore implies that a ranking of alternatives is needed in order to determine priorities to arrive at the most effective investments for the business to undertake with the limited supply of capital available.

Target returns

An alternative method used by businesses to initially screen investment proposals is to set a target return which the proposal must achieve in order for it to be considered. This can be set internally within the business or imposed from elsewhere. Such a target provides a criterion for the initial evaluation of capital investment proposals and any proposal which fails to project such a return will be rejected by the company as it will not help it to meet its target return. This is also known as the hurdle rate, which we referred to earlier. Thus any proposal which fails to meet the target will be rejected and this provides a means of initially screening investment proposals. Those which meet the target will either be accepted if the resources available to the business are sufficient to meet all the proposals, or be subject to further evaluation to decide between alternatives if the total resources are insufficient for all proposals.

Methods of depreciation

When a capital investment has been undertaken, it is included as an asset in the balance sheet of the business. Because it has a finite life, however, it will be depreciated over the expected life of that asset. There are two main methods of depreciating an asset which we will consider here, although other methods also exist. These two methods are:

1 straight line depreciation;
2 annuity depreciation.

In order to see the difference between the two methods let us consider the first option available to Dogfood plc, that of investing £3 500 000 in a canning plant which will have a useful life of 10 years. This company has a cost of capital of 12 per cent.

The straight-line method of depreciation is based on depreciating the capital cost of the investment in equal instalments throughout its life. Thus for our example the depreciation charge for the new equipment would be:

Capital cost of equipment: £3 500 000

Life of asset: 10 years

$$\text{Annual depreciation charge}: \frac{£3\,500\,000}{10} = £350\,000$$

The annuity method of depreciation takes into account both the capital cost of the investment and the cost of capital associated with that investment. Its aim is to equalise the total cost of the investment, in terms of principal and interest, throughout the life of the investment. The annual depreciation charge will thus vary from year to year. Calculating this charge is based upon the use of an annuity factor, which can be found from the tables in Appendix 2.

For our example the calculation would be as follows:

Capital cost of equipment: £3 500 000

Life of equipment: 10 years

Cost of capital: 12%

Therefore annuity factor: 5.650

Thus the depreciation charge can be calculated as follows:

$$\text{Annual payment} = \frac{\text{Capital cost}}{\text{Annuity factor}}$$

$$= \frac{3\,500\,000}{5.650}$$

$$= 619\,469$$

Calculation

Year	Annual payment (£)	Interest charge (£)	Capital payment (£)	Capital outstanding at end of year (£)
1	619 469	420 000	199 469	3 300 531
2	619 469	396 063	223 406	3 077 125
3	619 469	360 255	259 214	2 817 911
4	619 469	338 149	281 320	2 536 591
5	619 469	304 391	315 078	2 221 513
6	619 469	266 582	352 837	1 868 676
7	619 469	224 241	395 228	1 473 448
8	619 469	176 814	442 655	1 030 703
9	619 469	123 695	495 474	536 229
10	619 469	83 240	536 229	–

Where:
Interest charge = Capital outstanding at end of previous year × Cost of capital (15%)
Capital payment = Annual payment − Interest charge
NB: capital payment equals the annual depreciation charge.

The annuity method of depreciation seeks to take into account the time value of money. The two methods of depreciation have quite different effects as far as evaluating capital investment proposals is concerned.

Quantitative accounting methods of investment appraisal

All capital investment proposals need to be evaluated in order to assess the net benefit to the business of undertaking the investment. A variety of methods of evaluation are available to the business. In this chapter we will consider the following basic methods of investment appraisal:

- Payback
- Return on investment

- Accounting rate of return
- Residual income
- Net present value
- Internal rate of return.

In order to be able to evaluate the relative merits of each method we will use the example at the start of the chapter and apply each technique to our evaluation.

Payback

The payback method is the simplest method of evaluating a capital investment proposal. Research has shown, however, that it is one of the most frequently used methods in the UK for capital investment appraisal. Payback is expressed in terms of time and is simply the length of time required for the stream of cash benefits from an investment to recover the initial cash outlay.

Thus for Dogfood plc this would be calculated as follows:

	Option 1	Option 2
Capital cost of equipment	3 500 000	800 000
Net cash flow year 1	2 350 000 × 40%	385 000 + 50 000 − 25 000
	= 940 000	= 410 000
Balance remaining	2 560 000	390 000
Net cash flow year 2	2 350 000 × 40%	275 000 + 35 000 − 25 000
	= 940 000	= 285 000
Balance remaining	1 620 000	105 000
Net cash flow year 3	2 350 000 × 40%	190 000 + 30 000 − 20 000
	= 940 000	= 200 000
Balance remaining	680 000	

Therefore:

Payback period for Option 1 = 3 years + $\left(\dfrac{680}{940}\right)$ year = 3 years 9 months

Payback period for Option 2 = 2 years + $\left(\dfrac{105}{200}\right)$ year = 2 years 7 months

On the basis of this calculation therefore Option 2 is the preferred project as it has the shorter payback time.

Assessing investment with the use of the payback method favours those projects which produce early substantial cash in-flows. The decision rule is to rank order projects under consideration from the shortest to the longest period in which the initial investment is paid back with net receipts. This method divides the life of a project into two portions: payback portion and beyond the payback portion and it is important to note that the method ignores the post-payback portion and thus does not consider all the relevant information. It tends to advocate the less risky projects on the basis that risk is time-related and so the shorter the time scale, the lower the risk and so inevitably advises to reject the project where the recovery of cash takes longer and the benefits, however long-lasting and necessary, cannot produce early cash inflows.

Payback, for all its faults, is a very popular method of investment appraisal, possibly because it is easily understood by people with little theoretical knowledge of finance. It acts as a first-time screening device and through its emphasis on liquidity provides useful criteria for choice in times of great uncertainty and in capital refinancing.

Its use is favoured by risk-averse managers, particularly those whose rewards and incentives are tied to short-term financial performance indicators rather than long-term health and prosperity of the firm. The use of payback method for assessing investments has also been accused of encouraging short-termism: the point of view that adopts short-time horizons for decision-making.

Return on investment

Return on investment (ROI) is calculated as the total cash benefits from the investment expressed as a percentage of the cost of the investment. It is measured on a year by year basis.

Thus for Dogfood plc this would be calculated as follows:

Year	Option 1			Option 2		
	Capital outstanding (£)	Net cash flow (£)	ROI (%)	Capital outstanding (£)	Net cash flow (£)	ROI (%)
1	3 500 000	940 000	26.8	800 000	410 000	51.2
2	3 150 000	940 000	29.8	640 000	285 000	44.5
3	2 800 000	940 000	33.6	480 000	200 000	41.7
4	2 450 000	940 000	38.4	320 000	150 000	46.9
5	2 100 000	940 000	44.8	160 000	80 000	50.0
6	1 750 000	940 000	53.7	0		
7	1 400 000	940 000	67.1			
8	1 050 000	940 000	89.5			
9	700 000	940 000	134.3			
10	350 000	940 000	268.6			
11	0					

What should be noticed from this method of evaluation is that the ROI will increase as the investment ages, as long as cash flows remain the same as they do for Option 1. Thus these calculations give no real basis for comparing alternatives. Nevertheless many organisations are evaluated by this method and the consequence is that there is an incentive not to make investment as this will tend to reduce the ROI achieved. The most obvious consequence of this is that a firm is discouraged from investing in replacement equipment which is likely to be more efficient, and probably less polluting also.

Accounting rate of return (ARR)

The choice of the method to assess investment is, or at least ought to, reflect immediate financial objectives. Whereas payback method with its emphasis on liquidity suggests that cash generation is the primary objective, accounting rate of return which considers profits rather than cash in-flows suggests that the objective is the augmentation of shareholders' wealth. It is essentially a refinement of ROI which seeks to calculate average returns over the life of a project.

The formula for calculating the ARR is:

$$\text{ARR} = \frac{\text{Average net cash inflow}}{\text{Average net investment}}$$

where these averages are taken as the average over the expected life of the project.

Thus:

$$\text{Average net cash flow} = \frac{\text{(Incremental cash flow/Incremental costs)}}{\text{Expected life of the project}}$$

and

$$\text{Average net investment} = \frac{\begin{array}{cc} \text{Total cost of} & \text{Residual value} \\ \text{investment} & \text{at end of life} \end{array}}{\text{Expected life of the project}}$$

The superiority of this method lies in the fact that, unlike payback, it considers all of the relevant financial information over the entire life of a project but the method only considers accounting profits, which being determined by arbitrary accounting conventions; for example, straight-line depreciation, instead of net cash flows is not a good investment appraisal technique.

Thus for our example of Dogfood plc, ARR would be calculated as follows:

Option 1

$$\text{Average net cash flow} = \frac{\text{(Incremental cash flow/Incremental costs)}}{\text{Expected life of the project}}$$

$$= 940\ 000$$

$$\text{Average net investment} = \frac{\text{Total cost of investment} \, {}^{-} \, \text{Residual value at end of life}}{\text{Expected life of the project}}$$

$$= \frac{18\ 250\ 000}{11\ \text{(taking start and finish values of each year)}}$$

$$= 1\ 659\ 091$$

$$\text{ARR} = \frac{\text{Average net cash inflow}}{\text{Average net investment}}$$

$$= \frac{940\ 000}{1\ 659\ 091}$$

$$= 56.7\%$$

Option 2

$$\text{Average net cash flow} = \frac{\text{(Incremental cash flow/Incremental costs)}}{\text{Expected life of the project}}$$

$$= \frac{1\ 125\ 000}{5}$$

$$= 225\ 000$$

$$\text{Average net investment} = \frac{\text{Total cost of investment} \, {}^{-} \, \text{Residual value at end of life}}{\text{Expected life of the project}}$$

$$= \frac{2\ 400\ 000}{6}$$

$$= 400\ 000$$

$$\text{ARR} = \frac{\text{Average net cash inflow}}{\text{Average net investment}}$$

$$= \frac{225\ 000}{400\ 000}$$

$$= 56.25\%$$

Using this method of project evaluation we can see that there is little difference between the two projects. This is not obvious if ROI is used. So ARR is a more reasonable method of evaluation which does not mitigate against investment because of the low ROI in early years.

Residual income

None of the methods of evaluation we have considered so far take into account the cost of capital but this is important. If an investment is to create value for the business then the return achieved must be greater than the cost of capital. We therefore turn now to a method which recognises this, namely residual income (RI). In this context, RI is the net cash flow from a project less a charge for cost of capital. Thus:

$$RI = \text{Net cash flow from project} - \text{Cost of capital employed}$$

Residual income can be used to evaluate capital investment proposals by calculating the RI from the proposal for each year and then summing to find the total net RI. If the calculation shows a net positive RI then the investment proposal adds value to the company.

Thus for Dogfood plc this would be calculated as follows:

Year	Option 1				Option 2			
	Capital outstanding (£)	Net cash flow (£)	Cost of capital	Residual income (%)	Capital outstanding (£)	Net cash flow (£)	Cost of capital	Residual income (%)
1	3 500 000	940 000	420 000	520 000	800 000	410 000	96 000	314 000
2	3 150 000	940 000	378 000	562 000	640 000	285 000	76 800	208 200
3	2 800 000	940 000	336 000	604 000	480 000	200 000	57 600	142 400
4	2 450 000	940 000	294 000	646 000	320 000	150 000	38 400	111 600
5	2 100 000	940 000	252 000	688 000	160 000	80 000	19 200	60 800
6	1 750 000	940 000	210 000	730 000	0			
7	1 400 000	940 000	168 000	772 000				
8	1 050 000	940 000	126 000	814 000				
9	700 000	940 000	84 000	856 000				
10	350 000	940 000	42 000	898 000				
11	0							

Any positive RI indicates that the investment adds value for the company and should therefore be undertaken, if creating value for shareholders is the objective. It will be noticed again, however, that this method of evaluation provides little help in comparing alternatives.

Although RI takes into account the cost of capital it does not take into account the time value of money. One problem with most investments is that the expenditure is incurred at the commencement of the project while the benefits accrue at a later date. This can mean that the RI of a project in its early period may well be negative, even though the overall RI is positive. When targets are set in terms of RI, a project with a negative RI in its early years may well be rejected as failing to meet the target even though it is ultimately beneficial to the business.

Time value of money: compounding and discounting

You may have felt while reading the above explanations that there is a certain inconsistency in the logic of the comparisons used in the calculations of pay-back, ARR and RI. Each of the methods ignores the idea known as the time value of money. The time value of money means that expenditure incurred at the present time costs more than the expenditure that would incur in the future, and the further into the future the expenditure is incurred, the less is the cost. Equally the closer to the present that income is received, the greater is its value. This is because a firm has alternative uses for all of its funds and so incurring expenditure in the present prevents an alternative use of these funds. In practice the alternative use of any cash is considered to be the return which could be achieved from investing the cash, and the time value of money can be equated to the opportunity cost of that money. Using these methods of evaluation therefore means that projects with the same average inflow would be evaluated as the same even if the inflows for one project occurred mostly early in the life of the project while for the other they occurred mostly in the later life of the project.

This obvious fact appears to be outside the consideration of these methods which compare the money spent today to the money obtained from an invest-ment in future, as though their respective values were unaffected by the pas-sage of time.

Compounding and discounting are two techniques that help us adjust values of money according to the timing of their receipt.

Compounding is calculating the future value of money invested today at a certain rate of interest, in this instance say 10 per cent:

Today	Year 1	Year 2	Year 3
£1000	£1100	£1210	£1331

The accumulation of value will only happen if both capital and interest remain untouched. Discounting is the precise reverse of the above process; we start with an amount of money we expect to obtain in the future, future val-ues, and then attempt to establish their values in today's terms, present value, again assuming a certain cost of capital which, to make matters simple, we will assume to be 10 per cent.

Year 3: £1000
Today: £1000 × 0.751 = £751

Thus the present value of £1000 which we are promised to receive in three years has today's present value of only £751. The 0.751 multiplier is called a discount factor and has been extracted from the present values of £1 (or dis-count) table, usually attached to most accounting textbooks.

Discounting cash flows (DCF) is a technique used by the two remaining investment appraisal methods: net present value and internal rate of return.

Net present value

In order to take into account the time value of money it is necessary to undertake an evaluation which recognises that the further in the future a cash inflow occurs the less value it has to the business. Such techniques are based upon the discounted cash flow technique. This is a technique which attempts to calculate the present value of a future cash flow. This requires the use of a discounting rate to calculate the present value. This discounting rate equates to the rate of return which can be expected from an investment, and thus it is normal to use the cost of capital as a discounting rate. Thus for Dogfood plc a discounting rate of 12 per cent would be used.

The present value of a future cash flow can be calculated from the following formula:

$$PV = \frac{fv_n}{(1 + k)^n}$$

where:

PV = present value;

fv_n = future cash flow for the year;

n = the number of periods in the future;

k = discounting rate (in decimal form).

Present values can be calculated using this formula but can also be calculated using the discounting factor tables provided in Appendix 2.

The net present value (NPV) of an investment is arrived at by discounting all future cash inflows and outflows to arrive at present values and then summing to give the NPV.

Thus for Dogfood plc this would be calculated as follows:

Year	Option 1			Option 2		
	Net cash flow (£)	Discount factor	Present value (£)	Net cash flow (£)	Discount factor	Present value (£)
1	940 000	0.8929	839 326	410 000	0.8929	366 089
2	940 000	0.7972	749 368	285 000	0.7972	227 202
3	940 000	0.7118	669 092	200 000	0.7118	142 360
4	940 000	0.6355	597 370	150 000	0.6355	95 325
5	940 000	0.5674	533 356	80 000	0.5674	45 392
6	940 000	0.5066	476 204			
7	940 000	0.4523	425 162			
8	940 000	0.4039	379 666			

Year	Option 1			Option 2		
	Net cash flow (£)	Discount factor	Present value (£)	Net cash flow (£)	Discount factor	Present value (£)
9	940 000	0.3606	338 964			
10	940 000	0.3220	302 680			
Total			5 311 188			876 368
Initial investment			3 500 000			800 000
NPV			1 811 188			76 368

A positive NPV, that is one where the NPV of future expected cash flows less the initial investment is greater than zero, indicates a cash benefit to the firm and therefore a potentially worthwhile investment which creates value for shareholders. Investments are chosen in rank order from the highest to the lowest NPVs until the capital budget is exhausted. All investments with negative NPVs should be rejected for the reason that all investment should produce benefits which are higher than the cost of funding the project. In our example, when the cash flows are discounted this demonstrates that both options create value for the business but that Option 1 – the canning plant – creates much more value. This therefore is the option which should be chosen.

By indicating the likely returns, the NPV method emphasises the objective of shareholders' wealth maximisation, and so conforms to the criterion of shareholder wealth maximisation. Other advantages of using NPV as a method of assessing projects are:

● It takes full account of timing of all relevant financial information.
● It gives unequivocal signals to decision-makers.

While NPV is a method of investment appraisal which takes into account the time value of money, the value of the calculation is dependent upon the discounting factor selected. Changing this factor can alter the respective NPVs of alternative investments and so lead to a different decision being made. The choice of discount factor by the business is therefore of crucial importance in the evaluation of capital expenditure proposals and needs to reflect the opportunity cost of capital. In practice a business often uses a calculation of the WACC as its cost of capital.

Internal rate of return

Internal rate of return (IRR) is an alternative technique which also takes into account the time value of money. It represents the true interest earned by an investment over its life. The internal rate of return (or hurdle rate) is the discount rate which yields a zero NPV. It is a method of project evaluation which uses the rate of return on a proposed investment calculated by finding the discount rate that equates the present value of future cash inflows to the investments cost.

Internal rate of return can be found by an iterative process of using a number of different discount rates until one is found for which the NPV equals zero. Thus for Dogfood plc this might be calculated as follows:

Year	Option 1			Option 2		
	Net cash flow (£)	Discount factor = 12%	Present value (£)	Net cash flow (£)	Discount factor = 12%	Present value (£)
1	940 000	0.8929	839 326	410 000	0.8929	366 089
2	940 000	0.7972	749 368	285 000	0.7972	227 202
3	940 000	0.7118	669 092	200 000	0.7118	142 360
4	940 000	0.6355	597 370	150 000	0.6355	95 325
5	940 000	0.5674	533 356	80 000	0.5674	45 392
6	940 000	0.5066	476 204			
7	940 000	0.4523	425 162			
8	940 000	0.4039	379 666			
9	940 000	0.3606	338 964			
10	940 000	0.3220	302 680			
Total			5 311 188			876 368
Initial investment			3 500 000			800 000
NPV			1 811 188			76 368

Year	Option 1			Option 2		
	Net cash flow (£)	Discount factor = 25%	Present value (£)	Net cash flow (£)	Discount factor = 25%	Present value (£)
1	940 000	0.8000	752 000	410 000	0.8000	328 000
2	940 000	0.6400	601 600	285 000	0.6400	182 400
3	940 000	0.5120	481 280	200 000	0.5120	102 400
4	940 000	0.4096	385 024	150 000	0.4096	61 440
5	940 000	0.3277	309 038	80 000	0.3277	26 276
6	940 000	0.2621	246 374			
7	940 000	0.2097	197 118			
8	940 000	0.1678	157 732			
9	940 000	0.1342	126 148			
10	940 000	0.1074	100 956			
Total			3 357 270			700 516
Initial investment			3 500 000			800 000
NPV			−142 730			−99 484

Interpolating the two values:

Option 1

$$1\,811\,188 + 142\,730 = 1\,953\,918$$

Therefore

$$\text{IRR} = 12 + \left(\frac{1\,811\,188}{1\,953\,918} \times 13\right)$$

$$= 24.1\%$$

Option 2

$$76\,368 + 99\,484 = 175\,852$$

Therefore

$$\text{IRR} = 12 + \left(\frac{76\,368}{175\,852} \times 13\right)$$

$$= 17.6\%$$

NB: Further iterations would be used to obtain a more accurate approximation.

Internal rate of return produces a relative measure which makes it easier to compare different projects of different values and with different time scales. Thus although this still shows that Option 1 – the canning plant – produces a higher return, the relative difference is more apparent than merely calculating the NPV.

Because the cash flows in the case of Option 1 are equal for each year, however, we can calculate the IRR by using the table at Appendix 2 in conjunction with the following formula:

$$\text{Discounting factor} = \frac{\text{Investment cost}}{\text{Annual cash flow}}$$

Thus for our example this would be calculated as follows:

$$\text{Discounting factor} = \frac{\text{Investment cost}}{\text{Annual cash flow}}$$

$$= \frac{3\,500\,000}{940\,000}$$

$$= 3.7234$$

From the tables this shows a rate of return of approximately 23.5%. Therefore, IRR = 23.5%.

With a cost of capital of 15 per cent, a rate of return of 7 per cent from this investment indicates that the investment should not be undertaken.

Calculating the IRR can be a tedious process but fortunately the use of computers, or even programmable calculators, makes such a calculation a realistic possibility for investment appraisal, even for large and complex proposals.

The IRR also has a technical problem associated with it. Most projects have a net cash outflow at the start of the project and this is followed by a stream of net cash inflows. However, if circumstances are different and some of the future years also have net cash outflows then the calculation will produce more than one value for the IRR. Care must be taken in interpreting results in such a situation. Techniques have been developed to overcome this technical problem, which are outside the scope of this course. However, you should be aware of this technical problem with IRR.

Whenever a firm is considering investing in only one project but is currently considering a number of investments, they are said to be mutually exclusive. In each case the project which can earn the largest NPV should be selected, but sometimes the evaluation can be made more complicated because the NPV and the IRR give different returns. In such cases the project which can earn the highest NPV should be chosen. This is because the NPV and the IRR are based upon different assumptions.

The IRR assumes that the net cash flows are reinvested at the IRR whereas the NPV method assumes that they are invested at the firm's required rate of return or hurdle rate. If the hurdle rate is correct, then it will reflect the firm's opportunity cost of capital and is, therefore, the correct reinvestment rate for the firm. This is so because in a competitive market the future returns earned from a similar investment will be zero, and so the reinvested cash flows will equal the hurdle rate. This is why the NPV should take precedence over IRR whenever management is considering either mutually exclusive projects or single projects should the two methods give rise to different returns.

The IRR can be modified by finding the discount rate at which the present value of a project's cost is equal to the present value of its terminal value, where the terminal value is found as the sum of the future values of the cash inflows, compounded as the firm's cost of capital. However, the NPV is the only method which shows whether shareholder wealth will be increased and that is why it is theoretically the best investment appraisal technique.

The difference between the rate of return on a project and the rate of return on an investment with a guaranteed rate of return, is known as a reward for risk, and is the recognition of the level of risk attached to a project. It should be high where the risk attached to the investment is also high.

Choosing the method of evaluation

We have looked at a number of different techniques of accounting which can be used to evaluate different investment alternatives. Using the example of Dogfood plc we have seen that most show the building of the canning plant to be the better alternative but that the payback method shows the opposite. The question therefore arises as to which is the most appropriate method to use.

For finance theory there is no dispute – the theoretically correct method to use is based upon discounted cash flow – either NPV or IRR. These alone show which decisions create the most value for shareholders.

Nevertheless empirical evidence shows that firms do not place their reliance totally upon these methods. Research by Cooper *et al*. (2001) shows that all firms use several methods to appraise investment alternatives before making a decision. Prominent among these is NPV but payback also features to a considerable extent and there is evidence for all methods being used. The probable reason for the use of multiple methods of appraisal is that investment decisions tend to be so large, and hence significant, for a firm that its managers are reluctant to base any decision solely upon one evaluation.

Making investment decisions

The above methods used in investment appraisal are based on quantitative information alone and provide only the quantitative indicators regarding the acceptability (or otherwise) of projects. Yet we know that most decisions are made on the basis of consideration of both quantitative and qualitative factors. It is important to recognise therefore that, although capital investment will not normally be undertaken without an evaluation using one or other of these methods, this will not be the sole basis for appraising capital investment proposals and the decision between alternatives will not be made solely on the basis of this evaluation. Other factors which need to be considered are:

- the objectives of the business;
- availability of finance in terms of quantity and timing;
- cash flow effects and their incorporation into the overall cash budget;
- qualitative factors and non-quantifiable costs and benefits.

Not all the advantages of undertaking investment lend themselves easily to being expressed in terms of positive net cash flows. For example, investing in schemes enhancing employees' welfare or community projects may not necessarily translate themselves into additional cash inflows. Moreover we sometimes rely on the less rational but often equally valid bases for making decisions: experience, intuition, moral conviction and the more trivial reasons entrenched in business politics – turf wars, power struggles, personal self-aggrandisement and the like.

Not all factors can be described completely in financial terms therefore and these non-quantifiable factors may be of significance to the value of the investment. Possible non-quantifiable benefits can be classed as:

- *Social benefits*: e.g. the provision of a new canteen for workers;
- *Ethical benefits*: e.g. the provision of new safety facilities in the production environment;
- *Environmental benefits*: e.g. investment to reduce pollution;

- *Community benefits*: e.g. landscaping the environment or providing leisure facilities which can be enjoyed by local inhabitants;
- *Public relations benefits*: e.g. the provision of a visitors centre.

These types of investment will have financial aspects which can be incorporated into the analysis. They may also have future benefits in terms of sales or customer relations. There will remain, however, a non-quantifiable element and this may outweigh the financial factors in the decision-making process.

The socially responsible evaluation of investment alternatives

Accounting methods of evaluation are designed to measure the impact of a decision upon the firm itself, and therefore to evaluate the effect upon shareholders. A socially responsible approach, however, would recognise that all other stakeholders to the business are important. Consequently the effects of these decisions upon all stakeholders need to be taken into account. An accounting evaluation alone is unable to achieve this. We need therefore to consider alternative methods of evaluation which might be appropriate for this.

One such technique exists within the public sector and this is known as cost benefit analysis (CBA). In our discussion of investment appraisal, the implicit assumption has been that the ultimate purpose of any investment project is the maximisation of owners' wealth. Yet this objective would be almost entirely irrelevant in the case of investment decisions undertaken by the public sector where the improved welfare and quality of life of citizens are the ultimate objectives. Thus the public sector and other organisations whose primary objective is not the creation of wealth need a different analytical tool which would scrutinise the planned projects. The purpose of CBA is to systematically evaluate projects where the criteria for acceptance or rejection are expressed in qualitative terms. It aims to take into account all the effects of a decision and not just those which can be quantified or those which affect the firm itself. This can be modelled as follows:

Cost benefit analysis

Present value of the effects upon the firm + Present value of effects upon other stakeholders + Non-quantifiable costs and benefits = Total cost/benefit.

A socially responsible approach to investment decisions would be based upon this approach and would look at the whole life of the project. This approach is problematic of course as the quantification of effects upon stakeholders is difficult to achieve. Furthermore when non-quantifiable effects are taken into account an impartial evaluation of alternative investments is difficult to achieve and the decision must be based upon judgement. Having said that, however, such judgement, based upon managerial experience, is an essential part of any investment decision and so it is only the extent of concern for other stakeholders which differs.

Turning to Dogfood plc, we must address the question of which alternative should be chosen. Accounting evaluations seem to show that the firm should invest in a new canning plant. A concern with social responsibility would suggest, however, that the firm should invest in energy recovery equipment. A CBA approach may well show that the non-quantifiable benefits would make this the preferred option and the Managing Director certainly seems to be of this opinion. It has been argued by some (e.g. Covalenski and Dirsmith 1986) that accounting functions as a means for legitimating decisions made elsewhere. Others have argued (e.g. Birnbeg *et al*. 1983) that one of the consequences of accounting is to reduce uncertainty in the management of a business through the way in which data is structured. Similarly, Bhaskar and McNamee (1983) have argued that proxy measures are used as a means of quantifying performance against the planned course of action. On this basis it would seem reasonable to support the wish of the Managing Director and propose that the firm should invest in energy recovery equipment and provide an accounting evaluation which supports this. Given the considerable element of uncertainty in any evaluation this could be seen to be a responsible (as well as politically expedient) approach. It certainly fits with a socially responsible approach.

Further evaluation of investment appraisal

It is accepted that the choice of a method is a good predictor of what are the firm's ultimate business objectives and so, for example, the use of payback reflects the emphasis on liquidity whereas the use of NPV focuses on the creation of wealth. The current economic climate of uncertainty and change and the environment of fierce competitiveness in the global business have been instrumental in the loss of security of employment, which has further aggravated the unwillingness of managers to consider long-term effects in decision-making. The conventional methods of investment appraisal with their emphasis on cash generation are often criticised for excessively focusing on the short term at the expense of future economic welfare and thus contributing to the creation and persistence of the climate of short termism.

The real problem with any investment appraisal technique is that it is based on forecasts. If these forecasts prove to be incorrect so will the consequent results and, unfortunately, investment appraisal techniques on their own cannot predict whether or not a new product or service will be successful. We can see, however, that accounting can help a business manager to make capital investment decisions but that accounting alone does not lead to an appropriate method of optimising decision-making, particularly when a social responsibility approach is adopted.

Further reading

Bhaskar, K. and McNamee, P. (1983). Multiple objectives in accounting and finance. *Journal of Business Finance and Accounting*, 10 (4), 595–621.

Birnbeg, J.G., Turopolec, L. and Young, S.M. (1983). The organizational context of accounting. *Accounting, Organisations and Society*, 8 (2/3), 111–129.

Cooper, S., Crowther, D., Davies, M. and Davis, E.W. (2001). *Shareholder or Stakeholder Value*. London: CIMA.

Covalenski, M.A. and Dirsmith, M.W. (1986). The budgetary process of power and politics. *Accounting, Organisations and Society*, 11 (3), 193–214.

Dearden, J. (1969). The case against ROI control. *Harvard Business Review*, 47 (3) 124–135.

Emmanuel, C.R. and Otley, D.T. (1976). The usefulness of residual income. *Journal of Business Finance and Accounting*, 3 (4), 43–51.

Friedman, M. (1970). The social responsibility is to increase its profits. *The New York Times Magazine*, September, 32–33.

Hirshleifer, J. (1958). On the theory of optimal investment decisions. *Journal of Political Economy*, 66, 329–372.

Additional questions

Question 11.1

(a) Although many different methods are used by firms to evaluate capital investment proposals, theoretical arguments suggest that NPV is the best method of appraisal. Explain why this is so.

(b) Research evidence suggests that payback period is a method of evaluation commonly used by firms in evaluating capital investment proposals. Explain why firms might wish to use this method of evaluation.

(c) Marple Manufacturing Ltd is proposing to purchase a new machine to enhance its manufacturing capacity through the making of a new product. The machine would have a 4-year life with no residual value; it would cost £100 000 and would require also an additional investment in working capital of £60 000. Estimated benefits during its life are as follows:

	Year 1	Year 2	Year 3	Year 4
Additional sales (units)	1600	2000	2400	2400
Selling price per unit (£)	55	65	65	65
Variable cost per unit (£)	30	30	25	25

The company has already spent £75 000 on research and development to ensure that the new product will be successful.

If the new machine is purchased, an existing product, giving an annual contribution of £16 000, will have to be withdrawn.

The company uses a weighted average cost of capital of 15 per cent.

You are asked to calculate the NPV of the proposed investment and its IRR.

Question 11.2

Ukec plc, a company of diverse interests, is considering the purchase of a factory on the European mainland in order to take advantage of the greater market opportunities that changes in European Community regulations will bring. The following information is available on the factories under consideration:

	Factory A (£ million)	Factory B (£ million)	Factory C (£ million)
Purchase cost	50	100	90
Estimated net cash inflows			
Year 1	3	10	15
Year 2	6	15	19
Year 3	14	30	26
Year 4	16	45	40
Year 5	20	60	45

Factory A was still only 70 per cent complete and it is estimated that a further £25 million would be needed to complete the factory ready for production in year 1.

The cost of capital of the company is estimated at 10 per cent.

Subsequent to the preparation of the forecast data above, the company's economic research department has provided the following information:

• The country in which factory B is located will devalue their currency against the £ by 15 per cent on 1 January of year 4. It is estimated that the currency/volume effect on estimated net cash flows for factory B would be to reduce them by 5 per cent.
• Accelerating wage inflation in the country where factory C is located would probably reduce net cash inflows by the following amounts:
   Year 2: £2 million;
   Year 3: £3 million;
   Year 4: £4 million;
   Year 5: £6 million.

It is assumed that net cash flows arise at the end of the relevant year and that factory A can be completed in time for commencement of operations at the beginning of year 1.

Required:
(a) Calculate the NPV for each of the factories under consideration.
(b) Calculate the payback period for each of the factories under consideration.
(c) Advise the managing director as to which factory should be purchased, paying particular attention to the risk involved in each option.

12
Responsibilities towards Stakeholders

Learning objectives

After studying this chapter you should be able to:

- explain stakeholder influences on accounting;
- describe the relevance of social issues and their effects and implications to a business;
- explain and critique the principle of externalisation;
- explain regulation and its implications;
- describe the development of social and environmental accounting;
- critique the principles of social and environmental accounting;
- explain the principles involved in the measurement of environmental impact, including environmental auditing;
- describe the principles upon which environmental accounting is based.

Introduction

Although a concern with financial management is crucial to the general and strategic management of every organisation, it is of course not the only concern. We have seen throughout this book that financial management cannot be considered in isolation from other issues of importance to the organisation. Indeed, financial decision needs to be considered in the context of all these other issues in order for the most appropriate decisions to be taken. One issue which is of importance – indeed of increasing importance for the financial management of an organisation – is that of social responsibility and we have shown how this can be incorporated into the use of accounting.

The development of accounting

In order to set the scene, we need to consider briefly the history of the development of accounting. This shows that only certain effects of the actions of companies are generally considered to be the concern of the accounting of organisations. Anything else is considered to be irrelevant – and this includes the social and environmental effects of the actions of companies. It is the purpose of this chapter to show that this is not the case and that business performance can be improved by considering these effects. Social and environmental accounting is concerned with the measurement and reporting of these effects and the way they impact upon business performance.

All commercial enterprises have some form of accounting function. Indeed, accounting has become the universally adopted system of communicating economic information relating to an organisation and its activities – through the measurement and reporting of performance in financial terms. The notion of accounting, however, is far from being a new phenomenon. Accounting records dating back to ancient civilisations have been located, including building accounts for the Parthenon in Athens which have been found on marble tablets. Similarly, ancient Greek records exist illustrating an early form of stewardship accounting known as 'charge and discharge accounting': charge representing the amounts received and discharge being the amount expended. This system was further developed in Italy throughout the thirteenth and fourteenth centuries. The development included the practice of distinguishing between debit and credit entries and the use of two-sided accounting entries. The origins of double-entry bookkeeping system thus began to take form based upon the ideas of Paccioli.

It is into this world that accounting was born on the basis that there was a need to record the actions of the individual, and the effects of those actions as a basis for the planning of future action. This need was brought about by the separation of the public and private actions of an individual and the need to record, and account for, the public actions because of the involvement of others in these public actions. Thus the medieval methods of bookkeeping, with the indistinguishability of public from private actions were inappropriate to this modern world in which Capitalist enterprise was beginning to arise.

Capitalism required the ability to precisely measure activities and this was the founding basis of management accounting. Indeed it has been argued that Capitalism and the Industrial Revolution would not have been possible without the techniques of double-entry bookkeeping and its subsequent metamorphosis into management accounting. This accounting provided the mechanism to make visible the activities of all involved in the capitalist enterprise and to record both the effects of past actions and the expected results of future actions.

In so doing, however, a need was created to control the efficiency of the processes when combined and to attach an internal price, or more precisely a cost, to the processes now performed within the organisation. These systems thus provided quasi-market metrics that enabled managers to gauge the efficiency of the economic activity taking place within the organisation.

This was of particular importance for the development of management accounting as early cost management systems emphasised the need to control the level of input resources consumed per output unit. This was particularly true of labour, as a unit of resource consumed, because labour normally comprised the greatest factor cost of production in any nineteenth-century industrial organisation. Different industries developed control measures to serve their own particular requirements: thus, for example, railways used cost per ton-mile while distributors/retailers used gross margins and stock turnover.

The budget is probably the most widely used management accounting tool. It was developed in order to depict an organisation's plan in quantitative terms. Budgets and budgeting have developed considerably since these techniques were introduced and nowadays financial models have been increasingly used to produce and test the strength of proposed budgets. In order to construct such models it is necessary to define the various processes within the organisation and detail causal relationships between the factors within the financial information. An understanding of these relationships is important for social and environmental accounting also as we will demonstrate – except that these relationships may need to be understood differently.

It has been suggested that the typical assumptions made within management accounting are that there is a predictable and stable external environment, that individuals' behaviour is predictable and mechanistic, and also that the accounting data used as input is accurate. Given these assumptions it is implicitly possible for a model to accurately predict the future from a given set of inputs. Furthermore, financial packages are set up so that historical data can be input and analysed in an attempt to extract the relevant relationships that have previously been present. These same relationships, which are assumed to continue to be appropriate into the future, can then be used to project the financial position of the organisation.

Accounting thought can be considered to be based largely on ideas of causality, rationality and separability; this leads to the prescriptive nature of accounting models. As such these models have been used as tools to identify and adjust controllable variables, and thereby to purposefully influence an organisation's future position. Common to all accounting techniques which are generally accepted in practice, there is a shared epistemology – that is to say a shared understanding of knowledge and how it originates. This is located within the rational-economic understandings of modernity. As far as management accounting is concerned we can say that the effect is to enable us, through the techniques of accounting, to present a knowable, predictable, and hence calculable future.

Thus, the modernist reason of accounting journeys into the future and then back again, bringing with it information that allows 'rational' managers to make 'logical' decisions. These decisions are based upon our ability to calcu-late and predict with a degree of certainty. Thus the expectation of organisa-tional performance tomorrow can be reduced through accounting techniques to an algorithm today. For this to be a tenable position the procedures that constitute accounting must be able to capture the future, and this supposes that it can be predictably modelled. Such an assertion rests upon the notion of a degree of stability in the external environment – in accepting this we ignore the possibility of future ruptures, and unforeseeable contingencies. Further-more, it assumes a constant, objective reality. In social and environmental accounting the techniques are applied differently to take into account these uncertain future possibilities.

Stakeholder influences on accounting

Modern accounting therefore came into being when firms became so large that ownership was necessarily divided and with external investment becoming necessary. The traditional view of accounting as far as an organisation is con-cerned is that the only activities with which the organisation should be con-cerned are those which take place within the organisation, or between the organisation and its suppliers or customers – these are the only activities for which a role for accounting exists. Consequently it is considered, as far as trad-itional accounting is concerned, that these are the only activities which need to be taken into account as far as the accounting of an organisation is concerned.

This view of accounting places the organisation at the centre of its world and the only interfaces with the external world are concerned with acquisition of resources (raw materials, labour, capital, etc.) at the commencement of the organisation's processing cycle and selling its wares (goods or services and associated marketing costs) at the end of the processing cycle. This view of accounting is particularly pertinent for management accounting, which is essentially concerned with the transformational process within the organisa-tion, and the management of that transformational process.

Here therefore is located the essential dichotomy of accounting – that some results of actions taken are significant and need to be recorded while others are irrelevant and need to be ignored. Social and environmental accounting, however, recognises that the organisation operates in a society in which its actions affect that society and its members. This accounting seeks to recognise the interrelationship between a business and society and to account for the activities of the business in such a way that both the business and the society gain from the actions of the firm.

Traditional accounting, however, remains focused upon the actions of the organisation and upon reporting the effect of those actions upon the organisa-tion and its performance. In doing so it ignores the effects of the organisation upon its external environment.[1] A growing number of writers, however, have recognised that the activities of an organisation impact upon the external envir-onment and have suggested that one of the roles of accounting is to report upon the impact of an organisation in this respect – in other words the accounting of organisations should be more outward looking.

The start of an outward-looking aspect to accounting can probably be identified in the immediate post-war period when organisations developed their reporting orientation towards the attraction of inward investment. This did not, however, herald a concern with the effect of the actions of the organisation upon its external environment. Such a suggestion probably first arose in the 1970s and a concern with a wider view of company performance is taken by some writers who evince concern with the social performance of a business as a member of society at large. This concern was stated by Ackerman (1975) who argued that big business was recognising the need to adapt to a new social climate of community accountability but that the orientation of business to financial results was inhibiting social responsiveness. Indeed, at around the same time it was argued that companies were no longer the instruments of shareholders alone but existed within society and so therefore had responsibilities to that society. Furthermore there was a general acceptance of a shift towards the greater accountability of companies to all stakeholders. Recognition of the rights of all stakeholders and the duty of a business to be accountable in this wider context therefore has been a relatively recent phenomenon and the economic view of accountability only to owners has only recently been subject to debate to any considerable extent.

It is apparent, however, that any actions which an organisation undertakes will have an effect not just upon the organisation itself but also upon the external environment of that organisation. In considering the effect of the organisation upon its external environment it must be recognised that this environment includes:

- the business environment in which the firm is operating;
- the local societal environment in which the organisation is located;
- and the wider global environment.

These effects of the organisation's activities can take many forms, such as:

- the utilisation of natural resources as a part of its production processes;
- the effects of competition between itself and other organisations in the same market;
- the enrichment of a local community through the creation of employment opportunities;
- transformation of the landscape due to raw material extraction or waste product storage;
- the distribution of wealth created within the firm to the owners of that firm (via dividends) and the workers of that firm (through wages) and the effect of this upon the welfare of individuals.

It can be seen therefore from these examples that an organisation can have a very significant effect upon its external environment and can actually change that environment through its activities. It can also be seen that these different effects can in some circumstances be viewed as beneficial and in other circumstances be viewed as detrimental to the environment. Indeed, the same actions can be viewed as beneficial by some people and detrimental by others. This is why planning enquiries or tribunals, which are considering the possible effects of the proposed actions by a firm, will find people who are in favour and people who are opposed. This is of course because the effects of the actions of an organisation upon its environment are viewed and evaluated differently by different people.

Social issues and their effects and implications

This growing concern with the effects of the actions of an organisation on its external environment is based upon a recognition that it is not just the owners of the organisation who have a concern with the activities of that organisation. There are also a wide variety of other stakeholders who have a concern with those activities, and are affected by those activities. Indeed, those other stakeholders have not just an interest in the activities of the firm but also a degree of influence over the shaping of those activities. Also it has been argued that the power and influence of these stakeholders is such that it amounts to quasi-ownership of the organisation. Based upon this there has been, by some people, something of a challenging of the traditional role of accounting in reporting results. Such a challenge considers that, rather than an ownership approach to accountability, a stakeholder approach, recognising the wide stakeholder community, is needed.

The desirability of considering the social performance of a business was not at this time, however, universally accepted. Rather it was the subject of much debate, as the following quotations illustrate:

> There is no reason to think that shareholders are willing to tolerate an amount of corporate non-profit activity which appreciably reduces either dividends or the market performance of the stock. (Hetherington 1973)

> . . . every large corporation should be thought of as a social enterprise; that is an entity whose existence and decisions can be justified insofar as they serve public or social purposes. (Dahl 1972)

Over time, however, the performance of businesses in a wider arena than the stock market, and its value to shareholders, has become an issue of increasing concern. This concern led initially to the development of social accounting:

> Social accounting is an approach to reporting a firm's activities which stresses the need for the identification of socially relevant behaviour, the determination of those to whom the company is accountable for

its social performance and the development of appropriate measures and reporting techniques. (Fetyko 1975)

Social accounting recognises that different aspects of performance are of interest to different stakeholder groupings; it distinguishes, for example, between investors, community relations and philanthropy as areas of concern for accounting. It also considers various areas for measurement, including consumer surplus, rent, environmental impact and non-monetary values. (Klein 1977)

These writers consider, by implication, that measuring social performance is important without giving reasons for believing so. Indeed, one of the origins of social accounting is based upon ideological grounds. Other reasons exist and as far as the business itself is concerned the reasons for measuring objectively the social performance of a business include:

- to aid rational decision-making, and therefore improved performance;
- as a defensive measure.

Recognition of the rights of all stakeholders and the duty of a business to be accountable in this wider context therefore has been largely a relatively recent phenomenon. Generally its origins are considered to be in the 1970s.

 ## Environmental issues and their effects and implications

When an organisation undertakes an activity which impacts upon the external environment, it affects that environment in ways which are not reflected in the traditional accounting of that organisation. The environment can be affected either positively, through for example a landscaping project, or negatively, through for example the creation of spoil heaps from a mining operation. These actions of an organisation impose costs and benefits upon the external environment. These costs and benefits are imposed by the organisation without consultation, and in reality form part of the operational activities of the organisation. These actions are, however, excluded from traditional accounting of the firm,[2] and by implication from its area of responsibility. Thus we can say that such costs and benefits have been externalised. The concept of externality therefore is concerned with the way in which these costs and benefits are externalised from the organisation and imposed upon others.

Such externalised costs and benefits have traditionally been considered to be not the concern of the organisation, and its managers, and hence have been excluded from its accounting. It must be recognised, however, that the quantification of the effect of such externalisation, particularly from an accounting viewpoint, is problematical and not easy to measure, and this is perhaps one reason for the exclusion of such effects from the organisation's accounting. It is probably fair to state, however, that more costs have been externalised by the organisation than benefits. Hence a typical organisation has gained from such externalisation and the reported value creation of such an organisation has been overstated by this failure to account for all costs and benefits. This is achieved by restricting the accounting evaluation of the organisation to the internal effects. Indeed one way in which an organisation can report, through its accounting, the creation of value is by an externalisation of costs, which are thereby excluded from the accounting of the organisation's activities.

As far as the externalisation of costs is concerned it is important to recognise that these can be externalised both spatially and temporally. Spatial externalisation describes the way in which costs can be transferred to other entities in the current time period. Examples of such spatial externalisation include:

- environmental degradation through spoil heaps or through increased traffic imposes costs upon the local community through reduced quality of life;
- causing pollution imposes costs upon society at large;
- waste disposal problems impose costs upon whoever is tasked with such disposal;
- removing staff from shops imposes costs upon customers who must queue for service;
- just in time manufacturing imposes costs upon suppliers by transferring stockholding costs to them.

In an increasingly globalised market one favourite way of externalising costs is through transfer of those costs to a third-world country. This can be effected by a transfer of operational activities, or at least those with environmental impacts, to such a country where the regulatory regime is less exacting. In this respect it should be noted that the arguments regarding reducing labour costs are generally used for such a transfer of operational activities but at the same time less exacting regulatory regimes also exist.

The temporal externalisation of costs describes the way in which costs are transferred from the current time period into another – the future. This thereby enables reported value creation, through accounting, to be recorded in the present. Examples of temporal externalisation include:

- deferring investment to a future time period and so increasing reported value in the present;
- failing to provide for asset disposal costs in capital investment appraisal and leaving such costs for future owners to incur;
- failure to dispose of waste material as it originates and leaving this as a problem for the future;
- causing pollution which must then be cleaned up in the future;
- depletion of finite natural resources or failure to provide renewable sources of raw material will cause problem for the future viability of the organisation;

- lack of research and development and product development will also cause problem for the future viability of the organisation;
- eliminating staff training may save costs in the present at the expense of future competitiveness.

It can be seen that such actions have the effect of deferring the dealing with problems into the future but not of alleviating the need to deal with such problems. In this respect it must be recognised that it is not always apparent in the present that such costs are being temporally externalised, as they may not be recognised as a problem at the present time. For example, the widespread use of asbestos in the 1930s to 1960s was considered to be beneficial at the time and was only later found to be problematic. This temporal externalisation of costs, through causing the clean-up problems and costs of a later time period, was therefore incurred unintentionally. Equally such costs may at the present time be in course of being transferred into the future through actions taken in the present which will have unanticipated consequences in the future. Nevertheless it is reasonable to suggest that such actions may be taken in the present for cost minimisation purposes with little regard for possible future costs.

We can see therefore that if we take externalities into account that the decisions made and actions taken by firms may be very different. We can equally see that the recognition of the effect upon these externalities of actions taken by an organisation can have significant impact upon the activities of the organisation and that the way in which an organisation chooses to internalise or externalise its costs can have a significant impact upon its operational performance.

Regulation and its implications

Although it has been stated earlier that the disclosure of the actions of the firm in terms of their impact upon the external environment is essentially voluntary in nature this does not necessarily mean that the actions themselves are always voluntary. Nor does it mean that all such disclosures are necessarily voluntary.[3] The regulatory regime which operates in most countries means that certain actions must be taken by firms which affect their influence upon the external environment. Equally certain actions are prevented from being taken. These actions and prohibitions are controlled by means of regulation imposed by the government of the country – both the national government and the local government.

Equally regulations govern the type of discharges which can be made by organisations, particularly when these are considered to cause pollution. Such regulations govern the way in which waste must be disposed of and the level of pollutants allowed for discharges into rivers, as well as restricting the amount of water which can be extracted from rivers.

The regulatory regime which operates in every country is continuing to change and becoming more restrictive as far as the actions of an organisation and its relationship with the external environment are concerned.[4] It seems reasonable to expect these changes to continue into the future and concern for the environmental impact of the activities of organisations to increase. These regulations tend to require reporting of the activities of organisations and such reporting also involves an accounting connotation. This accounting need is not only to satisfy regulatory requirements but also to meet the internal needs of the organisation. This is because the managers of that organisation, both in controlling current operations and in planning future business activities, must have accounting data to help manage the organisational activities in this respect. The growth of environmental data, as part of the management information systems of organisations, therefore can be seen to be, at least in part, driven by the needs of society at large. In this way it is reflected in the regulations imposed upon the activities of organisations. As the extent of regulation of such activities can be expected to increase in the future, the more forward looking and proactive organisations might be expected to have a tendency to extend their environmental impact reporting in anticipation of future regulation, rather than merely reacting to existing regulation.

It should not be thought, however, that the increase in stature and prominence accorded to socially responsible behaviour by organisation is driven entirely by present and anticipated regulations. To a large extent the external reporting of such environmental impact is not determined by regulations – these merely require reporting to the appropriate regulatory body. Nor can it be argued that the increasing multinational aspect of organisational activity, and the consequent need to satisfy regulatory regimes from different countries, has alone driven the increased importance of environmental accounting. Organisations which choose to report externally upon the impact of their activities on the external environment tend to do so voluntarily. In doing so they expect to derive some benefit from this kind of accounting and reporting. The kind of benefits which organisations can expect to accrue through this kind of disclosure will be considered throughout this book. At this point, however, we should remember the influence of stakeholders upon the organisation and it can be suggested that increased disclosure of the activities of the organisation is a reflection of the growing power and influence of stakeholders, without any form of legal ownership, and the recognition of this influence by the organisation and its managers.

The development of social accounting

Implicit in the development of social accounting is a recognition that the activities of an organisation have effects not just upon the organisation but also upon its wider environment. Thus social accounting shows a concern with the effects of the actions of an organisation on this external environment. This is based upon the recognition that it is not just the owners of the organisation who have a concern with the activities of that organisation. Additionally there are a wide variety of other stakeholders who justifiably have a concern with those activities, and are affected by those activities. Indeed, those other stakeholders have not just an interest in the activities of the firm but also a degree of influence over the shaping of those activities. Such stakeholders can include:

- suppliers of raw materials and other resources;
- customers for the organisation's products or services;
- employees;
- the local community;
- society at large;
- the government of the countries in which the organisation is based or conducts its activities.

This influence is so significant that it has been argued that the power and influence of these stakeholders is such that it amounts to quasi-ownership of the organisation. Indeed the traditional role of accounting in reporting results has been challenged. This challenge argues that accountability should be based upon a stakeholder approach, recognising the whole stakeholder community rather than an ownership approach. The benefits of incorporating stakeholders into a model of performance measurement and accountability have, however, been extensively criticised. Thus different schools of thought exist, however, as to whether there is any benefit in taking into account the needs of all stakeholders in the management of a company. Thus, for example, the techniques of VBM (which we considered in Chapter 6) are based upon the premise that the way to maximise the performance of a company, for the ultimate benefit of all stakeholders, is by focusing upon the creation and maximisation of shareholder wealth. On the other hand, the stakeholder management school of thought disagrees and argues that performance of an organisation can only be maximised when the organisation addresses directly the needs of all stakeholders. This debate is ongoing without any firm evidence to provide a resolution to the debate.

Social accounting first came to prominence during the 1970s when the performance of businesses in a wider arena than the stock market, and its value to shareholders, tended to become an issue of increasing concern. This concern was first expressed through a concern with social accounting. This can be considered to be an approach to reporting a firm's activities which stresses the need for identification of socially relevant behaviour, the determination of those to whom the company is accountable for its social performance and the development of appropriate measures and reporting techniques. Thus social accounting considers a wide range of aspects of corporate performance and encompasses a recognition that different aspects of performance are of interest to different stakeholder groupings. These aspects can include:

- the concerns of investors;
- a focus upon community relations;
- a concern with ecology.

Measuring performance in terms of these aspects will include, in addition to the traditional profit-based measures, such things as:

- consumer surplus;
- economic rent;
- environmental impact;
- non-monetary values.

Many writers consider, by implication, that measuring social performance is important without giving reasons for believing so. Solomons (1974), however, considered the reasons for measuring objectively the social performance of a business. He suggests that while one reason is to aid rational decision-making, another reason is of a defensive nature.

Unlike other writers, Solomons not only argued for the need to account for the activities of an organisation in terms of its social performance but also suggested a model for doing this, in terms of a statement of social income. His model for the analysis of social performance is as follows:

	£
Statement of social income:	
Value generated by the productive process	xxx
+ Unappropriable benefits	xxx
− External costs imposed on the community	xxx
Net social profit/loss	xxx

Though this model seems to provide a reasonable method of reporting upon the effects of the activities of an organisation on its external environment, it fails to provide any suggestions as to the actual measurement of external costs and benefits. Such measurement is much more problematic and this is one of the main problems of any form of social accounting – the fact that the measurement of effects external to the organisation is extremely difficult. Indeed, it can be argued that this difficulty in measurement is one reason why organisations have concentrated upon the measurement through accounting for their internal activities, which are much more susceptible to measurement.

It therefore becomes important to consider social accounting and reporting in terms of responsibility and accountability. These can be classified as:

- the internal needs of a business, which are catered for by management accounting;
- the external needs, which are addressed for shareholders by financial reporting but largely ignored for other stakeholder interests.

Social accounting is an attempt to redress this balance through a recognition that a firm affects, through its actions, its external environment (both positively and negatively) and should therefore account for these effects as part of its overall accounting for its actions.

The measurement and reporting of performance

The evaluation of the performance of an organisation is partly concerned with the measurement of performance and partly with the reporting of that performance. If a greater importance is given to social accountability then changing measurement and reporting needs of an organisation must also be recognised. Social accounting is an attempt to measure and report upon organisational performance from a variety of perspectives, and hence to supply various diverse groups, with different needs for information. Thus it has been argued that there is a need for several distinct types of accounting to perform such a function. This argument is based upon a consideration of the limitations of the traditional economic base of accounting; it questions some of the premises of this economic base, such as:

● the desirability of continuing economic growth;
● the existence of rational economic man, making rational economic decisions;
● the exclusion of altruism from any decision-making process;
● the exclusion from consideration of the way in which wealth is distributed.

These factors are argued to be such that there is a need for a new paradigm. In this new paradigm the environment is considered as part of the firm rather than as an externality. Thus the concept of sustainability, together with a consideration of the use of primary resources, is given increased weighting as far as accounting for the actions of a firm is concerned. Indeed some writers go further and argue that there is a need for a new social contract between a business and the stakeholders to which it is accountable, and a business mission which recognises that some things go beyond accounting.

Accountability and social activity

It is generally recognised that power is an essential component of accountability and that greater accountability is recognised towards those stakeholders which have more power. In this respect organisations can be considered as externalising machines suited to self-preservation. Thus when faced with conflicting pressures a company will act in the interests of self-preservation by choosing the option with smaller risk but less benefit. It is also argued that the power of businesses is increasingly being consolidated into the hands of the executives, rather than owners, as it is they who have the expertise to assess this risk. One of the problems with this concern with power is that society at large, and the environment in particular, tend not to be powerful stakeholders. It is perhaps for this reason that social accountability tends not to be a feature of organisations.

Research has, however, been undertaken with regard to the relationship between managers and employees and the use made of accounting information in this respect. This research has been concerned with the disclosure of accounting information to trade unions. Different conceptualisations of the relationship between management and employees can generate different conclusions regarding the disclosure of accounting information during industrial relations bargaining. Findings from such research demonstrate that increased disclosure can lead to reduced opposition from employees, greater commitment and loyalty, and increased legitimacy for intended action. This evidence therefore seems to suggest that greater disclosure of information can actually bring about benefits to the organisation as well as to the stakeholders involved. This is in line with the concepts of social and environmental accounting which are concerned with greater disclosure of the activities of an organisation but with an emphasis upon disclosure of actions and the way in which they impact upon the external environment.

Much of this research and argument is undertaken by people who start from the presumption that such accountability, and consequent reporting, is desirable without giving any reasons why this should be so. The benefits which ensue therefore go to the various stakeholders who benefit without any discernable benefit to the organisations themselves. One way to achieve this is through legislation and this is the approach taken by various countries around the world, with mixed results.

Another approach, however, is to demonstrate the benefits to an organisation itself from such social responsibility, and this is the approach taken in this book. These benefits can take place in the short term or in the long term. Generally speaking they can be in any of the following forms:

- increased information for decision-making;
- reduced operational costs or increased revenue;
- more accurate product or service costing;
- improved strategic decision-making;
- improved image;
- market development opportunities.

Each of these will be considered throughout this book. First, however, we will consider parallel developments in environmental concern.

The principles of social accounting

The approach to measuring organisational activity through an accounting for the actions of a firm in relation to the external environment, and the impact of the activities of the firm upon external stakeholders, is generally known as environmental accounting. Such accounting recognises that the actions taken by a firm impact upon its external environment and consequently can be, and should be, accounted for. This is in contrast with the traditional view of accounting, grounded in classical liberalism, that what happens to the firm is of relevance to the firm, and should therefore be accounted for, while what happens outside the firm, whether affected by the firm or not, is irrelevant to the firm and not therefore a proper subject for accounting as far as the firm is concerned. Forms of accounting which reflect the actions of the firm upon its external environment are generally labelled social accounting, which has been defined as

> . . . the process of communicating the social and environmental effects of organisations' economic actions to particular interest groups within society and to society at large, beyond the traditional role of providing a financial account to the owners of capital, in particular, shareholders. Such an extension is predicated upon the assumption that companies do have wider responsibilities than simply to make money for their shareholders. (Gray *et al.* 1987)

and as

> Voluntary disclosures of information, both qualitative and quantitative made by organisations to inform or influence a range of audiences. The quantitative disclosures may be in financial or non-financial terms. (Mathews 1993)

There are some essential features of this form of accounting which distinguish it from traditional accounting. These features are based upon three principles:

1 It is an attempt to report upon the effects of the actions of the firm upon the societal environment which is external to the firm itself.
2 It is aimed at an audience external to the firm, and which has no legal ownership of that firm.
3 It is voluntary in nature.

In this respect it differs from traditional accounting in terms of its audience and its voluntary nature. One consequence of this is that not all firms feel the need for reporting this aspect of their operations and such reporting as does take place is by no means uniform in its approach.

Environmental accounting

One subset of social accounting is that form of accounting which is concerned with reporting the actions of the firm insofar as they relate to the environment in a physical rather than social sense. This is collectively known as environmental accounting. Environmental accounting can be defined in the following terms:

> ... it can be taken as covering all areas of accounting that may be affected by the response to environmental issues, including new areas of eco-accounting. (Gray *et al.* 1993)

and

> Environmental accounting can be defined as a sub-area of accounting that deals with activities, methods and systems for recording, analysing and reporting environmentally induced financial impacts and ecological impacts of a defined economic system. (Schaltegger *et al.* 1996)

Just as the definitions of such forms of accounting vary from one person to another, so too does the way in which such accounting is operationalised within different firms. Indeed this variation can be found not just through inter-firm comparison but also through longitudinal study. Environmental accounting is a relatively recent phenomenon and Mathews (1997) suggests that its roots go back only to the 1970s. Since that time interest in such accounting has grown considerably and the applications, perceived relevance and techniques of environmental accounting have developed considerably. Indeed the purposes of environmental accounting have also changed. It has been argued that such forms of accounting were used in the past to placate external environmental activists. Now, however, it is regarded as an important source of information for the internal management of the firm. In this book we will provide proof for this statement but it will also be suggested that one of the prime uses of environmental accounting data is for external consumption rather than for internal decision-making purposes.

It must be stated at this point, however, that difficulties surround the nature and purposes of environmental accounting. This is equally true with regard to the nature and purpose of traditional accounting, and the appropriateness of any measures suggested for either. Nevertheless it is clear that social and environmental accounting is significantly different from traditional accounting because of its attempt to include an accounting for the effects of the actions of the organisation upon the external environment. Thus the organisation, although recognised to be a discrete entity, is only one part of a system which transcends the organisational boundary and negates the internal/external binarism of traditional accounting. This different focus both distinguishes such accounting from its traditional role and leads to the need for different measures of performance.

The measurement of environmental impact

The techniques of environmental accounting have been subject to continual development over the years, and we will consider them in detail in the rest of this book. Growth in the techniques offered for measuring environmental impact, and reporting thereon, has also continued throughout the last 25 years during which the concept of environmental accounting has existed. However, the ability to discuss the fact that firms, through their actions, affect their external environment and that this should be accounted for has often exceeded any practical suggestions for measuring such impact. For example, it has been suggested using the concept of social overhead to be offset against reported results from traditional measures of income, without suggesting how this might be calculated. Equally a model for such accounting, based entirely upon non-financial quantification, has been suggested. Other suggestions include a conceptual model for the categorisation of various forms of socially oriented disclosure which included the separation of socially responsible accounting from total impact accounting. Various models for sustainability accounting have also been suggested.

At the same time as the technical implementation of environmental accounting and reporting has been developing, the philosophical basis for such accounting has also been developed. Thus the extent to which accountants should be involved in environmental accounting has been the subject of considerable discussion. Similarly it has been argued that such accounting can be justified by means of the social contract as benefiting society at large. Some have argued that sustainability is the cornerstone of environmental accounting while others have stated that environmental auditing should be given prominence.

More critical authors have viewed traditional accounting from a labour process perspective; they view it as a mechanism to support the dominance of capital over labour interests. Such authors have tended to view social and environmental accounting as a mechanism for benefiting non-traditional users of accounting information.[5] Thus it has been argued by some that there is a need to prevent the institutionalisation of such environmental accounting by its adoption and absorption by the accounting profession into normal accounting. Such critical views, however, conflict with the declared aims of environmental accounting – namely of measuring and reporting upon the effect within the external environment of the activities of the firm. In order to do so effectively, environmental accounting needs to be absorbed within mainstream accounting and utilised by practising accountants as a part of their normal activities. Environmental accounting cannot therefore be both a radical vehicle for change as well as a mechanism for incorporating externalities into the reporting of the firm through its accounting.[6]

Environmental accounting can be seen to be a topical issue from a variety of perspectives, but to be useful in measuring and reporting upon the impact of the actions of the firm it must necessarily be absorbed into the repertoire of accounting practitioners and into the systems of organisational control and reporting, rather than remaining as a critical external discourse. In other words, to be of use to businesses it is not appropriate to consider environmental accounting as a means to provide a basis for the criticism of organisational activity and behaviour. Such accounting becomes relevant and practical only when its benefits are established and built into organisational accounting. It is the purpose of this book, not to show that such accounting provides a vehicle for criticism but rather to demonstrate its practical utility.

The terms social accounting and environmental accounting can therefore be seen to have a variety of meanings and uses which for some people are revolutionary in their implications but for others are merely concerned with the ways in which business performance can be improved. In summary, the terms have two major dimensions to their use:

- They can refer solely to those costs and benefits which directly impact upon the bottom-line profitability of the company. These can be termed private costs and benefits.
- They can refer to the costs and benefits which affect individuals, society and the environment for which a company is not accountable. These can be termed societal costs and benefits.

In this chapter we are concerned primarily with the private costs and benefits, partly because this is where organisations starting to implement social or environmental accounting typically begin and partly because any justification for the implementation of such accounting must have a demonstrable benefit to that organisation. Much of what we consider will, however, be applicable to societal costs and benefits, and where there are obvious benefits to the organisation these will also be considered.

A primer produced by ACCA[7] claims that environmental accounting arises in three distinct contexts:

1 *National income accounting*: In this context such accounting refers to the consumption of a nation's resources, both renewable and non-renewable.
2 *Financial accounting*: In this context the concern is with the disclosure of environmental liabilities and material environmental costs.
3 *Management accounting*: In this context the concern is with the identification of costs and benefits which affect the organisation's decision-making processes.

It is this third context which we will concentrate upon, although there will be some implications for the other two contexts which will be mentioned.

The starting point for any consideration of the implications for the decision-making processes of an organisation is the identification of the relevant costs and benefits. These can be identified through an environmental audit.

The environmental audit

Before the development of any appropriate measures can be considered, it is first necessary for the organisation to develop an understanding of the effects of its activities upon the external environment. The starting point for the development of such an understanding therefore is the undertaking of an environmental audit. An environmental audit therefore is merely an investigation and recording of the activities of the organisation in order to develop this under-standing. Such an audit will address, inter alia, the following issues:

- the extent of compliance with regulations and possible future regulations;
- the extent and effectiveness of pollution control procedures;
- the extent of energy usage and possibilities increasing for energy efficiency;
- the extent of waste produced in the production processes and the possibilities for reducing such waste or finding uses for the waste necessarily produced;
- the extent of usage of sustainable resources and possibilities for the develop-ment of renewable resources;
- the extent of usage of recycled materials and possibilities for increasing recycling;
- life cycle analysis of products and processes;
- the possibilities of increasing capital investment to affect these issues;
- the existence of or potential for environmental management procedures to be implemented.

The undertaking of such an audit will require a detailed understanding of the processes of an organisation. The audit will therefore need to be detailed, and cannot be undertaken just by the accountants of the organisation. It will also involve other specialists and managers within the organisation who will need to pool their knowledge and expertise to arrive at a full understanding. Indeed, one of the features of environmental accounting is that its operation depends to a significant extent upon the co-operation of the various technical and managerial specialists within the organisation. Thus environmental accounting cannot be undertaken by the accountants alone, and one of its bene-fits is that it involves all these specialists in the pooling of knowledge and understanding.

The objectives of an environmental audit are:

- firstly to arrive at a complete understanding of the effects of organisational activity;
- secondly to be able to assign costs to such activity.

The audit should also enable the managers of the organisation to consider alternative ways of undertaking the various activities which comprise the operational processes of the organisation. It should also enable them to con-sider and evaluate the cost implications, as well as the benefits, of undertaking such processes differently. Such an audit will probably necessitate the collec-tion of information which has not previously been collected by the organisa-tion, although it may well be in existence somewhere within the organisation's data files. A complete environmental audit is a detailed and time-consuming operation but there is no need for such an exercise to be completed as one operation. Indeed, the review of processes and costs should be a continuous part of any organisation's activity. In this way it can lead to the implementation of better processes or control procedures without any regard to environmental implications. Thus the way to approach this audit is to extend the normal routines of the organisation to include a consideration, and quantification, of environmental effects on an ongoing basis.

Once this audit has been completed, it is possible to consider the development of appropriate measures and reporting mechanisms to provide the necessary information for both internal and external reporting. The measures which are used need to be based upon the principles of environmental accounting, as outlined in p. 291. It is important to recognise, however, that such an environmental audit, while the essential starting point for the development of such accounting and reporting, should not be viewed as a discrete isolated event in the developmental process. Environmental auditing needs to be carried out on a recurrent basis, much as is financial or systems auditing, in order to both review progress through a comparative analysis and establish where further improvement can be made in the light of progress to date and changing operational procedures.

The framework of accounting

Social and environmental accounting is normally considered to be concerned with the compilation of the effects of the activities of organisations from a different perspective, and the reporting of those effects to a wider range of stakeholders. These effects will tend to be different from those covered by mainstream accounting and will cover a wider range of effects and people affected. If such accounting is to be useful to organisations, however, there is a need for this social and environmental accounting to be incorporated into the normal accounting and reporting mechanisms of the organisation. Thus there is a need for a framework under which this can operate and which incorporates such accounting into the normal mechanisms of the organisation. While it is possible to operate a separate accounting system to deal with the concerns of social and environmental accounting this is costly in terms of resources. Moreover, it does not help an organisation to understand how the addressing of the concerns of this form of accounting yields practical benefits to the performance of the organisation.

Any such framework therefore needs to integrate the concerns of social and environmental accounting into the main accounting systems of the organisation. This is necessary in order to maximise the benefits from this accounting as far as the organisation is concerned. These benefits are twofold:

- to ensure that the benefits are yielded to the organisation and can be reflected in the bottom line of the organisation;
- to ensure that the decisions made within the organisation are made with full acquaintance with the facts and their implications.

Separate systems may result in sub-optimal decisions being made because all the facts are not integrated and reported upon.

An integrated accounting system, however, depends upon the development of an appropriate framework. The development of such a framework, in turn, may necessitate the presentation of information in a way which is different from how information is normally reported. It will certainly require the integration of accounting and non-accounting information. Such a framework needs to be built upon a recognition of the principles of environmental accounting and so it is to these that we now need to turn our attention.

The principles of environmental accounting

In order to understand the rationale for environmental accounting, and the basis on which it is suggested that such accounting operates, it is necessary therefore to consider the principles upon which environmental accounting operates. There are three basic principles which are generally regarded as underpinning to environmental accounting:

1 sustainability
2 accountability
3 transparency.

and each will be considered in turn.

Sustainability

Sustainability is concerned with the effects which actions taken in the present have upon the options available in the future. If resources are utilised in the present then they are no longer available for use in the future, and this is of particular concern if the resources are finite in quantity. Thus raw materials of an extractive nature, such as coal, iron or oil, are finite in quantity and once used are not available for future use. At some point in the future therefore alternatives will be needed to fulfil the functions currently provided by these resources. This may be at some point in the relatively distant future but of more immediate concern is the fact that as resources become depleted, the cost of acquiring the remaining resources tends to increase, and hence the operational costs of organisations also tend to increase. Similarly once an animal or plant species becomes extinct, the benefits of that species to the environment can no longer be accrued. In view of the fact that many pharmaceuticals are currently being developed from plant species still being discovered, this may be significant for the future.

Sustainability therefore implies that society must use no more of a resource than can be regenerated. This can be defined in terms of the carrying capacity of the ecosystem and described with input–output models of resource consumption. Viewing an organisation as part of a wider social and economic system implies that these effects must be taken into account, not just for the measurement of costs and value created in the present but also for the future of the business itself.

Measures of sustainability would consider the rate at which resources are consumed by the organisation in relation to the rate at which resources can be regenerated. Unsustainable operations can be accommodated either by developing sustainable operations or by planning for a future lacking in resources currently required. In practice, organisations mostly tend to aim towards less unsustainability by increasing efficiency in the way in which resources are utilised. An example would be an energy efficiency programme.

It might be considered to be unrealistic for any organisation to change to a fully sustainable method of operations, at least in a reasonable time scale. Thus what is of concern is the level of unsustainability of operations and the way in which this unsustainability can be reduced by making changes. A concern with sustainability inevitably implies a longer-term focus upon the operations of the organisation than is normally the case and a constant concern with alternatives which are available.

Accountability

Accountability is concerned with an organisation recognising that its actions affect the external environment. It therefore implies the assuming of responsibility for the effects of those actions. This concept therefore implies a quantification of the effects of actions taken, both internal to the organisation and externally. More specifically the concept implies a reporting of those quantifications to all parties affected by those actions. This implies a reporting to external stakeholders of the effects of actions taken by the organisation and how they are affecting those stakeholders. This concept therefore implies a recognition that the organisation is part of a wider societal network and has responsibilities to all of that network rather than just to the owners of the organisation. Alongside this acceptance of responsibility therefore must be a recognition that those external stakeholders have the power to affect the way in which those actions of the organisation are taken and a role in deciding whether or not such actions can be justified, and if so at what cost to the organisation and to other stakeholders.

Accountability therefore necessitates the development of appropriate measures of environmental performance and the reporting of the actions of the firm. This necessitates the incurring of costs on the part of the organisation in developing, recording and reporting such performance. Naturally in order to be of value to the organisation, the benefits derived must exceed the costs. Benefits must be determined by the usefulness of the measures selected to the decision-making process and by the way in which they facilitate resource allocation, both within the organisation and between it and other stakeholders. Such reporting needs to be based upon the following characteristics:

- understandability to all parties concerned;
- relevance to the users of the information provided;
- reliability in terms of accuracy of measurement, representation of impact and freedom from bias;
- comparability, which implies consistency, both over time and between different organisations.

Inevitably, however, such reporting will involve qualitative facts and judgements as well as quantifications. This qualitativeness will inhibit comparability over time and will tend to mean that such impacts are assessed differently by different users of the information, reflecting their individual values and priorities. A lack of precise understanding of effects, coupled with the necessarily judgmental nature of relative impacts, means that few standard measures exist. This in itself restricts the inter-organisation comparison of such information.

Such accountability will inevitably involve the disclosure of information about the organisation which is not traditionally disclosed and may involve the provision of information, over and above what is normally provided, concerning such things as the prevention or reduction of pollution, the extent of community service undertaken, the effects of actions upon employees and the products or services of the company. More specifically, it will involve accounting in more than merely financial terms and reporting for different purposes. Such disclosure by companies has increased over time and has been shown to lead to benefits not just to the stakeholders who are reported to but also to the organisation itself. This is because of the greater amount of information which is captured by the organisation and reported upon. This in itself leads to better informed decisions on the part of the organisation.

Transparency

Transparency, as a principle, means that the reporting of the external impact of the actions of the organisation can be ascertained from that organisation's reporting and pertinent facts are not disguised within that reporting. Thus all the effects of the actions of the organisation, including external impacts, should be apparent to all from using the information provided by the organisation's reporting mechanisms. Transparency is of particular importance to external users of such information as these users lack the background details and knowledge available to internal users of such information. Transparency therefore can be seen to follow from the other two principles. Equally it can be seen to be a part of the process of recognition of responsibility on the part of the organisation for the external effects of its actions and part of the process of transferring power to external stakeholders.

Principles of environmental reporting

These principles will reflect not just in the decision-making processes of the organisation and in its accounting systems but also in its reporting systems. This leads to a consideration of the principles which need to apply to these reporting systems. These can be summarised as:

- *Relevance*: to meet this criterion the target audience must be considered when providing information to ensure that the appropriate information is being reported upon.

- *Comprehensibility*: this means that the target group must be able to interpret the information correctly and the information supplied must therefore be adapted to the needs of the audience.
- *Verifiability*: it must be possible to check the exactness and precision of the data.
- *Completeness*: both positive and negative information must be included.
- *Comparability*: to be comparable, the figures reported must be given in a consistent manner and reports must be made at regular intervals.

It can be seen, however, that more effort is needed in such reporting to ensure the accuracy and comprehensiveness of such reporting. This inevitably has implications for the accounting systems of the organisation. We will consider this in more detail in the next chapter, but this accuracy and completeness can be seen to depend upon the correct identification of any social and environmental costs which might be incurred by the organisation. We need therefore to turn our attention to the identification of such costs.

Identifying social and environmental costs

A starting point for social and environmental accounting is the identification of those costs which are properly classified as social or environmental. The recognition of such costs is important for appropriate management decisions, as will be considered in more details in the next chapter. The definition of such a cost, however, depends to a large extent upon the intended use of the information; thus an environmental cost may be defined differently depending upon whether the information is going to be used for:

- capital budgeting purposes;
- product design purposes;
- cost allocation purposes;
- other management decisions.

Equally such costs will certainly include current costs but may well also include future costs and even potential costs, depending upon the use to which such information will be put in the management decision-making processes of the firm. These costs can be described as follows:

- *Current costs*: those costs which are currently being incurred and are therefore included in the accounting of the organisation.
- *Future costs*: those costs which are not currently being incurred but can be expected to be incurred at some point – at this point they will be included in the accounting of the organisation.
- *Potential costs*: those costs which may or may not be incurred – these will only be included in the accounting of the organisation if and when they are actually incurred.

It is important to recognise that, in the identification of environmental costs, the nature of costs is not necessarily so clear-cut that they can be readily classified as a social or environmental cost or not. Often the situation is unclear and the cost may be partly social or environmental and partly not. What is important, however, is to ensure that all costs are recognised and that they receive appropriate attention.

The terminology of environmental accounting often uses such terms as full or total cost, true cost or life cycle cost in an attempt to emphasise that traditional approaches are incomplete in their scope because of the way in which they overlook or hide important social and environmental costs. These terms, however, are not particularly helpful in identifying and focusing attention upon relevant costs for decision-making purposes. The Global Environmental Management Initiative[8] therefore uses terms such as direct, hidden, contingent liability and less tangible costs to focus attention more appropriately. We will therefore consider each of these classifications of costs in more detail.

Direct costs

Traditional accounting identifies these costs separately but they are not normally considered in terms of environmental costs. It will be apparent, however, that there can be environmental implications. For example, the decreased use of raw materials or a reduction in wastage has environmental implications. So too does the use of renewable resources rather than non-renewable resources. It is therefore important to identify which direct costs can be considered to be environmental costs as this can affect the business decisions made. Examples of such environmental costs which need to be identified separately, but are often overlooked, for environmental accounting purposes include:

- raw materials consumed;
- utility resources consumed;
- waste and reworking costs;
- salvage values.

Hidden costs

Many costs to a business are classified as overhead costs or general costs of operating a process or facility. Some of these can have significant environmental implications. Equally many costs are hidden in capital costs which have environmental implications. It might also be important to distinguish these costs between those incurred because of past actions, those incurred because of current operations and those incurred, or prevented, due to future intentions. These can be subdivided into four classifications as follows:

Regulatory costs

For most companies these are treated as overhead costs within the general overhead cost pool. This makes their magnitude more difficult to determine.

Moreover, their treatment in this manner makes it more likely that they will not receive the management attention which they deserve. Examples include:

- monitoring costs;
- reporting costs;
- training and inspection costs;
- labelling;
- pollution control costs;
- waste management costs;
- insurance and remedial work;
- protective equipment costs.

Voluntary costs

These are costs which are incurred over and above compliance costs and regulatory costs. They are often treated in the same way as regulatory costs and thereby lost within a general overhead cost pool. Examples include:

- community relations costs;
- landscaping and habitat protection costs;
- environmental audits;
- financial support to charities and environmental groups;
- reporting (e.g. annual environmental reports);
- recycling initiatives;
- feasibility studies;
- some R&D expenditure.

Lifecycle costs

These can be considered from two aspects:

Upfront costs

These are incurred prior to the introduction of a process or facility or prior to the commencement of a capital project and can relate to design costs, evaluation of alternatives or siting issues. These tend to be incorporated into either overhead costs or R&D costs and their significance is lost through such treatment. Examples include:

- site studies;
- site preparation;
- some R&D expenditure.

End of life costs

These costs are often not incorporated into cost systems or project evaluations at all even though they can be expected to be incurred at some point in the future. They are therefore essentially future costs or potential costs. Such costs would include decommissioning costs, asset replacement costs and anticipated future regulatory costs. Such costs tend to be overlooked because they are not well researched and documented and not included in traditional accounting systems. Examples include:

- closure and decommissioning costs;
- asset replacement costs;
- disposal costs;
- remedial or landscaping costs;
- post-closure care costs.

Contingent liability costs

These are costs which may or may not be incurred at some point in the future. As such they can best be treated probabilistically in terms of an expected value. They tend to arise because of unexpected consequences from the actions of the firm, such as accidents or subsequent discoveries. They would include remediation, compensation and litigation costs. These costs do not need to be identified for other purposes and therefore tend to be excluded from traditional accounting systems. As a consequence they tend to be excluded from the decision-making processes of the firm unless included in risk management procedures. Examples include:

- penalties and fines;
- compensation for damage to property or personal injury;
- legal costs;
- economic loss costs;
- future compliance costs.

Less tangible costs

Such costs are intangible and not readily subject to quantification because of their subjective nature. They tend to be concerned with the perceptions of such stakeholders as customers, employees, communities, the government and regulators. As such they are often defined as corporate image or relationship costs. What makes these costs intangible is not so much that the costs incurred cannot be identified but rather that the associated benefits almost certainly are. Examples include:

- costs of image creation of loss;
- costs of maintaining relationships with suppliers and customers;
- costs of employee relations;
- cost of relationships with local communities and society at large;
- costs of relationships with the investor and lender communities.

The classification of environmental costs

There are many costs, as previously mentioned, which cannot be completely identified as environmentally related or not related. This is not a reason for not undertaking such accounting. The objective of environmental accounting is to increase the amount of relevant information that is available to decision-makers who need such information. The success of environmental accounting is not therefore dependant upon the complete identification and classification of all the costs which a firm incurs; rather the benefit arises from a more accurate consideration of all the costs incurred.

Approaches which have been taken by firms to the classification of such indeterminate costs include:

- allowing costs to be treated as environmental for one purpose but not for another;
- treating costs as environmental when it is considered that more than 50 per cent of the cost is environmentally related;
- apportioning the costs of an item or activity and treating part as an environmental cost.

Such mechanisms will of course increase costs within the firm by imposing an increased burden upon the accounting system and its operatives. It is important to be sure that the costs incurred are outweighed by the benefits to be gained. These benefits of course may well be realised in the future and it is therefore important that appropriate time scales are applied to the consideration of the benefits of such action. Equally it is important that all benefits are recognised, even if not capable of accurate quantification, to ensure that the correct decision regarding the application of such classification is made.

It is equally important to recognise that the purpose of environmental accounting is to improve the quality of decision-making for the organisation, by considering all relevant factors. The aim is to improve the performance of the organisation, either in the immediate present or in the longer-term future. Thus the effects can be felt through cost reduction, either in current operations or in future operations, or through increased revenue or returns in the future.

Environmental accounting can of course be applied differently in different organisations and it is therefore important to consider the scale and scope of operations to which such accounting should be applied. The scale of use will depend upon the nature of the organisation as well as its needs and interests, its resources and its objectives. Thus it can be applied at different levels which include the following:

- at corporate level;
- at divisional, geographical or regional level;
- at departmental, facility or location level;

- for particular systems (such as power utilisation, packaging or emission control);
- at individual process level;
- at product or product-line level.

As far as scope is concerned there is a need for the firm to consider what such accounting is designed to achieve. It may be appropriate to apply such accounting only to those costs and benefits which affect profitability, and hence the bottom line. Equally it may be appropriate to consider issues regarding image and stakeholder relationships or to consider future and contingent costs and benefits. Different firms will take a different approach to this issue of scope depending upon the factors which are important to the company as well as the magnitude of such costs and benefits. It will certainly be the case, however, that all organisations can derive some benefits from the introduction of some form of environmental accounting, although the scale and scope will change from one organisation to another.

 # The implementation of environmental accounting

Environmental accounting can be used by any organisation to gain some benefits in its operations and performance, although the form it takes will depend upon the needs of the company. In any firm, however, the successful implementation of such accounting will depend upon the following:

- The support of the top management of the firm. This is because environmental accounting is likely to involve a new way of looking at the performance of the firm and the decision made regarding its operation. Commitment from the top management is likely to be necessary to ensure a culture for successful implementation.
- The establishment of an appropriately cross-functional team. Environmental accounting is not just an issue for accountants. It requires information which is not merely financial but arises from a wide range of specialisms within a company and the bringing together of a wide range of knowledge about the operational activities of the firm. This information needs to be acquired and shared so that an appropriate environmental accounting system can be implemented which will ensure the maximisation of benefits to the company.

Environmental accounting naturally has a part to play in any environmental management system which a company has because it provides a decision support tool for such a system. Companies who have introduced environmental accounting have, however, found that it has a part to play in many other systems or business tools. Examples of systems which have been improved by the use of environmental accounting techniques include the following:

- Total quality management systems;
- Life cycle design and costing systems;
- Cost of quality models;
- Design models for products or processes;
- Business process re-engineering programmes;
- Cost reduction programmes;
- Activity-based management systems;
- Activity-based costing systems.

The objectives of environmental accounting

We have seen therefore that the objective of environmental accounting is to measure the effects of the actions of the organisation upon the environment and to report upon those effects. In other words, the objective is to incorporate the effect of the activities of the firm upon externalities and to view the firm as a network which extends beyond just the internal environment to include the whole environment. In this view of the organisation the accounting for the firm does not stop at the organisational boundary but extends beyond to include not just the business environment in which it operates but also the whole social environment.

Environmental accounting therefore adds a new dimension to the role of accounting for an organisation because of its emphasis upon accounting for external effects of the organisation's activities. In doing so this provides a recognition that the organisation is an integral part of society, rather than a self-contained entity which has only an indirect relationship with society at large. This self-containment has been the traditional view taken by organisations as far as their relationship with society at large is concerned, with interaction being only by means of resource acquisition and sales of finished products or services. Recognition of this closely intertwined relationship of mutual interdependency between the organisation and society at large, when reflected in the accounting of the organisation, can help bring about a closer, and possibly more harmonious, relationship between the organisation and society. Given that the managers and workers of an organisation are also stakeholders in that society in other capacities, such as consumers, citizens and inhabitants, this reinforces the mutual interdependency.

Environmental accounting also provides an explicit recognition that stakeholders other than the legal owners of the organisation have power and influence over that organisation and also have a right to extend their influence into affecting the organisation's activities. This includes the managers and workers of the organisation, who are also stakeholders in other capacities. Environmental accounting therefore provides a mechanism for transferring some of the power from the organisation to these stakeholders. It is considered that this voluntary surrender of such power by the organisation can actually provide benefits to the organisation. Benefits from increased disclosure and the adoption of environmental accounting can provide further benefits to the organisation in its operational performance, beyond this enhanced relationship with society at large. These benefits can include:

- an improved image for the organisation which can translate into additional sales;
- the development of environmentally friendly or sustainable methods of operation which can lead to the development of new markets;
- reduced future operational costs through the anticipation of future regulation and hence a cost advantage over competitors;
- decreased future liabilities brought about through temporal externalisation;
- better relationships with suppliers and customers which can lead to reduced operational costs as well as increased sales;
- easier recruitment of labour and lowered costs of staff turnover.

It needs to be recognised, however, that there are increased costs of instituting a regime of environmental accounting and that these additional costs need to be offset against the possible benefits to be accrued. These increased costs are concerned with the development of appropriate measures of environmental performance and the necessary alterations to the management information and accounting information systems to incorporate these measures into the reporting system. This is particularly problematical for the organisation in terms of justification because the increased costs are readily quantifiable but the benefits are much more difficult to quantify.

This leads to one of the main problems with the accounting for externalities through social and environmental accounting. This problem is concerned with the quantification of the effects of the activities of the organisation upon its external environment. This problem revolves around four main areas:

1 determining the effects upon the external environment of the activities of the organisation;
2 developing appropriate measures for those effects;
3 quantifying those effects in order to provide a comparative yardstick for the evaluation of alternative courses of action, particularly in terms of an accounting-based quantification;
4 determining the form and extent of disclosure of those quantification so as to maximise the benefits of that disclosure while minimising the costs of the disclosure and the possibility of knowledge of the firm's operational activities being given to competitors.

These are problems which have been addressed by proponents of this form of accounting. It is fair to say, however, that these problems have primarily been recognised to exist rather than being satisfactorily solved. Those that argue in favour of an increased extent of disclosure in this area tend to consider the advantages of the disclosure from the point of view of external stakeholders rather than from the point of view of the organisation itself. Indeed, one of the features of the environmental accounting discourse is the polarisation of views between those concerned with the firm, and its owners and managers, and those concerned with the environmental and thereby certain external stakeholders. Nevertheless it is increasingly apparent that these environmental issues are recognised by organisations as being of importance and the extent of environmental reporting by organisation is increasing and seems likely to increase further in the future. The changing nature of reporting will be considered later, in the next chapter, but first we need to consider ways in which these problems can be addressed.

The drivers of environmental accounting

There is a general belief, not only among stakeholders but also among the internal managers of a business, that environmental accounting can have a significant effect upon business performance. Equally it is generally held that the measurement of such performance can help manage and improve the environmental impact of the business. This belief is driven by a number of factors, which can be classified as external factors and internal factors.

External factors

These can be summarised as follows:

- demands for information by regulators and other government agencies;
- public concerns regarding risks to health and to the ecological environment;
- the need to reassure investors and lenders that their financial interests are not being jeopardised by environmental problems;
- the exerting of pressure by industry associations and other business interests to improve performance;
- pressure from environmental groups and customers for increased information concerning environmental performance.

Internal factors

The internal business benefits of environmentally related measurement of performance have been summarised by the European Green Table report[9] as follows:

- providing the management of a company with concise and quantifiable environmental information;
- improving the basis for setting a company's environmental policy objectives and performance targets;
- improving the basis for a company's internal and external environmental reporting as well as communication regarding environmental issues;

- enabling companies to define their significant environment-affecting aspects and to describe and measure their environmental performance;
- allowing companies to focus upon, and to demonstrate, improvement in environmental performance;
- providing a valuable mechanism for those aiming to achieve ISO 14001 and EMS certification;
- complementing existing social performance by including the development of indicators for health and safety;
- improving the basis for internal and external benchmarking.

Many of these benefits can be seen to be concerned with making a more effective response, through internal actions, to the external pressures listed above. Internal environmentally related performance measurement is not, however, simply about reacting to external pressures and many organisations can be seen to be becoming more proactive in the setting of their own agendas for environmental performance improvement. This is because of the perceived benefits from such a course of action. Much criticism has, however, been levelled at the internal drivers of environmental performance, both from environmental pressure groups and from academics. Common criticisms have been concerned with the following:

- Many companies are driven by the need to comply with existing or anticipated legislation rather than by any real concern with the environment.
- Much corporate environmental action is concerned with publicity and image rather than with the environment, and is therefore little more than a public relations exercise.
- Internal motivations for environmental improvement are often prevented or diluted by budgetary and other business constraints which prevent significant action being taken; consequently external compulsion, through legislation or regulation, is necessary to bring about effective action by a company.
- Measures of environmental performance tend to be selectively chosen to demonstrate improvement rather than to provide a balanced picture of environmental performance.
- A concern with measurement and quantification can, in itself, be symptomatic of a managerialist discourse which seeks to impose its own limits on the environmental debate and thereby to effectively silence alternative points of view.

While any action by companies is open to such interpretation, and there is an element of truth in such interpretations, there is nevertheless sufficient evidence to show that companies are to a large extent genuinely concerned with their environmental performance. This is not just because such companies recognise their social duties as corporate citizens but also because they recognise the business benefits which can follow an improving environmental performance. These business benefits inevitably feed through into the bottom-line performance of the organisation.

Financial reporting and management accounting

There is a significant part of the discourse of accounting which argues that a focus upon financial accounting for external reporting purposes can lead to an inadequacy of data for internal decision-making purposes. This applies to environmentally related reporting as well as to financially related reporting. It is argued that this is for the following reasons:

- The financial perspective considers that the main aim of performance measurement is the collection of data for the provision of information to external stakeholders. This can compromise the collection and use of data for internal decision-making purposes.
- Data disclosed through annual reporting can be misleading or inappropriate when applied to internally for environmental management purposes.
- A focus upon financial reporting rather than management accounting can lead to a lack of integration of financial and environmental data into the general decision-making process of the organisation.

Environmental management and performance measurement needs to be linked to the broader issue of business management and performance measurement for the following reasons:

1 The environment is an important strategic issue for many companies which needs to be considered as part of a balanced scorecard of business performance measures.
2 Environmentally related performance measures can lead to insights into other areas of performance measurement and hence have practical applications in other areas of the business.
3 The effects of environmental performance spread throughout the organisation and thereby provide experience with dealing with some of the generic problems of the measurement of performance, such as:

- the inevitable balancing between simple measures of performance which can be easily collected and understood but which do not capture a complete picture of performance and more complex measures which capture this complete picture but are difficult to collect and understand;
- the extent to which performance measurement should be concerned with solely quantitative data and the extent to which qualitative data is important in the performance measurement process;
- the extent to which the purpose of performance measurement is concerned with control as opposed to motivation or the creation of continuous improvement.

While there is some validity to the criticisms which have been expressed there is nevertheless a strong body of evidence which demonstrates that the linking of financial reporting to the needs of business management leads to better performance on the part of an organisation. Moreover, the incorporation of environmental accounting information increases this performance.

Notes

1 Indeed this is consistent with financial accounting theory, and its concern with the boundary of the organisation, and with GAAP.
2 They are of course included in the costs of the firm's activities and thereby in its accounting but all the costs and benefits resulting from such action are not fully recognised through traditional accounting.
3 This is particularly the case in countries which have more vigorous regulatory regimes.
4 In other words the extent of regulation in this area has increased in recent years and is continuing to increase.
5 In other words stakeholders other than the professionals for whom external reporting has been considered to be effected.
6 The academic discourse of environmental accounting debates this dilemma to a great extent but this dilemma is not translated into the discourse of corporate reporting. My reading of the academic discourse is that there is a general agreement concerning what is desirable in such accounting and the debate is concerned with the means of achieving that outcome – whether incremental change or revolutionary change is the preferred means of securing the desired outcome.
7 *An introduction to environmental accounting as a business tool* which was a reprint of the primer developed by the United States Environmental Protection Agency (1995).
8 These terms are used in *Finding Cost-effective Pollution Prevention Initiatives: Incorporating Environmental Costs into Business Decision Making*, 1994.
9 The European Green Table produced a report entitled *Environmental Performance Indicators in Industry: Report 5, Practical Experiences with Developing EPIs in 12 Companies* in 1997. This report was based upon a study of Norwegian and Swedish companies and their implementation of environmental performance indicators.

References

Ackerman, R.W. (1975). *The Social Challenge to Business*. Cambridge, MA: Harvard University Press.
Dahl, R.A. (1972). A prelude to corporate reform. *Business and Society Review*, Spring, 17–23.
Fetyko, D.F. (1975). The company social audit. *Management Accounting*, 56 *(10)*.

Gray, R.H., Bebbington, J. and Walters, D. (1993). *Accounting for the Environment*. London: ACCA.

Gray, R., Owen, D. and Maunders, K. (1987). *Corporate Social Reporting: Accounting and Accountability*. London: Prentice-Hall.

Hetherington, J.A.C. (1973). *Corporate Social Responsibility Audit: A Management Tool for Survival*. London: The Foundation for Business Responsibilities.

Klein, T.A. (1977). *Social Costs and Benefits of Business*. Englewood Cliffs, NJ: Prentice-Hall.

Mathews, M.R. (1993). *Socially Responsible Accounting*. London: Chapman & Hall.

Mathews, M.R. (1997). *Twenty-five years of social and environmental accounting: is there a silver jubilee to celebrate?* Paper presented at the British Accounting Association National Conference, Birmingham, March 1997.

Schaltegger, S., Muller, K. and Hindrichsen, H. (1996). *Corporate Environmental Accounting*. Chichester: John Wiley & Sons.

Solomons, D. (1974). Corporate social performance: a new dimension in accounting reports? In H. Edey and B.S. Yamey (eds), *Debits, Credits, Finance and Profits*. London: Sweet & Maxwell, pp. 131–141.

Further reading

Cooper, S., Crowther, D., Davies, M. and Davis, E.W. (2001). *Shareholder or Stakeholder Value*. London: CIMA.

Crowther, D. (2000). *Social and Environmental Accounting*. London: Financial Times/ Prentice-Hall.

Crowther, D. (2002). *A Social Critique of Corporate Reporting*. Aldershot: Ashgate.

Crowther, D. and Rayman-Bacchus, L. (eds) (2003). *Perspectives on Corporate Social Responsibility*. Aldershot: Ashgate.

Additional questions

Question 12.1

'Every large corporation should be thought of as a social enterprise: that is as an entity whose existence and decisions can be justified insofar as they serve public or social purposes' (Dahl 1972).

Discuss the implications of this statement for the accounting systems of an organisation.

Question 12.2

'Environmental accounting can be defined as a sub-area of accounting that deals with activities, methods and systems for recording, analysing and reporting environmentally induced financial impacts and ecological impacts of a defined economic system.' (Schaltegger *et al*. 1996).

Evaluate the main features which distinguish environmental accounting from traditional accounting and the problems associated with the implementation of such a form of accounting.

13

Accounting in a Business Context

Learning objectives

After studying this chapter you should be able to:

- describe the purpose of strategic planning and the steps in the planning process;
- explain the nature of emergent strategy;
- discuss the relationship between strategy and organisation structure;
- describe the effect of IT upon the role of a business manager;
- critique the role of accounting in the planning process.

Introduction

As we have seen in this book, planning is an essential element of the work of a manager. Planning is a future-oriented activity with the objective of making the right decisions to ensure that the firm can meet its objectives. Equally we have seen that a crucial part of planning is concerned with financial planning. The objectives of financial planning are to:

- evaluate alternative courses of action in order to select the optimal course, in terms of the organisational objectives;
- assess the consequences of the future activities of the firm;
- ensure sufficient resources are available to undertake the planned course of action.

Financial planning therefore puts some detail into the corporate strategic plan. It therefore tends to have shorter-term horizon than does a strategic plan. In general terms, the financial plan will cover a number of years but will be more detailed for the immediate period than it will for future periods.

There are a number of elements of financial planning which are important:

- Budgeting
- Cash flow management
- Investment appraisal
- Performance measurement and evaluation.

In this book we have investigated the way in which accounting can help the business manager to perform his/her job better through:

- planning the operations of the business;
- controlling the plan in operation;
- making decisions which will help in the operation of the business.

All of these functions are vital to a business but are essentially inward looking and concerned with the internal operating of the business. A business manager, however, must be concerned not just with the internal running of the business but must also be concerned with the external environment in which the business operates – that is with his/her customers and suppliers, with competitors, and with the market for the products or services supplied by the business.

Such concerns of a business manager comprise the strategic element of the manager's job and a manager must therefore be familiar with this aspect of management, and with the way in which accounting can help in this area. This chapter therefore is concerned with a consideration of the external environment of a business and with the strategic part of a manager's job.

Strategic planning

Strategic planning is concerned with the future of the business and with how the firm can best supply what the market desires. This requires an analysis of the market in which the business is operating in order to decide what the market (i.e. potential customers) wants and what price it is willing to pay for the satisfaction of its wants. This is then followed by an analysis of what the firm is able to produce and supply (and at what price). This then determines how the firm will organise its activities in order to provide these goods or services.

Strategic planning is not concerned with the present but rather with the future and is therefore especially concerned with changes to current patterns of demand, and with ensuring that the firm's capabilities change to meet the changes in market demand. Thus strategic planning is concerned with ensuring the future of the business by ensuring that the firm changes to reflect changed market conditions. This can be modelled as shown in Figure 13.1.

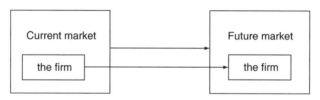

Figure 13.1 Strategic planning and market development

Without strategic planning there is a danger that the market would change without the firm being aware of this change and reflecting it in its own pattern of changing operations. Thus the firm would find itself outside the market, as shown in Figure 13.2. As a result, the firm would effectively go out of business.

Strategic planning therefore is concerned with the future direction of the business. This planning must of course ensure that the business has the capability of achieving whatever direction and objectives are determined in this planning stage. Thus the strategic plan must define a set of objectives for the business and the steps necessary to ensure the achieving of these objectives – in other words, an implementation plan. Most managers of organisations, at the commencement of their strategy development process, start with a vision of where they see the organisation being in the future. This is known as a 'strategic vision' and is often promulgated throughout the organisation in the form of a Mission Statement, which sets in very broad terms the reason for the firm's existence.

Thus the strategic planning process can be modelled as shown in Figure 13.3.

The implementation plan will involve the following aspects of planning:

Operations plan. To ensure that the firm has the resources (i.e. manpower, capital investment, working capital) and capabilities to achieve the objectives of the plan. These capabilities include:

- technological capability;
- capacity planning;
- ability to produce required costings.

Marketing plan. To ensure that the firm is able to:

- produce the required amount and maintain adequate stocks;
- to price the product correctly.

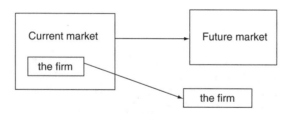

Figure 13.2 Market development without strategic planning

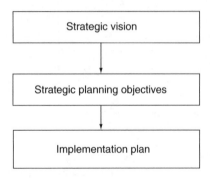

Figure 13.3 The strategic planning process

Figure 13.4 The components of the strategic plan

Financial plan. To ensure that the firm has the financial resources to:

● manage operations;
● undertake any necessary capital investment.

Thus the strategic plan will need to be as shown in Figure 13.4.

Corporate planning

The strategic plan sets out the objectives of the business for the future in outline terms and considers the options available to the business and the capabilities of the business to meet this plan. Once the future direction of the business has been determined by this planning, there is a need to change this plan into a more definite plan which can be expressed in quantitative terms. This is the function of the corporate plan, which provides a detailed plan for the firm, and its component parts, in order to enable the organisation of the future activities of the firm and to communicate this planning throughout the firm. This in turn leads to the development of the short-term plan, or budget, of the firm.

Thus the planning stages of the organisation are as shown in Figure 13.5.

Figure 13.5 Stages in the corporate planning process

The environmental analysis will enable a firm to develop its strategic plan through an examination of the external environment in which the firm is operating. An examination of the internal environment will enable a firm to translate this plan into a corporate plan for implementation. Part of this analysis will comprise a GAP analysis which will inform the managers of the firm of the ability of the firm to meet the plan and any gaps in resources which need to be addressed. Thus this GAP analysis will enable the managers of the business to determine what resources are needed in order to implement the plan and this will feed into both the operating budget and the capital investment budget.

We can see that the business manager needs to be involved at all stages of this planning process and that the accounting techniques which we have discussed have an important part to play in helping at all levels and all stages of the planning process. Thus management accounting is of importance to a business and its managers, not just operationally but also strategically.

Planned and emergent strategy

Although an organisation develops its strategy through this planning process, it is often the case that the effects of this strategy do not materialise in the manner intended. While following this strategy the managers of the business will continue making decision on a day-to-day basis. These decisions will inevitably

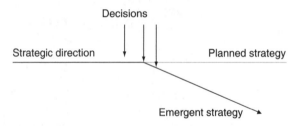

Figure 13.6 Planned and emergent strategies

affect the strategic direction of the organisation and may cause changes in the way the strategy is manifest in the operations of the organisation. This is known as emergent strategy, and can be modelled as shown in Figure 13.6.

Accounting and organisational design

An important part of strategic planning is to ensure that the organisation is structured in such a way that the plan can be achieved, and that the control systems of the organisation provide appropriate feedback to managers. This feedback is necessary in order to ensure that managers are able to measure performance against the plan and take corrective action as necessary. Thus the structure of an organisation needs to be determined by its planning while its control systems need to be determined by its structure, as illustrated in Figure 13.7. The control systems, in turn, provide a feedback loop as shown in Figure 13.8.

Organisational design is therefore dependent upon the planning of the business and accounting information is used to provide managers with feedback via the control systems in order to measure performance. Although each

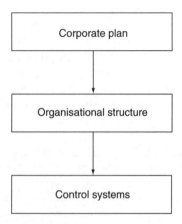

Figure 13.7 Planning and control systems

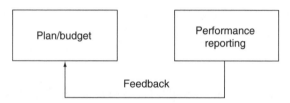

Figure 13.8 The feedback loop

organisation tends to be unique in its structural design and control systems, various attempts have been made to classify organisations according to their structural design and control systems. One such classification was undertaken by Miles and Snow (1978) who classified organisations according to the way in which they responded to their external environment. They identified four types of organisation:

1 *Defenders*: These organisations are strong on control systems, operate in stable markets where growth is slow and incremental, and tend to have hierarchical structures.
2 *Prospectors*: These organisations are concerned with exploiting market opportunities and therefore tend to have little formal structure, and control systems which are only concerned with overall results rather than detail.
3 *Analysers*: These organisations tend to operate in a matrix structure rather than hierarchically, and tend to have extensive planning systems, and elaborate control systems to measure performance against budgets.
4 *Reactors*: These organisations react to market changes rather than planning their strategy. Their structure and control is therefore viewed as often inappropriate to their needs and their performance is consequently below that achieved by other types of organisation.

Organisation theory is also concerned with other issues such as whether an organisation is centralised or decentralised and whether this affects the performance of the organisation. Decentralisation tends to be a key feature of modern organisations and this has had the effect of giving more responsibility to individual managers. Such managers therefore have more decisions to make and so need to understand the techniques which we have considered in order to be able to use them to help in managing their individual areas of responsibility.

One further trend in organisational design which is of significance to modern business managers is the trend away from hierarchical organisations towards a flatter structure with fewer levels of management. This is known as delayering and has been a feature of organisational design in the 1990s. This trend too has had the effect of giving greater responsibility to individual managers. It has also had the effect that the accounting department of an organisation has been delayered, thus providing the individual managers with less technical support from accountants. This too means that all business managers need to have a sound grasp of the techniques of management accounting and to be able to apply these techniques to appropriate business problems without relying upon the support of other expertise in the organisation.

The impact of IT upon business management

One of the features of business in recent years which looks set to progress into the future is the increasing use of IT by the firm as a whole and also by individual business managers. One feature of the increasing use of IT is that the techniques of management accounting which we have considered have become easier to use because of the processing capabilities of the IT available to managers. This is particularly true of the more statistical and mathematical techniques which we have considered. Thus analysis prior to decision-making has become easier and this has given a business manager the opportunity and ability to undertake more detailed analysis and to compare alternative decision outcomes in greater detail. This should have the effect of improving managerial decision-making by providing better support for these decisions. It has also had the effect of increasing the role of management accounting in managerial decision-making.

Another feature of the increased use of IT, however, is that it has made much more information available to the manager and has meant that the information provided is not just more detailed but also more speedily produced and hence more up to date. This improved feedback is valuable from the point of view of measuring performance and enabling corrective action to be taken when necessary. Also because the information is more up to date, corrective action can be taken earlier and therefore tends to need to be less dramatic. One problem with this increased volume of data available to managers, however, is that of information overload. This means that it is more difficult to identify the significant information from within the increased volume of data available. It might be argued therefore that although the quantity and speed of feedback from control systems have improved, the quality of that feedback has deteriorated. This means that the skill of a manager to identify and react to the relevant and significant information needs to be increased. As much of this information is financial in content this too means that the accounting expertise of each individual manager needs to be higher, as well as his/her IT competence.

This trend looks set to continue into the future and it means that the required skill level of each manager, as far as management accounting is concerned, appears to be continuing to increase.

Ensuring the numbers make sense

Although the subject matter of this book is managing finance, it is important to recognise that this must be set within the context of the strategic decision-making process of an organisation. The message therefore is that the best decisions are made when based upon analysis. This implies:

- strategic analysis
- financial analysis
- judgement.

In this book we have looked at various techniques of financial analysis and it is important to remember at all times that the reliability of the decision is dependent upon the assumptions made in the analysis. Thus there are a number of points to bear in mind in undertaking such analysis:

1 Strategic analysis requires an understanding of the market, the competition and customers.
2 Planning is future-oriented and not necessarily a continuation of the present.
3 Strategic analysis cannot be undertaken in isolation because competitors are also developing strategy and making decisions, rather than merely reacting to our decisions. Consequently anticipation is part of analysis.
4 A strategy creates value if the post-strategy value of the business exceeds its pre-strategy value but this involves:

- the identification of options;
- testing the validity of assumptions;
- determining the cost of capital;
- considering the uncertainty of projections;
- evaluating risk;
- using judgement.

5 In financial planning it is important to remember that calculations complement rather than replace strategic analysis. Thus analysis informs decision-making and informed judgement is the key to successful strategic decision-making.

 ## The causes of the crisis in modern management accounting

It has been argued at length, by Johnson and Kaplan amongst others, that today's management accounting systems fail to provide accurate product costs and information to aid cost control. Indeed Johnson and Kaplan (1987) note that the early interest of companies in accurately tracing costs to products had virtually disappeared by the First World War. They suggest that this was caused by the inability of firms, and their managers, to justify the high data collection costs in relation to the benefits which might be yielded from information on product costs. At that time businesses were not subjected to the current global competition in their domestic markets and could, notwithstanding the absence of accurate product costs, therefore earn reasonable profits from their activities.

Around the time of the disappearance of the quest to trace the consumption of resources to the products that caused their consumption (we will refer to this as internal costing), inventory costing emerged. Inventory costing was developed to serve different interest groups and different purposes to those of internal costing. We saw earlier that at the turn of the eighteenth century the rapid growth in companies trading with limited liability status created the demand for annual published accounts verified by independent accountants. For carrying out this verification process, accountants needed a simple method to separate costs to be charged in the period from those that would be taken to inventory and thereby carried forward to a future period. To accomplish this, inventory costing was developed. The principal aim of inventory costing was that of separating period costs from inventory costs in order to enable auditors to vouch the value of inventory, and this aim was in complete contrast with the aims of internal costing concerning the use of resources. Internal costing had a completely internal bias aimed at assessing and controlling internal process efficiency together with determining accurate product costs. The main difference in the two methodologies centred around the treatment of indirect overhead costs. Inventory costing created aggregated indirect cost pools which were then allocated to products using one common driver such as direct labour hours. Internal costing, in contrast, sought to identify the causes of indirect costs and to then trace these costs to the product.

Johnson and Kaplan claim that accounting courses and textbooks of that era universally adopted the inventory costing methodology, and so widespread did its teaching become that most modern-day accountants can recall nothing else. The unfortunate consequence of this is that companies now use inventory costing to make strategic product-cost decisions – a purpose for which its design was never intended. In addition, since accounting standards allow only manufacturing costs to be taken to inventory there has been little attention paid to methods of tracing the expenses of selling, research and development, and finance to products.

The environment in which management accounting operates has, however, changed radically over the last few decades but management accounting has largely failed to develop new systems to serve the new needs of its environment. Management accounting continues to apply performance measurement systems that emphasise short-term objectives.

The changing environment of accounting

In the nineteenth and early twentieth century, Western business enjoyed considerable success from the application of mass production. Mass production relied upon a combination of both stable product markets and processes. Markets were supplied and satisfied with standardised products. As an example of this standardisation, it is worthwhile recalling Henry Ford's famous remark that consumers could have any colour car they desired providing it was black. Product stability in this environment enabled companies to reap the rewards of economies of scale. Stable processes were scrutinised to discover the best way to accomplish tasks, building on the foundations of Taylor's principles of scientific management and Henry Ford's newer ideas in the field of mass production. In this environment processes were taken as given and efforts channelled towards their optimisation. The aim was thus to break processes down into simplified tasks, apply motion studies to determine the best way to carry out the tasks involved and then to use time study to ascertain the time that should be taken in the task. Mass production took scientific management a step forward by substituting machinery for labour and allowing machines to set the pace of work. Hounshell (1988) recognises that Ford applied Taylorist ideas of motion study in the layout of machining and assembly lines.

The system served Western business well for many years. Over recent decades, however, American and European markets have come under attack from Japanese products that offer superior quality at lower prices. Japanese business has achieved this competitive advantage, in part, by overturning the tenet of stable processes in mass production. Instead they introduced the notion of continuous improvement. Processes were no longer regarded as given, but instead subjected to attack in any area that was considered to be either wasteful or to not add value to the product. Inventory, for example, considered as wasteful and inefficient needed to be reduced and if possible eliminated and this was achieved through the application of JIT management principles. Similarly total quality management (TQM) forms an integral part of the JIT philosophy.

The Accounting implications of these changes

Global competition has ensured that Western businesses have had to respond to the challenge outlined above. This has been attempted by adopting the manufacturing techniques and philosophies applied so successfully by the Japanese. The result has radically changed the face of, and restored the importance of, manufacturing, which is now seen as a means of providing competitive advantage. The imperatives now emphasised are quality, reduced inventory levels, continuous improvement of processes, removal of all forms of waste and an improved quality of workforce committed to the achievement of company goals. Unfortunately, the accounting systems utilised in this new environment have not changed to reflect these new imperatives. Instead cost accounting philosophy remains embedded in the traditions of scientific management. Romano (1987) suggests that current cost accounting practice is subject to a 'time phase delay' which is 'needed . . . for cost accounting to catch up with factory developments'. Notwithstanding this time delay however, there exists little evidence to suggest that accounting systems are changing to any great extent in response to these changes in operational activities. This may well be because accountants remain cautious in their resistance to the introduction of radical changes to tried and tested systems, or it may be that the replacement of existing systems would involve large investment with a dubious payback. It is clear, however, that change in accounting techniques is necessary. Kaplan (1984) suggests 'outdated accounting and control systems can distort the realities of manufacturing per-formance . . . and place out of reach most of the promised benefits'. If manage-ment accounting systems are to regain their relevance they must be built around a model that reflects the particular manufacturing system which they seek to control and monitor.

It is worth considering at this point why it is that accounting systems have to change to meet the needs of the new manufacturing environment and what new measurement and control systems may be needed. In order to illustrate this we have adopted a framework which first reflects the purposes of cost accounting systems. Howell and Soucy (1987) list such purposes as:

- cost management and control;
- inventory valuation;
- the determination of product costs.

The first impact that the new environment has on cost accounting is to weaken further the case for the continued application of inventory costing sys-tems. Inventory costing was neither designed for nor capable of providing accurate product costs and is similarly incapable of assisting managers in cost control. Its only purpose is, therefore, to provide inventory valuations for external reporting. Whilst external reporting of inventory values remains important in the new environment, the reduced level of stockholding implicit with JIT means that valuation of inventory will clearly have a minimal impact on reported results. In these circumstances it is possible to satisfy the external reporting requirements by devising simplified methods of assigning over-heads to inventory. This would pave the way for the removal of the inventory valuation model of cost accounting and allow the introduction of systems that are capable of fulfilling the other more important purposes of cost accounting systems. Kaplan (1988) argues that it is impossible for one cost system to sat-isfy all of the above purposes and advocates the adoption of several systems that draw on one database.

The second impact JIT has on accounting is to alter the costing method used. With JIT manufacturing there is an increase in the number of batches processed since the ultimate aim of JIT is to achieve a batch size of one. This aim is achieved through improved flexibility of operations, reducing set-up times and improving the flow of materials through the factory. In these cir-cumstances it is no longer appropriate, or feasible, to use works orders to col-lect costs since this would involve an immense amount of paperwork. Accordingly, when JIT is adopted there is a move away from works order/job costing towards process costing (McNair et al. 1988; Swenson and Cassidy 1993). The shift from job to process costing will generally necessitate a revision of the current cost centre structure of the business. The process layout adopted with JIT is usually a flow line or cell dedicated to the production of one prod-uct or product family requiring common processes. The revised cost centre structure will model this and usually the whole flow line or cell will become a cost centre. Unit costs are then determined by dividing the costs incurred within the cell or flow line during the period by the number of units processed. One complicating feature of adopting process costing in this environment is that, as noted, JIT seeks a flexible manufacturing capability suitable for producing a variety of products. Traditional process costing on the other hand envisages the assignment of costs to large numbers of identical products (Horngren *et al.* 1994).

There are a number of other inconsistencies between conventional cost systems and the new manufacturing environment, one of the most striking being the reporting of labour costs. Labour costs have traditionally held a position of prominence in the costing system. Many of the JIT philosophies overturn this position. JIT emphasises employee flexibility and even flow production. In such a setting labour is expected to be flexible and move from job to job as required. This can also include moving between direct and indirect tasks. Similarly, within the cell the worker is expected to perform both the direct production tasks and also indirect tasks such as basic machine maintenance. Tracking labour costs in this setting is difficult if not impossible. Many companies in such an environment now treat labour as a fixed period cost for the whole cell or flow line.

The concept of labour efficiency variances is also called into doubt. Given the objective of even flow production it is possible to have workers standing idle on certain tasks. This arises if there is an imbalance between operations. Traditionally, workers would be expected to overcome the imbalance by producing for stock. This would ensure high labour efficiency but this solution is anathema to JIT, where idle labour is considered preferable to building for stock. The same principle applies also to machine utilisation since once again it is not uncommon to find machines standing idle if work is not being pulled through the system.

If accounting systems are to remain relevant they must seek to devise systems that measure the critical success factors within the new manufacturing environment. Instead of material price variances the system should focus on supplier performance and consider variables such as the percentage of deliveries made on time. Quality is of particularly crucial importance, yet few systems regularly report the cost of quality non-conformance, and Bromwich and Bhimani (1994) suggest ways of collecting quality costs. Also significant in this environment are both the throughput times and set-up times for the processes involved. Systems that report on these variables are also needed. In a JIT setting there will be a high degree of visual control monitoring, observing problems and correcting them immediately before variances appear. The new management accounting systems (MAS) have to exist side by side with such monitoring systems and support these real-time monitoring mechanisms. The new MAS will also need to be able to offer useful trend information to supplement the real-time systems.

One final and important aspect of the new manufacturing environment is the trend towards higher levels of machine automation and utilisation of computer technology. Many machines now incorporate robotic features that have replaced the previous significant interaction between labour and machine.

There are varying degrees of manufacturing automation ranging from the now almost common use of computer numerically controlled (CNC) machines through to the more revolutionary computer integrated manufacturing (CIM) systems. Whatever the degree of automation, however, the impact on manufacturing is the relentless replacement of labour by machinery. This trend has the effect of radically changing the cost structure of the business. More of the firm's costs become fixed and since the capital is greatly increased, the issue of charging the cost of capital to products becomes more important.

Activity-based costing (ABC) is also considered to be particularly appropriate to JIT. We noted earlier that with JIT, any non-value-adding activities are treated as wasteful and eradicated. Traditional costing systems adopt factory-wide overhead pools and seek to allocate these on the basis of direct labour hours. This treatment does not attempt to identify what is causing overheads to be incurred. In contrast, ABC recognises that most overhead costs are transaction-driven and seeks to pinpoint cost drivers. Only by recognising the root cause of overheads can action be taken to reduce or eliminate the cost. In this respect, ABC techniques are consistent with those of JIT.

Traditional cost systems fail to provide accurate product costs

We noted earlier that the inventory costing method, so widely used by businesses today, is not capable of accurately tracing the cost of resources consumed to the products that cause their consumption. The application of inventory costing thus results in product costs that are so heavily distorted that, at best, they cannot aid strategic product decision-making and at worst may cause managers to make inappropriate decisions. Given inventory costing has been used for several decades it is reasonable to question why it is only now that academics and practitioners are so vociferous regarding its inadequacies. Innes and Mitchell (1996) suggest the reasons why traditional costing systems now produce inaccurate product costs are threefold:

1 the growth in overhead costs and the diminution of labour costs in modern businesses;
2 the continued use of volume-related bases for overhead absorption;
3 a shift towards overheads that vary with factors other than volume.

Cooper and Kaplan (1988) add to the above the fact that traditional cost systems were developed at a time when companies manufactured a limited range of products, and labour and material costs were of greater significance than at present. They suggest that in that simpler environment, costs could be traced to products with greater ease and less distortion.

We will briefly consider each of the above factors given by Innes and Mitchell.

Firstly, we need to consider the reasons for the increase of overheads in relation to direct labour costs. Earlier we noted the trend towards the automation of the production function. Automation has the joint aims of reducing direct labour requirements and of ensuring consistency of output. However, whilst automation may reduce the requirements for direct employees it increases the demand for employees with the ability to programme and maintain the equipment. So as direct labour decreases with automation, indirect staff, categorised as overhead, actually increases in proportionate terms. There are varying degrees of automation, ranging from the isolated use of CNC machines and robotics through to the use of CIM. Manufacturing seems to be moving inexorably towards CIM and 'dark factory' production and thus the trend towards continued replacement of direct labour by skilled software staff seems inevitable.

The effective use of JIT techniques also leads to direct labour reductions. Aggarwal (1985) states that Japanese companies that have used kanban for upwards of 5 years have seen a 30 per cent increase in labour productivity and a 90 per cent reduction in rejection rates. Indeed, one feature, often noted by observers of Japanese manufacturing, is the particularly demanding pace of work.

Apart from the aforementioned steady reductions in the usage of direct labour, there was also a major shake-out of direct labour during the recessionary years of the 1980s. Management showed ruthless devotion to eliminating direct labour wherever possible. Surprisingly, in the same period little headway was made in overhead reduction.

Management attention was drawn towards direct labour reduction rather than overhead reduction for four reasons:

1 most managers were well versed in the concepts of scientific management which focus on achieving the most from direct labour;
2 machines could often be readily introduced to replace manual tasks;
3 the widespread use of direct labour hours to absorb overhead caused managers to have a bias towards reducing labour costs;
4 a general belief existed that overheads were fixed and could not be reduced.

The reduced significance of direct labour and the converse increase in indirect costs over time can be illustrated by the following:

	Direct labour as % of total product cost	Overhead as % of total product cost
1850	50	50
1900	40	60
1950	40	60
1960	33	67
1975	28	72
1985	25	75
1995	20	80

This chart shows average figures for the UK industry and illustrates how direct labour has reduced as a percentage of product cost, whilst during the same period overhead has increased. It should be remembered, however, that this does not necessarily reflect an overall reduction in labour used; part of the effect has been achieved by the increased use of indirect labour concomitant with the reduction in direct labour.

The proportionate cost shift from labour to overhead has led, indirectly, to a further distortion of product costs. This has arisen through the continued use of labour hours as the basis of absorbing overheads, despite a cost shift that has resulted in labour representing only a small proportion of total overhead costs. Miller and Vollmann (1985) quote the use of burden rates (the ratio of overhead costs to direct labour costs) of 1000 per cent. Such figures are meaningless. We cannot expect to achieve accurate product costs using an absorption base that represents such an insignificant proportion of the costs to be allocated. A further flaw exists in using labour hours to absorb overheads in that it suggests that overheads are driven by volume: we know that often this is not the case. Rather, it is transactions that drive overheads. Miller and Vollmann acknowledge that whilst there may be a correlation between volume and overheads, no causal link exists. Instead, they define four transaction types which they suggest drive overheads:

1 *Logistical transactions*: the ordering, execution and confirmation of material movement;
2 *Balancing transactions*: matching the supply of labour, material, machines and capacity with demand;
3 *Quality transactions*: ensuring that processes and outputs comply with specification;
4 *Change transactions*: dealing with various changes including product design and schedule changes.

The determination of accurate product costs requires an understanding of the causes of each type of cost. Managers are well versed in the causes of labour and material costs, but ill-equipped for grasping the driving force of overhead costs. Miller and Vollmann, therefore, offer certain tools for understanding and controlling overheads. These tools are stable manufacturing, automation and transaction analysis. Understanding the causes of overheads requires a detailed analysis of the transactions that drive these costs. Once the causal link of overhead costs has been determined it should be possible to more accurately trace those costs to products. Unfortunately, traditional costing methodology offers no guidance on the causes of overhead. This is a key reason why continued reliance on simple, but inappropriate, volume-driven bases for absorbing overheads will cause distortion of product costs. The effect of this distortion is that high volume products tend to be overstated in cost and thereby cross-subsidising low volume products which tend to be understated in cost.

The following example illustrates both how high volume products are over-costed and how the use of appropriate transaction type bases can lead to more accurate product costs:

The Manufacturing Co. Ltd produces two products, Alpha and Beta, in volumes per period of 1000 units and 1500 units respectively. Each product consumes 10 hours of direct labour in its production and labour is paid at the rate of £5 per hour. Each unit of Alpha requires 5 hours of inspection compared with 1 hour per unit for Beta. The total cost of the inspection department is £65 000.

Calculating product costs using traditional absorption costing based upon direct labour hours results in the following:

	Alpha	Beta
Number of units	1 000	1 500
Labour cost	£50 000	£75 000
Inspection cost	£26 000	£39 000
Total cost	£76 000	£114 000
Unit cost	£76	£76

Calculations

Labour cost

Product Alpha: 1000 units × 10 hours × £5/hour = £50 000
Product Beta – 1500 units × 10 hours × £5/hour = £75 000

Inspection cost

Total cost: £65 000
Total labour hours: (1000 units + 1500 units) × 10 hours = 25 000 direct hours

Absorption rate: $\dfrac{£65\,000}{25\,000 \text{ hours}} = £2.60/\text{hour}$

Product Alpha: 1000 units × 10 hours × £2.60 = £26 000
Product Beta: 1500 units × 10 hours × £2.60 = £39 000

Calculating product costs using an activity-based method of absorbing overhead costs gives the following:

	Alpha	Beta
Number of units	1 000	1 500
Labour cost	£50 000	£75 000
Inspection cost	£50 000	£15 000
Total cost	£100 000	£90 000
Unit cost	£100	£60

Calculations

Labour cost

Product Alpha: 1000 units × 10 hours × £5/hour = £50 000
Product Beta: 1500 units × 10 hours × £5/hour = £75 000

Inspection cost

Total cost: £65 000

Total inspection hours and cost

   Product Alpha: 1000 units × 5 hours = 5000 hours × £10/hour = £50 000
   Product Beta: 1500 units × 1 hour = 1500 hours × £10/hour = £15 000

   Absorption rate: $\dfrac{£65\,000}{6500\ \text{hours}}$ = £10/hour

Comparative product unit costs:

	Alpha	Beta
Using direct labour	£76	£76
Using inspection hours	£100	£60

This shows the effect of altering the method of absorption of overheads from one of volume-based to one of transaction-based can give significantly different product cost calculations and this can obviously make a significant impact upon decision-making. These differences are based upon relatively small differences in product volumes between the two different products. With larger volume discrepancies between the products manufactured, these differences can be expected to become even greater. General recognition of the shortcomings of traditional costing methods, based upon volume absorptions, has led accountants to express interest in alternative methods of costing such as ABC.

A re-evaluation of product costing

Conventionally product cost development comprises two stages:

1 tracing direct costs to the product;
2 allocating indirect costs to the product.

   Tracing direct costs, such as materials, to products is generally quite straightforward. It is in the allocation of indirect costs to products where cost distortion can arise. To understand how this distortion occurs we will consider the allocation process in greater detail. According to Cooper (1987a,b) there are two stages to cost allocation. Firstly, indirect costs are charged to cost centres, and Kaplan (1986) suggests that the first stage of this process is accomplished reasonably well. The second stage involves allocating the costs of cost centres to products.

   Conventional cost systems use a volume-related base, such as labour hours, to allocate indirect costs to products. The result is an overhead allocation that is in direct proportion to each product's consumption of direct labour hours. Horngren *et al.* (1994) refer to this as 'peanut-butter costing' to illustrate the uniform spreading of overheads across products. There would be no problem with this approach if products did indeed use overhead resources in direct proportion to direct labour hours. Unfortunately, they rarely do.

We can use the example of the Manufacturing Co. Ltd, considered earlier, to illustrate how costs are distorted by the use of volume-based absorption factors. Note how in the example, the use of direct labour hours as an allocation base results in an equal spread of overheads between products. Products Alpha and Beta consume the same level of direct labour hours so the volume-based absorption denominator simply allocates overheads in the same proportion. The underlying assumption then is that there is perfect correlation between the consumption of labour hours and demand for overhead resources. Note also that the resultant unit cost of each product is therefore identical. This follows because the consumption of direct labour hours is identical which in turn leads to equality in the absorption of overheads.

We can see from the example, however, that products Alpha and Beta actually demand different levels of overhead resource, as reflected in their need for inspection time. The inspection time of product Alpha is five times the duration of product Beta. Under a volume-based driver system the product costing does not reflect this, instead Beta cross-subsidises Alpha.

One of the features of the conventional system is that a variety of overhead costs will be allocated to cost centres. Given the heterogeneity of accumulated costs it is unlikely that a single allocation base will be the true cost driver in any situation, or even a reasonable reflection thereof. Activity-based costing offers a method of attributing costs to products with greater accuracy. The price to be paid for this increased accuracy is that the cost of administering the system is far greater than that of traditional systems. This is so since there are typically more cost pools and cost drivers with ABC than with a conventional system. The justification for incurring the additional cost can arise only when the benefits derived from ABC outweigh the cost. It is impossible to generalise when this will be so. However, as a guide, Cooper (1988) offers three important decision factors:

1 the sophistication of the firm's information systems;
2 the cost of errors;
3 product diversity.

The problems of performance measurement

We noted earlier how new manufacturing initiatives have rendered traditional operational performance measures inappropriate. In particular, we cited labour efficiency and machine utilisation as being poorly suited to the new manufacturing setting. We suggested, therefore, that management accounting needed new operational measures with greater relevance to the new environment. Whilst there is considerable variety in the metrics used by companies to assess operational performance, there is greater uniformity in the use of financial metrics as the ultimate measure of success.

In order to commence our review of the shortcomings of accounting it is first necessary to identify the role of, and context in which, performance measurement operates in an organisation. Nowadays, it is common for firms to adopt a mission statement and such statements explain the firm's raison d'être. They define purpose, scope and boundaries, and should accord with the desires of the major stakeholders of the firm. By their nature, however, mission statements are very broad and generalised and this may cause a problem for managers attempting to understand how they can contribute to the success of the mission. To overcome this problem mission statements need to be made more specific. The firm will achieve this in two ways:

1 through the adoption of goals that assist it in moving towards its mission: the quantification of these goals establishes specific objectives;
2 through the development of a strategy that will determine the actions needed to achieve its stated objectives.

Once the company has embarked upon its strategy it will need a system to assess regularly its success in implementing that strategy. This is where performance measures feature. Performance measurement provides this assessment system. Coates *et al.* (1993) state that performance measures serve the following purposes:

● directing and motivating managers to adopt goal-congruent actions;
● indicating the effectiveness of current strategies;
● providing a control mechanism for comparison of actual v. target performance;
● providing a basis of remuneration, promotion and incentives.

They note, however, that often there is a difference between the definition of the overriding purpose given in the mission statement and the performance measures adopted to judge success. Thus, whilst marketing imperatives figure predominantly in mission statements few companies use measures that specifically assess market success. Instead, financial performance measures are commonly adopted.

The performance measures adopted by traditional management accounting emphasise efficiency and cost reduction as the route to greater profitability. We have seen, however, that these traditional measures do not sit comfortably with JIT which advocates higher levels of discretionary expenditure on employee training and development and tolerates low machine utilisation rather than accepting increases to inventory. Nevertheless, firms adopting JIT principles enjoy performance improvements and this appears paradoxical to traditional measurement systems. Fox (1984) reports comments from the father of JIT, Taiichi Ohno, that traditional cost accounting has no explanation for the success of JIT. Similarly, Skinner (1986) has noted that despite improvements in efficiency and cost reduction achieved by certain firms, this has not resulted in improvements in profitability. These are indications that traditional performance measures are failing to function effectively.

Every business will develop a number of performance measures that it considers are key indicators of operational success. These tend to be tailored to the particular firm. For example, an engineering firm may judge its operational success to depend upon labour utilisation and high yield from raw materials whereas a retailer may focus on margins and stockturn. Accordingly, each firm will develop various performance metrics targeted at the perceived critical variables. Whilst there is a degree of variability in these operational measures there is far more uniformity in the use of financial performance metrics. We will consider a number of the measures commonly used.

Most companies, and where appropriate their divisions, use the level of profits earned as a measure of performance. Whilst the level of profit is important, on its own it is poor indicator of performance. Instead, profit adequacy requires expression in relation to the amount of capital resource utilised in the generation of that profit. The most common method of achieving this evaluation is through the measure of return on capital employed (ROCE). This is determined by the result of the firm's or division's net earnings before tax (NEBT) divided by the capital employed in the economic unit. Thus:

$$\text{ROCE} = \frac{\text{NEBT}}{\text{Capital employed}}$$

The widespread use of ROCE reflects the fact that the measure has many positive features. Specifically, it uses routinely collected accounting data, and as such it benefits from having low data-collection cost and having the objectivity that is inherent in financial accounting numbers. In addition, ROCE makes possible performance comparisons across divisions of different size and business activity. However, ROCE does suffer from several weaknesses which are well documented by Dearden (1969). For example, without specific adjustment, ROCE fails to recognise the effect of price changes. Thus, whilst profits relate to the current review period the asset base may be valued at costs incurred several decades ago. Apart from the technical weaknesses inherent in the measure, ROCE may also lead to dysfunctional manager behaviour. This dysfunctionality may manifest itself in a number of ways. It will be apparent that the achievement of an improved ROCE is possible by either increasing profits or reducing the level of asset employment. Managers may consider the manipulation of either, or both, of these variables to improve local short-term divisional results. This manipulation may, however, be detrimental to the long-term well-being of the overall company.

This can be illustrated with the following two examples:

Firstly, managers may decline to invest in worthwhile projects. Traditional financial theory suggests that a company should adopt new projects that yield a positive NPV after being discounted at the firm's cost of capital. However, if the cost of capital is below the division's current ROCE, it is possible for an adopted project to yield a positive NPV whilst lowering the ROCE. In these circumstances, managers judging on ROCE performance may be reluctant to embark upon a project which whilst beneficial for the company leads to a deterioration of its own ROCE.

Secondly, managers may decline to incur discretionary expenditure. Such actions, whilst enhancing short-term results, may cause damage to the longer-term well-being of the company. Within this category of discretionary expenditure are the costs of employee training and development, research and development, advertising expenditure and plant and building maintenance. Managers can decide to reduce, or in some cases eliminate, discretionary expenditure in the short term with little apparent disadvantage. In the longer term, however, this expenditure creates the intangible assets that provide the company with its competitive advantage.

We may question why ROCE, introduced in the 1920s by the Du Pont organisation and successfully applied by many organisations for several decades since, has now run into problems in its application. Johnson and Kaplan offer six possible reasons:

1 There is currently greater pressure for good short-term results than prevailed several decades ago.
2 In the past managers were promoted less frequently and as such had to live with the consequences of their decisions over longer periods.
3 Decisions were more transparent in the smaller organisations of the past.
4 Businesses are frequently run by managers with much more limited experience of the associated technology than was the case in the past.
5 Managerial bonus and incentive schemes are commonly linked to accounting measures of performance.
6 Changes in the competitive, global macroeconomic and technological environments of the present render traditional measures inappropriate.

These factors are considered in greater details throughout this book.

In order to overcome the consequences of the dysfunctional behaviour of rejecting projects that have positive NPVs but which result in returns below the current ROCE, some companies have adopted residual income as a performance measure. This approach was first introduced by the General Electric Company around the turn of the Second World War. Interestingly, the concept did not appear in management accounting literature, however, until the 1960s (Anthony 1965; Solomons 1965).

Residual income is determined by deducting a charge for the cost of capital from the NEBT. Using residual income as a performance measure overcomes the problem of the rejection of positive NPV projects. This is clear since a project that yields a positive NPV will be able to absorb a charge for the cost of capital and still increase residual value. An additional positive feature residual income has over ROCE is that it is possible to apply different costs of capital to projects with varying degrees of risk. The concept is, therefore, in accord with the risk – reward tradeoff adopted by the capital asset pricing model. Residual income thus has the ability to recognise different risk profiles whereas ROCE has no such ability. Residual income does have a downside, however, compared with ROCE in that it does not recognise the impact of size on an economic unit. It is clearly easier for a large division to earn a given residual income than a smaller division. To overcome this problem companies often specify absolute target levels of residual income for their divisional companies.

Modern financial theory holds that the objective of the firm is shareholder wealth maximisation (Rappaport 1986). It might appear appropriate, therefore, at this point to consider the utilisation of a performance measure with the capability to assess success in satisfying this objective. The firm achieves this firstly by evaluating strategic options to determine which of the available strategies should maximise shareholder wealth. The evaluation process utilises DCF techniques more commonly used in the evaluation of individual investment projects. The SWM model, however, utilises DCF techniques to evaluate the strategies of the whole firm rather than simply that of individual projects. The firm then adopts those strategies that the evaluation process suggests will maximise the NPV of the firm as a whole. The pursuance of NPV-maximising strategies should in turn maximise the firm's share price and hence the wealth of its shareholders.

The ordinary share price is usually taken as a proxy for SWM. The theory holds that the share price represents the future dividend flow and capital gains enjoyed by ownership of the share. Implicit in this model is that the stock market is efficient. Accordingly, the share price is always correct, encompasses all risk and reward expectations and quickly incorporates new information. The market should thus correctly evaluate the NPV-maximising strategies adopted by the firm and the share price should reflect the use of such maximising strategies.

The evaluation of strategies using DCF techniques is, however, difficult in practice. It assumes that strategy formulation is a rational planned process whereas modern strategic theory suggests that in a complex and rapidly changing environment, strategy is more likely to emerge through 'logical incrementalism' (Quinn 1980). The strategic planning process involves the firm positioning itself to take advantage of opportunities as they emerge rather than the pre-planned process assumed by Ansoff (1988). The incrementalist view holds that managers will not commit the firm to particular strategies at the outset, but instead will wait for a clearer picture to emerge as strategic options unfold. Thus, we can observe that the SWM model is actually attempting to evaluate options and the DCF model is unsuitable for option evaluation.

A number of features should be apparent from the foregoing. Firstly, performance measurement systems can influence the behaviour of managers. We have also seen that many of the traditional measures can cause dysfunctional behaviour. By contrast, an effective performance measurement system should have a positive impact on behaviour. Secondly, businesses operate in a dynamic environment typified by the following features:

- global competition
- mass customisation
- shortened product life cycles

- total quality management
- continuous improvement.

An effective performance management system should be capable of assessing the various imperatives critical to success in this dynamic setting. Clearly, simple financial measures cannot on their own convey how a firm is performing across this multitude of variables. In addition, financial measures suffer from being backwards focused. In other words they provide an indication of how well the firm has done in the past, but do not address the firm's position to be successful in the future. Supplementary measures are, therefore, needed to assess how the firm is managing the factors that are critical to the future success of the firm.

Kaplan and Norton (1992, 1993, 1996a,b) have put forward the 'balanced scorecard' as a new performance measurement system. They claim that this system offers a balance between short-term financial performance goals and operational measures that are the drivers of future financial success. Earlier, we stressed how the new competitive environment requires a business to invest in its intangible assets such as product and process innovations and employee development. We have also noted how such expenditures cut across short-term financial results. The scorecard provides a mechanism which enables companies to balance their short-run and long-run goals. It also highlights where results have been achieved by a tradeoff of other objectives.

Each business that adopts the approach develops its own purpose-built scorecard that reflects its 'mission, strategy, technology and culture'. The strength of the system is that it measures the success in achieving the strategies cascaded down by top management. Earlier in this chapter we noted how there may be a divergence between mission statements, strategies and performance measures. The scorecard offers a mechanism to avoid this divergence. The scorecard could, for example, take a mission statement that has a customer focus and convert generally stated goals into specific objectives and then develop associated performance measures. In this example the measurement system may seek an interface with the customer's management information system. If the customer has a system for capturing data that assesses its suppliers, the firm could attempt to capture this information to enable it to judge its performance through the customer's eyes.

Social responsibility and accounting

We have looked at some of the problems in the use of accounting for strategic decision-making purposes. For a business which is seeking to follow a socially responsible approach to business these problems become more acute because the implications for social responsibility are less subject to financial analysis. Thus the judgement element of strategic decision-making becomes even more important. This is particularly true because, as we have seen in preceding chapters, it is less certain what course of action is the most socially responsible one when different stakeholders seek different objectives. Approaches such as the balanced scorecard attempt to provide a rigorous methodology for identifying the important factors for business success and social responsibility can be built into such a scorecard but inevitably there is a need to recognise socially desirable activity in the objectives of the organisation, and thereby into the planning of the organisation.

Conclusions

In this chapter we have undertaken a review of the way in which management accounting has developed and the ways in which modern manufacturing has continued to develop without management accounting responding to the changing needs by continuing to develop. We have considered the problems currently existing in the use of management accounting both in terms of providing costing information for operational control purposes and in terms of providing information for the measure of performance. We have highlighted a number of problems with both aspects of accounting and have highlighted a number of weaknesses inherent in financial performance measures. We have also seen how the use of these measures can adversely influence managerial behaviour.

Managing a business, or part thereof, is a complex process, as we have seen, and requires a manager to address a variety of problems. So it requires him/her to possess a variety of skills. In this book we have considered a variety of problems which business managers face in the course of their work, and looked at the ways in which the use of the techniques of accounting can help the manager in finding solutions to these problems. We have considered both the strengths and weaknesses of these techniques and see that, on balance, the use of these available techniques will enable a manager to arrive at a better solutions to these business problems, and so to manage the business better than is possible without the use of these techniques. We have therefore also considered the relevance of these techniques of accounting to managers in all areas of a business and see that they are equally relevant to all areas of management. It is hoped therefore that you, as a prospective business manager, will become a better manager through the use of these techniques in appropriate situations.

References

Aggarwal, S.C. (1985). MRP, JIT, OPT, FMS? Making Sense of Production Operating Systems. *Harvard Business Review*, September–October, 8–16.

Anthony, R.N. (1965). Accounting for capital costs. In R.N. Anthony, J. Dearden and R.F. Vancil (eds), *Management Control Systems: Cases and Readings*. Homewood, IL: Irwin.

Anssoff, H.I. (1988). *Corporate Strategy*. London: Pelican.

Bromwich, M. and Bhimani, A. (1994). *Management Accounting Pathways to Progress*. London: CIMA.

Coates, J.B., Davis, E.W., Longden, S.G., Stacey, R.J. and Emmanuel, C. (1993). *Corporate Performance Evaluation in Multinationals*. London: CIMA.

Cooper, R. (1987a). The two-stage procedure in cost accounting: Part one. *Journal of Cost Management for the Manufacturing Industry*, Summer, 43–51.

Cooper, R. (1987b). The two-stage procedure in cost accounting: Part two. *Journal of Cost Management for the Manufacturing Industry*, Fall, 39–45.

Cooper, R. (1988). The rise of activity-based costing: Part two: when do I need an activity-based cost system? *Journal of Cost Management for the Manufacturing Industry*, 3 (Fall), 41–48.

Cooper, R. and Kaplan, R.S. (1988). Measure costs right: make the right decisions. *Harvard Business Review*, September–October, 96–103.

Dearden, J. (1969). The case against ROI control. *Harvard Business Review*, May–June, 124–135.

Fox, R.E. (1984). Main bottleneck on the factory floor?. *Management Review*, November, 55–61.

Horngren, C.T., Foster, G. and Datar, S.M. (1994). *Cost Accounting – A Managerial Emphasis*. London: Prentice-Hall.

Hounshell, D.A. (1988). The same old principles in the new manufacturing. *Harvard Business Review*, November/December, 54–61.

Howell, R.A. and Soucy, S.R. (1987). Cost accounting in the new manufacturing environment. *Management Accounting (USA)*, August, 42–48.

Innes, J. and Mitchell, F. (1996). A review of activity-based costing practice. In C. Drury (ed.), *Management Accounting Handbook*. London: CIMA.

Johnson, H.T. and Kaplan, R.S. (1987). *Relevance Lost: The Rise and Fall of Management Accounting*. Boston, MA: Harvard Business School Press.

Kaplan, R.S. (1984). Yesterday's accounting undermines production. *Harvard Business Review*, July/August, 95–101.

Kaplan, R.S. (1986). *Cost Accounting for the 90's: The Challenge of Technological Change Proceedings*. Montvale, NJ: National Association of Accountants.

Kaplan, R.S. (1988). One cost system isn't enough. *Harvard Business Review*, January/February, 61–66.

Kaplan, R.S. and Norton, D.P. (1992). The balanced scorecard – measures that drive performance. *Harvard Business Review*, January/February, 71–79.

Kaplan, R.S. and Norton, D.P. (1993). Putting the balanced scorecard to work. *Harvard Business Review*, September/October, 134–147.

Kaplan, R.S. and Norton, D.P. (1996a). Using the balanced scorecard as a strategic management system. *Harvard Business Review*, January/February, 75–85.

Kaplan, R.S. and Norton, D.P. (1996b). *The Balanced Scorecard: Translating Strategy into Action*. Harvard Business School Press.

McNair, C.J., Mosconi, W. and Norris, T. (1988). *Meeting the Technology Challenge in a JIT Environment*. Montvale, NJ: National Association of Accountants.

Miles, R.E. and Snow, C. (1978). *Organisational Strategy Structure and Process*. London: McGraw-Hill.

Miller, J.G. and Vollmann, T.E. (1985). The hidden factory. *Harvard Business Review*, September–October, 142–150.

Quinn, J.B. (1980). *Strategies for Change*. London: Irwin.

Rappaport, A. (1986). *Creating Shareholder Value*. New York: Free Press.

Romano, P.L. (1987). Manufacturing in transition: the turning point for cost management practice: Part III. *Management Accounting (USA)*, November, 63–64.

Skinner, W. (1986). The productivity paradox. *Harvard Business Review*, July–August, 55–59.

Solomons, D. (1965). *Divisional Performance and Control. New York:* Financial Executives Research Foundation.

Swenson, D.W. and Cassidy, J. (1993). The effect of JIT on management accounting. *Journal of Cost Management,* Spring 7 *(1),* 39–47.

Further reading

de Ste Croix, G.E.M. (1956). Greek and Roman accounting. In A.C. Littleton and B.S. Yamey (eds), *Studies in the History of Accounting.* London: Sweet and Maxwell.

Mintzberg, H. (1994). *The Rise and Fall of Strategic Planning.* London: Prentice-Hall.

Peters, T.J. and Waterman, R.H. (1986). *In Search of Excellence.* New York: Harper & Row.

Porter, M.E. (1985). *Competitive Advantage:* New York: Free Press.

Smith, T. (1992). *Accounting for Growth.* London: Century Business.

Additional questions

Question 13.1

The managing director of Cable Co. Ltd is concerned that the strategy of the company as determined by the board never seems to materialise exactly as planned. He attributes this to a faulty planning process. Do you agree with him?

Question 13.2

Accounting information provides detail which is essential to the planning of a business but only considers the internal operations of the business. A successful business manager needs also to be concerned with the external environment in which a business is operating. Discuss.

Appendix 1

Chapter 1

Answer to Question 1.1

Main inputs

- materials
- labour
- capital (i.e. plant and machinery, etc.)
- finance.

Main outputs

- products or services
- profit.

Answer to Question 1.2

Data – a set of facts
Information – the basis of decision-making
Key elements of information

- meaningfulness
- relevance
- timeliness

- accuracy
- format.

Chapter 2

Answer to Question 2.1

	£	£
Sales		150 000
Production expenses		
Labour	30 000	
Raw materials	45 000	
Overheads	12 000	87 000
Fixed costs		11 000
Net cash inflow		52 000

Answer to Question 2.2

	Oct. (£'000)	Nov. (£'000)	Dec. (£'000)
Receipts			
Sales*	197	245	285
Mortgage receipts		100	
Total	197	345	285
Payments			
Direct costs:			
Materials	70	80	80
Labour	56	36	32
Overheads:			
Production	38	26	14
Sales	29	30	39
Admin.	20	24	16
Dividend	50		
Mortgage repayment			5
Deposit on m/c		4	
Total	263	200	186
Net cash flow	(66)	145	99
Balance b/f	16	(50)	95
Balance c/f	(50)	95	194
*Sales:			
Cash	24	32	40
Credit 1 month	162	195.4	259.2
Credit 2 months	10.8	18	21.6
Total	196.8	245.4	284.8

Chapter 3

Answer to Question 3.1

Suggested financial analysis

Ratio analysis

In all financial analysis we are concerned with comparisons. It is not possible to tell whether a ratio shows a good position or not without knowing what the industry norms for this type of company are expected to be. In this case we do not have such information and so we are not in a position to make such observations. What is equally important in this kind of analysis is to see how the position of the company is changing over time and this we can do by comparing the ratios over the 4 years for which we have information.

Let us turn to the analysis and interpretation. The answer here has been structured in accordance with the four types of ratios:

1 Measures of profitability
2 Measures of efficiency
3 Measures of liquidity
4 Measures of risk.

For each of these types of ratio we have calculated the ratios which are possible to calculate and drawn some conclusions.

Measures of profitability

	Year 4	Year 3	Year 2	Year 1
Return on capital employed	11.2%	12.7%	13.2%	11.0%
Return on equity	15.5%	19.4%	19.8%	16.6%
Return on sales	8.1%	9.9%	10.1%	8.3%

There is no information concerning share price and so ratios such as EPS, price-earnings ratios, dividend yield and market-to-book ratios cannot be calculated. While these figures seem to be quite respectable we are unable to comment about this without knowing what the industry norms are for this type of company. Looking at the figures, however, we can see a decline in these ratios from year 2 onwards and this suggests that the company might be having some problems causing its declining profitability. Let us therefore continue with our analysis.

Measures of efficiency

	Year 4	Year 3	Year 2	Year 1
Stock turnover	18.0	17.7	19.9	18.9
Debtor turnover	9.3	9.1	11.1	9.9
Average collection period	39.5	37	34.6	–

Here too the figures look problematic as the collection of money from debtors seems to be taking longer. Stock turnover seems to be much the same. The figures show that stock is being turned over approximately every three weeks during this period. This is quite a low stock level to have but for this type of business then the purchase of raw materials on a regular basis would be expected.

Measures of liquidity

	Year 4	Year 3	Year 2	Year 1
Current ratio	0.88	1.04	1.07	1.00
Quick ratio	0.69	0.83	0.84	0.80

These figures seem to show a problem with the company. It seems that there is a shortage of working capital in general but a shortage of cash in particular.

Measures of risk

	Year 4	Year 3	Year 2	Year 1
Debt to equity ratio	0.39	0.53	0.50	0.51

The only change here is that the ratio has decreased in year 4. This may be because some loans have been repaid during the year. These figures seem to give no cause for concern.

Answer to Question 3.2

- No established measures;
- No requirement to report anything except charitable donations;
- No commonality between companies – or even by one company for different years.

Consequently indicators of socially responsible performance must be used as proxy measures. Examples include:

- Measures used in the environmental report;
- Production of an environmental reports itself;
- Written information in the annual report.

Chapter 4

Answer to Question 4.1

Value based management is based upon the assumption that maximising the value of a firm to its shareholders also maximises the value of that firm to society at large.

Stakeholder theory is based upon the following arguments:

- It is an accurate description of how management works.
- It is more morally and ethically correct for organisations to consider wider needs than purely concentrating on the needs of one group.
- The reason for managing your stakeholders is to create shareholder wealth.

Answer to Question 4.2

Rappaport (1986) argues that accounting profit fails to measure changes in the economic value of the firm, citing the following reasons:

- alternative accounting methods can be employed to give different figures;
- risk is excluded from the analysis;
- future investment requirements are excluded;
- the dividend policy in force is not considered;
- the time value of money is ignored.

Chapter 5

Answer to Question 5.1

Prime cost = Direct material + Direct labour

		£
Direct materials		
	Steel	4 000
	Plastic	1 800
	Other	750
		6 550

Direct labour	8 000
Prime cost	14 550

Total cost = Prime cost + Overheads (i.e. indirect costs)

Overheads	
Factory rent	2500
Admin.	800
Insurance	350
Cleaning materials	75
	3725

Total cost = 14 550 + 3725
$$= 1825$$

Answer to Question 5.2

Direct costs
  steel used in product manufacture
  wages of machine operators
  patent royalties on product manufactured
  overtime payments for machine operators.
Indirect costs
  floppy discs for the office computer
  wages of factory security guard
  tools for maintenance mechanics
  painting of the factory gates
  tyre replacement for the delivery van
  telephone rental.

Chapter 6

Answer to Question 6.1

(1) Contribution

	£'000
Sales−	5000−
V C	3500
Contribution	1500

$$\text{Contribution per unit} = \frac{1500}{100} = £15$$

$$\text{B E level of production} = \frac{FC}{\text{Contribution}}$$

$$= \frac{900\,000}{15}$$

$$= 60\,000 \text{ units}$$

(2) (a)

	£'000	£'000
Sales (1 00 000 units)		5000
Direct materials	1000	
Direct labour	1000	
Variable production overheads	700	
Variable selling and distribution overheads	450	
Fixed production overheads	900	
Fixed selling and distribution overheads	200	4250
Net profit		750

(b)   Current price = £50

New price = 50.00 − (150 000/100 000) = £48.50

(3)   £

Increased sales revenue	300
Increased fixed costs	250
Increased profit	50

New profit level = £650 000

(4) New selling price = £55
New sales volume = 95 000
New sales revenue = £5 225 000
New profit level = £825 000

Answer to Question 6.2

$$\text{Contribution per unit} = \text{Price} - \text{Variable cost}$$
$$= 10 - 8$$
$$= 2$$

$$\text{No. of units sold} = \frac{\text{Sales revenue}}{\text{Price per unit}}$$

$$= \frac{350\,000}{10}$$

$$= 35\,000$$

$$\text{Fixed costs} = \text{Break even point (units)} \times \text{Contribution per unit}$$
$$= 35\,000 \times 2$$
$$= 70\,000$$

New break even point:

$$\text{BEP} = \frac{f}{(p - v)}$$
$$= \frac{50\,000}{2}$$
$$= 25\,000 \text{ units}$$

$$\text{Margin of safety} = \frac{\text{Actual sales} - \text{Break even sales} \times 100\%}{\text{Break even sales}}$$
$$= \frac{35\,000 - 25\,000 \times 100\%}{25\,000}$$
$$= 40\%$$

Answer to Question 6.3

	£
Costs of production	
Variable costs (180 000 × 14)	2 520 000
Fixed costs	792 000
	3 312 000
Sales revenue (180 000 × 20)	3 600 000
Profit	288 000

$$\text{BEP (units)} = \frac{f}{p - v}$$
$$= \frac{792\,000}{(20 - 14)}$$
$$= 132\,000$$

$$\text{BEP (revenue)} = \frac{f}{(p - v)/p}$$
$$= \frac{792\,000}{(20 - 14)/20}$$
$$= 2\,640\,000$$

$$\text{Margin of safety} = \frac{\text{Actual sales} - \text{Break even sales} \times 100\%}{\text{Break even sales}}$$

$$= \frac{180\,000 - 132\,000 \times 100\%}{132\,000}$$

$$= 36\%$$

Increased costs due to labour cost increase:

$$\text{Variable} = \left(\frac{14}{2}\right) \times 10\%$$

$$= 0.7$$

$$\text{Fixed} = 792\,000 \times 0.2 \times 0.1$$

$$= 15\,840$$

$$\text{BEP (units)} = \frac{f}{p - v}$$

$$= \frac{(792\,000 + 15\,840)}{20 - 14.7}$$

$$= 152\,423$$

Answer to Question 6.4

	Current (£)	−5% (£)	−10% (£)	−15% (£)
Price	20	19	18	17
Variable cost	14	14	14	14
Contribution per unit	6	5	4	3
Total contribution	120 000	100 000	80 000	60 000
Fixed costs	65 000			
Breakeven sales (units) (i.e. fixed costs/contribution per unit)	10 834	13 000	16 250	21 667
Margin of safety (i.e. [current sales − breakeven sales]/breakeven sales)	85%	54%	23%	—

$$\text{Current profit} = \text{Contribution} - \text{Fixed costs}$$

$$= 120\,000 - 65\,000$$

$$= 55\,000$$

Sales to maintain current profit:

	Current	−5%	−10%	−15%
Sales	20 000	24 000	30 000	40 000
Additional sales	–	4 000	10 000	20 000

Chapter 7

Answer to Question 7.1

Factors to consider:

- methods of apportioning joint costs – physical units or sales value;
- treatment of by-products as cost reduction;
- problems of absorbing overheads generally.

Answer to Question 7.2

	£
Costs of producing batch 36:	
Raw materials (2.40 × 400)	960
Direct labour [(400/20) × 6.80]	136
Machine overheads [(400/20) × 2.50]	50
Machine set-up	32
Rectification work:	
Labour (10 × 6.80)	68
Machine overheads (10 × 2.50)	25
Machine set up	36
	1307
Less scrap (20 × 0.80)	16
	1291

$$\text{Units produced: } 400 - 20 = 380$$

$$\text{Cost per unit: } \frac{1291}{380} = 3.40$$

	£
Cost of defective work:	
Raw materials (2.40 × 400)	960
Direct labour [(400/20) × 6.80]	136
Machine overheads [(400/20) × 2.50]	50
Machine set-up	32
	1178

$$\text{Cost of defective work} = (1291 - 1178) + \frac{20}{400} \times 1178$$

$$= 172$$

Answer to Question 7.3

$$\text{Direct labour hour rate: } \frac{25\ 800}{2600} = £9.92 \text{ per direct labour hour}$$

$$\text{Direct materials rate: } \frac{25\ 800}{12\ 800} = 202\% \text{ of direct materils cost}$$

$$\text{Direct wages rate: } \frac{25\ 800}{7200} = 358\% \text{ of direct wages cost}$$

$$\text{Unit rate: } \frac{25\ 800}{1075} = £24.00 \text{ per unit}$$

Answer to Question 7.4

	Cutting (£)	Finishing (£)	Maintenance (£)	Canteen (£)
Actual overheads	71 500	47 300	25 100	24 300
Allocate canteen costs	14 580	7 290	2 430	(24 300)
	86 080	54 590	27 530	—
Allocate maintenance costs	20 647	5 506	(27 530)	1 377
	106 727	60 096	—	1 377
Reallocate canteen costs	918	459	—	—
	107 645	60 555	—	—

NB – Final reallocation on the basis of 60:30 to the service departments in order to prevent further iterations.

Chapter 8

Answer to Question 8.1

Fixed manufacturing overhead absorption rate

	Production depts		Maintenance dept. (£'000)	Stores dept. (£'000)	Total (£'000)
	1 (£'000)	2 (£'000)			
Allocated	360	470	240	170	1240
Reallocated					
Stores dept.	59.5	85	25.5	(170)	
			265.5		
Service dept.	45.51	60.69	(106.2) (40%) labour		
	81.92	77.38	(159.3) (60%) m/c		
	546.93	693.07			
/150 000	£3.65	£4.62 per unit			

Total cost per unit
   Direct materials: 6.00
   Direct labour: 7.50
   Variable manf. oheads: 2.40
   Fixed manf. oheads
      Dept. 1:   3.65
      Dept. 2:   4.62
                 24.17

Profit statement – absorption costing
   Sales: 144 000 × 35 = 5 040 000
   Cost of sales: 144 000 × 24.17 = 3 480 480

   Gross profit: 1 559 520
   Non-manf. costs: 765 000

   Net profit: 794 520
   Less
   Under absorbed overheads
      Dept. 1: 20 000 + 4000 × 3.65 =   34 600
      Dept. 2: 4000 × 4.62 =   18 480

   Net profit: 741 440

Profit statement – marginal costing
   Sales: 144 000 × 35 = 5 040 000
   Variable cost of sales: 144 000 × 15.90 = 2 289 600

   Contribution: 2 750 400
   Fixed costs
      Manf. 1 240 000 + 20 000 1 260 000
      Non-manf.   765 000

   Profit   725 400
Nb: difference is in stock valuation.

Answer to Question 8.2

Calculation of fixed manufacturing cost overhead absorption rate

	Production depts		Service dept. (£)	General factory overheads (£)
	1 (£)	2 (£)		
Allocated	360 000	455 000	220 000	230 000
Gen. factory	103 500	80 500	46 000	(230 000)
	463 500	535 500	266 000	–
Service dept.	51 722	128 728	(133 000) – based on labour hours	
	73 379	59 621	(133 000) – based on machine hours	
	588 601	723 846	–	
/150 000	3.92	4.83 (cost per unit)		

Total cost per unit	£
Direct materials	6.00
Direct labour	6.50
Manufacturing overheads	3.00
Manufacturing overheads	
Dept. 1	3.92
Dept. 2	4.83
	24.25

Profit statement

	£
Sales (146 000 × 40)	5 840 000
Less cost of sales (24.25 × 146 000)	3 540 500
Gross profit	2 299 500
Less non-manufacturing costs	920 000
	1 379 500
Less under absorbed overheads	
Dept. 1 (25 000 + 3.92 × 4000)	15 680
Dept. 2 (4.83 × 40 000	19 320
Net profit	1 344 500

Answer to Question 8.3

Absorption costing method

	Product A (£)	Product B (£)	Product C (£)
Materials	17.00	12.00	20.00
Labour	4.00	8.00	10.40
Overheads	24.00	36.00	60.00
	45.00	56.00	90.40

ABC method
Total machine hours = 1000 × 1 + 1500 × 1.5 + 6000 × 2.5 = 18 250
Total overhead cost = 18 250 × 24 = 438 000

Cost driver activity

	Product A	Product B	Product C	Total
Machine hours	1000	2250	15 000	18 250
Set-ups	100	120	350	570
Materials movements	15	12	65	92
Inspections	100	240	500	840

Cost driver rates

	Total cost	Total activity	Unit cost
Machine hours	153 300	18 250	8.40
Set-ups	131 400	570	230.52
Materials movements	65 700	92	714.13
Inspections	87 600	840	104.29
	438 000		

Overhead cost per unit

Product A		£
Machining	8.40 × 0.5	4.20
Set-ups	$230.52 \times \dfrac{100}{1000}$	23.05
Materials movements	$714.13 \times \dfrac{15}{1000}$	10.71

Inspections	$104.29 \times \dfrac{100}{1000}$	10.42
		48.38
Product B		
Machining	8.40×1.5	12.60
Set-ups	$230.52 \times \dfrac{120}{1500}$	18.44
Materials movements	$714.13 \times \dfrac{12}{1500}$	5.71
Inspections	$104.29 \times \dfrac{240}{1500}$	16.68
		53.43
Product C		
Machining	8.40×2.5	21.00
Set-ups	$230.52 \times \dfrac{350}{6000}$	13.45
Materials movements	$714.13 \times \dfrac{65}{6000}$	7.74
Inspections	$104.29 \times \dfrac{500}{6000}$	8.69
		50.88

Product cost

	Product A (£)	Product B (£)	Product C (£)
Materials	17.00	12.00	20.00
Labour	4.00	8.00	10.40
Overheads	48.38	53.43	50.88
	69.38	73.43	81.28

Chapter 9

Answer to Question 9.1

	£	£
Sales		150 000
Production expenses		
Labour	30 000	
Raw materials	45 000	
Overheads	12 000	87 000
Fixed costs		11 000
Net cash inflow		52 000

Answer to Question 9.2

	Month 1 (£)	Month 2 (£)	Month 3 (£)
Income			
Cash sales (75%)	45 000	60 000	82 500
Credit sales (25%)		15 000	20 000
Total cash inflow	45 000	75 000	102 500
Expenditure			
Raw materials*	80 000	48 000	48 000
Labour	20 000	20 000	36 000
Overheads	4 000	4 000	4 800
Fixed factory costs**	8 000	8 000	8 000
Selling and admin. expenses**	2 500	2 500	2 500
Total cash outflow	114 500	82 500	99 300
Net cash flow	(69 500)	(7 500)	3 200
Cumulative cash flow†	(69 500)	(77 000)	(73 800)

* Raw materials cost = requirements for following month but for month 1 equates to requirements for first two months.
** Cash costs exclude depreciation.
† Cumulative cash flow = working capital requirement

Answer to Question 9.3

Advantages of budgeting:

- It provides a formal way in which the objectives of the organisation and its long-term plan can be translated into specific plans and tasks, providing clear guidelines to managers regarding current operations.
- It facilitates the comparison and selection between alternative courses of action and their evaluation.
- It provides a means of communicating organisational plans to all members of the organisation.
- Constraints upon production capability are highlighted (the limiting factor(s)).
- Preparing budgets provides an opportunity to review operations and revise if necessary.
- Performance at all levels of the organisation can be measured and evaluated against an accepted yardstick of the budgeted plan.

Problems associated with budgeting:

- As a planning tool budgeting is only as good as the calculations made and limitations on managerial calculation affect this.

- The budgeting process can be viewed as a competitive bidding for funds rather than as a planning process.
- The existence of detailed budgets can cause inflexibility and a resistance to adapting to changed business circumstances.
- Variations require explanation and this may use managerial time ineffectively if these explanations do not help future performance.
- Control through budgets can only be exercised by an 'after the event' comparison of actuals with budgets and this may be of little help as a guide to current operations.

Chapter 10

Answer to Question 10.1

Problems:

- lack of motivation due to non-involvement;
- targets set may be unrealistic;
- budget includes costs which are not controllable;
- bonus not directly linked to controllable performance.

Essential features of a budgeting system:

- setting of agreed targets;
- mechanisms for feedback;
- ownership of budget;
- goal congruence;
- recognising achievements.

Answer to Question 10.2

Main points to consider:

- Targets set need to be regarded as achievable by managers; targets set are imposed centrally without regard as to whether or not managers regard them as achievable.
- Ownership of targets is best achieved through participation in target setting; targets are set centrally without the involvement of managers.
- Individuals set more difficult targets for themselves than those allocated to them, and this could lead to an improvement in company performance as the managers would be motivated to achieve these targets; the managers have no motivation to achieve targets imposed upon them and this is one reason for their failure to achieve the targets set.
- Allocation of resources is optimised through using the expertise of those involved in operations; this is not the case in this firm.

- Managers should only be held responsible for performance which they can influence; i.e. they should only be accountable for their performance with respect to controllable costs.
- Central management appears to assume Theory X behaviour by the imposition of targets; perhaps the assumption of Theory Y would lead to improved performance.
- Feedback needs to be timely to enable corrective action to be taken; there is no indication of what feedback is given and under what time scale.
- Performance measurement needs to promote goal congruence and the feedback and reward systems need to be allied to this objective; the motivation of managers is dependant on this and this is one reason why targets fail to be met.

Chapter 11

Answer to Question 11.1

(a)
- Time value of money
- Risk premium.

(b)
- Cash flow implications
- Scarce resources.

(c)

	Year 0	Year 1	Year 2	Year 3	Year 4
Investment	(100 000)				
Working capital	(60 000)				60 000
Contribution		40 000	70 000	96 000	96 000
Lost cont.		(16 000)	(16 000)	(16 000)	(16 000)
Net cash flow	(160 000)	24 000	54 000	80 000	140 000
@ 15%		0.869	0.756	0.657	0.571
	(160 000)	20 856	40 824	52 560	79 940
	NPV = 34 180				
@ 30%		0.769	0.591	0.455	0.350
	(160 000)	18 456	31 914	36 400	49 000
	NPV = (24 230)				

$$\text{IRR} = 15\% + \frac{34\ 180}{(34\ 180 + 24\ 230)} \times 15 = 23.8\%$$

Answer to Question 11.2

(a) Cash flows

	Factory A (£ million)	Factory B (£ million)	Factory C (£ million)
Year 0 purchase cost	(50)	(100)	(90)
Year 0 addnl cost	(25)		
Year 1	3	10	15
Year 2	6	15	17
Year 3	14	30	23
Year 4	16	42.75	36
Year 5	20	57	39

NPV

	d.f.	Factory A (£ million)	Factory B (£ million)	Factory C (£ million)
Year 0		(75)	(100)	(90)
Year 1	0.909	2.73	9.09	13.63
Year 2	0.826	4.96	12.39	14.04
Year 3	0.751	10.51	20.49	17.27
Year 4	0.683	10.93	29.20	24.59
Year 5	0.621	12.42	35.40	24.22
		(33.45)	6.57	3.75

(b) Payback period   never   4.1 yrs   4 yrs

(c) Factory C has a positive NPV and the shortest payback period. There is greater risk attached to this project, however, because of the uncertainty surrounding the inflation forecast. Factory B has the highest NPV but again uncertainty is attached to the forecast of devaluation effects. Normally factory B would be selected but factory C has the lowest initial cost and higher short-term returns than factory B – perhaps this should be chosen.

Chapter 12

Answer to Question 12.1

Main points:

- stakeholder v. legal ownership and power;
- value creation and appropriation;

- business ethics;
- value creation and distribution;
- cost externalisation;
- life cycle analysis;
- sustainability;
- accountability;
- transparency.

Answer to Question 12.2

Main points:

- impact upon society v. impact upon organisation;
- value creation and distribution;
- accounting for externalities;
- life cycle analysis;
- sustainability;
- accountability;
- transparency;
- problems of measurement;
- conflicting perspectives upon environmental performance;
- changes in understanding over time.

Chapter 13

Answer to Question 13.1

Important factors:

- Strategy is affected by day-to-day decision and so emergent strategy becomes manifest.
- Changes in the external environment affect the way in which strategy is manifest in its implementation.
- Budgeting and control affect the strategic process through feedback control.

Answer to Question 13.2

The main purposes of management accounting are:

- planning the operations of a business;
- making decisions about the business;
- controlling operations;
- reporting on performance.

These inevitably are concerned primarily with the internal operations of a business. A business manager must, however, be concerned also with the external environment in which a business operates, i.e. the market, customers, competitors and suppliers. While these are largely outside the scope of management accounting they fall within the scope of strategic planning. Management accounting assists strategic planning and the budgeting and performance reporting aspects of management accounting provide assistance to business managers whatever area of business they are concerned with.

Appendix 2

Discount table: present value of £1

Discount rate

Years	1%	2%	4%	5%	6%	8%	10%	12%	14%	15%	16%	18%	20%	22%	24%	25%	26%	28%	30%	35%	40%
1	0.990	0.980	0.962	0.952	0.943	0.926	0.909	0.893	0.877	0.870	0.862	0.847	0.833	0.820	0.806	0.800	0.794	0.781	0.769	0.741	0.714
2	0.980	0.961	0.925	0.907	0.890	0.857	0.826	0.797	0.769	0.756	0.743	0.718	0.694	0.672	0.650	0.640	0.630	0.610	0.592	0.549	0.510
3	0.971	0.942	0.889	0.864	0.840	0.794	0.751	0.712	0.675	0.658	0.641	0.609	0.579	0.551	0.524	0.512	0.500	0.477	0.455	0.406	0.364
4	0.961	0.924	0.855	0.823	0.792	0.735	0.683	0.636	0.592	0.572	0.552	0.516	0.482	0.451	0.423	0.410	0.397	0.373	0.350	0.301	0.260
5	0.951	0.906	0.822	0.784	0.747	0.681	0.621	0.567	0.519	0.497	0.476	0.437	0.402	0.370	0.341	0.328	0.315	0.291	0.269	0.223	0.186
6	0.942	0.888	0.790	0.746	0.705	0.630	0.564	0.507	0.456	0.432	0.410	0.370	0.335	0.303	0.275	0.262	0.250	0.227	0.207	0.165	0.133
7	0.933	0.871	0.760	0.711	0.665	0.583	0.513	0.452	0.400	0.376	0.354	0.314	0.279	0.249	0.222	0.210	0.198	0.178	0.159	0.122	0.095
8	0.923	0.853	0.731	0.677	0.627	0.540	0.467	0.404	0.351	0.327	0.305	0.266	0.233	0.204	0.179	0.168	0.157	0.139	0.123	0.091	0.068
9	0.914	0.837	0.703	0.645	0.592	0.500	0.424	0.361	0.308	0.284	0.263	0.225	0.194	0.167	0.144	0.134	0.125	0.108	0.094	0.067	0.048
10	0.905	0.820	0.676	0.614	0.558	0.463	0.386	0.322	0.270	0.247	0.227	0.191	0.162	0.137	0.116	0.107	0.099	0.085	0.073	0.050	0.035
11	0.896	0.804	0.650	0.585	0.527	0.429	0.350	0.287	0.237	0.215	0.195	0.162	0.135	0.112	0.094	0.086	0.079	0.066	0.056	0.037	0.025
12	0.887	0.788	0.625	0.557	0.497	0.397	0.319	0.257	0.208	0.187	0.168	0.137	0.112	0.092	0.076	0.069	0.062	0.052	0.043	0.027	0.018
13	0.879	0.773	0.601	0.530	0.469	0.368	0.290	0.229	0.182	0.163	0.145	0.116	0.093	0.075	0.061	0.055	0.050	0.040	0.033	0.020	0.013
14	0.870	0.758	0.577	0.505	0.442	0.340	0.263	0.205	0.160	0.141	0.125	0.099	0.078	0.062	0.049	0.044	0.039	0.032	0.025	0.015	0.009
15	0.861	0.743	0.555	0.481	0.417	0.315	0.239	0.183	0.140	0.123	0.108	0.084	0.065	0.051	0.040	0.035	0.031	0.025	0.020	0.011	0.006
16	0.853	0.728	0.534	0.458	0.394	0.292	0.218	0.163	0.123	0.107	0.093	0.071	0.054	0.042	0.032	0.028	0.025	0.019	0.015	0.008	0.005
17	0.844	0.714	0.513	0.436	0.371	0.270	0.198	0.146	0.108	0.093	0.080	0.060	0.045	0.034	0.026	0.023	0.020	0.015	0.012	0.006	0.003
18	0.836	0.700	0.494	0.416	0.350	0.250	0.180	0.130	0.095	0.081	0.069	0.051	0.038	0.028	0.021	0.018	0.016	0.012	0.009	0.005	0.002
19	0.828	0.686	0.475	0.396	0.331	0.232	0.164	0.116	0.083	0.070	0.060	0.043	0.031	0.023	0.017	0.014	0.012	0.009	0.007	0.003	0.002
20	0.820	0.673	0.456	0.377	0.312	0.215	0.149	0.104	0.073	0.061	0.051	0.037	0.026	0.019	0.014	0.012	0.010	0.007	0.005	0.002	0.001

Discount rate

Years	1%	2%	4%	5%	6%	8%	10%	12%	14%	15%	16%	18%	20%	22%	24%	25%	26%	28%	30%	35%	40%
21	0.811	0.660	0.439	0.359	0.294	0.199	0.135	0.093	0.064	0.053	0.044	0.031	0.022	0.015	0.011	0.009	0.008	0.006	0.004	0.002	0.001
22	0.803	0.647	0.422	0.342	0.278	0.184	0.123	0.083	0.056	0.046	0.038	0.026	0.018	0.013	0.009	0.007	0.006	0.004	0.003	0.001	0.001
23	0.795	0.634	0.406	0.326	0.262	0.170	0.112	0.074	0.049	0.040	0.033	0.022	0.015	0.010	0.007	0.006	0.005	0.003	0.002	0.001	
24	0.788	0.622	0.390	0.310	0.247	0.158	0.102	0.066	0.043	0.035	0.028	0.019	0.013	0.008	0.006	0.005	0.004	0.003	0.002	0.001	
25	0.780	0.610	0.375	0.295	0.233	0.146	0.092	0.059	0.038	0.030	0.024	0.016	0.010	0.007	0.005	0.004	0.003	0.002	0.001	0.001	
26	0.772	0.598	0.361	0.281	0.220	0.135	0.084	0.053	0.033	0.026	0.021	0.014	0.009	0.006	0.004	0.003	0.002	0.002	0.001		
27	0.764	0.586	0.347	0.268	0.207	0.125	0.076	0.047	0.029	0.023	0.018	0.011	0.007	0.005	0.003	0.002	0.002	0.001	0.001		
28	0.757	0.574	0.333	0.255	0.196	0.116	0.069	0.042	0.026	0.020	0.016	0.010	0.006	0.004	0.002	0.002	0.002	0.001	0.001		
29	0.749	0.563	0.321	0.243	0.185	0.107	0.063	0.037	0.022	0.017	0.014	0.008	0.005	0.003	0.002	0.002	0.001	0.001			
30	0.742	0.552	0.308	0.231	0.174	0.099	0.057	0.033	0.020	0.015	0.012	0.007	0.004	0.003	0.002	0.001	0.001	0.001			
35	0.706	0.500	0.253	0.181	0.130	0.068	0.036	0.019	0.010	0.008	0.006	0.003	0.002	0.001	0.001						
40	0.672	0.453	0.208	0.142	0.097	0.046	0.022	0.011	0.005	0.004	0.003	0.001	0.001								
45	0.639	0.410	0.171	0.111	0.073	0.031	0.014	0.006	0.003	0.002	0.001	0.001									
50	0.608	0.372	0.141	0.087	0.054	0.021	0.009	0.003	0.001	0.001	0.001										

Discount table: present value of £1 received annually for N years

Discount rate

Years	1%	2%	4%	5%	6%	8%	10%	12%	14%	15%	16%	18%	20%	22%	24%	25%	26%	28%	30%	35%	40%
1	0.990	0.980	0.962	0.952	0.943	0.926	0.909	0.893	0.877	0.870	0.862	0.847	0.833	0.820	0.806	0.800	0.794	0.781	0.769	0.741	0.714
2	1.970	1.942	1.886	1.859	1.833	1.783	1.736	1.690	1.647	1.626	1.605	1.566	1.528	1.492	1.457	1.440	1.424	1.392	1.361	1.289	1.224
3	2.941	2.884	2.775	2.723	2.673	2.577	2.487	2.402	2.322	2.283	2.246	2.174	2.106	2.042	1.981	1.952	1.923	1.868	1.816	1.696	1.589
4	3.902	3.808	3.630	3.546	3.465	3.312	3.170	3.037	2.914	2.855	2.798	2.690	2.589	2.494	2.404	2.362	2.320	2.241	2.166	1.997	1.849
5	4.853	4.713	4.452	4.329	4.212	3.993	3.791	3.605	3.433	3.352	3.274	3.127	2.991	2.864	2.745	2.689	2.635	2.532	2.436	2.220	2.035
6	5.795	5.601	5.242	5.076	4.917	4.623	4.355	4.111	3.889	3.784	3.685	3.498	3.326	3.167	3.020	2.951	2.885	2.759	2.643	2.385	2.168
7	6.728	6.472	6.002	5.786	5.582	5.206	4.868	4.564	4.288	4.160	4.039	3.812	3.605	3.416	3.242	3.161	3.083	2.937	2.802	2.508	2.263
8	7.652	7.325	6.733	6.463	6.210	5.747	5.335	4.968	4.639	4.487	4.344	4.078	3.837	3.619	3.421	3.329	3.241	3.076	2.925	2.598	2.331
9	8.566	8.162	7.435	7.108	6.802	6.247	5.759	5.328	4.946	4.772	4.607	4.303	4.031	3.786	3.566	3.463	3.366	3.184	3.019	2.665	2.379
10	9.471	8.983	8.111	7.722	7.360	6.710	6.145	5.650	5.216	5.019	4.833	4.494	4.192	3.923	3.682	3.571	3.465	3.269	3.092	2.715	2.414
11	10.368	9.787	8.760	8.306	7.887	7.139	6.495	5.938	5.453	5.234	5.029	4.656	4.327	4.035	3.776	3.656	3.544	3.335	3.147	2.752	2.438
12	11.255	10.575	9.385	8.863	8.384	7.536	6.814	6.194	5.660	5.421	5.197	4.793	4.439	4.127	3.851	3.725	3.606	3.387	3.190	2.779	2.456
13	12.134	11.348	9.986	9.394	8.853	7.904	7.103	6.424	5.842	5.583	5.342	4.910	4.533	4.203	3.912	3.780	3.656	3.427	3.223	2.799	2.468
14	13.004	12.106	10.563	9.899	9.295	8.244	7.367	6.628	6.002	5.724	5.468	5.008	4.611	4.265	3.962	3.824	3.695	3.459	3.249	2.814	2.477
15	13.865	12.849	11.118	10.380	9.712	8.559	7.606	6.811	6.142	5.847	5.575	5.092	4.675	4.315	4.001	3.859	3.726	3.483	3.268	2.825	2.484
16	14.718	13.578	11.652	10.838	10.106	8.851	7.824	6.974	6.265	5.954	5.669	5.162	4.730	4.357	4.033	3.887	3.751	3.503	3.283	2.834	2.489
17	15.562	14.292	12.166	11.274	10.477	9.122	8.022	7.120	6.373	6.047	5.749	5.222	4.775	4.391	4.059	3.910	3.771	3.518	3.295	2.840	2.492
18	16.398	14.992	12.659	11.690	10.828	9.372	8.201	7.250	6.467	6.128	5.818	5.273	4.812	4.419	4.080	3.928	3.786	3.529	3.304	2.844	2.494
19	17.226	15.678	13.134	12.085	11.158	9.604	8.365	7.366	6.550	6.198	5.877	5.316	4.844	4.442	4.097	3.942	3.799	3.539	3.311	2.848	2.496
20	18.046	16.351	13.590	12.462	11.470	9.818	8.514	7.469	6.623	6.259	5.929	5.353	4.870	4.460	4.110	3.954	3.808	3.546	3.316	2.850	2.497

Discount rate

Years	1%	2%	4%	5%	6%	8%	10%	12%	14%	15%	16%	18%	20%	22%	24%	25%	26%	28%	30%	35%	40%
21	18.857	17.011	14.029	12.821	11.764	10.017	8.649	7.562	6.687	6.313	5.973	5.384	4.891	4.476	4.121	3.963	3.816	3.551	3.320	2.852	2.498
22	19.660	17.658	14.451	13.163	12.042	10.201	8.772	7.645	6.743	6.359	6.011	5.410	4.909	4.488	4.130	3.970	3.822	3.556	3.323	2.853	2.498
23	20.456	18.292	14.857	13.489	12.303	10.371	8.883	7.718	6.792	6.399	6.044	5.432	4.925	4.499	4.137	3.976	3.827	3.559	3.325	2.854	2.499
24	21.243	18.914	15.247	13.799	12.550	10.529	8.985	7.784	6.835	6.434	6.073	5.451	4.937	4.507	4.143	3.981	3.831	3.562	3.327	2.855	2.499
25	22.023	19.523	15.622	14.094	12.783	10.675	9.077	7.843	6.873	6.464	6.097	5.467	4.948	4.514	4.147	3.985	3.834	3.564	3.329	2.856	2.499
26	22.795	20.121	15.983	14.375	13.003	10.810	9.161	7.896	6.906	6.491	6.118	5.480	4.956	4.520	4.151	3.988	3.837	3.566	3.330	2.856	2.500
27	23.560	20.707	16.330	14.643	13.211	10.935	9.237	7.943	6.935	6.514	6.136	5.492	4.964	4.524	4.154	3.990	3.839	3.567	3.331	2.856	2.500
28	24.316	21.281	16.663	14.898	13.406	11.051	9.307	7.984	6.961	6.534	6.152	5.502	4.970	4.528	4.157	3.992	3.840	3.568	3.331	2.857	2.500
29	25.066	21.844	16.984	15.141	13.591	11.158	9.370	8.022	6.983	6.551	6.166	5.510	4.975	4.531	4.159	3.994	3.841	3.569	3.332	2.857	2.500
30	25.808	22.396	17.292	15.372	13.765	11.258	9.427	8.055	7.003	6.566	6.177	5.517	4.979	4.534	4.160	3.995	3.842	3.569	3.332	2.857	2.500
35	29.409	24.999	18.665	16.374	14.498	11.655	9.644	8.176	7.070	6.617	6.215	5.539	4.992	4.541	4.164	3.998	3.845	3.571	3.333	2.857	2.500
40	32.835	27.356	19.793	17.159	15.046	11.925	9.779	8.244	7.105	6.642	6.234	5.548	4.997	4.544	4.166	3.999	3.846	3.571	3.333	2.857	2.500
45	36.095	29.490	20.720	17.774	15.456	12.108	9.863	8.283	7.123	6.654	6.242	5.552	4.999	4.545	4.166	4.000	3.846	3.571	3.333	2.857	2.500
50	39.196	31.424	21.482	18.256	15.762	12.234	9.915	8.305	7.133	6.661	6.246	5.554	4.999	4.545	4.167	4.000	3.846	3.571	3.333	2.857	2.500

Index